and the **Wilderness** *shall* **Blossom**

and the Wilderness shall Blossom

Henry Benjamin Whipple

CHURCHMAN
EDUCATOR
ADVOCATE FOR THE INDIANS

Anne Beiser Allen

AFTON HISTORICAL SOCIETY PRESS

AFTON PRESS is grateful to the following generous donors who have made possible the publication of

and the Wilderness Shall Blossom

Henry Benjamin Whipple

CHURCHMAN, EDUCATOR, ADVOCATE FOR THE INDIANS

Robert and Mary Anderson
Sharon Avent
Frank and Laura Budd
Caroline Bye
James and Joanie Delamater
Episcopal Diocese of Minnesota
Tom and Lorraine Evans
Barbara Forster
Gary F. Gleason
Harry and Pat Haynsworth
Louis and Kathrine Hill
Ben and Pat Jaffray
James and Marilyn Jelinek
Gary Johnson and Joan Hershbell
James E. Johnson
John and Elaine Killen
John and Judy Kinkead
Nan Lightner
George and Dusty Mairs
Andy McCarthy
Walter McCarthy and Clara Ueland
Malcolm and Patricia McDonald
Dick and Joyce McFarland
Howard and Janet McMillan
Dick and Nancy Nicholson
Ford and Catherine Nicholson
Ben and Lynn Oehler
Judy Oehler
John T. Richter
Elizabeth McMillan Ringer
St. Andrew's-by-the-Lake, Duluth
St. John the Evangelist Church, St Paul
St. Paul's Episcopal Church, Duluth
Jon and Susan Seltzer
Mac and Mary Seymour
Harry and Virginia Sweatt
Gedney and Emily Anne Tuttle
Angus and Margaret Wurtele
Irma Wyman

Edited by Michele Hodgson
Copyedited by Ashley Shelby
Designed by Mary Susan Oleson
Production assistance by Beth Williams
Printed by Pettit Network Inc.

Library of Congress Cataloging-in-Publication Data
Allen, Anne Beiser, 1941-
And the wilderness shall blossom: Henry Benjamin Whipple, bishop, educator, advocate for the Indians / by Anne Beiser Allen.—1st ed.
    p. cm.
ISBN 978-1-890434-75-5 (hardcover: alk. paper)
1. Whipple, Henry Benjamin, 1822-1901. 2. Bishops—Minnesota—Biography.
3. Missionaries—Minnesota—Biography. 4. Episcopal Church. Diocese of Minnesota. Bishop (1859-1901: Whipple) 5. Episcopal Church—Missions—Minnesota—History. 6. Church work with Indians—Episcopal Church—History. 7. Indians of North America—Missions—Minnesota. 8. Indians of North America—Minnesota—Social conditions. I. Title.

BX5995.W48A44 2008
283.092--dc22
[B]

                                                2007014309
printed in China

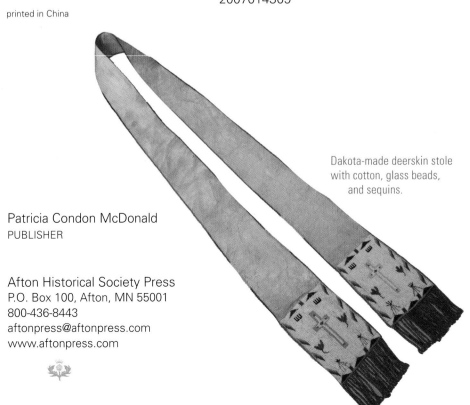

Dakota-made deerskin stole with cotton, glass beads, and sequins.

Patricia Condon McDonald
PUBLISHER

Afton Historical Society Press
P.O. Box 100, Afton, MN 55001
800-436-8443
aftonpress@aftonpress.com
www.aftonpress.com

table of contents

acknowledgments

THIS BOOK WOULD NOT HAVE BEEN completed so readily without the help of many people. James Zotalis, dean of the Cathedral of Our Merciful Saviour in Faribault, was especially generous with his time and resources. Joe Bjordal, manager of news and information at the Episcopal Diocese of Minnesota, provided valuable encouragement and support. Ben and Judy Oehler as well as Al and Paul Jefferson, descendants of Bishop Whipple, provided family materials and encouragement. Doctors John Joyce and Edward Rosenow of the Mayo Clinic reviewed the bishop's recorded symptoms and suggested possible diagnoses concerning his ailments. Ben Scott and Robert Neslund provided their insights into the bishop's life. The rectors and staff of Zion Church in Rome, New York; Trinity Church in St. Augustine, Florida; and the Church of the Good Shepherd in Maitland, Florida, supplied me with histories of their parishes.

The staff at the Minnesota Historical Society library in St. Paul were very helpful in providing access to the bishop's papers and those of other people whose lives intersected with his. Richard Mammana and his Anglican Web site were invaluable resources for information on Anglican history around the world. Jim Kolster and Julie Sullivan of the Diocese of Florida's Cuba Committee provided background and images of the Cuban church. Ted Neuhaus clarified some issues on church politics in the nineteenth century. Stephen Schaitberger provided insights on the Ojibwe mission. Bill McMahan located the Hill Memorial School in Athens for me. Dick Nicholson supplied several letters between Whipple and James J. Hill. Carrie Zeman helped date the Whipple/Lincoln meeting. Tilly Laskey, curator at the Science Museum of Minnesota, and photographer Craig Thiesen supplied images of Whipple's Native American artifacts. Mollie Harris pointed us to the Indian drawings from Fort Marion. Marilyn Jelinek, wife of James Jelinek, bishop of Minnesota, photographed the pectoral cross worn by Whipple and his successors.

I am grateful to Afton Historical Society Press for believing in my book and making it happen, especially to publisher Patricia McDonald, director of operations Chuck Johnston (who also helped with photography), editors Michele Hodgson and Ashley Shelby, designer Mary Sue Oleson, and production assistant Beth Williams. Thanks also to John and Mary for letting me use their home as a base while I worked at the MHS library, and to that unnamed person who serves as my personal reference librarian, chauffeur, and copyeditor, whose patience and support made it all possible. —*Anne Beiser*

the publisher adds her thanks to the many people who made this book possible financially, people like Bob and Polly McCrea who invited us to entertain potential donors, including Bishop Jim and Marilyn Jelinek, at their home in Long Lake one fine summer evening. In Duluth, Laura and Frank Budd invited their friends and fellow parishioners to meet us at a friend-raising, fundraising reception at the Kitchi Gammi Club. In St. Paul, my husband Malcolm and I hosted a reception at our home church, St. John the Evangelist, where friends and fellow parishioners added their support.

Donors at the $1,000 level or above are recognized on the copyright page of *and the Wilderness shall Blossom*, which is intended as a gift to Diocese of Minnesota on the occasion of its 150th anniversary. Parishioners in several churches pooled their contributions to total $1,000, in which cases the parish is recognized. Some donors asked to remain anonymous.

To all of our generous donors, and especially to Bishop Jelinek, who blessed this project with his unstinting help including financial support, I hope this beautiful biography of Henry Benjamin Whipple lives up to your every expectation. It has been a pleasure and an honor to help shape it and publish it. Thank you from my heart. —*Patricia McDonald*

foreword: CRUX, LUX, DUX

HENRY BENJAMIN WHIPPLE, the first Episcopal bishop of Minnesota, loomed larger than life on the nineteenth-century stage of national and international history. More than a century after his death, the story of his complex life—as churchman, educator, and advocate for Native Americans in the fragile, pioneering years of the American westward movement—looms just as large. As the Episcopal Diocese of Minnesota commemorates its sesquicentennial in 2008, we are poised to revisit the inspiring life and witness of Bishop Whipple. But where to begin?

It seems fitting to start by meeting the man through his cross—the bishop's cross that he wore around his neck every day, the cross that has been handed down to his successors, the cross that I have worn as bishop of Minnesota for the past fourteen years, the cross that I will one day hand to my successor. It is a Celtic cross, made of sterling silver and inscribed with three Latin words: *Crux, Lux, Dux,* or Cross, Light, Leadership. In those words—words to which I can only imagine Bishop Whipple often clung by physically grasping that cross in his hand—we find our deepest, personal understanding of the man.

Crux—the cross on which Jesus died—reveals the heart of it all, the bishop's heart. Jesus showed extraordinary compassion throughout his life and ministry, but particularly from the cross—loving even those who were killing him and asking that they be forgiven. It is the kind of compassion we see in Bishop Whipple, not only for those who are neglected, shunned, or persecuted in society, but even for those who are the enemies of peace and reconciliation. It is in the compassion of the cross that Whipple found his reason for being.

Lux—the light of Christ—illuminated the bishop's way. The vision that Jesus gave his disciples came from his own awareness of the breadth of God's heart, a heart filled with compassion, equality, and justice for all people. It was the light of this message that helped Whipple see his way through the dark days of challenge.

Dux—leadership through faith—defined the bishop's work. Jesus led by example as he preached peace, compassion, and justice in the name of God. From the beginning of his episcopate, Whipple was determined that all who lived in the Diocese of Minnesota, European settlers and Native Americans alike, should live in peace and know the love of God. Whipple was a champion for others, but more important, he was their companion in the ardors and joys of life's journey. His lifelong dedication to Christ's principles made him a leader in the United States and abroad.

I am deeply grateful to Afton Historical Society Press and to Anne Beiser Allen for their beautifully illustrated and richly detailed look at Henry Benjamin Whipple, who led the Episcopal Diocese of Minnesota as bishop for a remarkable forty-two years. It is my privilege to follow in the footsteps of this great man who lived his faith—a man who brought discomfort to those who would and did diminish others while he brought hope to those who had little or none. A man of his culture yet ahead of his time. A man whose legacy of love and leadership continues to influence both the Episcopal Church and society.

I thank God for Bishop Whipple, who shaped not only the diocese but also the state of Minnesota by his passion, energy, and commitment, all of which came out of his abiding faith. This is his story, and the story of those courageous pioneers of faith who served with him. It is a story that can light our way and rekindle in us the courage, compassion, and generosity to be God's agents of reconciliation and peace for a world in need.

Faithfully,
James L. Jelinek
VIII BISHOP, EPISCOPAL DIOCESE OF MINNESOTA

Dacotah Village, watercolor drawing by Seth Eastman, ca. 1850. Located close to rivers or lakes, Dakota villages were comprised of ridge-roofed houses twenty to thirty feet long. Made of poles lashed together with withes and basswood bark and covered with elm bark, the houses were shared by four or more related families. In fair weather, much of the Indians' social life took place outdoors, under the scaffolds in front of their houses, which provided shade and were used for storage, drying corn or furs, and sometimes also for sleeping.

Abraham Lincoln sat in his office in the White House on the afternoon of September 16, 1862.[1] His desk was piled high with reports from military officers, cabinet members, legislators, and civil servants. Most of the reports related to the war between the states. A series of humiliating defeats had been followed by a reshuffling in the high command, and now General Robert E. Lee's army was encamped north of the Potomac, on the banks of Antietam Creek, near Sharpsburg, Maryland, barely fifty miles from the capital. The next day's battle of Antietam would produce unprecedented numbers of casualties on both sides, but would result in Lee's withdrawal to Virginia.

Lincoln was awaiting a visit from the Episcopal bishop of Minnesota, Henry B. Whipple. Whipple was a cousin of Lincoln's commander-in-chief, Major General Henry Wager Halleck, who had requested this meeting on his cousin's behalf. Bishop Whipple wanted to discuss the recent Dakota Indian war in Minnesota, which had come as an unpleasant distraction to a president preoccupied with a far larger conflict.

Exasperated by the government's persistent failure to fulfill the terms of treaties signed with their people over the past decade, the Dakota of Minnesota had erupted into warfare on August 18, raiding frontier farmsteads, looting, and killing. They attacked Fort Ridgely and nearby New Ulm, although without success, and took more than two hundred captives before they were defeated on September 23 by a force led by Minnesota's former governor, Henry H. Sibley.

When Lincoln had removed General John Pope from his command of the Army of the Potomac on September 5, after the latter's disastrous showing at Bull Run the week before, the president sent him to Minnesota to deal with the Dakota threat. Partly as a sop to the general's pride, Lincoln created a Department of the Northwest and gave its command to Pope. Once again, however, Pope failed to satisfy his president's expectations. Although he wisely left the prosecution of the war against the Dakota to

Abraham Lincoln, ca. 1863, a few months after Bishop Henry Whipple's visit. Preoccupied with the weak performance of his army in northern Virginia, the president was suddenly forced to also deal with a Dakota Indian uprising in Minnesota in August 1862.

Instructed by Bishop Jackson Kemper, missionary bishop of the Northwest since 1835, to "remember the red man," Whipple (ca. 1862) visited Minnesota's Ojibwe and Dakota Reservations to talk with the native people. What he learned reinforced his conviction that the nation's Indian policies were misguided and, if not changed, would lead to disaster.

Colonel Sibley, Pope's reports to Washington contained overtones of the same kind of panic he had shown at Bull Run. Claiming that all of the Indians in Minnesota were up in arms, he demanded additional troops and supplies, even though he knew Lincoln could not afford to divert them.[2]

Despite Pope's fears, the fighting did not spread to Minnesota's other two resident Indian tribes, the Ojibwe and the Winnebago. Although they also had serious complaints about the way they had been treated by the government, they appear to have preferred to wait and see whether the Dakota were successful before committing themselves to open warfare. An attempt by the Ojibwe chief Hole-in-the-Day to stir up violence against whites during this time never gained support among his fellow tribesmen.[3]

Bishop Whipple feared that the outrage of the white community against the Dakota, fueled by panic and uncertainty, would divert attention from the all too real grievances that lay at the heart of the Dakota outbreak. He wished to make sure the president understood the context in which the war had taken place.

The man who entered the president's office with General Halleck was tall, well built, and self-confident, with a genial manner. A stiff white collar showed beneath his well-cut black clerical suit. He was clean-shaven and wore his hair long, brushed back from what novelists of the day would have called a "noble brow." His firm jaw was marked by a noticeable cleft. Deep-set eyes gazed steadily at Lincoln. His voice was strong yet pleasant. It would be easy to imagine him speaking from the pulpit, compelling faith by the earnest forthrightness of his discourse. He was neither overawed by the president's rank nor condescending. Like Lincoln, Henry Benjamin Whipple took men as he found them.

The president offered his guests chairs and sat back to listen to what the bishop had to say.

Whipple had been an Episcopal minister for thirteen of his forty years and bishop of Minnesota for the last three. Since his consecration in October 1859, he had met often with the Native Americans living in his diocese and heard their stories of broken promises and outright fraud perpetrated on them by representatives of the American government in the half-century since the white man first made his way into their country. During the past two months, he had been one of the very few voices of reason in a state made frantic by tales of atrocities committed by the Dakota. In speeches and letters to the press, he had insisted that the government's treatment of the Dakota was largely responsible for their resorting to war. For this view, he was widely reviled by his fellow Minnesotans.[4]

Whipple had firsthand knowledge of the devastation caused by the war. When hostilities began, he was returning from a trip with his missionaries through Ojibwe country in the northern half of the state. He then traveled to southern Minnesota to spend several weeks in St. Peter, where refugees had gathered under the protection of Colonel Sibley, who was gathering his forces there. Whipple's hand still showed signs of an injury he had received while ministering to the wounded settlers. In mid-September, he had come east to attend his church's upcoming national convention and to raise money for the refugees, stopping en route to visit the First Minnesota Regiment on the battlefield at Antietam.

But Whipple also recognized the validity of the Dakota side of the dispute. It was only a little more than ten years since the eight thousand Dakota living in Minnesota had agreed to sell their lands—compromising some thirty-five million acres—to the United States for $1,665,000. This sum was to be meted out over fifty years in annual payments of money and goods. The Dakota were also to be provided with mills, blacksmith shops, and schools for their children. Men were to be hired to teach them farming and other agricultural trades. The Dakota retained only a strip of land, one hundred miles long and twenty miles wide, along the upper reaches of the Minnesota River. In 1858 they had given up half of that territory in exchange for an additional $266,000.

But the annuities were often delayed, much of the money vanished into the pockets of licensed traders at the agencies, and no schools had been established. Uprooted from the villages along the Mississippi and lower Minnesota Rivers where they had lived for generations, the Dakota were finding it difficult to adjust to the economic realities of life on a constricted reservation. Only a few of them had chosen to become farmers; most still followed their

General Henry Wager Halleck was Lincoln's commander-in-chief of the Union Army from 1862 to 1864. Halleck introduced Whipple, his cousin, to the president when the bishop asked to intercede for the Dakota who had attacked Minnesota's white community in 1862. A graduate of West Point, Halleck wrote a textbook on war (published in 1848) that was widely used.

time honored practice of hunting and gathering for subsistence. With their Minnesota hunting grounds severely restricted, they were dependent upon the annuity payments for survival.

Whipple had written to Lincoln in March, reiterating points he had raised with President James Buchanan two years earlier about the shortcomings of the government's notoriously corrupt Indian policies. Now the bishop had come to plead with the president in person, not only for leniency toward the captured warriors, but for an overhaul of the nation's Indian program.

Indian affairs had not been high on Lincoln's agenda when he was inaugurated on March 4, 1861. Not only was the nation on the brink of war, but a host of Republican supporters were expecting to be rewarded for their roles in electing the Illinois lawyer to the country's highest office. The Office of Indian Affairs was one of the plums of the political patronage system. Bishop Whipple was not exaggerating when he wrote that "an Indian agent with fifteen hundred dollars a year can retire upon an ample fortune in four years."[5] Agents arranged contracts for the supplies the Indians received under treaty agreements and approved licenses for the traders who sold goods at the agencies. The opportunities for bribes, kickbacks, and sharp trading were virtually unlimited. The new agents appointed in 1861 for Minnesota's Dakota and Ojibwe tribes had promptly set to work to make their fortunes at the expense of those they were charged to help.[6]

While corruption in the Office of Indian Affairs was not new, and the Republican appointees were no more avaricious than many of their predecessors, conditions in the rest of the country made the situation more critical. The Civil War was the chief concern of everyone in Washington. Congress had delayed voting on the appropriations for the Dakota annuities until late in the session, and the Dakota had run out of food. Their new Republican agent, Thomas Galbraith, had little experience with Indians and had not handled the situation well.

By mid-August the annuity money, previously paid in June, still had not arrived at the Dakota agencies. The delay had prevented the Dakota from making their usual hunting trip to the Dakota plains for buffalo. They had spent two months waiting near the agency buildings, their tempers growing steadily shorter. By then, many of them were on the verge of starvation.

Whipple listed in considerable detail the wrongs committed against the Indians by administrations dating back to the earliest days of the republic: treaties broken, laws not enforced, funds siphoned by government officials and licensed traders. He asked permission to inspect the Indian bureau's files and pressed the president for assurances that the mistakes of the past would not be repeated.

Lincoln "was deeply moved," Whipple later wrote in his autobiography, *Lights and Shadows of a Long Episcopate.* He agreed that "it needs more than one honest man to watch one Indian Agent." The president gave Whipple a note addressed to Secretary of the Interior Caleb Smith, who had jurisdiction over the bureau, instructing Smith to give the bishop "any information he desires about Indian affairs." The two men shook hands and the bishop departed, satisfied that he had done what he could.

Lincoln later told an acquaintance, "Bishop Whipple . . . came here the other day and talked with me about the rascality of this Indian business until I felt it down to my boots. If we get through this war, and I live, this Indian system shall be reformed!"[7]

The Dakota War lasted thirty-seven days. Sibley appointed a five-man military tribunal that condemned 303 Dakota warriors to death. Sixteen more were sentenced to imprisonment. Some of the trials lasted less than half an hour.

Whipple's words apparently still echoed in Lincoln's mind when the president received the list of the condemned on November 5. Commissioner of Indian Affairs William P. Dole urged clemency for those who had surrendered in the expectation of being treated as prisoners of war.[8] As General John Sanborn of Minnesota later put it, "A people who could make a treaty could break it at will and go to war, and no offense could be committed until the laws of war were violated."[9] Lincoln instructed Sibley and Pope to do nothing until he had reviewed the evidence himself.

When the reports arrived, the president had two young clerks read through them carefully, checking the facts. When they finished, Lincoln reduced the number of men to be executed from 303 to 39, one of whom was later reprieved. Two were convicted of

The hanging of thirty-eight Dakota men at Mankato, Minnesota, in December 1862 ranks as the largest mass execution in American history.

rape, the rest of murder. The Dakota reservation was abolished, and Lincoln sent orders to remove those tribal members not convicted of criminal behavior to a new reservation on the upper Missouri River in the spring.

On December 26, 1862, thirty-eight Dakota men were hanged before a cheering crowd in Mankato, Minnesota. It was the largest mass execution ever held in the country. Thirty-six of them accepted Christian baptism from clergymen who had ministered to them in the weeks before their deaths. The condemned painted their faces and sang a traditional death song as they stood on the gallows. At 10:15 a.m., the officer in charge ordered three slow, measured beats on the drum. The executioner—a man whose family had been killed in the conflict—cut the rope holding the scaffold, and seconds later thirty-eight bodies hung suspended. They were buried in a mass grave.[10]

Bishop Henry Whipple emerged from this tragedy into the nation's consciousness as a leading advocate of justice for Native Americans. It was the first step along a path that would define his life.

Main Street, Adams, N.Y.

Adams, the small town in upstate New York where Whipple was born, was founded around 1800 by New Englanders on land relinquished by the Iroquois in 1788. Primarily a farming community, its population in 1820 was little more than 2,400.

enry Benjamin Whipple was born February 15, 1822, in Adams, New York, a small farming community in western Jefferson County, near the place where Lake Ontario empties into the St. Lawrence River. He was the oldest of six children born to John Hall Whipple, who had come to Adams two years earlier with his bride, Elizabeth Wager, to open a general store. The Whipples and Wagers had long and distinguished histories in America; the future bishop took pride in the fact that at least sixteen of his ancestors had fought in the Colonial and Revolutionary Wars.[11]

Henry had three sisters—Sarah Brayton, born in 1824, Susan Letitia, born in 1826, and Frances Ransom, born in 1835—and two brothers—John, born in 1828, and George Brayton, born in 1830. John Whipple's widowed mother, Susannah Hall Whipple, also made her home with the family until her death in 1840.[12]

The Whipple family was close knit. John Whipple took a loving interest in his children's welfare, writing conscientiously to them when they were away from home. In July 1833, when eleven-year-old Henry was at school in Clinton, New York, his father wrote, "I know you do not know how to be prudent yet without advice from some one. . . . Write me what you want to do [with the money you want] and if best I will send it. My son you know I do not want to pinch you but I want you to learn that you do not know best. . . . Remember my son I want to do for your good." As long as John Whipple lived, Henry would make a point of consulting his father whenever he had a major decision to make—even though he did not always follow John's advice.

His mother also had a prominent place in Henry Whipple's heart, and he always spoke of her with deep affection. "I owe much to my holy mother," he wrote in his autobiography, "whose unfaltering voice in speaking of Divine truth saved me from scepticism." He fondly recalled the time she told him, "My dear boy, it is always right to defend the weak and helpless."

As a boy, Henry enjoyed walking in the woods and fields around Adams, fishing in its streams, and listening to the tales of old Peter Doxtater, who had

Whipple's father, John Hall Whipple, was a merchant in Adams. Born in Albany, John was one of ten children of Benjamin and Susannah Hall Whipple. As a boy, he served as clerk to his cousin George Brayton, a merchant in Western, just north of Rome, New York. There John met Elizabeth Wager, whom he married in 1820. A respected businessman, he served two terms as township supervisor.

Whipple's mother, Elizabeth Wager Whipple, was the daughter of one of the New York electors who chose Thomas Jefferson as president in 1800. Her older sister Catherine was General Henry Wager Halleck's mother.

been kidnapped by Mohawks during the Revolutionary War and lived with them for three years. He also liked hearing the letters that came to Adams from Frederick Ayer, who had been a clerk in Henry's father's store before becoming a Congregationalist missionary to the Ojibwe in far-off Minnesota in 1831.[13]

The Whipple family attended the Presbyterian church, which, until 1828, was the only church in town. Henry's blind grandmother, however, was a devout Episcopalian. Her grandson often read to her from the *Book of Common Prayer*. He was thus exposed at a young age to two strains of Protestant theology: the Calvinism of the Presbyterians, with its heavy emphasis on individual salvation, and Anglicanism, with its stately liturgy and preference for community worship.[14]

Religious sentiment was especially active in western New York during Henry Whipple's childhood, when the phenomenon known as the Second Great Awakening swept through the area. This widespread religious revival of the 1820s and 1830s (echoing a similar revival that had occurred in the previous century) was a reaction to the deism of the 1790s, and by its contention that "heaven on earth" was possible, resulted not only in increased church attendance but also in the development of secular reform movements (abolitionism, temperance, public education, etc.). Western New York became known as the "Burnt-Over Area" because of the fiery preaching of ministers at the mass revivals held frequently in every community. New sects sprang up like wildflowers: Mormons, Unitarians, and William Miller's eschatological Seventh-Day Adventists all had their beginnings in upstate New York at this time. Enthusiasm for church and mission work even increased among the already-established churches: Congregationalist, Presbyterian, Methodist, Baptist, Episcopalian, and Roman Catholic.[15]

As Adams' first public school would not be built until 1876, Henry learned his three R's from an independent teacher.[16] Not having had the opportunity for higher-level schooling himself, John Whipple wanted his son to get a good education and enter one of the professions, perhaps as a lawyer. When Henry was ten, he was sent to a boarding school run by Professor Charles Avery in Clinton, New York, some seventy miles from home.[17] Then, in 1836, a group of Presbyterians founded the Black River Literary and Religious Institute in Watertown, only fifteen miles northeast of Adams, and John Whipple enrolled his son there. Young Henry was a diligent student, already showing signs of the enthusiasm and strong desire to please that would mark his later years.[18]

In the fall of 1837 Henry enrolled in Mr. Grosvenor's school in Rome, a thriving canal town in Oneida County, with the intention of going on to Union College, which his cousin Henry Halleck had attended. Instead, a few months later, his father sent him to Oberlin, Ohio, where he entered the preparatory department of Oberlin College. (His uncle, George Whipple, was the preparatory department's principal and professor of mathematics.)[19]

The road to Ohio was a busy commercial thoroughfare where Irish immigrant laborers manhandled heavy barrels and wooden cases from wagons to boats and back again and families headed west in search of a better life. Whipple later recalled the excitement of looking out of a stagecoach window, watching boats loaded with supplies for the "border settlers" in the wilds of Michigan.[20]

Unfortunately, the academic pace at Oberlin proved too great for young Henry. In 1840, he became seriously ill and was sent home before he could finish his second year. The doctor told John Whipple that his son had been studying too much. What he needed was "to be put into active business with a good deal of outdoor life. . . . Thus ended my dream of Yale," Whipple later observed.

Henry Whipple had always been "a frail and delicate boy." Throughout much of his life he suffered recurrent bouts of bronchitis and similar respiratory ailments, probably a result of bronchiectasis, an abnormal dilation of the bronchi that often followed a pneumonia episode.[21] His "frailty" was not physical weakness. In his early years in Minnesota, he undertook grueling journeys by buggy and canoe and on foot, often amazing his contemporaries with his endurance. But he had a persistent habit of facing challenges with single-minded intensity and may well have spent so much time over his books that he collapsed into a state of nervous exhaustion.

Back in Adams, eighteen-year-old Henry went to work in his father's general store. He was an outgoing young man with a knack for making friends easily. John Whipple began to use him as his factor, sending him to Syracuse, Buffalo, and other distribution centers to acquire goods for the local market, which the steadily improving transportation system was constantly expanding.[22]

Whipple spent time with the state militia, which he had joined when he was sixteen. "It afforded many pleasant hours of recreation," he recalled, "with the fuss and feathers of military equipage. During the Patriot rebellion in Canada [in 1838] we were ordered to the defense of the frontier, but the Government had wisely sent out some regulars who settled the matter before we entered upon actual service, and our military reputation was saved."[23]

Politics ran a close second to religion as the chief topic of conversation in western New York in the 1840s, and Henry Whipple quickly became active in

The Erie Canal, which was completed in 1825, brought goods from New York City to Syracuse within days rather than weeks. Housewives in upstate New York began to expect to find the same goods in their stores that their relatives had back home, and in equal abundance, making it possible for them to entertain on the same level. This painting of the Erie Canal was made in 1829 by John W. Hill.

the local political scene. He attended the 1840 Whig convention in Utica, when Thurlow Weed engineered the ouster of Henry Clay in favor of Benjamin Harrison as the party's presidential nominee. Whipple became a close acquaintance of Weed and other party stalwarts such as Horace Greeley and Edwin Croswell. But he soon became disillusioned with Whig politics and came to identify himself with the conservative wing of the Democratic Party, along with John A. Dix and Horatio Seymour. He accompanied Dix around New York in 1844 during Dix's gubernatorial campaign.

Whipple never considered running for office himself, believing that his involvement in his father's business would present a conflict of interest. The only elective post he held was one term as inspector of schools in Adams.[24] The Democrats found him useful, however. His genial manner and honesty made him popular among all kinds of people, from immigrant Irish laborers to members of the highest social circles. He had a gift for persuading others to support his point of view—and to part with cash for a good cause.

On October 5, 1842, Henry Whipple married Cornelia Wright, daughter of Benjamin Wright, a prominent local lawyer and surrogate judge. The six Wright children—Cornelia, Sarah, Charles, Benjamin, John, and Lavina—had attended school with the young Whipples in Adams. A "remarkably handsome" young woman, Cornelia Wright possessed a serene competence that endeared her to all whose lives she touched. Known as Nell to her friends and family, she was intelligent and practical, with a "great amiability." These were admirable qualities for a merchant's wife; for a clergyman's wife, they would be invaluable.[25]

The Wrights were Episcopalians, and Cornelia encouraged her new husband to join her church. "She led me to the Saviour," Whipple recalled fondly. He claimed that Cornelia influenced him primarily by example; it was her brother Benjamin who lectured him on religion. At their insistence, Whipple agreed to read the Bible and found its message compelling.[26]

Until his marriage, Whipple had not been especially religious, having been turned off by the enthusiasm of the revivalists.[27] Now, rereading the *Book of Common Prayer,* he found the church's ancient liturgy appealing, its focus on communal worship a welcome relief from the frenzied individualism of the revival movement. "The Puritan delighted to dwell on the Sovereignty of God rather than on the Fatherhood; and when

Cornelia Wright Whipple as a young woman. Cornelia attended Emma Willard's Female Academy in Troy, New York. When her father ran into financial difficulties before she graduated, she was allowed to finish her classes and pay for them later. Upon graduation, she went to South Carolina to teach the children of Governor Richard Manning. It was Cornelia who brought Henry Whipple into the Episcopal Church.

he believed that he was the chosen of God, elected from all Eternity to share in God's favor, it made him strong; but the poor soul who believed that he was not one of the elect was driven to despair." Episcopal theology seemed more benign to him: "I love the Book of Common Prayer for its sincere, fervent piety, its clear declaration of the truth of the Incarnation, and because it everywhere teaches the blessed doctrine of justification alone by the merits of our Lord and Saviour, Jesus Christ. I love it because it breathes a spirit of tender compassion for the erring."

Henry Whipple realized that he had found his spiritual home. His father's business associate,

William Pierrepont, arranged for him to be baptized by the Reverend Josiah H. Bartlett of Zion Episcopal Church in Pierrepont Manor, not far from Adams. Cornelia's brother Benjamin was baptized with him. In 1843 the two young men were confirmed by the Right Reverend William Heathcote DeLancey, Episcopal bishop of Western New York. Whipple suggested that Wright change his course of study from law to theology and (with Cornelia's enthusiastic approval) offered to help support him financially while he prepared for the ministry.

That fall, Whipple became seriously ill with a respiratory infection. His doctor operated on his throat and advised him that, if he wanted to save his life, to spend the winter in the more moderate climate of the South.[28] Leaving Cornelia and their infant daughter, Sarah Elizabeth (Lizzie), behind in his father's care, Henry set sail on October 20 for Savannah, Georgia.[29] The journey took nine days, during which Whipple suffered from seasickness and the frustration of adverse winds, which, on one day, held their progress to less than four miles in twenty-four hours of sailing.

During his two days in Savannah, he saw his first slaves, who appeared "happy and cheerful" but lazy, by his account. A steamship then took him down the inland passage to St. Augustine, Florida, where Cornelia's sister Sarah and her husband, George Fairbanks, lived. Whipple remained in St. Augustine for the next two months, living in a boardinghouse run by Mrs. Robert Reid.[30]

"The air and climate of St. Augustine," Whipple wrote in his diary, "is one of the finest in the world, and were it home I would love to live and die in this sunny land, this land of flowers as it is named." The twenty-one-year-old man was charmed by the hospitality of the plantation owners and businessmen whom he met through Fairbanks, then a clerk in the U.S. Circuit Court for northern Florida. He was easily convinced that Florida's slaves were not, after all, as miserable as his abolitionist uncle George Whipple believed, and he accepted at face value his hosts'

assurances that they would gladly abolish slavery were they not compelled to continue it by economic necessity. He observed, however, that owning slaves appeared to sap the energy of white slave owners, whose lack of economic initiative was shocking to a Yankee. Noting that it took a larger number of slaves to complete a task than it would a single northern laborer toiling for wages, he concluded that blacks were not capable of supporting themselves independently and, therefore, their transition to freedom should be gradual. "That it is right for men to be free none can doubt," he wrote, but it was "better to prepare them for freedom & then & not till then give them that precious boon which otherwise would be a curse."

Not until he attended a slave sale in Mobile, Alabama, did the cruelty of the system show itself to him: "The pitiful faces of those to be sold, the jokes & witticisms heard on all sides, the indecent remarks which one is obliged to listen to at times, all make it an unpleasant sight. . . . Never have I seen more sad and sorrowful faces than I have seen at these sales."

His deepest sympathy, however, was aroused not by the plight of slaves, but by tales of the recently concluded Seminole War in Florida. Led by Osceola, the Seminoles had fought for two years to keep from being moved against their will to the Indian Territory, now the state of Oklahoma. Mrs. Reid, whose husband had been actively involved in the Seminole War, gave Whipple a graphic account of Osceola's capture in 1837 while carrying a flag of truce. The Seminole chief died of malaria not long afterward in a prison at Fort Moultrie, South Carolina. Those Seminoles who continued to resist removal had fled deep into the southern swamps, and in 1844 the army was still trying to capture them and remove them from the state.

"When will the cupidity and cruelty of white men cease?" Whipple wrote in his diary, then answered himself sadly, "Not until the last lone Indian has

The plight of Seminole chief Osceola stirred Whipple during the winter of 1844–1845, which he spent in Florida for his health. Osceola led his people's resistance to the government's attempt to move them out of Florida in 1835. He was captured in 1837 and died of malaria at Fort Moultrie in South Carolina in 1838. His followers continued to fight sporadically until 1858, by which time most of the tribe had been relocated to the Indian Territory. Painting by George Catlin, 1838.

gone to the spirit land." War and the corruption accompanying it were costing the government hundreds of thousands of dollars, he complained, just "to expatriate the poor Seminole." He concluded his thoughts on the subject with the observation that "Christianity loses its lovely appearance when exhibited to the barbarian in garments of blood."

Whipple spent the winter comfortably, taking walks and horseback rides and visiting Jacksonville and St. Mary's, Georgia, by stage and steamer. He talked with planters, "crackers" (poor whites), and slaves, and found them all fascinating. Gradually his health improved, although he was still troubled occasionally by "poor weak nerves." On January 6, 1844, he noted in his diary that he had regained eleven pounds and now weighed 155. His twenty-second birthday came and went. With a touch of guilt, he noted, "This is the first winter I have ever tried the sweets of continual idleness, & I fancy will be the last, for all miseries deliver me from the ennui of being idle."

His stern Yankee upbringing is nowhere more evident than in his disapproving comments on the southerners' lack of religious feeling and their love of entertainment. He disliked their fondness for the theater, gambling, and blood sports, and their willingness to transact business and pursue pleasure on Sundays. Yet he enjoyed some of the pastimes his hosts urged on him, especially the costumed miming that was a part of the Epiphany season in Florida.

In February Whipple began a leisurely trip home. He spent a month in New Orleans, whose cathedral evoked the observation that "altho' full of blind bigotry yet there is a beautiful lesson of faith to be learned even from the misguided Catholics." The people of the sophisticated, multicultural city seemed hopelessly addicted to the pursuit of pleasure. Dueling was still practiced, and horse racing took place even on Sundays, as did cockfights, boxing matches, military parades, and opera performances. He counted twenty "glaring violations of this holy day and each participated in by hundreds & thousands."

Slavery in New Orleans wore a more vicious face than in rural Florida; Whipple saw slaves in the pillory and on chain gangs. He learned that slaves came in all shades of skin tone. "We have at our boarding house a boy as white as 9/10 of the boys at the north and yet this boy is & always will be a slave." It made Whipple uncomfortable: "I for one can never be reconciled to this heterogeneous mingling of colours."[31]

On March 30, he embarked on a steamboat to travel up the Mississippi. Sermons, lectures, concerts, and even a ball helped pass the time as the boat wound its way up the river. St. Louis, Missouri, where he paused for a day or two, was "a very fine city," with "good schools & churches & some fine hotels," though it possessed "a very large foreign population who exercise a very deleterious effect upon the city." At Cairo, Illinois, he changed to a smaller packet, noisy and crowded, to steam up the Ohio River to Cincinnati.[32]

By April 12, Whipple was heading east by stagecoach

The New Orleans riverfront probably looked much like this when Whipple visited the city in the spring of 1844. Two large flatboats have brought freight down the river, while the masts of clipper ships testify to the city's ocean trade. The steam-powered riverboat was a forerunner of the new steam age, which was revolutionizing travel on the rivers and oceans of the world. Whipple took a steamboat upriver on his journey home. The two church spires in the background are the First Presbyterian Church (the spire) and St. Patrick's Catholic Church (the square tower). Christ Episcopal Church, founded in 1803, stood on the riverside corner of Canal and Bourbon Streets, but it does not appear in this drawing.

View of the Cincinnati riverfront in the 1870s. Whipple disembarked in Cincinnati on his way home from Florida in 1844 and continued his journey east by stagecoach.

along the recently macadamized National Turnpike over the Allegheny Mountains to Cumberland, Maryland, where he boarded a train to Baltimore. His companions on this stretch of his journey, a boisterous bunch, were members of Ohio's delegation to the Whig National Convention in Baltimore.

Whipple spent two days sightseeing in Washington, D.C., admiring the Capitol, the Treasury, the Patent Office (especially the National Institute Museum, now the Smithsonian, on its second floor), and the White House. The seeming inactivity of members of the House of Representatives outraged him. "I expected to find much talent, but I certainly see but little exhibited," he remarked. He found that the senators displayed a

William Heathcote DeLancey, bishop of Western New York, was Whipple's mentor and ordained him to the priesthood in 1849. When Whipple later became a bishop, DeLancey advised him to "never be separated from your luggage."

greater dignity: "I never spent a more pleasant morning than the one I spent in the Senate."

A friend introduced him to Samuel Morse, inventor of the telegraph, who was ensconced in the basement of the Capitol. Morse sent the message "Mr. Whipple of New York is here" over the wire to a room in a nearby hotel and showed Whipple how to read the response from the series of dots and dashes that appeared on a coil of paper. "Tell Mr. Whipple," the reply said, "that he is looking upon an invention which will revolutionize the commerce of the world."[33]

After several days in Philadelphia, where he visited the chief tourist sites and was appalled by the crowds of "foreign scum," Whipple arrived in Adams in mid-May 1844 and resumed his business and politi-

cal activities.[34] Two more daughters joined the family: Cornelia Ward in 1845 and Jane Whiting in 1847.[35]

In 1847, Whipple served as secretary of the Democratic Convention in Syracuse, where the "Barnburners" and the "Hunkers" battled for control of the party in New York. The chief point of contention was America's involvement in the Mexican War, an expansionist act that brought California into the American fold but exacerbated the slavery issue when an effort was made to outlaw slavery in any new territories acquired by the war. It was Whipple's last partisan political endeavor.

As time went by, Whipple was finding the siren call of the church hard to ignore. Despite what he considered an attractive offer of a job as broker for a grain dealer in Chicago, he decided in January 1848 to enter the Episcopal priesthood. He wrote to Bishop DeLancey and inquired about the requirements for ordination. With a wife and three children to support, he could not afford to attend the General Theological Seminary in New York City. Would it be possible, he asked, to get his theological education without leaving western New York? The bishop arranged for him to study privately with the Reverend W. D. Wilson, rector of Christ Church in Sherburne, and even offered him a dispensation that would shorten his course work. This last Whipple declined, insisting he was perfectly capable of taking the entire course, under Wilson's tutelage. His father and wife supported his decision, although his political friend Thurlow Weed "hoped a good politician had not been spoiled to make a poor preacher."[36]

Leaving his family in Adams, Whipple spent the next year and a half in Sherburne (some eighty-five miles south of Adams), completing his studies in June 1849. Returning to Adams, he spent the summer working for his father and acting as lay reader at the new Episcopal church organized the previous February. As lay reader, he was authorized to lead prayer services but not to perform rites of the church.

On August 26, 1849, Bishop DeLancey ordained Henry Whipple to the diaconate at Trinity Church in Geneva, New York.

Whipple was never an innovative theologian. His sermons broke no new theological ground, and he doesn't seem to have questioned accepted doctrines. It was diligence, not brilliance, that enabled him to complete his theological training within such a short time—that and the individual attention of Dr. Wilson. But he had a sincere belief that he was able to convey to his listeners, and that made him a popular preacher. His God was a kind and loving figure, the kind of father he had known in John Whipple: forgiving, sustaining, always accessible. He was convinced that mankind was lost without Christ: "God is a necessity of thought." His simple language, gauged to the intellectual level of his audience, lacked the oratorical flourishes beloved by so many of his colleagues. His imagery was often romantic, as when he called the sacrament of communion "the trysting place of love."[37]

His colleagues spoke of his "childlike love" and "genuine humility," which showed themselves in an obvious gratitude "for any word of appreciation." They were charmed by the "youthful hope and high courage" shining from his "clear-cut and ecclesiastical" face and by the musical quality of his voice "that, without an effort . . . filled the largest of English cathedrals."[38]

His theological outlook expressed itself in his behavior toward his fellow Christians. Nothing pained him so much as disputes among believers; he often urged argumentative colleagues to seek common ground on which they could lay aside their quarrels. At a gathering of church notables, he once placed his right arm around the shoulders of an extreme supporter of High Church ritual and his left around those of one of the staunchest evangelical Low Churchmen, smiled, and exclaimed, "Here are two of the best men in the whole church. I don't know which I love the more, and they are just beginning to find out how much they

Whipple with daughter Jane (known as Jennie), ca. 1849, before he became a priest. Jane Whiting Whipple married Henry A. Scandrett in May 1872. Having acquired tuberculosis during the Civil War, Scandrett had come to Minnesota to recover his health. For many years, he sold insurance in Faribault and served as treasurer of the Seabury Mission. In 1881, when his illness grew worse, the family moved to New Mexico. They returned two years later, and Scandrett died in Faribault.

love each other!" Unable to move, the two men had no choice but to smile at one another, and, claimed Whipple, from that moment they became fast friends.[39]

Despite his mercantile background, Whipple seems to have had little interest in acquiring personal wealth. The money that came to him from benefactors went for the work of the church. His family lived modestly, although he saw that his children were well educated in church-sponsored boarding schools. He gave freely of his time and possessions, though he could drive a shrewd bargain when necessary and could wheedle generous donations for his causes out of the most hesitant giver.[40]

Called to serve at Zion Church in Rome, New York, soon after his ordination, Henry Benjamin Whipple set out at last upon his life's work.

Zion Church in Rome, New York, for which Whipple raised construction funds. Designed in the neo-Gothic style by leading Episcopal Church architect Richard Upjohn, it featured a ceiling open to the rafters, buttresses on the outside walls, and a double belfry on the roof.

*H*enry Whipple received his call to Zion Church in Rome, New York, in the fall of 1849, not long after the birth of his fourth child, Charles.[41] Although the parish was relatively small, Whipple was paid $500 a year, plus $125 toward the rental of a house—a decent enough salary in a time when missionaries often earned less than half that. Many of his relatives lived in the town or nearby, and he still had friends there from his school days.[42]

Set amid a thriving agricultural district in central New York, Rome in the early 1850s was a bustling community of 7,920 souls. It boasted a number of small factories—canneries, knitting mills, and the nation's first modern cheese-processing plant. The Erie Canal and the railroad both passed through the town.[43]

Founded in 1825 as a mission of New York City's Trinity Church, Zion Church in 1849 was a "feeble" parish, Whipple felt, though "loyal and true." He saw not weakness but potential. Within four months of his arrival, the vestry voted to purchase an abandoned public school lot upon which to build a new church. They sent Whipple to New York to consult with Richard Upjohn, the designer of Trinity Church who was acquiring a reputation as the Episcopal Church's leading architect. Upjohn accepted Zion's commission and produced a neo-Gothic plan to be constructed of "unhewn stone of a dark blue shade" and "crowned with a double belfry."[44]

Whipple's experience as a merchant and politician served him well in his new role as the builder of a young parish. Unlike many of his colleagues, who came out of seminary filled with enthusiasm for their faith and little more, he understood the practical business of administering a community and raising funds to support it. He was already acquainted with many of the state's most wealthy and influential men, and he quickly got to know the others. Never embarrassed to ask for money for a good cause, he seemed to have a sixth sense for finding donors willing to trust him with their funds.[45]

Original Zion Church in Rome, New York, Whipple's first parish. It was built in 1826 in cooperation with the Masonic Order. When membership in the Masons declined after 1830, Zion parish purchased the property and renovated it in the colonial style. At the building's dedication on September 15, 1833, Zion's membership consisted of twenty-seven families. Frequent clergy turnover and financial troubles were "a recurring source of concern."

Whipple returned to New York in November 1850 to solicit financial aid for his parish's building project and came home with private pledges and donations, including "sundry gifts of prayerbooks for reading desk and altar," but no substantial funds from Trinity Church. A second appeal made toward the end of the construction process was no more successful. Whipple felt it was the absence of John A. Dix, his friend and an influential member of Trinity's vestry, that blocked his request at the time it was made. Construction began on August 15, 1850; a year later the first service was held in the new building. Unfortunately, donations were $2,800 short of what was needed to complete the job. Whipple's skill at fundraising was put to its first major test as he struggled to find the resources to pay off the debt. With the help of the vestry, he scraped together nearly $1,700 in additional local subscriptions.

Meanwhile, he had been lobbying friends among New York's political elite, including Governor Horatio Seymour, who agreed to write to Trinity Church's vestry, asking them to support Zion's request for aid. Dix later told Whipple that when Zion's appeal was discussed at the vestry meeting in the fall of 1851, five members in turn rose and read out letters they had received. Finally, one vestryman said, "I suspect that we each have a letter in behalf of this application. I move that no more letters be read, but that the grant be made unanimously." Thus Whipple wrested a loan of $1,000 from Trinity to settle the last of Zion's debt. When challenged by Trinity's comptroller as to the morality of his strategy, Whipple quoted Jesus's parable of the unjust judge who grants the poor widow justice to get her to stop pestering him. The comptroller smiled and invited Whipple to dine with him the following day.

Whipple had begun his service at Zion as a newly ordained deacon; he held services, performed marriage, funeral, and baptismal rites, and assisted at the Eucharist. He was also authorized as a missionary pastor and supported in part by the national church's Board of Missions. He was ordained a priest at Christ Church in Sackets Harbor, near Adams, in February 1850. As priest he could now preside at the Eucharist and grant absolution. Nine months later, he became Zion's first rector, chosen and paid by the parish with the approval of Bishop William DeLancey.

Whipple was instituted on September 26, 1851, the day after the dedication of the new church by Bishop DeLancey. The sermon for the occasion was preached by Whipple's former mentor, the Reverend W. D. Wilson. "A happier life God never gave to man than that of a shepherd of Christ's flock," Whipple reflected years later. This was especially true at Zion. "No pastor ever had a more loving and devoted parish." To this day, he is remembered by Zion as "a man of dynamic energy and inspiration."[46] He made a point of ministering not only to the "men and women of culture and note" in his parish, but also to the "large population of extreme poor" in the city's shantytowns.

Whipple was proud that he had never refused Communion to anyone who had been baptized, no matter what church they usually attended, even though it was customary in most parishes to limit Communion to "communicants" (baptized and confirmed adults who attend church regularly and take communion at least three times a year). One of Whipple's communicants had married a man who was a prominent member of the local Presbyterian church, and they attended services alternately at one another's churches. One day, the husband told Whipple, "I do not like to turn my back on the Lord's Table. May I go to the Communion with my wife?"

Whipple answered, "It is not our Communion Table, it is the Lord's. If you have been baptized in the name of the Blessed Trinity, hear the invitation, 'Ye who do truly repent and desire to come'; it is your privilege." When he asked DeLancey if he had done the right thing, the bishop said he had, quoting Bishop John Henry Hobart of New York as his authority.

Whipple learned to preach, as priests often do, by listening to the comments he received from his congregation. Early in his career, while substituting for the rector of a church in another town, he attempted to impress the congregation by delivering what he considered his best sermon. Afterward, one of his parishioners, who had known him from his childhood, put his hand on Whipple's shoulder and told him earnestly, "Henry, no matter how long you live, *never preach that sermon again!*" He never did.

Whipple's standard routine for preparing a sermon began on Monday with reading the services, lessons, collect, Epistle, and Gospel for the following Sunday. "There is a lesson inwrought and underlying the service for each Sunday, Festival and Fast day," he explained, "which a prayerful consideration will bring out. Selecting my text, I have made my notes as full as if I were to preach extempore. Then destroying the notes I have reviewed the subject and made other notes, often repeating this several times. When my heart was full of my subject, after earnest prayer, I have written my sermon." Even on those occasions when he preached an unwritten sermon, he followed the same process, "always

with the prayer that the words spoken might by the Holy Spirit help some poor soul to find peace."

The popular young preacher was soon receiving offers from churches in Chicago and Milwaukee, as well as Terre Haute, Indiana, and Buffalo and Oxford, New York. He turned them down. He was happy in Rome, the "one bright oasis in a careworn life." He made many lifelong friends in the city and returned frequently to the end of his life.

In 1853, not long after the birth of Frances (Fannie),[47] Cornelia became seriously ill with typhoid fever. Her doctor recommended a mild climate for the winter. Henry decided to take her to Florida, where the tropical air might speed her recovery, as it had his a decade earlier. The vestry voted him a six months' leave, and Cornelia's sister, Sarah Fairbanks, invited them to stay with her in St. Augustine.

While the Whipples were in New York looking for a ship to take them south, Henry stopped in at the General Convention, which was being held there at the time. He encountered Florida's Bishop Francis H. Rutledge, who had been rector of Trinity Church in

St. Augustine, Florida, in 1855, shortly after the Whipples wintered there while Cornelia recovered from typhoid fever. Trinity Church, where Whipple served as interim rector, appears at left rear. The state had changed considerably since Whipple's visit a decade earlier. In 1853 it led both Georgia and South Carolina in cotton production, and its population grew, between 1850 and 1860, from 87,445 to 140,424, 40 percent of whom were slaves.

George R. Fairbanks, Whipple's friend and one-time brother-in-law. Fairbanks' first wife was Cornelia's sister, Sarah; his second wife, Susan Beard, was the widow of Cornelia's brother, Benjamin. A lawyer by profession, Fairbanks served in the Florida territorial legislature before the Civil War and was later a major in the Confederate army. In 1868, he helped to found the University of the South at Sewanee, Tennessee, where he taught history and served on the board of trustees as commissioner of buildings and lands. Fairbanks, who maintained homes in both Florida and Tennessee, was a promoter of the citrus industry, served as editor of the *Florida Mirror*, and wrote several histories of Florida, one of which was used for many years in the state's public schools.

St. Augustine during Whipple's previous visit. Rutledge told Whipple that his diocese was suffering from a severe shortage of clergy and asked if he would undertake mission work in east Florida during his stay there. Whipple agreed, no doubt pleased at the prospect of earning a salary during his stay.[48]

From November 1853 to April 1854, Whipple was interim rector at Trinity St. Augustine. As the parish at Jacksonville was also vacant, Whipple was the only Episcopal minister in all of east Florida that season.[49] While Cornelia recuperated, he traveled around the area, preaching and holding services. He raised money to enlarge and beautify Trinity Church, and founded a church in Palatka, twenty-six miles to the southwest. He preached a sermon at the state convention in Tallahassee. He also visited Charleston, South Carolina, at Bishop Rutledge's

request, to solicit funds for mission work in Florida.[50]

Florida had changed noticeably in the ten years since Whipple's first visit. Cotton plantations were spreading across the countryside, with sugarcane a close second in production. As both crops were labor-intensive, slaves made up 40 percent of the population. There were more towns, more roads, even a few colleges. Railroads were being built through the swamps and canebrakes, although it still took Whipple nearly a week to travel the two hundred miles from Jacksonville to Tallahassee, a journey that could be made only by stagecoach.[51]

Whipple's earlier enthusiasm for Florida was reinforced as he traveled around the area, holding services in plantation houses. He preached to slaves as well as to their masters, preparing a large class of "black servants" for confirmation in St. Augustine. Although still convinced that masters and slaves were frequently "united in bonds of affection," he criticized a man for complaining that his new slave was sullen after having been separated from his wife and children. "The negro is mad, as you or I would be," he remarked. The ambivalence of Whipple's attitude did not disturb Florida's slaves, however. They liked this New York preacher. When a group of them heard that he was raising money to improve the church in St. Augustine, they collected a large basket of eggs as their donation to the cause.[52]

Whipple had the greatest respect for his black sexton, David, who listened closely to the parson's sermons and then repeated them to those who couldn't come to the services. "Old David was a devout man who believed in Jesus Christ as if he had put his finger in the prints of the nails," Whipple recalled. "Jesus walked with him, was in his home and heard his prayers." The young priest was touched by David's simple, all-inclusive faith and eagerness to share it.[53]

When he returned to Zion in April 1854, Whipple attempted to tender his resignation, but the vestry refused to accept it. Again, he received offers from other churches, including one in Florida, and again he turned them down. But other forces were combining to change his life. In December 1856, shortly after he refused a call to Grace Church in Chicago, he received a letter from Albert E. Neely, who described a mission that he and his fellow members at Chicago's St. James Church hoped to begin among the city's railroad workers. The mission, to be called Holy Communion, would be a "free church," where both rich and poor could worship equally. Neely asked Whipple to take charge of the new parish.[54]

During his visits to New York on parish business, Whipple had observed the novel concept of "free" churches—churches that did not charge a fee for pew rental but welcomed all comers. In those days, pew rental was the accepted means of financing the parish's operations, including paying the rector's salary. In Rome, as in most communities at this time, Episcopal Church membership consisted largely of wealthy, influential people for whom the $8 to $12 annual pew rentals presented no real hardship. To abandon such a tried and true fiscal program required a leap of faith that most vestries were reluctant to take on behalf of their constituents.[55]

Whipple was intrigued by Neely's proposal. Much as he loved Zion, the challenge had gone out of his work there. He had always wanted to take God's word to the poor, the outcasts of society, to gather them back into the fold and make good middle-class Christians of them. In Rome's shantytowns and among Florida's "crackers" and slaves, the emotional response to his efforts was satisfying, much more so than the well-bred behavior of his middle- and upper-class congregants. But to take this position would be a major gamble. His father said his son had "no right to go to Chicago for an experiment." After all, Cornelia was expecting their sixth child in March. Bishop DeLancey questioned whether Whipple had received a real "call." Whipple worried about the climate in Chicago and whether it would endanger Cornelia's health. There were "consumptive tendencies" in her family, he told Neely.[56] After much soul-searching, Whipple turned down the

Trinity Church in St. Augustine, Florida, where Whipple served for six months as interim rector in 1853–1854. Its previous rector was Cornelia's brother Benjamin Wright, who had developed tuberculosis while serving at his first parish in Sackets Harbor, New York. He went to Florida in the vain hope of regaining his health, but he died in 1852.

Chicago job.

Almost immediately, he had second thoughts. After all, Rome's climate was not so very healthy either. Hadn't Cornelia contracted her severe typhoid there? Also, he was having trouble making ends meet. Although Zion was now paying him $1,000 a year, it was barely enough to support his growing family, especially as he hoped to send his oldest daughter away to boarding school in New Jersey. Neely had offered him $2,000 a year, plus moving expenses. And there were all those unchurched railroad workers in need of salvation. He reminded himself that he had become a priest because he wanted to minister to the spiritual needs of the community. Certainly, the rich had as many spiritual needs as the poor. But Christ had given his followers clear instructions to serve the poor, and Whipple would have that chance in Chicago. He wrote Neely in March and accepted the call.[57] He was unaware that he was beginning a journey that would lead him from the quiet life of a small town preacher toward the greater fame that awaited him.

Metropolitan Hall, where Whipple held his first services in Chicago, was on the third floor of the Metropolitan Building on the corner of Randolph and LaSalle Streets, shown here in 1858.

Albert Neely was delighted with Henry Whipple's decision. He wrote that he had found a hall in the heart of Chicago that could be rented for $550 a year. It was on the city's South Side, not far from the railroad yards, "easy of access to poor and rich." St. James Church would "lend" them the three members required by church law to form a parish.[58] Whipple went to Chicago in April, shortly after the birth of his second son, John, and pronounced himself satisfied with the arrangements.

Chicago in 1857 was a bustling young city with a population of more than seventy-five thousand. Founded twenty-four years earlier on the swampy land where the Chicago River flows into Lake Michigan, it had grown faster than any city in the nation. It was a natural meeting place for traffic between the eastern states and settlements on the Upper Mississippi, a situation that the nation's railroad builders had quickly recognized. By midcentury, Chicago was the center of the largest rail network in the world. Grain elevators, lumberyards, and meatpacking plants crowded along the waterfront.

It was not a beautiful city. There was no sewage system, and the river into which the roadside ditches drained was thick with a greasy sludge that stank in summer. Few of the streets were paved. Animals often lay for days where they died. State Street was a muddy alley lined with pawnshops, boardinghouses, saloons, and blacksmith shops. The main business district was on Lake Street, leading down to the wharves on Lake Michigan.

Poverty was widespread and extreme; 25 percent of the population controlled 100 percent of the city's wealth. The rest were crowded into ramshackle pine shanties, two to a lot, or lived in disreputable "patches" along the riverbanks. Gambling and prostitution were widespread. The Sunday closing laws for saloons were not observed. Outright worship of money was the city's chief characteristic.[59] From a young clergyman's point of view, this was a town in serious need of religion.

Whipple wrote to his daughters in June, describing the "very busy" city and its crowded wooden sidewalks. At the hotel where he was boarding, four hundred people ate every day. Metropolitan Hall, where the Church of the Holy Communion would begin its life, was large enough to seat twenty-five hundred people, though his small congregation took up only a fraction of the space. There were five other Episcopal churches in the city, but his was the only "free" one. He had about a dozen scholars in his Sunday school already, and he was confident the parish would grow. Whipple soon found a small but pleasant house for his family, only half a mile from the church, and they joined him in September.[60]

The young priest spent his weekdays at the railroad yards, talking with the men there and inviting them to come to his church. William J. McAlpine, chief engineer of the Galena Railroad, suggested that the men would be more likely to listen to Whipple if he knew something about railroading. So

George McClellan was chief engineer and vice president of the Illinois Central Railroad when he attended Whipple's Holy Communion Church. A Mexican War veteran, he served as general-in-chief of the Army of the Potomac from July 1861 to November 1862. In 1864, he ran against Lincoln on the Democratic ticket.

West Point graduate Ambrose Burnside, a railroad engineer who became a Civil War general, also attended Whipple's church. McClellan hired Burnside for the Illinois Central in 1858, and he became its treasurer in 1860. He was elected governor of Rhode Island in 1866 and served in the U.S. Senate from 1875 to 1881.

Whipple read a copy of *Lardner's Railroad Economy* from cover to cover. Soon he was able to discuss the merits of different locomotives with ease. Among the railroad men in Holy Communion's congregation were George McClellan and Ambrose Burnside, West Point–educated engineers with the Illinois Central, who would soon gain fame as Civil War generals.

Railroading was a hazardous occupation in those days, when the technology was well in advance of safety precautions. Whenever he heard of an accident, Whipple went to the superintendent of the line involved and asked the names of the injured so he could visit them. He also visited prisoners and social outcasts—prostitutes, actors, gamblers—inviting one and all to come to his church. This did not always sit well with his parishioners. There were objections when he proposed to baptize an actress and her baby. "Knowing the weak side of human nature, I was pained but not surprised," Whipple later recalled. At length, McAlpine and his wife offered to sponsor her and the dispute ended.

Whipple had no doubt that he had acted correctly. "Convinced of this woman's fitness to receive the sacraments of the Church, I would have received her had it left me with a congregation of one mother and babe," he wrote. Later, when he presented the woman for confirmation, Bishop Henry J. Whitehouse asked how he could be expected to confirm someone with such a notorious occupation.

"Bishop," Whipple said, "would you sustain me if I were to suspend a Communicant from the Holy Communion for attending the theatre?"

"Certainly not," Whitehouse replied.

"Then can I refuse to receive this pure woman who loves Jesus Christ, when she asks me for a home in the church?" asked Whipple.

Whitehouse smiled. "Certainly not," he said. And he confirmed the woman.

Whipple's knack for conversing with all sorts and conditions of men (and women) helped his missionary work quickly bear fruit. His simple, straightforward sermons, delivered in his beautiful, clear voice, were popular. Soon his congregations were so large that some of the other Episcopal churches accused him of "poaching" members from their parishes.

The rivalry between the church's High and Low factions was especially bitter in Chicago's Episcopal churches. Throughout much of the nineteenth century, the Episcopal Church was torn by a sharp theological dispute between its evangelical, or Low Church, wing, which traced its development back to the Calvinists of the Reformation period, and the High Churchmen, or ritualists, who revered the church's ancient liturgies, translated from Roman Catholic usage by the fathers of the church under Kings Edward VI and James I. Low Churchmen stressed personal faith and reading of the Scriptures; High Churchmen preferred communal worship through the *Book of Common Prayer.* Low Churchmen insisted on the need for individual conversion; High Churchmen preached general penitence and participation in the life of the church. Low Churchmen wore simple dress during services, supplemented the *Book of Common Prayer* with prayer meetings and revival-style preaching, and celebrated the Eucharist only on special occasions; High Churchmen wore long white linen surplices and black stoles, confined their worship to the services in the *Book of Common Prayer,* and celebrated the Eucharist frequently. Some High Churchmen were beginning to revive the use of decorative practices from the old Roman Catholic tradition, such as candles, embroidered altar cloths, and robed choirs. This offended the Low Churchmen, whose altars were unadorned tables holding no more than a simple wooden cross, with a plain linen cloth used during Communion, and who preferred congregational singing to trained choirs.[61]

In this struggle, Whipple constantly urged moderation and brotherhood. Although he considered himself a High Churchman, he tried not to impose his views on those Anglicans who differed from him. "Strife is an awful price to pay for the best results,"

Henry John Whitehouse was bishop of Chicago during Whipple's time there. Whitehouse's popularity was limited by his refusal to live in Illinois and his inability to control the theological squabbling among his clergy. Whipple made a point of not emulating the older man's administrative style.

he once wrote, "but strife among Christ's own kinsmen is a grievous sin." He was as distressed by the ardent Anglo-Catholics as by the passionate evangelicals. "While the Church should be careful to set forth in all its fullness the wondrous scheme of redemption," he insisted, "we should be careful not, by any possibility, to teach the unlearned such a reverence as may even border upon an idolatrous worship of the elements." High and Low Church were simply the reflection of "two classes of men, one magnifying the blessed Orders and Sacraments of the Church because they are the gifts of Christ and His channels of grace, the other magnifying the personal faith of the sinner in Jesus Christ and seeing in the sacraments witness of the love of the Saviour. Both hold opposite sides of Divine truth and ought to live together in love as members of one body."[62]

"It has always been a cause for thankfulness that God has given me the ability to put aside the petty annoyances which fret out life," Whipple wrote many years later. "It is worry, not work, that kills men; and the man is happy who can shut out troubles when the day's work is done, for burdens are not lightened by hugging them to the heart." His refusal to become involved in the dispute impressed many of his listeners, who were tired of hearing lengthy harangues about the theological merits of placing, or not placing, candles on the altar.

The High/Low Church dispute wasn't the only problem Bishop Whitehouse had with his diocese. The Episcopal Church at that time did not require bishops to reside in their dioceses, but only to make annual visitations to perform confirmations. White-house preferred to live in New York. This did not sit well with many of Whipple's parishioners. When the yearly diocesan convention passed an assessment of one dollar per communicant for sup-port of the bishop, Whipple's vestry at first refused to pay it. Whipple told them he would not preach an-other sermon in the parish until they accepted their

St. Ansgarius Episcopal Church in Chicago. Whipple preached often at this Scan-dinavian church at the re-quest of its Episcopal rector, the Reverend Gustaf Unonius.

canonical duty and paid up. Reluctantly, they obeyed. "No one felt more keenly than I did the non-residence of Bishop Whitehouse," Whipple admitted in his auto-biography, "but to me he was always the kindest and most affectionate of friends and bishops."

At least once each week, Whipple preached at St. Ansgarius Swedish Episcopal Church in Chicago. The massive Scandinavian immigration of the period had led the Episcopal Church to review the history of the Scandinavian Lutheran churches to see whether it might draw their members into the Episcopal fold. The Lutheran service used by Swedish and Norwe-gian churches resembled the English one, as both had been translated originally from the Catholic Mass. The church in Sweden, like the Anglican Church, had kept the tradition of choosing bishops in the ancient Catholic manner: by consent of a convocation of prelates. The Norwegian church, on the other hand, followed the German practice of electing bishops. Be-cause the Swedish church had not broken the line of succession, the Episcopal Church decided it could be recognized as an orthodox Christian community and its members accepted as properly confirmed. As Whipple put it, "With a valid ministry, a reformed faith and a liturgical service, they ought to be in commun-ion with us." The Norwegians would have to be con-firmed again by an Episcopal bishop, but they too could probably be brought into the church successfully.[63]

Bishop Whitehouse had written to Whipple in March 1857, describ-ing the large numbers of Swedish and Norwegian immigrants in Chicago and the proposed outreach being made to them under the leadership of the Reverend Gustaf Unonius, a graduate of the Episcopal Church's Nashotah House seminary in Wisconsin. Whitehouse had approved

Unonius's organization of St. Ansgarius Episcopal Church, which soon had a small congregation composed of Swedish and Norwegian immigrants.

But Swedes and Norwegians have different traditions, and St. Ansgarius's two nationalities did not always work in harmony. Unonius tended to side with his fellow Swedes. When he left Chicago to visit Sweden in 1858, he asked Whipple to look after his congregation and entrusted to him the Communion service that famed singer Jenny Lind had donated to St. Ansgarius. It had been given to the Swedes, Unonius told Whipple, and in the event that the Swedish and Norwegian congregations split, the service was to stay with the Swedes.[64]

Cornelia Whipple took an active part in the work of her husband's mission. She too felt a strong calling to serve the poor and bring them to Christ, a habit of mind that went back to her school days. The poor families in the back alleys of the Whipples' neighborhood soon became familiar with the cleric's wife who visited their sick and needy, and her efforts were highly appreciated by those she served.[65]

By the end of his first year, Whipple had gathered a large enough congregation to begin planning for a proper church building. In January 1858, St. James had moved to a new building and its members offered their old church to Holy Communion. A week later it caught fire, suffering nearly $2,000 worth of damage. Undaunted, Whipple forged ahead, and by February 1859 he had moved his parish into a sturdy wooden Gothic-style church on the old St. James site.[66]

After two years in Chicago, things were going well, and the Reverend Henry Whipple had no thought of changing his post in the immediate future. Then, one afternoon in July 1859, his friend, the Reverend Dr. Robert H. Clarkson of St. James, approached him, put his arm around Whipple's shoulder, and offered him his congratulations on having been elected bishop of the new diocese of Minnesota.[67]

A dumbfounded Whipple wrote in his diary that evening, "May God help me!"

HIGH CHURCH versus LOW CHURCH

THE QUESTION OF HOW MUCH ritual is proper to Christian worship has dogged the English church since its earliest days. Inspired by John Calvin, the evangelical extremists, who believed that faith alone was necessary for salvation and who laid a heavy stress on personal conversion, became known as Low Churchmen, while those who insisted that sacraments, penitence, and full involvement in the life of the church, with its ancient apostolic tradition, were more important, became known as High Churchmen. Both groups filled their Sundays with an extensive program of church-related activities, including Sunday school for all ages and sermons lasting up to an hour or more, supplemented by weekday lectures and services, especially among the evangelicals.

In the 1840s a group of radical liturgists centered at Oxford (sometimes called Tractarians for the tracts they published describing their views) argued that a sacred setting was as important to the reception of the Gospel as sincere preaching. They called for restoration of many practices (flowers and candles on the altar, robed choirs, vestments in seasonal colors, orders of deaconesses) denounced by the evangelicals as a "popish" preference for form over substance.

The Oxford Movement gained support among the ritualist High Churchmen, while it was fervently condemned by the evangelical Low Churchmen. Those High Churchmen who adopted a wide range of Catholic practices but remained Anglicans were called Anglo-Catholics. Those who, like Whipple, tried to find some common ground in the center became known as Broad Churchmen.

Imported into the American church by its theologians, the battle between High and Low Churchmen raged for half a century with much vindictive name-calling on both sides. In 1873, the most extreme wing of the Low Church broke away to form the Reformed Episcopal Church. By the mid-twentieth century, many of the disputed practices had become standard, but the Episcopal Church continues to feel the aftereffects of the struggle.[68]

St. Paul in 1859, when Whipple arrived as bishop. The state of Minnesota was then a year old; its population was about 172,000, not including 17,000 Indians. The state capital, St. Paul, had 10,401 inhabitants and two Episcopal churches.

The diocese that elected Henry Whipple as its bishop, like the state whose boundaries it shared, was a fairly new creation. Minnesota Territory, which included a large tract of land that had been part of the Louisiana Purchase, as well as the region along the western shore of Lake Superior, joined the Union in May 1858. The new state's 79,548-square-mile land area was nearly the size of Great Britain.

Until 1840, most of the white people in Minnesota were fur traders or soldiers. Major trading posts had been established at Traverse des Sioux on the Minnesota River and at Crow Wing on the Upper Mississippi. Fort Snelling, built in 1821, supported the trading posts along the Mississippi and its tributaries. Minnesota's extensive pine woods had begun to attract the attention of lumbermen already at work in northwest Wisconsin. By 1849, the territory's white population had grown to a little more than 4,000. By 1857, it exceeded 150,000, many of the newcomers establishing farms on the 1,468,434 acres of public land that had been purchased from the Dakota in the Treaty of Traverse des Sioux in July 1851. This flood of white immigration was beginning to strain relations with the Ojibwe and Dakota, who had made their homes in the territory for several centuries. As treaty after treaty was signed, the Native Americans relinquished ever-increasing amounts of land to the white newcomers, who firmly believed in their manifest destiny to occupy and "civilize" the continent from sea to sea.[69]

The Episcopal Church was just beginning to deal with the nation's expanding boundaries. For the first twenty-five years of its existence, it had been primarily an eastern church, preoccupied with the challenge of defining its role as an Anglican church no longer attached to England. A convocation was called in Connecticut in 1785 by Samuel Seabury, who had been consecrated the previous year in Scotland by Scottish Anglican bishops who were semi-independent of the English Church. Another group, led by William White, rewrote the *Book of Common Prayer* and devised an American liturgy, which it submitted to the archbishop of Canterbury in 1786. White and Samuel Prevoost were consecrated by the archbishop in 1787.

At its constitutional convention in 1789, the American church recognized Seabury's somewhat irregular consecration, set up rules for the organization of dioceses and parishes, approved the American version of the prayer book, and made other decisions necessary to create a proper Anglican church organization. Rejecting the authoritarian structure of the mother church, it provided for a General Convention to be held every three years. Every diocese would be required to send two lay and two clerical delegates to the convention to vote on issues of importance. A separate House of Bishops would have veto power over the convention's decisions. There would be no archbishop; the presiding bishop would have minimal administrative duties beyond those of his own diocese.[70]

America, however, did not wait for the Episcopal Church to organize itself. No sooner was the Treaty of Paris signed in 1783 than settlers made their way across the mountains into the interior of the continent, to Ohio and Kentucky, and beyond. The Baptists began sending missionaries west in 1785, and the Methodists had ten circuits set up in the West by 1789. The Congregationalists founded their first missionary society in 1800, followed in 1802 by the Presbyterians. These missionaries were primarily concerned with recruiting Euro-American Christians, but soon they began looking at the nonwhite field as well.

The vigorous sermons of the Second Great Awakening brought increased church attendance among Episcopalians as well as other denominations, and a strong demand arose for new priests to work both in the East and on the frontier. Seminaries were founded and missions established to work in Asia, Africa, and the American West. In 1820, the church founded the Domestic and Foreign Mission Society to oversee this work.

Acknowledging the need to provide services to its members on the frontier, the church appointed Jackson Kemper missionary bishop of the Northwest in 1835. He was given responsibility for the territories of Indiana and Missouri. Three years later, when Leonidas Polk was named missionary bishop for the southwest, Kemper's jurisdiction was expanded to include the territories of Wisconsin and Iowa, and "all other parts of the United States north of latitude 36 1/2 where the church is yet unorganized"—an area larger than all of Eastern Europe.[71] By then, the Episcopal Church had 22 dioceses, 18 bishops, and 772 clergy serving an estimated 40,000 communicants. (By contrast, the Methodists by 1838 had 6 bishops, 2,458 clergy, 638,784 official members, and perhaps 2 million unofficial constituents.)[72]

Kemper paid his first visit to Minnesota in 1843, where he met with Ezekiel Gear, the army chaplain

Jackson Kemper, missionary bishop of the Northwest from 1835 to 1859, whose district included Minnesota until 1857. Born in Pleasant Valley, New York, Kemper oversaw the organization of the Diocese of Minnesota and the election of Whipple as its first bishop.

at Fort Snelling and the only Episcopal minister in the region. From 1846 to 1848, the Reverend Ebenezer Greenleaf ran a small mission at Stillwater, a lumbering community on the St. Croix River, but there was little sustained activity by Episcopal missionaries in the territory until 1850, when James Lloyd Breck arrived in St. Paul with two companions to set up a mission.

Born in Philadelphia in 1818, Breck had decided to become a missionary while still in his teens. He and two colleagues founded a mission called Nashotah House on the shores of a lake near Prairieville, Wisconsin, in 1844. Modeling their undertaking on a medieval monastic pattern, the young men pledged themselves to celibacy, work, and worship, devoting themselves to preaching the Gospel in the surrounding countryside and recruiting young men to train for the priesthood while raising their own food and sharing domestic chores. It was a challenging program and difficult to maintain. As the area became more settled, the need for priests to serve parishes in the area put increased pressure on the school to provide them. When the seminary began to replace the mission as Nashotah's reason for being, Breck decided to start over with two new colleagues in Minnesota.[73]

When Breck's party arrived in June 1850, the Minnesota Territory consisted of three small settlements: St. Paul, with about 1,300 people; St. Anthony, with another 250; and Stillwater, with about 150. There were fewer than fifteen Episcopal communicants, six of whom lived in St. Paul. On a bluff overlooking the village of St. Paul, Breck built a twelve-by-seventeen-foot frame house for what he called the Associate Mission. During the next two years, he and his colleagues founded several missions in Minnesota—at Cottage Grove, Marine Mills, Sauk Rapids, and Prairie La Crosse (now La Crescent), as well as at Hudson in Wisconsin.

With Bishop Kemper's permission, Breck left St. Paul in the spring of 1852 to set up a mission among the Ojibwe at Gull Lake in central Minnesota. Although at first the mission (which Breck named St. Columba) seemed to thrive, Breck eventually came into conflict with a group of Ojibwe led by Hole-in-the-Day, and in 1857 he was forced to leave the region. He moved his headquarters to Faribault, a small town in south-central Minnesota, where he founded a school for training missionary clergy. He called it Seabury University.[74]

By that time, five more Episcopal priests had come, under Kemper's direction, to take charge of parishes that had been organized in the rapidly

James Lloyd Breck, Episcopal priest and missionary. Educated in Philadelphia by William Muhlenberg, a High Churchman whose fascination with liturgy predated the Oxford Movement, Breck dreamed of founding missions based on the medieval monastic model. In 1844 he founded Nashotah House in Wisconsin. Six years later, he came to St. Paul, where his Associate Mission was the first Episcopal establishment in Minnesota. After an unsuccessful attempt to organize a mission among the Ojibwe, Breck moved to Faribault in 1857 and founded Seabury Theological School.

The Associate Mission in St. Paul in 1850. Located on two acres of land in the block bounded by Summit, St. Peter, College, and Rice Streets, the mission initially consisted of three young clergymen (Breck, Timothy Wilcoxson, and J. Austin Merrick) and one teenaged scholar. The wood-frame mission building served as a school and chapel; the four men lived in the tent.

Consecrated in 1851, the original Christ Church on Cedar Street between Third and Fourth in St. Paul was the first Episcopal church built in Minnesota. The parish, organized under the aegis of the Associate Mission, chose James Lloyd Breck as its first rector. The earliest diocesan conventions, in 1856 and 1857 (at which the diocese of Minnesota was organized), were held here. Replaced with a stone structure in 1866, it was closed in the twentieth century.

in other areas of Bishop Kemper's jurisdiction, would be congruent with those of the proposed state. A meeting was held at Christ Church in St. Paul in May 1856, but nothing was settled until September 1857, when an even larger group of clergy and laity convened under Kemper's chairmanship to draw up a diocesan constitution. A third convention in May 1858 completed the process. It was decided to wait until 1859 to elect a bishop, since the national church would be holding its triennial convention at that time. Although bishops could be consecrated at any time, it was customary for consecrations to be held at the General Convention.[76]

Minnesota's diocesan convention met in St. Paul's Church, located at Olive and Ninth Streets

Located at Olive and Ninth Streets, St. Paul's Church was founded in the capital city's "lower town" in 1856. The conventions of 1858 and 1859, which completed the work of organizing the diocese and elected Whipple its first bishop, were held at St. Paul's.

growing towns of Minneapolis, Red Wing, Stillwater, St. Anthony, and St. Paul. Immigration to Minnesota was increasing exponentially. Every day at least three boatloads of settlers traveled up the Mississippi to Minnesota in 1856. Politicians were preparing a state constitution and lobbying in Congress for statehood. "Every man expected to be a millionaire," recalled one of the priests who came to Minnesota that year. "Everyone sought to be the founder of a city."[75] Not even the national financial depression that struck in October 1857 could stem the tide of settlement.

The territory's Episcopalians decided it was time to form an independent diocese. Its boundaries, as in St. Paul, on June 29, 1859. It was the second Episcopal church to be established in the city, whose population now exceeded 10,000. The parish had been founded less than three years earlier in the home of Captain Napoleon J. T. Dana, a retired army officer and banker, to serve the religious needs of the area known as the "lower town." When St. Paul's came to choose a rector, two names had been proposed: Dr. Andrew Bell Paterson and an unknown priest named Henry Benjamin Whipple. Paterson, who was already living in St. Paul, was chosen. The stone church was barely completed by the time the convention met. One of the convention's first orders of business was the official consecration of the new church by Bishop Kemper.

The bishop then called the convention to order. Twenty-one parishes were represented, all of them sending at least one lay delegate. Nineteen clergymen made up the clerical contingent: Ezekiel Gear, J. A. Russell, J. V. Van Ingen, Andrew Bell Paterson, Charles Woodward, E. Steele Peake, E. P. Gray, David B. Knickerbacker, Timothy Wilcoxson, James Lloyd Breck, Ezra Jones, Dudley Chase, J. S. Chamberlain, Solon Manney, Edward R. Welles, Joshua Sweet, John Williamson, Benjamin Evans, and Mark Olds.

In his address to the convention, Bishop Kemper announced that, having reached his seventieth year, he intended to resign his position as missionary bishop of the Northwest at the General Convention in October in Richmond, Virginia. Thereafter, he would limit his sphere of action to the diocese of Wisconsin. He added that he had promised to visit Kansas "before July has elapsed," but would proba-

bly have time to "attend to a few urgent calls" in Minnesota before he left, as he would continue to be responsible for the diocese until the consecration of the bishop "you expect to elect this week." The implication was clear: There must be no further delay in choosing a bishop to run the new diocese.[77]

After some discussion, the voting began. It was soon clear that two candidates stood out from the initial list of five nominees. Dr. Andrew Bell Paterson, rector of St. Paul's, was the choice of the laity, while the clergy preferred Dr. John Ireland Tucker of Troy, New York. The wealthy scion of a prominent family in Amboy, New Jersey, Paterson had come to St. Paul's in 1857 and taken a leading role

Dr. Andrew Bell Paterson, rector of St. Paul's Church, nominated Whipple as bishop of Minnesota. Born to a wealthy family in New Jersey, Paterson first visited Minnesota in 1849 and contributed two-thirds of the money for the construction of Christ Church. In 1857 he became rector of St. Paul's.

in organizing the diocese. Tucker, whom Bishop Horatio Potter of New York had recommended, was the author of a popular hymnal and a strong advocate of free churches. He was supported by the "upper town," as the area upstream was called, which included Christ Church and "the friends of the Bishop Seabury Mission." Paterson's support came from the "lower town," where St. Paul's was located.

It had been agreed beforehand that if a candidate was not elected by both the laity and the clergy after two ballots, his name would be dropped from consideration. Two formal ballots were taken on two succeeding days. Both times, Dr. Tucker received a strong majority of votes from the clergy, but in each case the laity (voting by parish) rejected him by a vote of eleven to ten. Tucker was thus eliminated from consideration. The clergy retired to see if they

Ezekiel Gear was the first Episcopal priest in Minnesota. Gear had been a missionary since 1810, working first among the settlers and the Oneida in western New York under Bishop John Henry Hobart. He made his way to Galena, Illinois, and in 1837 became army chaplain at Fort Snelling on the Minnesota River. Although his primary responsibility was to minister to the soldiers, he also served Episcopalians in the civilian population around the fort before Reverend James Lloyd Breck's arrival in 1850. In 1860 Gear became the chaplain at Minnesota's Fort Ripley.

Napoleon Jackson Tecumseh Dana, the layman who supported Whipple's nomination as bishop. A West Point graduate, Dana served in the Mexican War and supervised Fort Ripley's construction. Leaving the army, he went into banking and served on the diocesan standing committee. He donated the lots on which St. Paul's Church was built in 1856. During the Civil War, he served in the First Minnesota Regiment, commanded the Third Brigade at Antietam, and was major-general of the Department of the Mississippi. After the war, he became a railroad executive and deputy commissioner of pensions.

could come up with a more viable candidate. Someone suggested the Reverend Dr. Arthur Cleveland Coxe, a well-known religious writer, but one of the delegates from Christ Church said that he knew Coxe well and was certain he would never accept the position.[78]

At this point, Solon Manney (the army chaplain at Fort Ripley, in Crow Wing County) remarked that in

each canvas, while the other two candidates had received most of the votes, one vote had been cast for a Reverend Henry B. Whipple. Could the man who cast that vote explain it? Dr. Paterson admitted that, unwilling to cast a vote for himself and yet not satisfied that his rival was sufficiently worthy, he had recalled something he had been told during a recent visit to Chicago. An acquaintance had asked him whom Minnesota would choose as its bishop, and when Paterson admitted he didn't know, the man said there was no one more fit to be bishop of a western diocese than the young rector of Holy Communion parish. Paterson had visited Holy Communion and been duly impressed.[79] He described Whipple's talents and history, which he had taken the time to discover.

Ezekiel Gear then recalled having met Whipple in 1856, when Whipple had come to Minnesota to visit his brother John, then a land agent in Crow Wing.[80] In fact, Gear had been corresponding with Whipple, trying to persuade him to take on one of the new churches in the state. James Lloyd Breck was also familiar with him, as Whipple had been sending money from his parishes to support Breck's missions since his days in Rome. When the clergy voted again, Whipple received fourteen of eighteen votes.[81]

Captain Napoleon Dana was also familiar with Whipple's work in Chicago, having previously suggested him as a rector for St. Paul's.[82] During the laity meeting held to discuss the clergy's latest vote, Dana gave Whipple an enthusiastic tribute. E. T. Wilder, H. T. Welles, and Isaac Atwater, all prominent members of the diocese's lay leadership, also urged his election. The lay members then voted unanimously for Whipple, and he was elected bishop.

"Believing that the call was from God," Whipple accepted.

Before long, the rest of the world would agree with his conclusion.

Eli T. Wilder, lay leader and judge, was a longtime member of the diocesan standing committee and later served on the church's national boards. He was a trustee of St. Mary's and also contributed generously to Seabury and Shattuck schools.

Henry Welles, a lumber/railroad/real estate entrepreneur, was the first mayor of Minneapolis. A member of Gethsemane parish, he funded Holy Trinity Church's construction in St. Anthony Falls in 1855. The St. Mary's Hall trustee also contributed to the Faribault schools.

Isaac Atwater was a leading layman who served on the diocesan council for many years. He was an early member of Gethsemane Church in Minneapolis, a benefactor of the Faribault schools, a university regent, a newspaper editor, and state Supreme Court justice.

The members of the House of Bishops at the General Convention in Richmond, Virginia, in 1859, when Whipple was consecrated bishop of Minnesota.

hipple did not accept the Minnesota episcopacy immediately. He received formal notice of his election on July 2, 1859, and on July 4 he left Chicago for Adams, New York, to discuss this unexpected honor with his father and Bishop DeLancey, his closest adviser in matters of religion. For the next two weeks Whipple wavered. After all, he had barely begun his work at Holy Communion. He had been criticized by friends and relatives for taking his family to Chicago, and now he was being asked to take them even farther into the wilderness. He would have to take a cut in salary, just as his second daughter was preparing to join her sister at boarding school.[83]

He would be responsible for an area nearly eighty thousand square miles in size, with few roads, widely scattered settlements, and few modern conveniences. No railroads yet connected Minnesota with the outside world; the telegraph would not reach St. Paul until 1860. Whipple would have to build up the apparatus of diocesan administration almost from scratch when so far he had never run anything larger than a single parish.

But Henry Whipple had always liked a challenge. And there were the Indians to consider.

An estimated seventeen thousand Native Americans lived in Minnesota in 1859; the Ojibwe occupied the northern lakes region, the Dakota the southern prairies, and the Winnebago a small reservation near the state's southern border. The three tribes were often antagonistic toward one another. The Ojibwe and the Dakota in particular had a long history of competition over the hunting grounds of central Minnesota. Their periodic wars were a source of frustration to the government agents who worked with them.[84]

Whipple's fascination with America's native peoples, which had begun in his childhood, had been reinforced by stories he heard about the Seminoles during his visits to Florida. But his family responsibilities prevented him from considering missionary work among them. The pay was inadequate and the living conditions unacceptable. Even mission work among the poor in Chicago had its unpleasant moments. As a bishop, however, he could minister to the Indians without having to live among them on a daily basis.

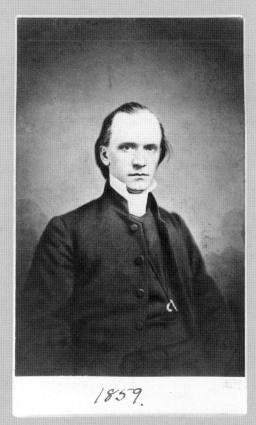

1859.

Henry Benjamin Whipple was thirty-seven-years-old in 1859, when he was elected bishop of Minnesota.

Minnesota's climate, which was said to be exceptionally healthy, also attracted him. In the first decades of its existence, the state attracted large numbers of the chronically ill, particularly tuberculosis sufferers hoping to find relief for their condition in its clean, fresh air. After two years in Chicago's polluted air, the prospect of Minnesota's uncontaminated woods and lakes must have sounded like heaven to a man always concerned for his own health and that of his family.

On July 12, 1859, Whipple wrote his friend Robert Clarkson in Chicago, "You can never know what a sore trial this election of Bishop has been to me." But, he added, "Those whose godly counsel I most highly prize have said I must accept it and as a call of God my own sense of duty says the same." The same day he wrote to the Minnesota standing committee, accepting the position.

He returned to Chicago on July 20 to put things in order and prepare for his consecration, which would take place in October at the General Convention in Richmond, Virginia. Bishop Kemper was the presenting bishop at his consecration, accompanied by eight other bishops, including William DeLancey of Western New York and Henry Whitehouse of Illinois. Bishop George Burgess of Maine spoke feelingly of the "heavy burdens" awaiting the new bishop, who would "often find no help but in Jesus Christ." Kemper urged him not to forget the "wandering Indians" who lived in his diocese. DeLancey offered him some eminently practical advice: "Never allow yourself to be separated from your luggage."[85]

Returning to Chicago, Whipple celebrated his first confirmation at Holy Communion Church. Then he set off for Minnesota, traveling by train to Prairie du Chien and up the Mississippi by steamboat. On November 1, the boat stopped at Wabasha, Minnesota, where he held his first service in his new diocese at a Baptist church, baptizing the thirteen-month-old son of a settler named William Wright.[86]

At last, on November 12, 1859, Bishop Whipple arrived in St. Paul. He was met by members of the diocesan standing committee, under the chairmanship of Captain Napoleon Dana. Whipple learned that his new diocese consisted of four self-supporting parishes (all in the Minneapolis/St. Paul area), one Ojibwe mission at Gull Lake (run by a native deacon after Breck's departure), a school, and thirty-four missions among white settlers in outlying towns, only seventeen of which had church buildings. There were four parochial clergy (supported by their parish) and sixteen missionary clergy (supported by missionary societies). The diocese counted 476 communicants in good standing, 165 of them outside the Twin Cities. Sunday school attendance was around 500, one-fifth of them at Breck's school in Faribault. The yearly offerings came to $8025.23. The highest rector's salary (at Gethsemane Church in Minneapolis) was $800 a year. The missionary clergy received stipends of between $250 and $300 a year from the Domestic and Foreign Missionary Society, headquartered in New Haven, Connecticut. Whipple's $1,500 salary would have to come out of the diocesan treasury. Dependent as it was on the generosity of parishes already strapped for funds to support their own priest and build a church, there was no guarantee that he would be paid regularly.

As bishop, Whipple would license clergy to serve within his diocese and authorize the formation of parishes and the construction of churches. He would approve applications to study for the ministry and ordain men to the diaconate and priesthood. He would oversee all missionary activity within his jurisdiction, whether financed by the diocese or the national church. He would license lay readers to preach and hold prayer services in the absence of clergy. He would confirm baptized persons who had reached the age of maturity and were prepared to make a public affirmation of their faith and a commitment to the church. He could suspend a priest for cause, subsequently notifying his fellow bishops of his action so that the priest could not be licensed elsewhere with-

A former fur-trading post, Crow Wing (ca. 1863) was the gateway to Minnesota's Ojibwe country for many years. James Lloyd Breck described it as a town with "only 32 dwellings . . . but seven whiskey shops." As the only white settlement in the area, it became the county seat *pro tem* of the newly formed Crow Wing County in 1857, when the county's white population was only 176. It faded away after the Ojibwe moved to White Earth in 1869 and the railroad passed it by.

out having the case reopened. Every three years, he was expected to attend the General Convention as a member of the House of Bishops, where he would help select new bishops, whether elected by their dioceses or appointed as missionaries. It was a heavy responsibility, and Whipple took it seriously.

During his first few days in St. Paul, the new bishop visited churches in St. Anthony and Minneapolis. He was especially pleased to learn that Gethsemane had voted to become a free church the preceding year. St. Mark's, a small mission founded in 1858 in north Minneapolis, was also free. Neither of these towns was as yet very large, but Gethsemane parish boasted 82 communicants, Holy Trinity 30, and St. Mark's 11. The two churches in St. Paul (Christ and St. Paul's) claimed 186 communicants between them.

At St. Anthony, Whipple met John Johnson Enmegabowh, the Native American deacon who led St.

Columba's Mission at Gull Lake. Enmegabowh invited him to visit the mission, which he said had a congregation of 128 baptized Ojibwe.

Eager for a glimpse of the diocese's only mission to the native peoples, Whipple agreed. Accompanied by Breck and Enmegahbowh, he set off in late November on his first visit to the Ojibwe country. He didn't let Enmegahbowh send word ahead of his coming. "I had heard so many doubts expressed concerning Indian missions that I desired to see it in its everyday and not its holiday dress."

It was a long, tedious journey, more than a hundred miles each way by steamboat, horse-drawn buggy, and foot, and took a full week to complete. The route followed the Mississippi River, past logging camps and the military encampment at Fort Ripley, and through deep forest filled with lakes of varying sizes. Crow Wing, a former fur trading post a few miles above the juncture of the Crow Wing River with the Mississippi, was the last white settlement on their path. It was a squalid place, populated primarily by white traders, lumbermen, and entrepreneurial mixed-blood shopkeepers who made their living from the Ojibwe and soldiers at Fort Ripley. Peake, the Crow Wing missionary, and army chaplain Solon Manney joined Whipple's party as it made its way to Gull Lake, ten miles north of the little settlement. It took them two days to reach, walking on the narrow footpaths used by the Ojibwe.

On approaching the settlement, Whipple was appalled by the abject poverty and drunken men and

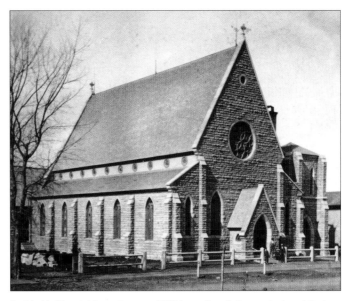

St. Mark's Church (shown here ca. 1850s) was founded as a mission of Gethsemane parish in north Minneapolis in 1858. It moved in 1863 to the corner of Fourth and Hennepin, and again in 1910 to its current location on Oak Grove overlooking Loring Park. Whipple's successor, Samuel C. Edsall, chose St. Mark's as his primary church in 1901. It became the official diocesan cathedral in 1941.

women he saw. A body lay abandoned beside the trail. Scalp locks hung from poles beside the doors of the wigwams. Syphilis, brought by the white men who also provided the illegal whiskey, was widespread.[87] He saw a woman scraping bark from a tree, and Enmegahbowh told him that she would probably feed it to her children, since she had nothing else to give them.

That evening, as Whipple held Thanksgiving Day services in the small log chapel and spoke at length with Enmegahbowh, he determined that he would do all within his power to save these people from the dire fate he saw hanging over them. "I resolved that, God being my helper, it should never be said that the first Bishop of Minnesota turned his back upon the heathen at his door." An interpreter helped him preach his sermon, which he found "at first difficult, but it compels the use of simple language in order to reach the heart." After confirming "several people," he celebrated communion, an emotional experience for the young bishop, who contemplated "the joy which would come to the Divine Heart of

St. Columba's Mission (ca. 1854) at Gull Lake in Minnesota was founded by James Breck in 1852. From 1854 to 1862 it was run by the Ottawa Episcopal deacon Enmegahbowh with the support of the Reverend E. Steele Peake in Crow Wing. It was vandalized by Hole-in-the-Day's followers in 1862 and burned down in 1864.

Holy Trinity Church, the first Episcopal church west of the Mississippi, was founded in 1851 in what was then called St. Anthony Falls. From 1852 to 1864 it was the headquarters of the missionary Jacob Chamberlain. The original church building was made of wood in the Gothic pointed style. The first convocation of clergy was held here in 1854, as well as the formation of the first standing committee. This second building was consecrated in 1855.

The original Gethsemane Church, founded in 1856. Whipple held his first diocesan convention here in June 1860. Under the Reverend David B. Knickerbacker, it established an outreach program to the Dakota at Mendota, founded a Minneapolis hospital (St. Barnabas), and was the home of the Brotherhood of Gethsemane, a laymen's service organization. It also fostered the development of several other churches and missions in the area, including St. Mark's.

After a year's work in the Minnesota River Valley, Ebenezer Steele Peake joined Breck's mission at Gull Lake in 1856 with his bride, Mary Augusta Parker. Peake moved to Crow Wing in 1857 as part of the Associate Mission team with Breck and Solon Manney. Peake was responsible for the mission's Indian work. From 1862 to 1865 he was chaplain to the Twenty-Eighth Wisconsin Infantry. Later he served in Austin, Minnesota; California; the area from Detroit Lakes, Minnesota, to Valley City, North Dakota; and Faribault.

the Saviour as He looked down upon these men of the trembling eye and the wandering foot, kneeling at his feet."

The party remained for several days, visiting "from wigwam to wigwam." One woman asked him to bury her child. After the service she brought him a lock of the child's hair, saying she had heard that white mothers sometimes had the hair of a dead infant made into a cross. Would the bishop make a cross of her child's hair for her? Deeply touched, Whipple agreed to do so, later writing, "I learned that an Indian mother's heart is like that of a white mother." Before he left, he baptized James Lloyd Breck Manitowaub, infant son of two of Enmegah-bowh's leading converts, Isaac and Rebecca Manitowaub.[88]

Returning to St. Paul, Whipple rested for three days, then set out to visit missions in Red Wing, St. Cloud, Sauk Rapids, Orono, Anoka, Shakopee, Belle Plaine, and St. Peter. Only Red Wing had a properly organized parish and full-time rector, both accomplished in October 1858. The parish had just finished building its first church, which Whipple consecrated on November 29. The Reverend Dudley Chase served the mission stations at St. Cloud and Sauk Rapids, on the Mississippi above Minneapolis, which had a total of eight communicants. The Reverend E. P. Gray had been in Shakopee, on the Minnesota River, since 1857 and claimed twenty-four communicants. Gray also looked after Belle Plaine, where two or three Anglicans met regularly for services at the home of Judge Andrew G. Chatfield. St. Peter's small chapel, where the Reverend Ezra Jones counted twenty-three communicants, had been built in 1857.[89] All these riverside towns had recently been built. The sound of hammers mingled with the cries of livestock roaming the dirt streets and the shouts of carters bringing loads up from the wharves on the river.

On December 18, Whipple ordained Charles W. Clinton to the diaconate at St. Paul's in St. Paul. On the following day, the bishop set out to rejoin his family in Chicago. When the boat stopped briefly at Wabasha at nine o'clock that evening, he received a telegram from Adams, notifying him that his father had died.

Whipple left the boat at La Crosse and caught a train that took him to Chicago by way of Milwaukee. After barely an hour with his family, he departed again for Adams, arriving on December 23. He had traveled nearly one thousand miles in five days—a far cry from the four weeks it had taken him to travel a similar distance from New Orleans to Baltimore fourteen years earlier. Railroads were bringing the frontier closer to the eastern seaboard every day. This was one reason that the population of new states like Minnesota grew so quickly. Although Minnesota had no rail lines as yet, its neighboring states, Wisconsin and Illinois, had several, and one line had crossed the Mississippi into Iowa a few years earlier at Rock Island.

In Adams, Whipple learned that his father's store had failed to recover from the 1857 crash and was forced into bankruptcy. "Merciless creditors drove him to death," he claimed of sixty-four-year-old John Whipple, who died of apoplexy. His death left his widow destitute, facing a host of debts she could not pay. Henry helped her to sell her house and most of her possessions, and settled her with one of his sisters before returning to Chicago to help Cornelia prepare for the family's move to Minnesota. The "dear old home is broken now," Whipple wrote in his diary, mourning "that dear father who so tenderly watched over my childhood." For years Whipple continued to receive requests for payment of his father's debts.

Returning to Minnesota in February, Whipple disembarked in Winona, helped to organize a parish in Rochester, and then went to Faribault to inspect Breck's school. He traveled over an unpaved stagecoach road across the open prairie and into the Big Woods, an 1,800-square-mile deciduous forest stretching in an elongated triangle formed by St. Cloud, Mankato, and Northfield. Along the way, he passed settlers busily chopping down oak, elm, and maple trees and plowing up the prairie for farmsteads.

Faribault at that time was reminiscent of Adams in the earliest days of Whipple's childhood. Located some seventy-five miles south of St. Paul, it had been founded at the junction of the Straight and Cannon Rivers six years earlier by the fur traders Alexander Faribault and Henry Sibley, with two others. Several mills and a nearby limestone quarry formed its first industries, and in 1856 it became the seat of Rice County. By 1857, it had twenty-three stores, four hotels, two livery stables, five wagon shops, two meat markets, a blacksmith, and a shoemaker. The Catholics, Congregationalists, and Episcopalians had built churches and the Baptists, Methodists, and Lutherans had organized faith communities. In February 1858, a Ladies Literary Society

Former fur trader Alexander Faribault founded the city of Faribault. The son of a French-Canadian fur trader and his Dakota wife, Faribault played an influential role in the treaties signed at Traverse des Sioux in 1851. He later served in the Minnesota Legislature, where he lobbied successfully for the establishment of the state schools for the deaf and blind in his town and for the rail line that passed through it.

The Alexander Faribault house in Faribault, Minnesota. Watercolor by Josephine Lutz Rollins, 1948.

Fowler's Store in Faribault, where Breck's mission held its first classes.

was formed. The 1860 census showed a population in Faribault of 1,520 souls.[90]

Finding affordable housing in Minnesota for his large family presented a major problem for Whipple. Although the Board of Missions and the diocesan council had assumed that he would live in St. Paul on the grounds of Breck's original mission, that site was no longer available, and the standing committee had not been able to locate a proper residence nearby; everything that seemed suitable was too expensive.

The inhabitants of Faribault offered him a solution. Alexander Faribault, who had founded the town on the site of his old trading post, had a large vision for its future. He had secured a promise from the state railway planners in 1858 that a railroad from Minneapolis to the Iowa border would pass through Faribault. But he dreamed of making his town an educational oasis. He persuaded his fellow state legislators to establish a school for the hearing impaired in Faribault, and was lobbying for a school for the blind. When Breck told him about his plan to found a theological school, Faribault gave him five acres on which to build it.[91]

As a Roman Catholic, Faribault understood the diocesan model of church government. He believed that a resident bishop, albeit a Protestant one, would enhance the town's fledgling cultural reputation. He and his fellow town fathers offered to build the bishop a house, free of charge, if he would locate his headquarters in Faribault.[92] Whipple thought it over for a few days, then accepted the offer. As he told the diocesan council, Faribault was located in the center of the area of the state then being settled, the school was there, and the house was free. Financially as well as logistically, Faribault was his best option.

In February 1860, the two-year-old Seabury University had two scholars, George Tanner and Samuel Hinman, and two professors, James Lloyd Breck and Solon Manney. There was also a preparatory program with 134 students, not all of whom attended classes regularly. Tanner and Hinman spent part of each day teaching preparatory classes and were also expected to do missionary work in the surrounding countryside. The mission also ran an Indian boarding school, Andrews Hall, where its pupils were instructed in Christianity and Anglo-American cultural habits. The Indian boys and girls lived with the Breck family, as did the two seminary students.[93]

It was a rustic setting. Three small, rough-hewn school buildings—the Breck home, the chapel/schoolhouse, and the dormitory for the preparatory schoolboys—stood in a clearing surrounded by thick woods, joined by dirt paths. Nearby was a small Dakota encampment. Years later, Whipple would recall witnessing his first scalp dance on the site of the future Shumway Memorial Chapel.

Whipple looked upon Breck's "university" and heaved a deep sigh. He approved of the concept of a diocesan theological school. If the diocese were to grow, it would need to train its own clergy. It could not depend on men from eastern schools sent out as missionaries at rock-bottom stipends; too often these were men who had failed elsewhere and came west because it was the only job they could get. It would be better to train local men, who already had a stake in the community. Nashotah could barely turn out enough men to supply Wisconsin's needs. Seabury would simply have to be reorganized on a more businesslike basis.[94]

The novice bishop had his work cut out for him. He had to set up an administrative structure for the diocese, encourage existing churches and missions and establish new ones, and recruit and train additional clergy so the church could keep up with the state's rapidly growing white population. In addition, the mission to the Ojibwe needed strengthening, and there was as yet no Episcopal mission among the Dakota or Winnebago. All of this would take time and money, much of which would have to come from outside the diocese, because the people of Minnesota were spending most of their money on building a new state.

Fortunately, it was the kind of challenge Henry Whipple liked best, and he settled into it with characteristic enthusiasm. His first act was to form a solid financial and educational foundation for Seabury; by the time he left Faribault on February 21, 1860, a charter had been drawn up and a board of trustees chosen.[95] He had also visited most of the existing missions and churches in his bailiwick and now had a fair idea of their strengths and weaknesses.

As he prepared Cornelia and the children to move to Faribault in April, Whipple's mind was already working out a strategy for the years to come.

Ballyhack, the dormitory James Lloyd Breck built at Faribault to house the preparatory students at Seabury University.

Bird's-eye map of Faribault, published in 1869. The Episcopal school campus is on the bluff overlooking the Straight River. The large building to the right is the state school for the blind and deaf. In the main part of town, slightly to the right of center, is the Episcopal Cathedral, shown with a pointed tower that was never built. Whipple's home and St. Mary's school were across the street from the cathedral to the east.

n July 1859, Whipple's father-in-law, Benjamin Wright, wrote to his brother Joseph, who raised horses in New York, suggesting that he might make the new bishop a present of a good horse. The present arrived in the form of a handsome eight-year-old black Arabian named Bashaw. His sire was a New York Black Hawk, his dam a Blucher mare, and he was first cousin to the celebrated racehorse George M. Patchen. Joseph Wright had once turned down an offer of $1,200 for him. Whipple described him as "a kingly fellow" with "a slim, delicate head, prominent eyes, small, active ears, large nostrils, full chest, thin gambrels, heavy cords, neat fetlocks."

Although Whipple had other horses, Bashaw was his favorite and his closest companion during those early years in Minnesota. Bashaw arrived in Faribault in November 1860, and by the time he died in October 1880, he had carried his master—on his back or in a buggy or sleigh—over more than fifty thousand miles of Minnesota woods and prairies. "Patient, hopeful, cheerful, he was a favorite of all the stage-drivers," his master boasted. The horse had a knack for finding his way under difficult conditions. His greatest challenge came one night in November 1861, when the bishop became lost in a snowstorm on his way to the Dakota mission at the Lower Sioux Agency on the Minnesota River.

"I . . . kept my horses headed in the direction which I thought to be that of the Agency," Whipple remembered. "I said my prayers, threw the reins over the dash-board, let the horses walk as they would. . . . Suddenly Bashaw stopped. I was confident that the wise fellow had struck a landmark, for he knew as well as I did that we were lost. . . . It proved to be an Indian trail. . . . Bashaw followed it, and when his mate was inclined to turn out he put his teeth into his neck and forced him into the path." Not long after, the bishop saw a light shining in the agency window, "and when Bashaw saw it, he leaped like a hound from her kennel." Moments later, Whipple was safe inside the mission house.

Whipple's travels around his new diocese began soon after he returned to Minnesota in February 1860, following his father's funeral. After deciding to make Faribault his home, he visited Stillwater. Although the parish there was one of the state's oldest, Whipple found it "feeble," its rector too busy with his work as superintendent of the public schools to give it the attention it needed. From Stillwater, Whipple made his way along the St. Croix to the Mississippi and up to St. Paul, stopping at several communities along the way. He visited the state prison and was "deeply impressed with the devout attention of the prisoners," even the murderers.

All sorts of people lived on the frontier in those early days: rough woodsmen, Indian traders, loggers, immigrants from Europe, and impoverished "people of culture" who hoped to recoup their financial reverses in the West. They were a hardy lot, "brave, hospitable and manly. . . . Their homes were widely separated, with little of social life, and the school-house meetings were *reunions.*" Whipple and his missionary clergy preached in one-room log cabins, roughly framed schoolhouses, primitive wayside inns, or "under the shade of forest trees." The long journeys between settlements had their positive side. "In the summer . . . the travel over the prairies was full of inspiration—wild flowers on every side, fowl springing up almost from under the horses' feet, and often the deer and elk in the distance; while in the winter, the clear sparkling weather, the wonderful sight of the sundogs and the rare game sent the blood tingling through the veins, and I could truly say that God had given me a lot in pleasant by-paths and abiding places." He also learned to beware of sloughs, marshy depressions on the open prairie where an unsuspecting wagon could be mired up to its wheel hubs in moments.

Some years later, when Whipple was visiting England, a young aristocrat asked him if it were true "that in the West it is not an uncommon thing for two men to sleep in the same bed." Replied Whipple, "It is quite true. I have thirty-five clergymen in my diocese; I have slept with sixteen of them, and it is quite possible that I shall sometime sleep with the remaining nineteen." (One of his clergymen, recalling the story years later, added, "My experience is that [the bishop] had the lion's share of the bed."[96])

These pioneers had a plain but instinctive faith. As one of them said, "A man can't live all alone with God, as we do, and say there is no God." It was also practical. Another man told how he had been on a sinking steamship, where his fellow passengers "were crying and confessing their sins like mad." He had grabbed a bucket and started bailing. "I thought God would think just as much of me if I was dipping water to save those miserable critters, as if I was a whining and a sniveling over my sins."

In March 1860, Whipple paid a second visit to the Ojibwe country, this time remaining for a week to become better acquainted with conditions at the mission. In April, he went to Chicago and officiated at the wedding of his widowed brother-in-law, George Fairbanks, to Susan Beard Wright, widow of Cornelia's brother Benjamin, before returning with his family to Faribault.

Whipple then settled into a routine that would consume much of his life for the next forty-one years. As bishop, he was required to visit each parish church in the diocese at least once a year to hold confirmation services. This included regular visits to the Indian missions. He preached in a different church every Sunday and often held services on weekdays as well. Even non-Episcopalians who attended relished his sermons. In 1861, he visited forty-five communities between April 21 and June 6, baptizing, marrying, and burying all who required such services.

His enthusiasm inspired the men under him, and by the time the 1861 diocesan convention convened in Red Wing on June 12, the number of mission stations in the state had almost doubled, with regular services being held at thirty new stations since Whipple's arrival. He licensed lay readers to assist the missionaries, with the goal of providing monthly services to "every village in the state." He taught a course in pastoral work at Seabury every spring. And he attended meetings—of diocesan committees, of the trustees of the Faribault schools, of the Minnesota Historical Society, and of other groups in which he took an interest. He was always in demand as a public speaker.

Whipple approached his first diocesan convention, held in St. Paul on June 13–14, 1860, with a certain degree of anxiety. It was the first time he had met all of his clergy in one place, and by now he knew of the rift between the evangelical clergy of the lower St. Paul faction, led by Dr. Paterson, and the High Church supporters of James Breck. The first sign of trouble came as the delegates were being seated. Dr. Paterson rose to challenge the right of John Johnson Enmegahbowh, the Ojibwe deacon, to vote.

That Enmegahbowh was a Native American probably had little to do with Paterson's raising the question. The issue rested on an interpretation of the fourth article of the diocesan constitution, which defined voting members of the convention as "the Bishop and canonically resident clergy with a lay representation from each parish." There had been some question at an earlier convention as to whether army chaplains (specifically Gear and Manney) were to be considered as "canonically resident" clergy, and it had been agreed that they were. But the status of deacons had not yet been decided. Whipple contended that they also came under the heading of "canonically resident" clergy.

When Paterson appealed the question, however, Whipple allowed it to come to a vote. Whipple's position was approved by a large margin, and in 1864 the article in question was amended to read "all presbyters *and deacons* having been canonically and actually resident within the diocese for the space of six months and that are not under canonical censure."[97]

Whipple later admitted that he could have simply stated that, as he had placed Enmegahbowh's name on the list, the issue was moot. But it had seemed to him that diplomacy was called for. As he put it, "I thought it time to decide whether a father was to quarrel with his children." No other disputes arose, and Whipple confided to his diary that evening that he had managed to keep the "flames down." He went on to his June 17 meeting with the diocesan missionaries with relief, a feeling shared by his fellow clergy. The two factions seemed satisfied that their new bishop would not favor one of them over the other and settled down to work in concert with him.

An observer at Whipple's first convention was David Anderson, the Canadian bishop of Rupert's Land, who was passing through Minnesota on his

Robert Machray, bishop of Rupert's Land in Canada from 1864 to 1904, often visited Whipple on his way through Minnesota to church meetings in Toronto. Established in 1844, Machray's province covered most of central Canada, with headquarters in Winnipeg. Until the Canadian Pacific Railway was constructed in the 1880s, the inhabitants of central Canada had to travel up the Red River into Minnesota to reach eastern Canada. From 1898 until his death, Machray was primate of the Canadian Church of England. He and Whipple often exchanged views on the mission efforts among the native peoples in their respective jurisdictions.

way east to a convocation of the Canadian church. Appointed to his post in 1849, Anderson oversaw an extensive mission program to the Native Americans of the region and the scattered fur traders in addition to the farmers of the fertile Red River Valley. He and Whipple became friends and began a lively correspondence. Anderson's successor, Robert Machray, arrived in 1864 and continued the relationship. Anderson and Machray were undoubtedly the source of Whipple's information on Canada's Indian policy, which he believed was superior to that of the United States.[98]

At the end of June 1860, Whipple went up the Minnesota River to visit the Dakota and Winnebago agencies. On the way back, he consulted with the Reverend Edward Livermore at St. Peter, who was beginning work among the scattered settlers in the Minnesota Valley between Mankato and Henderson. Whipple visited the Ojibwe Mission again in mid-July, bringing back a wagonload of twenty young Ojibwe to enroll at Andrews Hall.[99]

On one of these early visits, Whipple learned a valuable lesson about preaching to Indians. His sermon had been one he often gave to white men, calling on them to repent of their sins and beg forgiveness of God. Afterward, one of the chiefs took him aside and asked him why he was slandering the Ojibwe, calling them sinners. "*We* are not sinners," he said. It was the white men, who brought firewater and evil to the Ojibwe, who were the sinners, and Whipple would do better to talk to them. From then on, Whipple's sermons to Native Americans emphasized the love God had for them rather than their failure to follow God's rules.

On July 11, while on his way up the Mississippi to Crow Wing, Whipple stopped in Anoka to consecrate a church, baptize a child, and confirm two adults. Trinity Church Anoka was one of the mission parishes formed by Jacob S. Chamberlain, the energetic priest who ran the St. Anthony Falls Mission out of Gethsemane Church. Over the past eight years, Chamberlain had founded missions in Chanhassen, Hassan, Minnetonka Mills, Neenah, Orono, St. Alban's, Anoka, Monticello, Clearwater, Buffalo, Sauk Rapids, and St. Cloud. By 1860, the St. Anthony Falls Mission claimed 111 communicants—

a fifth of the entire diocesan membership. Chamberlain was a highly respected member of the diocesan clergy who had attended both the 1858 and 1859 organizational conventions and was a member of Dr. Paterson's lower St. Paul faction.

Independent and hot-tempered, he was also accustomed to running his mission without interference. His greatest fault, his colleagues felt, was overconfidence, a tendency "to look upon things that are not as if they were." Six months after he had consecrated the Anoka church, Whipple discovered that it had a $3,000 debt and only four communicants. The contractor, who had expected to be paid before the church was consecrated, was demanding his money. Whipple was furious. In February 1861, he went to St. Anthony to discuss the situation

Jacob Chamberlain's reluctance to receive direction from his new bishop led to his departure from the diocese in 1864 to become chaplain-general of the Union Army. Son-in-law of Bishop Philander Chase of Illinois, Chamberlain arrived in Minnesota in 1852 under the auspices of the Board of Missions. He was active in mission work in and around the Minnesota Valley and Minneapolis, where he founded Gethsemane Church, among many others.

with Chamberlain, who had visited the Anoka church only once since its consecration. The bishop received no satisfaction from Chamberlain, who informed him that he was leaving shortly on a fundraising tour of eastern cities. "He has openly refused to be guided by his Bishop & in defiance of his advice goes East to solicit aid," Whipple fumed in his diary that evening. On February 27, he wrote a fellow clergyman that Chamberlain "has raised large sums of money of which no accounting has ever been given to bishop or Standing Committee. Much of his church property is held by other than parochial or diocesan authority. Four of the churches built by him were to say the least where there is no congregation. The system is all bad . . . the church never designed such use of funds by one man."

When Whipple criticized Chamberlain's habit of building churches "in advance of populations," Chamberlain was outraged. The dispute between them simmered through the next year. At the 1862 diocesan convention, Whipple claimed that Chamberlain tried "once or twice" to introduce subjects that would divide the clergy from their bishop, but fortunately "God overruled." The following January, Chamberlain went so far as to request a meeting with a Judge Harlan; whether the meeting took place is unknown, but a truce seems to have been established. Chamberlain left the diocese in May 1864 to become chaplain general of the Union Army.[100]

Part of Chamberlain's troubles arose from the fluid nature of settlement during Minnesota's formative years. People would locate in a town for a short time, then move on, seeking better conditions elsewhere. Towns sprang up and vanished almost overnight. The little log church at St. Alban's on Lake Minnetonka, with its imitation stained-glass window over the chancel (made of painted linen), had a flourishing congregation with six full-fledged communicants in 1860; by 1861 the town had faded so much that the parish moved to Excelsior. The Civil War exacerbated the situation, as men left the frontier settlements to join the army. The Dakota War in the fall of 1862 caused thousands more to depart. By April 1864, shortly before he left the diocese, Chamberlain was holding services in only three locations: Orono, Excelsior, and Chanhassen.[101]

The dispute with Chamberlain was an anomaly in Whipple's relationships with his clergy. His benevolent, paternalistic style evidently went over well with the men with whom he worked, especially since he showed a willingness to work long hours to support their efforts. The priests tolerated his quirks with fond amusement, as when his fear of being late led him to arrive fifteen to twenty minutes early for services. A colleague observed that if he wanted to avoid being pestered by his bishop to start the service before everyone else was ready, the "wise rector hid himself till the right moment was reached." The bishop, an old friend once remarked, was "99 parts St. John, one part New York politician," combining the "wisdom of the serpent with the gentleness of the dove."[102]

Having experienced the bitterness of partisan churchly disputes when he lived in Chicago, Whipple was determined to prevent such a situation from developing in his diocese. An admitted High Churchman, he was proud to note that Holy Communion had been celebrated every Sunday in his diocese since 1850. Nevertheless, he drew a firm line on the question of adding unnecessary drama to the liturgy. Putting candles and colored hangings on the altar, using incense, and bowing before the altar were discouraged.[103]

Whipple explained his position on ritual to the House of Bishops in October 1866: "No one who desires to preserve order could recognize the right of any priest to alter the ritual of the church . . . [or] to introduce customs which have not been used in the Anglican Church for the last 300 years. . . . Nothing should be done which could justly be a cause of offense to other members of the fold." The Minnesota diocese, he said, was "a missionary body. . . . The people to whom we minister are the most practical people on the face of the earth. . . . They must be met by the beautiful simplicity of the doctrines of Christ and the realities of a living, working, missionary church."

This cautious approach served Whipple well. He later took pride in the fact that he had "conceded to the clergy all the liberty which the Church has given. . . . We have no right to question the opinions of any man who holds and teaches the Apostles' and Nicene Creeds and is loyal to the Church of Christ." Years later, he would boast that "in forty years of my episcopate, not one of my clergy has disobeyed the

The seal of the Diocese of Minnesota. Designed by Whipple with the assistance of a Reverend Hoffman, one of his clerical friends from back East, the seal expresses Whipple's hopes of bringing peace to the Indians in his jurisdiction as well as to the factions in his church and in the wider Christian community. The motto *Pax per sanguinem crucis* translates as "Peace through the blood of the cross."

godly advice of his bishop."[104]

By the fall of 1860, the Seabury Mission schools were a going concern. Manney and Breck made a good team; the students called them "Dr. Canon" and "Dr. Rubrics," in recognition of their theological specialties. The seminary now had three students, with three young women assisting them as teachers in the primary and secondary departments.[105]

Whipple refused to allow Seabury's theology to be too rigid: "From the first, I said that I would not be the head of a divinity school representing a party." He turned down offers of funding from groups who required the students to adhere to a particular theological position. "A young man who enters a theological school comes as a learner," he told

one such group. "I think it would be a wiser policy for you to look, not to the opinions of the young men, but to the piety, scholarship, soundness in faith, earnestness, and charity of the teachers to whom you confide these young men. . . . The Church . . . must not by any possibility allow her true position to be narrowed into limits which will surely produce parties."[106]

Nevertheless, he insisted that the Faribault schools maintain a religious character. "If the only end of school work is to teach certain branches of learning, there is no excuse for church schools," he said. "Every pupil who comes to us is a separate trust from God. . . . Nothing can be so sad as the thought that one of Christ's little ones may perish."[107] Church attendance was obligatory for all students. Except for the seminarians, they were not required to be Episcopalians. In fact, many students came from "other religious bodies." Whipple's goal was "to educate men to lead and guide our development in the coming future."[108]

In September 1860, Whipple started east on the first of his annual fundraising journeys for his diocese and the various programs it supported. The Board of Missions never seemed able to afford as many missionaries as he needed. Though their stipends ran between $200 and $300 a year, their expenses were often much greater, both with families to house and feed and with their work, and Whipple felt obliged to help them out when they ran short. At Faribault's schools, tuition never completely covered salaries, upkeep and construction of buildings, and room and board for the students. The Indian missions were always in need of more money. Whipple himself could not always count on his $1,500 salary being paid in a timely fashion, and he had to support his family (including three daughters now at boarding school), pay for his extensive travels, and come up with funds for diocesan programs when other sources were not immediately available.[109] On this first trip, he spoke in churches in

Chicago, Adams, Albany, Newburgh, New York City, and Brooklyn before attending the annual Board of Missions meeting in New Haven, Connecticut, on October 10, and afterward at several churches in the New York area and in Philadelphia.

It was mid-November before Whipple finally returned to Minnesota. As he waited in La Crosse for transport up the icebound Mississippi, Whipple reflected happily on the kind reception he had received from those generous eastern churches. He had also received encouragement from individual donors such as Dr. George Shattuck of Boston and merchant Robert B. Minturn of New York.

But the country's future was far from promising. While he was in the east, Whipple had gone to Washington, D.C., hoping to talk with government officials about the shortcomings of the nation's Indian policy. He had written to President Buchanan in April, setting out his concerns, but had received no reply. Now he brought with him letters from his

Officers of the First Minnesota Volunteer Infantry stand in front of the commandant's quarters at Fort Snelling before departure to serve with the Army of the Potomac in 1861. Pleading the needs of his diocese, Whipple turned down the unit's request to serve as regimental chaplain, but preached to them before they left for the front. In September 1862, he visited the regiment on the battlefield at Antietam and spent the night in General McClellan's tent.

Leonidas Polk, bishop of the Southwest from 1838 to 1841 and of Louisiana from 1841 to 1864, was a general in the Confederate Army. Educated at West Point, Polk had considerable influence among the army's ranks in the West, although he was not an outstanding general. He was killed in action at Pine Mountain.

would secede from the Union. "You will have to seek justice for your Indians from the Northern government," he concluded.[110]

It was an accurate forecast. Within weeks of Whipple's return home in mid-November, South Carolina seceded. Mississippi, Florida, Alabama, Georgia, Louisiana, and Texas followed. On April 12, 1861, the South Carolina militia fired on Fort Sumter, the Union fort blocking the entrance to Charleston harbor. Sumter surrendered on April 14. The next day President Lincoln proclaimed South Carolina in a state of insurrection and called for troops to put the rebellion down. America was at war.

Minnesota's young men rushed to form army units. In April 1861, Whipple addressed the Faribault Guards upon their enlistment. On May 12, he preached to the First Minnesota Volunteer Regiment at Fort Snelling, taking as his text, "If I forget thee, O Jerusalem, let my right hand forget thy cunning."[111]

At the June diocesan council meeting, Whipple recalled how bishops of north and south had joined together at his consecration only two years before and prayed that God would "make us once again one in love." His prayer seemed unlikely to receive a positive answer. In July the southern dioceses held a convention in Montgomery for the purpose of forming a separate Episcopal Church of the South.[112]

That same summer, Whipple was shocked to hear that Leonidas Polk, Episcopal bishop of Louisiana for the past twenty years, had accepted a commission as major general in the Confederate Army. Although he said nothing at the time, Polk's decision pained Whipple. He felt the taking up of arms was not consistent with a bishop's role, even if—as in Polk's case—he had received military training as a youth at West Point. "Educated at the south and thoroughly imbued with southern views both as to social and political views, he very early was committed to the plans of rebellion," Whipple wrote in his diary in August 1864, upon hearing of Polk's death in battle. "Having taken this step it was easier

friend J. K. Sass, president of the Bank of Charleston, who had generously supported the church's mission program for many years, to influential politicians, asking them to support the bishop's requests. He received little encouragement. "A prominent Southern statesman" whom Whipple approached explained that Lincoln's election was all but certain, and if he became president, the South to listen to the specious arguments to enter military service. In an evil hour he listened to these entreaties and gave up the peaceful vocation of a Shepherd of Christ to become a man of war. . . .We would gladly drop a mantle of charity over his sins but we can never forget what untold desolations came to our beloved land through the influence of himself and those who with him engaged in the work of rebellion, from which all true sons of the church cry 'Good Lord deliver us.'"

The unsettled times had their heroes and their villains. In the fall of 1861, failing health led the Reverend Benjamin Evans to resign as rector of St. Paul's Church in Winona. A few weeks later, Whipple received a letter from a J. W. Williams, who claimed to be a clergyman of the Church of England. Williams informed Whipple that he had received a call to St. Paul's of Winona. "The letter was so very pious," Whipple said, "that it excited my suspicion"—particularly its postscript, in which Williams declared that he was "a devoted admirer of yours,

and . . . not a Low Churchman." Williams was a personable man with some skill at preaching, but when Whipple asked him to present his credentials, Williams claimed that they had been lost in a fire aboard a steamboat. Whipple wrote to St. Paul's vestry, telling them he believed Williams was an imposter who could not be allowed to officiate. The angry vestrymen passed a vote of censure against their bishop. A few days later, Williams got drunk and was evicted from his hotel, and it was discovered that the woman with him was not his wife. An embarrassed vestry hastily withdrew its resolution of censure. In February another minister arrived in Winona, with the proper credentials, and Whipple duly instituted him.

Chamberlain's continuing antagonism, an imposter in Winona, increasing unrest among the Ojibwe and Dakota, and disappointing news from the East concerning the progress (or lack thereof) of the war made for a bad outlook for 1862.

The reality would be far worse.

Camp of the First Minnesota under the command of General Willis Gorman near Edward's Ferry in Maryland, January 1862.

Chippewa Burial Ground, painting by Cameron Booth, undated. Ojibwe burial houses commonly had open doorways for family offerings and spirit movement. The upright stone monument indicates the grave of a baptized Christian family member.

In 1862, Henry Benjamin Whipple was catapulted onto the national stage as a leading spokesman for the rights of America's native peoples. His role as their advocate, especially to the two major tribes inhabiting his diocese, had been evolving since his arrival in Minnesota three years earlier. For decades, the Ojibwe and Dakota's relationship with the Episcopal Church in Minnesota had been tenuous. Their dealings with white traders and federal agents were, at best, strained.

Christianity got off to a slow start among Minnesota's Ojibwe. Members of the widespread Algonquian linguistic family, the Ojibwe originated in the area around the eastern shores of Lake Superior. During the mid-seventeenth century, they were pushed westward by tribes that had been displaced from homelands farther east. Using the new firearms introduced to the region by French traders, the Ojibwe moved into northern Wisconsin, Minnesota, Manitoba, and western Ontario.

The tribe was organized in bands, made up of individual families and their allies. When the first government-sponsored explorers in America reached Minnesota in 1805, Ojibwe bands lived on eleven lakes: Red, Leech, Cass, Winnibigoshish, Sandy, Gull, Mille Lacs, Otter Tail, Rabbit, Rice, and Pokegama. A few had moved out of the forest into the Red River Valley around Pembina, North Dakota; some as far west as Turtle Mountain. Each band was autonomous, although relations among the various bands were close. Government was by consensus, with leadership comprised of elders and men of acknowledged ability.

The Ojibwe signed a treaty in 1837 ceding to the United States a strip of land 18 miles wide and 150 miles long along the northern shore of the Mississippi River. This gave white lumbermen access to the pine along the St. Croix and Chippewa Rivers. Further treaties in 1847, 1854, and 1855 led to other cessions of land along the Mississippi and St. Croix Rivers and Lake Superior. These lands were then acquired by settlers and logging interests.[113] Reservations were established, separating the remaining Indian land from that which the government could survey and sell. By 1859, when Whipple first visited them, an estimated seventy-eight hundred Ojibwes lived on nearly a dozen reservations within Minnesota's borders.[114]

Ojibwe culture was complex and highly successful, based on a cooperative social organization, a seasonal economic round of hunting, gathering, fishing, and gardening, and a religious tradition called the Grand Medicine. All of life—animal, vegetable, human, natural, and supernatural alike—was regarded as one unified sphere of existence, directed by a ruling spirit (*Kitchimanitou,* translated by Europeans as the Great Spirit), with the aid of lesser spirits. One communicated with these spirits through dreams and visions. By good conduct, and with the assistance of benevolent spirits, one could achieve *pimadaziwin,* which included long life, health, and good fortune. The Midewiwin, members of the Grand Medicine Lodge, were the human guides who instructed the people in their progress toward this goal.[115]

To the Ojibwe, the Christian missionaries who began working among them in the 1830s were nuisances. The missionaries either dismissed the Grand Medicine structure as pagan nonsense or tried to adapt parts of it—the acknowledgment of a Great Spirit, for example—to Christian imagery, redefining the terms to suit their own preconceptions. Believing that God was guiding history on an upward curve toward perfection, and that America was destined to become the New Jerusalem, they could not view Christianity apart from their own EuroAmerican culture. They insisted that converts cut their hair, dress in European-style clothing, establish permanent homes on individual farms, and abandon their ancient traditions. They objected to polygamy, which the Ojibwe regarded as a way of guaranteeing women economic security in the tribe and a means of extending kinship ties between rival groups. The expectation of gifts exchanged at frequent intervals seemed like begging.

By the time Henry Whipple arrived in Minnesota, Christian missionaries had been working among the Ojibwe for more than a quarter of a century. They were mostly Protestants. Although Catholic priests had visited the Ojibwe country periodically since the mid-1700s, they did not establish a resident mission until 1855; their early efforts were aimed primarily toward the mixed-blood offspring of French-Canadian fur traders, who were presumed to be of the Catholic faith. In 1832, the American Board of Commissioners for Foreign Mission sent a small group of missionaries to work among the Ojibwe. They were largely unsuccessful in weaning the

Ojibwe from their traditional faith, and in 1855 the board withdrew its missions.[116]

The most successful Christian missionary to Minnesota's Ojibwe was born on the shores of Rice Lake, near Peterborough, Ontario, around 1820. An Ottawa by birth, he had been trained in the practices of the Midewiwin by his grandfather, a member of the Lodge. A Methodist missionary persuaded the boy's father to send him away to school. Enmegahbowh (One Who Stands Before His People) converted to Christianity and was baptized John Johnson.[117] He came to Minnesota in 1839 as an interpreter with the American Board Mission.

Convinced that Christianity

John Johnson Enmegahbowh, the Ottawa priest who devoted his life to bringing Christianity to the Ojibwe in Minnesota. Born in Canada, he came to the territory in 1839 as an interpreter for the American Board Mission to Hole-in-the-Day's band. He was a lay delegate from St. Columba's Mission to the conventions of 1856, 1858, and 1859. Ordained to the diaconate in 1859, Enmegahbowh (One Who Stands Before His People) became the first Native American ordained as a priest in the Episcopal Church, in 1867.

held the answer to the Ojibwe's problems, Enmegahbowh preached diligently in the region over the next several years. At one point, depressed by the missionaries' lack of success, he decided to return to Canada, but a series of severe storms struck the ship taking him across Lake Superior, which he took as a sign that God wanted him to turn back. Ezekiel Gear, the army chaplain at Fort Snelling, persuaded him that the Episcopal version of the faith was more suitable to his needs than the Methodist and Presbyterian versions with which he had been previously acquainted.

By 1850, many Ojibwe had begun to think EuroAmerican-style farming might be the answer to their economic troubles. The number of fur-bearing animals had been decreasing throughout the region, due primarily to overhunting, as the natives competed with one another to supply the fur companies. No longer able to rely on the fur trade to provide them with metal cookware, steel knives, guns, ammunition, cloth, and other items not available in their environment, the Ojibwe had attempted, through various treaties, to offset their losses by selling land to the white man in exchange for annual payments of goods and money.[118]

The Ojibwe parted with their land reluctantly, however. They had watched native peoples to the east sell off their land bit by bit until they had none left. Wisconsin's Winnebago were a case in point. Treaty after treaty reduced their territory until, in 1840, they had to leave their home in the Green Bay area. Thinking to use them as a buffer between the warlike Dakota, to whom they were distantly related, and other tribes, the government sent the Winnebago first to northeast Iowa, then to the Crow Wing area, and finally to a reservation in southern Minnesota, near Blue Earth. Through a combination of wars with other Indians and pressure from the whites, the once populous Winnebago nation was reduced to barely eighteen hundred members.[119]

The Ojibwe had no desire to suffer the same fate. They decided that perhaps the time had come to learn to use the white man's farming methods and supplement their traditional diet of game, fish, wild rice, and maple sugar with cattle, wheat, and potatoes. They asked the government agent to send them teachers. It was in response to this request that James Lloyd Breck arrived to set up an Episcopal mission on Gull Lake.

The Gull Lake band was led by Hole-in-the-Day (Bugonaygishig), whose father had allowed the American Board to set up its mission twenty years earlier. Tall, handsome, and subtle, Hole-in-the-Day was both ambitious and devoted to the interests of his people. He managed to insert clauses in treaties that gave him an extra share of the tribal annuities, with which he built himself a fine house on a section

of land near Crow Wing, where he entertained army officers from Fort Ripley and other influential whites. He distributed money freely to his supporters and married the daughters of chiefs of nearly every other band. A talented orator, he sought to manipulate the tribe's relations with the U.S. government through cooperation, or, if that didn't work, through intimidation and threats of war.[120]

Reverend Breck opened his mission at Gull Lake in 1852. Although his methods of propagating the faith were similar to those of the American Board, Enmegahbowh was able to offset his superior's shortcomings by his own familiarity with the way things were done among the Ojibwe. By July 1855, Breck's St. Columba Mission had thirty-one Ojibwe students in its school, and several adults had accepted baptism, including the wives of several chiefs and a leading member of the Grand Medicine Lodge. The mission had at least ten white employees: a farmer, a blacksmith, a carpenter, and seven teachers, four of them women.[121] Encouraged by his success, Breck responded to a request

Enmegahbowh, Manitowaub, and James Lloyd Breck. Isaac Manitowaub was one of the Gull Lake Mission's first converts and a leading lay member. At his first visit to the mission, Whipple baptized Manitowaub's son, James Lloyd Breck Manitowaub.

Enmegahbowh's first wife, Charlotte (Biwabikogeshig-equay, or Iron Sky Woman) was a cousin of the younger Hole-in-the-Day, the Ojibwe chief whose antagonism caused the government a good deal of grief. Her family connections with the Gull Lake band led to the establishment of St. Columba's Mission there by Breck and Enmegahbowh in 1852. She and Enmegahbowh had at least twelve children, none of whom outlived their parents, though some left children whom Charlotte cared for. After Charlotte's death in 1895, Enmegahbowh married a woman named Mary, by whom he had at least one child, whose son later served as a priest at White Earth.

from the Leech Lake band by establishing a second mission at Leech Lake in 1856.

But then Breck unintentionally became entangled in Indian politics. He accepted the position of official government teacher, with a salary paid out of the tribe's education fund. Hole-in-the-Day objected strenuously to tribal annuity money being used to promote Christian doctrine. He asserted that, by hiring Breck, the government had abrogated tribal rights. The education fund belonged to the Ojibwe, he told the agent, and they alone had the right to select teachers for the tribe. Between 1854 and 1855, Breck received some $3,000 to operate schools at several Ojibwe villages. Although he then resigned, his reputation among the Ojibwe had been severely damaged.

Hole-in-the-Day began a campaign of harassment against Breck's missions. Cows were killed and mis-

sionaries threatened. Several warriors forced their way into the mission house, leaving only when the Ojibwe women inside ordered them out. At first, the missionaries blamed the Indians' "sauciness" on the alcohol that was so widely abused, but the violence escalated. By 1857, the situation had become so unstable that military authorities at Fort Ripley insisted the missionaries move into the fort. Then a German settler living in the area was murdered. When his Ojibwe killers were identified and arrested, a mob of whites seized them from the sheriff and lynched them. Fearing for the lives of his staff and family, Breck hastily withdrew. The Leech Lake post was abandoned, and the St. Columba Mission at Gull Lake (which had been vandalized by Hole-in-the-Day's warriors) was left in Enmegahbowh's charge. With the help of Isaac Manitowaub, White Fisher, and other faithful members of his flock, Enmegahbowh repaired the damaged mission building and went on with the work.

When Henry Whipple paid his first visit to St. Columba in November 1859, he was impressed by Enmegahbowh's faith and persistence, although he found the native deacon's methods unorthodox. It was a constant mystery to him how Enmegahbowh never seemed able to live on his salary. Charity was a noble thing, but Enmegahbowh—following the Ojibwe practice of gift giving and sharing one's goods with other members of the community— seemed at times to be supporting half the village. Enmegahbowh's long letters kept his bishop abreast of happenings among the Ojibwe people. Even when he did not completely accept Enmegahbowh's views, Whipple was often better informed than the government's resident agents.[122]

On his second visit in March 1860, Whipple spent more time talking with the Ojibwe than he had the previous November. Bad Boy, one of the tribal elders, a "graceful old man whose manner while speaking [is] impressive," told him that the tribe was poor, having had a bad harvest, and needed seed for the spring. He wanted a school and agricultural

White Fisher, a leading Ojibwe convert. Assistant to Bad Boy, chief of the Gull Lake band, White Fisher supported Breck's mission work.

Bad Boy, chief of the Gull Lake band, who told Whipple in 1860 that his people needed a school and agricultural training.

training for his people. Whipple assured him that "we came to them not to buy land or furs but to help Indians to Heaven."

From Gull Lake, Whipple accompanied Enmegahbowh to Mille Lacs, traveling on foot with a sledge to carry their supplies. The still-frozen earth made walking in moccasins uncomfortable, but the spell of the winter woods entranced him. "None can tell how deeply solemn prayer seems as you stand under the broad canopy of heaven, studded with stars and alone before God breathe out to him your faith, your wants, your warm gushing thoughts," he wrote in his diary. At night, the travelers built a palisade around a roaring campfire and slept on beds of fir and spruce branches. "There is nothing which so tests a man's temper as this wild, rough life," he reminisced years later. "If he has any cross-grained material about him it will come out, or if disposed to be a shirker it will be revealed."

On his return to St. Paul, Whipple wrote to President Buchanan, describing the failure of America's Indian policy as he saw it and listing specific actions he thought could be taken to repair the situation. The letter, dated April 9, 1860, was a distillation of facts and opinions he had gathered through talks with Breck, Gear, Enmegahbowh, E. Steele Peake, Judge Charles Flandrau, missionary Frederick Ayer, and others in Minnesota, and from his earlier study of the government's relations with the Seminoles and other tribes. He enclosed with it letters from prominent New York Democratic leaders endorsing his opinions.[123]

It was morally wrong, he told the president, for the government to make treaties with the Indian tribes as if they and the United States were equals; the differences in political strength between the two parties made such treaties a farce. It was also wrong to pay the Indians in cash, because the money was usually squandered within weeks, often on alcohol, which was a curse to them. The federal laws against selling liquor to Indians could not be enforced; the agents had no police powers and could not patrol the extensive borders of the scattered reservations to prevent liquor sellers from sneaking in. Even when

Bugonaygishig (Hole-in-the-Day), prominent chief of the Ojibwe during the 1850s and 1860s, inherited his name from his father, whose band was originally located just above Little Falls, Minnesota. Hole-in-the-Day forced Breck to abandon his mission at Leech Lake in 1857, and in 1862 tried to talk the Ojibwe into attacking Fort Ripley. His extravagant lifestyle included two homes, ostentatious dress, a hired bodyguard-interpreter, and several wives, including a white woman, Helen Kater, whom he met on his 1864 trip to Washington. He was murdered in August 1868, apparently by renegades from his own tribe, for reasons that are still not clear. No one was ever charged with the crime.

lawbreakers were caught, local judges often let them go. The government should use the army to enforce laws to protect the Indians, Whipple urged, and deal only with chiefs who did not drink. The Indians' only hope of survival as a race, he added, lay in their adopting Christianity and EuroAmerican civilization.

Whipple made eight specific recommendations: 1) treaties should regard Indians as "wards" and provide them with supplies "in kind as needed" rather than cash payments for their land; 2) U.S. commissioners with the authority to try all violations of Indian law should be appointed near all reservations; 3) agents should be instructed to take prompt action against all sales of liquor to Indians; 4) those of "intemperate habits" should be struck from the annuity rolls; 5) medals should be issued for sobriety; 6) all bands of a tribe should be concentrated on a single reservation, where they could be more efficiently served; 7) Indians should be encouraged to acquire individual title to land and to begin farming thereon; and 8) "practical Christian teachers" should be hired to teach the Indians agriculture and "the arts of civilization."[124]

Whipple would repeat these points (with the exception of 3, 4, and 5) again and again over the succeeding years in communications with government officials and private charitable organizations. He was particularly insistent on the government's duty to abide by the terms of all its treaties, and on the need to bring Indians under the rule of law to protect their lives and property. This particular letter, however, received little attention from Buchanan, who was preoccupied with the impending collapse of the Union. The debate raged between those who regarded the United States as a republic under a strong central government and those who saw it as a confederacy of independent states able to decide serious issues, like the continued existence of slavery (and its extension into new territories in the West), on an *ad hoc* basis. No one in Washington had time to reflect on the future of the Indians, who, it was believed, were a primitive, outdated society doomed to vanish within a generation or two anyway.

When Whipple returned to the Ojibwe country in July, he visited the more distant Pokegama and Sandy Lake bands, accompanied by Peake, E. P. Gray of the Shakopee Mission, Enmegahbowh, and William Superior, one of Enmegahbowh's converts. It was a "severe trial of strength," the bishop observed, "to carry 75 or 80 lbs on ones shoulders under a July sun." But he was too pleased with what he was discovering about the Ojibwe and their homeland to feel the pain. Years later, Enmegahbowh recalled, "The Indians said, 'We must not let [the bishop] do this. He will kill himself. He cannot work in this way and live.' But he would smile—oh how we loved that smile . . . and say, 'O, this is nothing! This does not tire me!' and his voice filled us with hope and courage."[125]

On the road, they met a group of men from Hole-in-the-Day's village at Leech Lake, who apologized for taking part in the destruction of Breck's mission house in 1857. Whipple's party accompanied the men to Leech Lake by canoe, battling a sudden storm. At the village, he met some Ojibwe who wore medals of the Virgin Mary. They told him that they had been baptized by a Roman Catholic priest.[126] When Whipple asked them if they knew about Jesus, they admitted they didn't. "What a comment on Romish teaching," he wrote in his diary that evening: no knowledge of Jesus, only a medal, and yet they had been baptized!

On March 6, 1861, two days after Abraham Lincoln's inauguration, Whipple wrote a letter to the new president, repeating many of the points he had made to Buchanan. By now the bishop had spoken with a number of Native Americans, and his initial

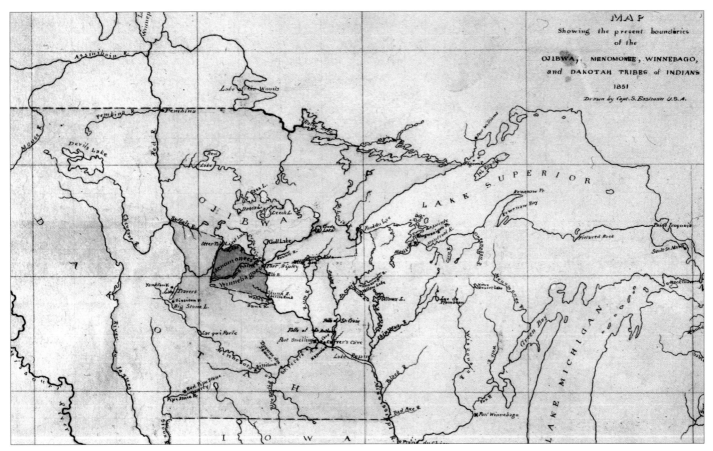

Frontier army officer and artist Seth Eastman made this colored pen-and-ink map showing the boundaries of the "Ojibwa, Menomonee, Winnebago, and Dakotah" tribes in 1851.

George Bonga, a trader of mixed African American and Ojibwe ancestry, often served as interpreter for the Ojibwe. He was among Whipple's informants on Ojibwe matters.

impressions were even more firmly grounded. "From the day of the treaty a rapid deterioration takes place," he declared. "The Indian agents . . . are generally selected without any reference to their fitness for the place. . . . Then follow all the evils of bad example, of inefficiency, and of dishonesty. . . . The Indian, bewildered, conscious of wrong, but helpless, has no refuge but to sink into a depth of brutishness. . . . The first thing needed is *honesty*. . . . The second step is to frame instructions so that the Indian shall be the ward of the Government. They cannot live without law. We have broken up, in part, their tribal relations, and they must have something in their place. . . . The schools should be ample to receive all children who desire to attend. . . . In all future

treaties it ought to be the object of the Government to pay the Indians in kind," to prevent government agents from succumbing to the temptation of skimming funds from the annuities. "Can these red men become civilized? I say, unhesitatingly, *yes*," but only if the government dealt with them honestly.[127]

The letter received little attention from the new president, who was facing the looming crisis at Fort Sumter. Undaunted, Whipple began a letter-writing campaign on the Indians' behalf to Secretary of the Interior Caleb Smith, who had oversight of the Office of Indian Affairs, and to Secretary of the Treasury Salmon P. Chase, who was responsible for annuity payments. Whipple also wrote to Commissioner of Indian Affairs William Dole and those members of Congress he hoped he could interest in his cause.

Smith replied that the problems Whipple raised were difficult to remedy without Congressional assistance. He hoped, he said, to get Congress to agree to isolate the Indians from white contact on one large reservation, dismantle the current trading system, and pay all Indian annuities in goods rather than cash.[128]

Morton Wilkinson, Minnesota's new Republican senator and a member of the Senate's Committee on Indian Affairs, sent Whipple a condescending letter assuring him that the situation was bound to improve under the new administration. He modestly acknowledged his role in selecting the new superintendent and agents and suggested that any errors were in the system, not the men. The Indians would have to change their way of life, he said, before they could benefit from the kind of education that missionaries like Whipple proposed.[129]

Cyrus Aldrich, chair of the House Committee on Indian Affairs, told Whipple that Minnesota's Indians were better treated than most, and while something certainly should be done, it was difficult to know just what. He added that he would welcome any concrete suggestions, but opined that Indians in general were incapable of civilization.[130] His colleague William Windom likewise showed little interest in the welfare of people who were not his constituents.

Even Uncle George Whipple, now living in New York as secretary of the American Missionary Association, hearing of his nephew's agitation on behalf of the Indians, wrote to criticize him. The old abolitionist told the bishop he would do better to interest himself on behalf of slaves.[131] Only Minnesota's Senator Henry M. Rice expressed any agreement with Whipple's views, but pointed out that, as a lame-duck Democrat, he was not in a position to do much good.[132]

The situation among Minnesota's Indian tribes became even more unstable in the wake of the Republican electoral victory of 1860. In the distribution of political patronage that followed Lincoln's election, all the old Indian bureau employees were turned out and replaced by loyal Republicans, many of whom had no experience in dealing with Indians. William Dole, the new commissioner of Indian Affairs, was an Illinois merchant who had helped nominate Lincoln. Clark Thompson, the new superintendent of the Northern District (whose headquarters was in Minneapolis), and his agents—Thomas J. Galbraith for the Dakota, Lucius C. Walker for the Ojibwe, and St. Andre D. Balcombe for the Winnebago—were likewise party stalwarts whose chief interest in their jobs seemed to be the opportunity to make their fortunes at government expense. To the dismay of Whipple and others sympathetic to the Indian cause, most of these new officials were more venal than their predecessors. Superintendent Thompson, who oversaw all government agents in Minnesota and Wisconsin, was rumored to be as deeply involved in shady dealings as the agents and traders.[133]

Hole-in-the-Day, whose aggressive stance in 1857 had brought him considerable political influence among his people, was ignored by the new Ojibwe agent, Lucius Walker. The outraged chief began complaining to anyone who would listen about the rampant frauds committed by government agents and traders. He demanded Ojibwe control of the annuity funds for which his people had sold land they needed to support their traditional way of life.

Painted in 1857 by artist George Healy, Henry M. Rice, a former fur trader and one of the founders of the city of St. Paul, helped negotiate treaties with the Winnebago in 1846 and the Ojibwe in 1847, 1854, and 1855. While sympathetic to the Indians, Rice was also committed to the establishment of Minnesota as a state. He was elected to Congress in 1853, where he secured legislation extending preemption laws over unsurveyed land in Minnesota Territory and proposed the act approving the state constitution in 1857. After two terms in the House of Representatives, he served as state senator from 1858 to 1862.

The Ojibwe were especially bitter about the 1847 treaty, by which they had ceded a tract on the western bank of the Mississippi for pennies an acre in the expectation that it would be turned over to the Winnebago, who had been moved out of Wisconsin the year before. When the Winnebago were sent to Blue Earth instead, the land was sold by the government to white settlers at the standard price of $1.25 per acre. Because of fraud and mismanagement in the Indian bureau, the Ojibwe seldom received the full amount of their annuities from additional land sold to the government in 1854 and 1855.[134]

Now the white man was at war, and Congress was less interested than ever in the welfare of its Indian allies. During the early months of 1862, feelings among the Ojibwe against the intruding white man once again began to run high. Their complaints were echoed even more stridently among the Dakota in the southern part of the state, where government incompetence was about to bring on a full-fledged war.

George Catlin's watercolor sketch of Cloud Man's Dakota village, ca. 1834, near Lake Calhoun in present-day Minneapolis. Congregationalist missionaries established the earliest mission to the Dakota in this village in 1834.

The Ojibwe had given up considerable land in the two decades leading up to 1862, but they were still living on their ancestral lakes and had retained enough to continue their traditional hunting/gathering/fishing economy, albeit on a smaller scale than in previous years. The Dakota of Minnesota were a different story.

Minnesota's Dakota belonged to the easternmost branch of the great Sioux nation, a warrior society whose territory extended in 1800 from the Mississippi River to the Rocky Mountains. Sometimes called Santee (from Isanti, the people of Knife Lake), the eastern Dakota were divided into four subtribes. Along the Mississippi and lower Minnesota Rivers were the Mdewakanton (people of the Mystic Lake, their name for Mille Lacs). They were a fairly numerous group with settled villages under Chiefs Little Crow, Wabasha, Shakopee, Red Wing, Good Road, and Black Dog. Inland from them were the Wahpekute (Leaf Shooters), a smaller, more nomadic group who hunted on the plains south of the Minnesota River. Farther up the Minnesota were the Wahpeton (Leaf People) and Sisseton (Swamp People), whose territory extended into the eastern ranges of what would become Dakota Territory.[135]

The seminomadic Dakota made their living from hunting, fishing, gathering wild plants, and raiding their traditional enemies, especially the Ojibwe. Only the Mdewakanton practiced gardening, having learned the skill from their Ojibwe neighbors. They also traded furs to the white men for weapons, iron cookware, and cloth. Each village was governed by a chief. The chieftainship usually passed from father to son, but the father could choose any of his sons he thought capable of governing, and his decision had to be approved by the village elders. If part of the village objected to a new chief, it could move away and choose its own leader. The chiefs ruled by consensus and strength of character, frequently making alliances with neighboring villages through marriage with the daughters of leading families. During a hunt, the men often formed a soldiers' lodge to enforce agreed-upon rules as to where, when, and how animals could be killed, thus preventing squabbles that could turn into blood feuds. The lodge also set rules for the hit-and-run warfare carried on against the Ojibwe and other tribes.[136]

The Dakotas' first encounter with American officialdom came in 1805, when Zebulon Pike negotiated with the Mdewakanton for a piece of land on which to build a fort. Pike purchased 100,000 acres of bluff land overlooking the junction of the Minnesota and Mississippi Rivers. The selling price was left blank in the treaty, and when Congress finally ratified it in 1808, the sum was fixed at $2,000, or two cents an acre—well below the dollar an acre Pike had suggested. The payment was to be made in goods, not cash, as the Dakota had no use for money at the time.[137]

In 1837, the Mdewakanton signed another treaty ceding title to their lands on the eastern

Fort Snelling in 1848, watercolor on paper by soldier-artist Seth Eastman, who served at this citadel overlooking the confluence of the Mississippi and Minnesota Rivers in the 1840s.

side of the Mississippi in exchange for $300,000, invested for their benefit in a twenty-year annuity paying $15,000 per annum. Additional payments for medicines, agricultural equipment, cattle, tools, and the salaries of white farmers, blacksmiths, and physicians brought the annual payments close to $25,000. Debts to the traders would be paid from this sum, and the government reserved up to one-third of the annual payment for an education fund to pay for teachers in each village. For various reasons, this education fund was never fully expended, and the issue became a major sticking point in later treaty negotiations.

The 1837 treaty was a great boon to the Mde-wakanton, who had been on the verge of starvation. Game had become scarce in their hunting grounds. Not only fur-bearing animals but also deer and buffalo had all but ceased to exist in the Dakota lands east of the Mississippi. With the creation of the Astor fur monopoly, prices at the trading houses had risen sometimes as much as three and four times, and most Dakota hunters were deeply in

debt. Now the government guaranteed them regular provision of food, as well as a means of paying off their debts to the traders. The Sisseton, Wahpeton, and Wahpekute, who were not parties to the treaty, were impressed and began to wonder if they could not sell off some land too.

While only a few villages were affected by the 1837 treaty, its economic impact was greater than the Dakota anticipated. The annuity, while improving their economic condition, made them dependent on the U.S. government for their livelihood. The government therefore could—and did—use annuity payments to pressure them into desired behaviors. Their relationship with the traders was also altered. Instead of paying for goods with furs, the Dakota now ran up cash debts against their anticipated annuities—and the prices continued to climb. Frequently, when payment day arrived, a Dakota found that he received nothing but a little food from the agent.[138]

By the end of the 1840s, white immigration into Minnesota Territory was beginning to affect the Dakota. Whiskey flowed freely from settlements on the Mississippi's eastern bank and was sold illegally by some of the less reputable independent traders operating in the wake of Astor's now-defunct American Fur Company. The agents' efforts to control the alcohol trade by licensing traders and using troops from Fort Snelling to enforce the laws were only sporadically successful.[139]

In the summer of 1851, another treaty was negotiated at the trading post at Traverse des Sioux on the Minnesota River. This time all four Dakota bands were involved. The Sisseton and Wahpeton signed in early July and the Wahpekute and Mdewakanton at the end of the month. In these treaties, the Dakota sold all their land within the territorial boundaries for $3 million, to be invested as before, with annual payments in goods and cash. The payments (amounting to about $20 a year per person) would be made for fifty years, then the principal would revert to the U.S. Treasury.[140] A reservation one hundred miles long and twenty miles wide along the upper Minnesota River was to be set aside for the tribe's permanent use. Schools, blacksmith shops, and mills would be set up on this reservation, where the Dakota could be instructed in farming, if need be.

As the treaties were being signed, the traders slipped in a second paper—which the chiefs signed, thinking it was another copy of the treaty—guaranteeing payment of the traders' claims (in an amount not listed) out of the funds to be paid to the Indians. Congress had ruled a few years earlier that payments to traders could no longer be included in treaties, and this was the traders' way of getting around the law. When the Dakota found out how they had been deceived, they were angry, but there was nothing they could do; the paper they had signed was a legal document.

The Senate had another surprise in store for the Dakota when it came time to ratify the treaties. There had been much criticism of the way in which the government had previously promised Indian tribes permanent reservations, only to come back a

few years later with new treaties moving them elsewhere. Before approving the Traverse des Sioux treaties, the Senate removed the "permanent home" clause and replaced it with one that guaranteed the reservation only "until the Executive shall deem it expedient to direct otherwise." This change, which in effect meant that they had given up *all* their land, not just most of it, also angered the Dakota. Chief Wabasha, who had opposed the treaties from the beginning, said, "There is one more thing which our great father can do, that is, gather us all together on the prairie and surround us with soldiers and shoot us down."[141]

The ink was barely dry on the Traverse des Sioux treaties before white settlers began pouring into the newly opened lands, sometimes staking claims to property in Indian villages that had not yet been removed.[142] Over the next few years, the Dakota packed up their belongings and moved to the new reservation along the Minnesota River, some twelve miles upstream from Fort Ridgely. The agency was

Pictured here in 1960, the Yellow Medicine (Upper Sioux) Agency served the Sisseton and Wahpeton bands.

Former fur trader Joseph Brown was the Upper Sioux agent from 1857 to 1860. He encouraged the Dakota to take up farming and adapt to EuroAmerican cultural patterns. His house on the Minnesota River midway between the Upper and Lower Agencies was demolished during the Dakota War.

White Dog (Shonka-sha), former head of the farmers at the Lower Agency and one of Whipple's converts, was executed in December 1862 for allegedly leading a detachment of soldiers from Fort Ridgely into ambush during the Dakota War. A few years after his death, his widow married Good Thunder. This portrait is part of a panorama painted by John Stevens in 1862.

moved from Fort Snelling to the Redwood area, and a subagency was established for the Sisseton and Wahpeton thirty-five miles upstream, where the Yellow Medicine River flows into the Minnesota.

The new reservation was not large enough for hunting to be economically feasible for the eight thousand Dakota who made it their home. It became even smaller in 1858, when they were persuaded to sell the land on the northern bank of the river. The government agents—Nathaniel McLean (1849–1853), Charles Flandrau (1856–1857), and Joseph R. Brown (1857–1860)—each made an effort to teach the Dakota to farm. Despite the reluctance of Dakota warriors to do "woman's work," the agents gradually succeeded in winning over some of them. One of Little Crow's men, White Dog, was hired by McLean in 1851 as a government farmer and encouraged to form a "farmer's society" among the Mdewakanton. By 1857, White Dog had twenty men engaged in farming near the Lower Agency. In July 1858, Chief Wabasha consented to have his hair cut (the symbol of acceptance of the new lifestyle), adding his prestige to what agent Brown called the "pantaloon band." By late 1861, even Little Crow, who had maintained a firm opposition to any attempt to undermine the cultural life of his people, was showing an interest, at least to the extent of having his wives learn the white man's farming methods and moving his family into a frame house.[143]

If the treaty conditions had been strictly adhered to, perhaps the situation would not have deteriorated quite so rapidly. But annuity payments were often late and the salaries offered by the Office of Indian Affairs were too low to keep farmers, blacksmiths, mill operators, and other white employees from turning over frequently. Fraud was rampant. The quality of the food and goods provided by the government was often poor. The traders continued to make excessive profits at the Indians' expense, and some of the agents—particularly Robert G. Murphy (1854–1856), who was removed on charges of

Congregationalists Samuel and Gideon Pond were the first missionaries to the Dakota. The brothers arrived in 1834 at White Cloud's Sisseton village on Lake Calhoun. Working independently at first, they later associated with the American Board Mission and served the Dakota until 1862. Samuel Pond created the first written form of the Dakota language.

incompetence and corruption—found ways to line their pockets too. Few Dakota men were yet willing to work on the farms, and when cutworms or other natural disasters damaged the crops, starvation often threatened the entire tribe.

The American Board established a mission among the Dakota in 1835, concentrating its efforts on the Sisseton and Wahpeton. They found the Mdewakanton less open to their message, which they blamed on the band's close contact with undesirable elements in the white community. The missionaries' major selling point was their assertion that adopting the white man's farm-based economy would protect the Dakota from starvation; but after the 1837 treaty the Mdewakanton were able to supplement their traditional economy with government-provided annuities.

The Dakota religion, like that of the Ojibwe, involved a close relationship between the seen and unseen worlds and between men and beasts, although the terms and traditions were quite different. There was no society of priest-healers like the Midewiwin, but there were medicine men of great power, *wicasta wakan,* who served as war leaders, spiritual guides, and healers. It was a holistic, animist faith with no formulated theology, relying heavily on an awareness of the presence of spirit *(wakan tanka)* in everything from rocks to people and accessible through vision quests, feasts, and sacred dances. It was difficult for the nineteenth-century Christian missionaries to find connections in this faith on which to build.[144]

Stephen Riggs, a Presbyterian missionary with the American Board Mission, came to Minnesota in 1837 with his wife, Mary. After several years at Lac Qui Parle, they moved to the Upper Agency area in 1851, where Riggs founded the Hazelwood Republic, made up of his Dakota converts, and published a Dakota dictionary and grammar book. After the 1862 Dakota War he assisted General Henry Sibley in processing the Dakota prisoners. His son, Alfred Riggs, later worked at the American Board mission on the Santee Reservation in Nebraska.

Nevertheless, by 1860, the American Board had begun to make some headway. A small group of converts had come into being near the Upper Agency, about one hundred of them having been admitted into church membership. In 1854, Stephen Riggs founded a community of Christian Dakotas that he called the Hazelwood Republic. Dr. Thomas Williamson's son, John, finished his theological training in 1860 and intended to open a mission at the Lower Sioux Agency.

Until that time, the Episcopal Church had not made any effort to convert the Dakota. E. Steele Peake had visited the Lower Agency in 1856, before joining James Lloyd Breck at Gull Lake, and baptized the daughter of Jared Daniels, the agency doctor. He had urged Bishop Kemper to send a missionary to the Dakota, but nothing came of it.

Shortly after his first diocesan convention ended, Whipple set out with Breck to visit the Dakota and Winnebago tribes. At the Lower Sioux Agency, he stayed with Dr. Daniels, who allowed him to hold services in his home. On Friday, June 22, 1860, Whipple confirmed a Captain DeRossey, an army officer stationed at Fort Ridgely. The service was held outdoors just as the sun set over the rolling prairie surrounding the agency. The Dakota, who had gathered at the agency to await their annuity payment, looked on with interest as the tall priest, garbed in a long, white surplice and an embroidered stole, laid his hands on the soldier's bare head and spoke solemn words in a rich, melodious voice. The following Sunday, a large number of them crowded into Daniels' home to hear Whipple preach. Thomas Robertson, a mixed-blood interpreter, translated Whipple's words into Dakota.

Earlier that day, three Mdewakanton chiefs—

The restored Lower Sioux Agency as it looks today. It was agency headquarters for the Dakota Reservation from 1852 to 1862. The Episcopal mission was established in 1860 among the Mdewakanton and Wahpekute Dakota who were served at this building. The Dakota War began with attacks on the agency and its adjoining trading posts.

Wabasha, Taopi, and Good Thunder—had asked to speak with Whipple. Wabasha was a prominent chief and Little Crow's principal rival as spokesman for the tribe. Taopi and Good Thunder were members of Little Crow's band, more open to the white man's ideas than their chieftain, who had joined the ranks of Indian farmers. The three men told Whipple of their concerns for the future. The government had promised them a teacher, they said, but none had been provided. They had heard Whipple say he had come from the Great Spirit to help his children. They asked him to send them a missionary.

As it happened, Whipple had one available: Samuel Dutton Hinman, then in his last year at Seabury. Whipple ordained Hinman deacon on September 20 and sent him to the Lower Sioux Agency. Hinman arrived at the agency in October, accompanied by his bride, Mary Bury, and Emily West, who had been with Breck at the Ojibwe Mission and had spent the past three years teaching at Andrews Hall. The three set briskly to work, and by the time of the bishop's next visit on December 12, they had thirty children in their school and a small but regular congregation of Dakota attending services at the mission, named for St. John the Evangelist.[145]

Hinman, having trained under Breck, was a staunch High Churchman, devoted to the use of liturgy as an aid to personal piety. In October 1860, as he was establishing the Dakota Mission, Whipple received a letter from G. T. Bedell, assistant bishop of Ohio and secretary of one of the church's larger missionary societies. An earnest member of the evangelical faction, Bedell offered support for the proposed mission to the Dakota—with certain reservations. "The religious instruction of those Indians is of as difficult, as it is vital, importance," Bedell wrote. "They must be kept away from all that tends to or looks like Roman Catholicism. . . . That whole system is too much allied to human nature in its depravity. . . . You must get for them some missionary who works upon that principle: in other words, tech-

nically speaking, an Evangelical man." He acknowledged Whipple's known High Church tendencies: "There need be no hesitation in your expressing a desire for Evangelical missionaries, even whilst you profess yourself an Evangelical High Churchman," he assured him, and suggested that Whipple apply to his missionary society for "both the man and the support."[146]

Samuel Hinman, the first Episcopal missionary to the Dakota, came west from Connecticut, and was one of the first graduates of Seabury. He and his bride, Mary, opened a mission near the Lower Agency shortly after he was ordained in 1860. He accompanied his flock to South Dakota in 1863 and later to the Santee Reservation in northeast Nebraska.

Whipple did not avail himself of Bedell's offer. As long as the Dakota Mission was under his oversight, he managed to support it out of diocesan mission funds and with donations acquired through speaking tours in the East.[147] He had been given the new diocese to run and he would run it his way—politely and diplomatically and according to his conscience, but without interference from his brother bishops or anyone else.

The Winnebago, whom Whipple visited on June 26 after leaving the Dakota agency, were polite but "seemed indifferent" to his message, he noted in his diary. In any case, he had no missionary for them. "Would God that a faithful man might be raised up for

Andrew Good Thunder (Wakinyanwaste), a minor chief under Taopi, was Whipple's first adult male Dakota convert. His daughter, Lydia Sigourney, briefly attended Andrews Hall, Whipple's Indian school at Faribault. Good Thunder's first wife, Snana (Margaret), saved the mission's Bible in August 1862; the couple separated around 1865.

the work," he wrote wistfully.

In 1861, Joseph Brown, who had been a trader in his earlier days and was married to a Dakota woman, was replaced as agent by the unknown Thomas Galbraith, whose chief qualification for the job was that he had campaigned diligently in Minnesota for the Republican Party. Galbraith made sweeping personnel changes at the agency. He dismissed White Dog as chief farmer, replacing him with Taopi, who came from the same village. While White Dog was said to have accepted the loss of his government salary without complaint, he was no more happy about it than any of the others who were discharged. Jared

Daniels and his brother Asa, who had served as agency physicians since 1855, were also replaced.

In June 1861, Whipple paid a second visit to the Dakota Mission, where he observed a "thrilling" maiden's feast celebration and confirmed seven persons. Good Thunder asked him to take his twelve-year-old daughter back to Faribault to educate her at Andrews Hall, and Whipple agreed. The girl was baptized Lydia Sigourney, after a popular poet and writer of edifying books for children. Unfortunately, Lydia became seriously ill in her first year at the school. Whipple sent for her father, who came immediately. The chief was distressed; his friends had told him that his daughter had been poisoned by Ojibwe girls at the school. Lydia assured him that the other girls had always treated her like a sister. "There are no enemies among Christ's children," she told him.

Good Thunder took his daughter home, where she died a few weeks later. Whipple was with the family when she passed away and heard her urge her father to become a Christian so they could be together in paradise. A belief in the soul's immortality was part of the Dakota religion, but it was understood that the Christian heaven and the Dakota one were not the same place. After the child's funeral, Good Thunder asked Whipple to baptize him. He took the Christian name Andrew. His wife, Snana, was baptized at the same time with the name Margaret.[148] The deaths of two of his children, both baptized by Hinman, brought Taopi into the church also. Like Good Thunder, he hoped to see them again one day in heaven.

Wabasha, however, resisted baptism. Whipple went to visit him in the house the government had built for the chief in his village two miles south of the agency. A scalp dance was going on at the agency when Whipple arrived, and he was told that it was in honor of a Dakota who had killed an Ojibwe. Outraged, Whipple complained to Wabasha, "You asked me for a school and a mission. . . . I come to visit you and I see . . . a horrible scalp dance. I know the man who was killed; he had a wife and children; the wife is asking for her husband; the children are asking for their father. Wabasha, the Great Spirit is angry! Some day He will look Wabasha in the face and ask him for his red brother."

Wabasha took a puff on his pipe, blew the smoke into the air, and replied, "White man goes to war with his own brother; kills more men than Wabasha can count all his life. Great Spirit look down and says, '*Good* white man; he has my Book; I have good home for him by and by.' Dakota has no Great Spirit's Book; he goes to war, kills one man, has a foolish scalp-dance; Great Spirit very angry. *Wabasha doesn't believe it!*"

Wabasha was referring to the Civil War, which had begun a few months earlier. The Dakota followed the news of the war with great interest. The more disaffected members of the tribe had recently formed a soldiers' lodge, where they gathered to discuss their grievances against the government. They taunted the farmer Indians, who they thought—rightly—were being favored by the agent. They complained that the traders were charging too much, although they had no way of proving it, as the traders were the only ones who kept records. They told one another that soon all the white soldiers would have to leave Minnesota, an argument that gained strength as the Union armies seemed to lose one battle after another. If the soldiers left, the settlers who had taken the Dakota's land would be left unprotected.

Red Owl, the tribe's leading spokesman, died in 1861.[149] Maneuvering quickly began among the surviving chiefs to take his place. The leading contenders were Wabasha, Little Crow, Big Eagle,

Wabasha was a leading Mdewakanton chief whose people lived on the Mississippi River near Winona, Minnesota, before the treaties of 1851 and 1858 were signed. Although he opposed the treaties, he came to believe that his people's survival depended on changing their lifestyle. Wabasha converted to Christianity following the 1862 war.

and Traveling Hail. An election was planned for the spring of 1862. The winter of 1861–1862 was extremely cold, with many storms and deep snow. Food supplies ran short in the Dakota lodges. Galbraith issued food from the warehouses only to the farmer Indians, which infuriated the others, although the farmers wisely shared what they could with their brothers. Rumors began to circulate that because of the war, the government would not be able to keep its commitments to the Indians in the coming year.

The stage was being set for a tragedy of epic proportions.

The Dakota attack on the Lower Agency, as portrayed in an 1893 panorama painted by New Ulm artists Anton Gág, Christian Heller, and Alexander Schwendinger. Sixteen men, mostly traders and agency employees, were killed here on the morning of August 18, 1862.

Henry Whipple cannot have welcomed the new year in 1862 with any great optimism, though there was no way he could have anticipated the degree of disaster that would ensue. He visited St. Columba in January, then toured some of the EuroAmerican communities that were springing up in southern Minnesota on land acquired eleven years earlier from the Dakota.

At the end of June, four women from Philadelphia—Catherine and Elizabeth Biddle, Caroline Harris, and Sarah Farnum—arrived in Faribault, eager to visit the Indian missions they had been supporting with donations. On July 1, the bishop escorted the visitors, plus his wife, his eldest daughter, Lizzie, and his son Charles, to St. John's Mission at the Lower Sioux Agency. Cornelia Whipple complained of the hot weather, mosquitoes, and bedbugs. "I could but wonder how your father could stand it, in all his long tramps," she wrote her two younger daughters, at school in New Jersey.[150]

The party was entertained by a Dakota monkey dance and later a begging dance at the agent's home, where the Dakota asked for the distribution of the annuity supplies that had been delayed. Unaware of the frustrations underlying the performance, the women found it picturesque. The next day, they traveled upriver to the Yellow Medicine Agency, where a group of Yanktonais (a Nakota tribe who lived just west of Minnesota's border) were visiting. The ladies were disappointed when the Yanktonais refused to sell them personal ornaments as souvenirs.

Returning to the Lower Sioux Agency, they took part in little Lydia Sigourney's funeral. It was a poignant event. The service, held in the Dakota language, included a Dakota version of the hymn "Nearer, My God, to Thee." The Dakota women had gathered hundreds of wild roses to line the grave. To Whipple, "paradise never seemed nearer."

During his visit, the bishop spoke at length with Wabasha, White Dog, Taopi, and Good Thunder. The chiefs were unhappy. The annuities were late, and there was much grumbling among the hungry Dakotas. White Dog, especially, was "in a querulous mood." Whipple thought it was because White Dog's wife objected to her husband's interest in Christianity, but the former head farmer may also have been still nursing a grievance over the loss of his job to Taopi the previous year.[151]

Taopi (The Wounded Man), who had been one of Samuel Hinman's first

Taopi, chief of the farmer Indians at the Lower Agency, was an early convert to Christianity. When the "friendly Sioux" moved to Santee in 1867, Taopi remained behind and died in poverty two years later at Faribault. His story was published in 1869 in *The Journal of the Reverend S. D. Hinman, or Taopi and His Friends*.

Beggar's Dance by Seth Eastman, ca. 1850. The object of the dancers was to solicit gifts of food, drink, or tobacco, either from their fellow tribesmen or white visitors. Whipple and his party witnessed a similar dance at the Lower Sioux Agency in the summer of 1862.

converts, was depressed because another of his children was dying, and the medicine man had told him that it was because Taopi had become a Christian.

One of the things that annoyed the Dakota most about the terms of their treaties was the pressure they were under from the agents to abandon their traditional way of life. Those who took up farming, accepted Christianity, or adopted the white man's style of clothing were often harassed by those who opposed the changes. There had even been a few deaths. Whipple did his best to reassure them that they were taking the right course.[152]

The bishop and his party were on the reservation for more than a week, visiting with the Dakota and laying the cornerstone for a church. Whipple baptized nine women and children, confirmed six persons, preached, and celebrated the Eucharist. The degree of discontent he saw among the Dakota worried him. "It seemed as if the very air was charged with materials for the cyclone of death," he later re-

called. Some of the men refused to shake hands with him, which he regarded as a bad omen.

Whipple spoke with the agent, Thomas Galbraith, who seemed to him an agreeable man. Galbraith had written him at the end of May, claiming he had uncovered a swindle being carried on by the "traders and unprincipled devils [who] control everything."[153] When the bishop asked Hinman about it, he replied that the rumors of a swindle were "but too true." It was done, he said, "through Commissioner [Charles] Mix who is still retained at Washington."[154] The "swindle" was a rumored plan to substitute greenbacks for gold in the annuity distribution. Although Galbraith was as deeply involved in skimming money from the government pot as anyone else, he seems to have been sincere about implementing the government's acculturation policy and expanding the area under cultivation on the reservation. To encourage the Dakota to cooperate, he intended to award annuity goods only to those who agreed to become farmers—a policy that would soon backfire.[155]

But in July, Galbraith felt confident. The harvest looked promising, and he had apparently been reassured that the annuity payment would be made in the usual gold. More and more Dakota were settling onto farms; even Little Crow, who was a medicine man as well as a chief and an outspoken advocate of traditional ways, had agreed to "become a white man."[156] If Galbraith shared Whipple's concern about the situation on the reservation, the agent apparently felt he had things under control at that point. Galbraith "entered fully into my plans" for the mission, the bishop confided to his diary, and promised to send him an "Indian suit" for his collection of native cultural items.

Returning to Faribault, Whipple presided over the July 16 commencement exercises at Seabury, ordained George Tanner (one of Seabury's first graduates) to the priesthood, and then laid the cornerstone for the Cathedral of Our Merciful Saviour. James Breck's wife had died in April, and as Whipple was preaching at her funeral, the idea of building a cathedral at Faribault (which he and the Brecks had discussed vaguely for some time) solidified in his mind. Funds were already coming in. On Easter Day, the congregation of the Good Shepherd parish at Faribault had collected $600 toward the cathedral's building fund.[157]

Whipple knew exactly what kind of church he wanted it to be. In his sermon at the laying of the cornerstone, he said, "The worship of this church

The Cathedral of Our Merciful Saviour under construction in 1862. The name was suggested by Whipple's friend and colleague, Bishop Arthur Coxe of Western New York.

The first Episcopal church at the Lower Sioux Agency was under construction when the Dakota War erupted in August 1862. The church was destroyed during the war, but stone from it was used in 1889 to build St. Cornelia's Church at Birch Coulee.

will be common worship. . . . The glorious Gospel of Jesus Christ will here be preached. . . . The Sacraments of Christ will here be set forth." It would be a free church, "for all for whom Christ died."[158]

July 16 was a day of "unalloyed joy," he wrote in his diary that evening, the "most delightful series of services of my episcopate." The following day, he laid another cornerstone, for Seabury Hall, the first permanent building of the new Divinity School.[159]

When the ceremonies were over, Whipple and his guests embarked on July 24 for the Ojibwe Mission. He spoke with Hole-in-the-Day at Gull Lake, sympathizing with his complaints against the agency. Hole-in-the-Day was not appeased; he demanded to know where the school was that Whipple had promised them. Whipple replied that he'd

tried to find a teacher, but no one wanted to come to a place where drunkenness was so widespread. That night, the Ojibwe held a scalp dance and whiskey flowed freely. It was, the bishop observed sourly, "a pandemonium of devils."

The ladies returned to Faribault while Whipple set off on a more extensive tour in the company of E. Steele Peake, Enmegahbowh, William Spencer (the mixed-blood sutler from Fort Ripley), and three Ojibwe guides. Traveling mostly by canoe, they visited Gull Lake, Leech Lake, and Red Lake between August 4 and 14. It was Whipple's first trip to some of the lakes, and he was fascinated by the beauty of the area, awed by the thousands of acres of wild rice. A local trader explained to him how government funds were siphoned off by collusion between the traders, the agent, and the commissioner in Washington: a claim would be made by the trader for $150,000 (although the Indians' debt was only $20,000), and the commissioner would allow the claim in return for half the profit.

At Red Lake, Whipple met the band's head chief, Madwaganonint, a tall man of kingly dignity. The chief told him that his people were reluctant to sign any treaty for fear they would lose their lands and become economically dependent on the government for survival, as had happened to their relatives farther south. Whipple was impressed by the prosperity of the Red Lakers, who were not yet affected by contact with the white man. "The condition of this people is so unlike that of Indians in treaty relations with the Government, that one cannot fail to see at a glance the iniquity which lies at the door of the Government," he wrote in his diary that night.

On August 4, as they were setting out on their tour, Peake had shown Whipple a letter from Little Crow to Hole-in-the-Day, warning the Ojibwe chief that some young Dakotas were itching for war against the Ojibwe and promising to try to keep them in check. On their return, a day out of Gull Lake, the party found a discarded Dakota moccasin, which the Ojibwe took as proof that Dakota warriors were in the vicinity and probably up to no good. But this time it was not the Ojibwe who were the target of the Dakota.

When Whipple returned to St. Paul on Monday, August 18, he learned that all hell had broken loose at the Lower Sioux Agency that morning.

The situation on the Dakota reservation had continued to deteriorate after Whipple's departure a month earlier. The annuities, expected in June, had still not been paid by mid-August. The Dakota had put off their summer hunt to await the distribution of money and food at the agencies and their families were growing hungry. The previous year's corn crop had been damaged by cutworms, and while the current crop was growing well, it was not large enough

to feed the whole tribe. Men sat idly around the campfires, rehashing old grievances against a government that had persuaded them to give up their homes and hunting grounds for money that had vanished into the pockets of the traders. The old question of the missing education fund was brought up again.

The food and other in-kind supplies arrived in early August and were placed in the agency warehouses to await the arrival of the gold that made up the remainder of the annuity payment. Agent Galbraith refused to distribute anything until the gold arrived. He told his superiors in Washington that he didn't want to have to go through the distribution process twice. "I held back, in order to save provisions, until the last moment," he wrote in his year-end report.[160] As the days passed, the thought of all that flour, pork, lard, sugar, and other provisions sitting behind locked doors was too much for the hungry Dakota.

On August 4, a group of warriors at the Yellow Medicine agency broke into the warehouse. They were driven off only when an army unit of one hundred men under Lieutenant Timothy Sheehan, on hand to provide security during the distribution, aimed a mountain howitzer at the rioters as they emerged from the warehouse door. A conference followed, and Galbraith was persuaded to make a partial distribution of supplies to keep the peace. Among those taking part in the conference was Little Crow, the influential Mdewakanton chief from the Lower Agency, who demanded that Galbraith make a similar distribution to his people. Galbraith agreed, but did not follow through.

It was apparently at this conference that the trader Andrew Myrick remarked, "If they're hungry, let 'em eat grass!" Myrick's comment was translated into Dakota by the American Board missionary John P. Williamson. The Dakota leaders were outraged. Myrick would soon regret his flippancy.[161]

Believing that the trouble was over, Galbraith

sent the soldiers back to Fort Ridgely. At the Lower Agency, the Dakota asked the traders to give them supplies on credit, but the traders (including Myrick) refused to do so until current debts were paid. At an August 15 conference between the traders, the agent, and the chiefs, the traders remained firm.

Despite the continuing unrest among the Dakota, Galbraith did not expect serious trouble. On August 16, he left the agency, taking fifty mixed-blood volunteers calling themselves the Renville Rangers to enlist in the army at Fort Snelling. On August 17, Samuel Hinman noted happily that Little Crow himself attended Sunday service at St. John's Mission. The chief even shook Hinman's hand on leaving the building.[162]

That evening, however, four young men came to Little Crow's home in his village near the Lower

Little Crow (Taoyateduta), leader of the Dakota people during the 1862 war. One of the tribe's leading spokesmen, he escaped capture at Wood Lake, fled to the Canadian border, and was killed the following fall near Acton. For many years, his skeleton was displayed at the Minnesota Historical Society. It was reburied in 1971 at Flandreau, South Dakota, where many of his descendants live.

Agency. The young men had been hunting, without much success. As they walked past the fence surrounding a white settler's field near the township of Acton, one of them found some eggs, which he ate. The others teased him, saying that the eggs belonged to a white man and that the white man would be angry with him for stealing them. The young man replied that if the white man objected, he would kill him. The others laughed. He wasn't brave enough, they said. He would show them, he retorted. Soon afterward, they came to a cabin

where three white men were sitting. The young man challenged them to a shooting match. The settlers shot at the target first, and after they had discharged their weapons, the young Dakotas shot them, as well as two women who were looking on.

Excited and a bit frightened by what they had done, the young men rushed back to their village, where they announced to their chief, Red Middle Voice, that they had started a war against the whites. Although Red Middle Voice was an outspoken member of the soldiers' lodge, he did not have much of a following outside his village. He knew that if the war was to have any chance of success, all of the villages would have to be involved, and they would need an influential chief to lead them—preferably Little Crow (also known as *Taoyateduta,* His Red People). Although Little Crow had lost the election for principal chief of the Mdewakanton to Traveling Hail the previous spring, he had played a leading role in the treaty negotiations of 1851 and 1858 and was widely respected as a spokesman for his people. His distrust of white men was well known.

Little Crow and the other leading chiefs—Wabasha, Big Eagle, and Traveling Hail—knew that their chances of success in a war against the white man's army were negligible. Little Crow had been to Washington and seen how many soldiers the Great Father Lincoln commanded. Although the war had diverted much of Minnesota's military establishment out of state, more army units were being formed every day. The Confederate victories had not wiped out the Union forces, and the white man's tactics and weaponry were far superior to those of the Dakota. For much of the night, the hastily gathered council debated what should be done. It was clear to the chiefs that the younger men were not inclined to let this opportunity pass by.

At length one of the braves accused Little Crow of cowardice. The Mdewakanton chief surged to his feet. He told them once more that the proposed war would inevitably end in failure. Then he added, "Taoyateduta is not a coward! If you want to die, I will die with you!"[163]

The next morning, Monday, August 18, the war began.

Although they were aware that the Indians were unhappy, the uprising took the white citizens of Minnesota by surprise. They had believed that the Indians would soon vanish, overwhelmed by the white man's superior civilization. They regarded the lands the Indians occupied as vacant territory that they had every right to claim and begin exploiting. The government made this easy by acquiring the land and selling it to them under the Homestead Act for a mere $1.25 an acre; the 1854 preemption act allowed even those who had taken up land before it was surveyed to keep it. The average settler regarded the government's rules and regulations as an inconvenience, mere bureaucratic pettifoggery to be evaded if possible, or at least manipulated to his advantage. Indians, like bears, wolves, and coyotes, were a nuisance, to be eradicated so that civilized communities might flourish. He was about to learn differently.

A large party of Dakota warriors descended upon the Lower Agency buildings early on Monday morning, killing several trading house employees, including Andrew Myrick, whose mouth they stuffed with grass. They broke open the warehouses and began looting them. The remaining whites in the settlement, including Samuel Hinman and Emily West from St. John's Mission, fled toward Fort Ridgely. The braves killed not only the traders with whom they had grievances, but the new agency doctor,

Philander Humphreys, and Philander Prescott, a government farmer whom they had known for years. Small war parties spread into the countryside, particularly north of the Minnesota River, where white settlers, many of them German immigrants, had established farms on land the Dakota had only recently relinquished. Men, women, and children were killed without warning, although some of the women and older children were taken back to the Dakota villages as captives.[164]

The Christian Dakota were in a particularly awkward situation. Adult men, like Taopi and Good Thunder, tried to distance themselves from the fighting. At the Upper Agency, John Other Day, Lorenzo Lawrence, and Paul Mazakutemane risked their lives to help the missionary families escape. Toward the end of the fighting, they were able to take the captives under their wing. Some of the children from Andrews Hall, who had been visiting relatives at the time, were made captives, and the Ojibwe withdrew their children from the school, fearing they would be killed by the Dakota if Faribault were attacked.[165]

When word reached Fort Ridgely's commandant, John Marsh, he led a detachment of forty-six men toward the agency to restore order. Inexperienced in Indian warfare, Captain Marsh reached the ferry unaware that the Dakota waited in ambush for him. White Dog appeared on the opposite bank and, according to survivors, encouraged Marsh to bring his men over. As they started to cross the river, the soldiers were mowed down and Marsh drowned trying to escape. The survivors returned to the fort around eight o'clock that night. When he heard their story, eighteen-year-old Lieutenant Thomas Gere, who had been left in command, sent an urgent message to Governor Alexander Ramsey, asking him to "send reinforcements without delay."[166]

Little Crow's initial plan seems to have been to attack the fort before reinforcements could arrive and then sweep down the Minnesota, driving all re-

John Other Day (Ampatutokacha), a Wahpeton chief and member of the Presbyterian mission, helped save many of the white refugees from the upper section of the reservation and later argued for the protection of the captives. He was awarded $2,500 by the government for his efforts. He later served as one of General Sibley's scouts and tried his hand at farming, but died of tuberculosis at Fort Wadsworth, South Dakota, in 1869, shortly before Whipple's relief caravan arrived.

sistance before him. But Indian warfare did not follow the same rules as those used by white men. In the council held to discuss the plan, Little Crow had to contend with those who wanted to attack New Ulm instead, where the opportunity for plunder was greater. Meanwhile, widespread depredations (carried out by small raiding parties) were taking place from Lake Shetek near the Iowa border through Brown, Kandiyohi, and Renville Counties, and as far north as Breckenridge on the Otter Tail River.[167]

By the time Little Crow had amassed enough men to attack the fort on Wednesday, it had been reinforced by an assortment of regular and volunteer troops, including Lieutenant Sheehan's detachment (which had been on its way north to Fort Ripley) and the Renville Rangers under Agent Galbraith's command. After several hours of heavy fighting, the

Dakota were driven off. An unsuccessful raid against New Ulm on Tuesday morning was followed by a larger attack on Saturday in which much of the town was destroyed, in part by defenders who set fire to outlying buildings to keep the Dakota from occupying them.

Despite the widespread dissatisfaction among the Dakota, not all of them were willing to take up arms. And while many atrocities occurred, some Dakota chose to save white people—warning them, hiding them, in some cases escorting them to safety. Some of them had developed friendly relations before the war with the settlers whose lives they saved; others were Christian converts who felt a loyalty to the missionaries working among them. The mixed-blood population—offspring of intermarriage between Dakota women and traders, soldiers, or other white men—found their loyalties split between the parties of their mothers and their fathers. When the war began, the "farmer" Indians and the mixed-bloods were threatened by the warriors, who insisted they join in the fighting. Some did so; others fought alongside the white soldiers.[168]

Most of the warriors came from the two Lower Agency tribes, the Mdewakanton and the Wahpekute. Wabasha continued to press for peace, but many of the young men from his village joined the warriors, and he had to choose between maintaining his position as a chief and being condemned as a traitor. He chose to stand with his men in the pitched battles at Fort Ridgely and New Ulm. The Wahpeton and Sisseton of the Upper Agency conferred and decided on a wait-and-see policy, although many individual warriors joined in the raiding.[169] A few visitors from the Winnebago reservation reportedly took part in the fighting, although this was never verified, and the Winnebagos as a tribe were not involved. Rumors that Little Crow had sent an appeal to Hole-in-the-Day, urging the Ojibwe to join the uprising, also were not verified.[170]

News of the massacres spread across the prairie

and through the frontier towns and villages. Thousands of people left their homes in panic-driven haste, some never to return. St. Peter, where Colonel Henry Hastings Sibley was assembling an army to oppose the Dakota, was bedlam: refugees sought safe passage downriver, injured survivors needed treatment, and volunteers with outdated weapons and few supplies demanded to be led into battle immediately.

Bishop Whipple left St. Paul on August 19, at Sibley's request, to ask Alexander Faribault to raise a company of men and join him at St. Peter. Riding all night, Whipple reached Faribault at sunrise with the first news of the uprising. He helped organize the town's volunteer company, which left just hours later.

Then word came from the Ojibwe country that the Gull Lake Mission had been destroyed by a war party led by Hole-in-the-Day. At church the following Sunday, a disconsolate James Lloyd Breck announced that the Indian missions were a failure. Whipple jumped to his feet and strode to the front of the chancel, crying, "Our Indian missions *cannot* be a failure, for if our missionaries are murdered, my young diocese will have the honor of writing in its history the names of martyrs for Christ!"

After the service, he retired to his study, where Solon Manney found him in tears.

"Manney," Whipple cried, "it is *not* a failure! We must not give up hope!"

"You are right, bishop," Manney replied quietly, "there is no failure. All we have to do is sow the seed; you have done that, and in His own good time God will permit you to see the harvest."

Much comforted, Whipple set about doing what he could to help the traumatized people of his diocese. On August 27 he went to St. Peter, taking the battered medical bag he carried on his journeys and assisting Dr. Asa Daniels in the makeshift hospitals set up around the town. Daniels "set the fractured limbs and performed amputations while I sewed up

wounds," Whipple recalled. In the process, he cut his own hand.

The trouble in the Ojibwe country, like that among the Dakota, arose largely as a result of the greed of the government's employees. Apparently, Superintendent Clark Thompson and his agents, Thomas Galbraith and Lucius Walker, had been involved in a conspiracy to skim a hefty sum off the annuities before the payments were made. In 1861, Walker had delayed the Ojibwe payment for nearly two months, then blatantly falsified the rolls.[171]

But Walker appears to have been as incompetent a crook as he was an agent. Not only had he made no effort to win the Ojibwes' confidence, he had also alienated Hole-in-the-Day by taking away the generous gifts and bonuses the chief had been receiving as the leading spokesman of his people. While not all Ojibwe regarded Hole-in-the-Day as their supreme chief, he was the most influential leader of the warrior faction and not a man to be trifled with. In addition, Walker had revoked the trading license of Clement Beaulieu, a mixed-blood trader of long standing in Crow Wing. Beaulieu uncovered the fraudulent 1861 payments by checking the payroll lists against the testimony of the Ojibwe.

Daniel Mooers, another trader, observed, "Very naturally the traders hated [Walker]; he got Hole-in-the-Day down on him; all the men that had any influence with the Indians in this upper country were against him, even the whiskey sellers of Crow Wing. I think the man was half crazy." Beaulieu tried to persuade some of the chiefs to go to Washington and complain to the Great Father, but they demurred. Hole-in-the-Day was not so circumspect. He went to Washington in June 1862 and demanded that Commissioner of Indian Affairs William Dole dismiss Walker from his post and correct "the wrongs practised or attempted upon his band . . . with a firm and unsparing hand."[172]

Dole apparently fobbed the chief off with vague promises to look into the matter and Hole-in-the-

Day returned home. Meanwhile, in response to Lincoln's call for an additional 600,000 volunteers, a company of young mixed-blood Ojibwes was enrolled in the Union army, reportedly while they were under the influence of liquor at Crow Wing. Hole-in-the-Day was alarmed, suspecting that this was the first step toward enforced enlistment of Ojibwes in the white man's army. As the weeks went by without any sign of action on Dole's part, Hole-in-the-Day began to suspect that the commissioner had no intention of investigating his charges. When Dole

came to St. Paul in August to make a treaty with the Red Lake Ojibwe band, Hole-in-the-Day decided to stir things up.

He sent word to his followers at Gull and Leech Lakes, urging them to slaughter all the whites in the area and take their horses and goods. He told Enmegahbowh that he intended to attack the agency and Fort Ripley, which at that time was defended by only thirty men. Enmegahbowh sent a warning to Daniel Mooers at Crow Wing, who passed the word on to Walker. Walker sent for soldiers from the fort

Commissioner of Indian Affairs William Dole and presidential secretary John Nicolay at their encampment on Big Lake en route to Crow Wing in 1862. Dole had come to make a treaty with the Red Lake Ojibwe when the Dakota War began. After a meeting with Hole-in-the-Day, Dole went back to Washington, leaving Agent Ashley Morrill to settle matters. The treaty with the Red Lake band was not signed until 1864.

to arrest Hole-in-the-Day, but the chief saw them coming and fled, the soldiers firing at him as he ran. This was on August 19.

At Gull Lake, Enmegahbowh's mission was ransacked and the missionary fled to Fort Ripley with his wife, children, and converts. "We barely escaped with our lives," he wrote to Whipple on August 25.[173] At Leech Lake, the traders were taken prisoner and freed only by the intervention of Buffalo, a wily old chief who advised caution. Shaboshkung, the Mille Lacs chief, sent one hundred warriors to Fort Ripley to protect it against Hole-in-the-Day's men. Commissioner Dole, then at Fort Ripley, was so grateful to them that he promised the band they would never have to leave their reservation.[174]

Things quieted down when word went out that Lucius Walker had committed suicide. The stress of having his malfeasance discovered and the evidence of growing anger among the Ojibwe seem to have unbalanced Walker's mind. He sent his wife by stagecoach to St. Anthony on August 20, telling her that he was "going out on business." He then rode south to the ferry at Monticello, stole the boat, and when challenged by the ferryman, cried that three hundred Indians were after him and rushed away. His body was found several days later with a bullet in his head and one bullet gone from the revolver that lay beside him.[175] With Walker's death, most Ojibwes felt that their greatest grievance had been removed.

Many of the chiefs distrusted Hole-in-the-Day because of his past behavior and preferred to negotiate their remaining complaints with William Dole and Clark Thompson, who returned to Crow Wing on August 29 to meet with them. It would be better, they felt, to wait and see how the Dakota fared. As Buffalo put it, "You can kill these men as well next week as today."[176]

Sibley's campaign against the Dakota was moving slowly but irrevocably forward. By August 28, his army had reached Fort Ridgely. On the 31st, a burial party was sent upstream under the command of

Buffalo, chief of the Leech Lake Ojibwe band. When Hole-in-the-Day asked him to join an attack on the white men in August 1862, Buffalo declined, observing, "You can kill these men as well next week as today."

Joseph Brown, the former Dakota agent and trader whose home along the river had been destroyed by Dakota marauders. Dr. Jared Daniels went with them. The party bivouacked for the night near Birch Coulee, a ravine leading into the Minnesota River, downstream from the agency and on the other side of the river. The site was poorly chosen. The next morning a large party of Dakotas attacked and pinned the detachment down for twenty-four hours before a relief force arrived. Sixteen men and more than a hundred horses were killed in this affair, the last major success the Dakota could claim.

Sibley moved on, driving the Dakota before him. On September 22, the two armies encamped just below the Yellow Medicine Agency. A final battle held the following day at Wood Lake ended the war. Little Crow, Red Middle Voice, the four young men who started it all, and many others fled across Minnesota's border onto the Dakota plains. Wabasha, Taopi, Good Thunder, White Dog, and many others surrendered. The 269 white captives were released on September 26, and more than 1,200 Dakotas, mostly women and children, were taken prisoner.[177]

As the freed captives and refugees began to tell their stories, Sibley felt pressured to identify and punish those Dakota responsible for the murders. General John Pope, who had arrived in St. Paul after the expedition was under way, ordered Sibley on September 28 to make no peace treaty with the Dakota: "The horrible massacres of women and children . . . call for punishment beyond human power to inflict. . . . It is my purpose utterly to exterminate the Sioux. . . . They are to be treated as maniacs or wild beasts."[178]

Sibley, who was promoted to brigadier general in recognition of his successful campaign, had already formed a military tribunal of five officers to try the accused Dakota. He informed Pope that he had sixteen prisoners in custody so far. "If found guilty they will be immediately executed, although I am somewhat in doubt whether my authority extends quite so far."[179]

Painting of the Birch Coulee battle, where soldiers were pinned down for twenty-four hours on September 2, 1862, resulting in the deaths of sixteen men and more than one hundred horses. (Detail from the Gág/Heller/Schendinger panorama.)

By November 5, the tribunal had examined the evidence against 392 prisoners—nearly all of the male Dakotas who had surrendered—and condemned 307 of them to death. Wabasha, Taopi, and Good Thunder were able to convince the tribunal that they had taken part in the war only under compulsion, and they were released. The three chiefs, who had contrived to gather many of the captives under their protection in the last days of the hostilities, were even promised rewards for saving many lives.[180] White Dog, however, was condemned for his part in the ambush at the ferry, even though he insisted that he had tried to warn the soldiers, not to lure them into the trap.[181]

The speed with which the trials were completed caused some concern among those who were not infected with lynch fever. Even Stephen Riggs, the American Board missionary from the Yellow Medicine Mission who acted as an interpreter and preliminary examiner of the evidence, felt that things had moved faster than justice required. In many cases, simply being present at one of the pitched battles was regarded as "proof" of guilt.[182]

Four of the cases were reconsidered; the final list sent to General Pope contained 303 names. Pope wired the list to the president, explaining that he intended to carry out the sentences as soon as possible. The telegram cost more than $400. (The *New York Times,* appalled at the expense, suggested that the amount be deducted from Pope's salary.) Lincoln wired back a request for the "full and complete record of their convictions" and added pointedly, "Send all by mail."[183]

The prisoners were taken under guard to Camp Lincoln, Sibley's winter camp on the Blue Earth River near Mankato. Their families were marched to Fort Snelling, where they were placed in a kind of concentration camp surrounded by a wooden stockade. This was partly for their protection, since the white population of Minnesota was in a vindictive mood. On their way to the fort, the Dakota women and chil-

General Henry Hastings Sibley, a fur trader who became Minnesota's first governor, commanded the military force that defeated the Dakota at Wood Lake in 1862. He tried nearly 400 of the warriors for rape and murder and condemned 303 to death. Later, he permitted the families of the "friendly Sioux," who had not taken part in the war or who volunteered to serve under him as scouts, to camp on his farm near Mendota. Sibley often helped Whipple work to secure better treatment for the Indians.

dren were attacked several times by angry mobs; not even the army escort could protect them completely. One infant was snatched from its mother's arms and subsequently died.[184]

Meanwhile, Sibley prepared to mount another expedition to pursue the fugitives into Dakota Territory in the spring. Good Thunder and several others offered their services as scouts and they were allowed to take their families out of the camp. Whipple brought several of them to Faribault, where

After Lincoln removed him from command of the Army of the Potomac following the disastrous second battle of Bull Run (Manassas), General John Pope was sent to Minnesota to take charge of the campaign against the Dakota. "It is my purpose," he told Sibley, "to utterly exterminate the Sioux."

Alexander Faribault allowed them to pitch their tipis on his property. Others camped at Sibley's estate near Mendota.[185]

Whipple had left Minnesota on September 8 to attend the Episcopal Church General Convention in New York and collect aid for Minnesota's injured settlers. He also intended to visit Washington and put in a good word for the Dakota. He had an unhappy personal duty to attend to as well: his father-in-law, Benjamin Wright, had died in Philadelphia and his body was being returned to Rome, New York, for burial. Cornelia asked her husband to read the burial service.

The next two months passed in a whirlwind of activity. Whipple attended the Illinois diocesan convention in Chicago on September 10; on September 15 he was in Philadelphia, talking with philanthropists; on the 16th he went to Washington and met with Lincoln. With the president's permission, Whipple read through the Department of Interior archives, examining the treaties and warrants regarding the government's relations with the Dakota. He learned that of the $1,665,000 promised the Dakota in the 1851 treaty, $30,000 had been set aside for the construction of schools, mills, blacksmith shops, and other beneficial objects (almost none of which had been built) and $6,000 per year had been earmarked for educational purposes (but not expended). The $266,000 promised for the land ceded in 1858 had not been appropriated until March 1861, and almost all of it had gone to pay claims presented by the traders, despite a clause in the treaty specifying that no debts should be paid unless first approved in a public council of the Dakota. No such council was held. In short, Whipple found that everything the Dakota had told him was true.[186]

On September 18 he visited the battlefield at Antietam, comforting the wounded, particularly in the Minnesota First Infantry, which had lost heavily in that action. The remains of the carnage at Antietam shocked him. "The field was covered with the dead, and the stone house and barn hard by were filled with the wounded and dying." Among the wounded was Colonel Napoleon Dana, commander of the First Minnesota, who had urged Whipple's election at the 1859 diocesan convention. "There was a hushed stillness which pervaded the camps," Whipple wrote to Ezekiel Gear in Minnesota. "The men had been too near heaven & hell to take their Maker's name in blasphemy." The wounded of both sides lay side by side "& talked like brothers."[187]

The General Convention opened on October 1. It was a "sad" occasion, Whipple confided to his diary, notable for the absence of the southern bishops and delegates. Despite the urging of several delegates, the convention voted against making any political statement in support of the Union, simply expressing its regret at the outbreak of war and a pious hope that peace would soon return.[188] In the South, the newly organized Southern Episcopal Church was preparing for its first General Convention in Augusta, Georgia, in November.[189]

Whipple prepared a letter to President Lincoln, asking that a commission be appointed to revise the nation's Indian policy, which he insisted was the true cause of the Minnesota outbreak. He asked his fellow bishops to sign it. One declined, saying piously, "I hope that you will not bring politics into the House." Others were not so sensitive, and he eventually collected the signatures of eighteen bishops, as well as twenty lay and clerical delegates. Among the latter were four Minnesotans and two men—William Welsh of Philadelphia and Boston's George Shattuck—whose names would be closely linked with Whipple's in the years ahead.[190]

Whipple also wrote an article, titled "Duties of Citizens Regarding the Indian Massacre," which he sent to the nation's newspapers. It reiterated his belief that U.S. government policy, not innate evil in the Indians, was to blame for the troubles. For his efforts, he was excoriated in the Minnesota press, which was calling for the extermination of every Indian within the state's borders.

On October 19, Whipple organized a committee of philanthropists to handle the $2,500 he had so far raised for relief of white victims of the violence in Minnesota. He then went on a tour of cities in New York, New Jersey, and Massachusetts, continuing his efforts. At the end of the month, he buried his father-in-law in Rome, then did more fund-raising in Pennsylvania. He returned to Faribault at the end of November. Whipple set out for Mankato, where the executions were to be held, on the morning of December 26, but his buggy broke down and he had to

General Burnside's attempt to wrest the Antietam Creek bridge from the Confederates allowed General Lee to shift troops to protect his defenses.

Minnesota's First Volunteer Infantry regiment was decimated at Antietam. More than four thousand Union and Confederate soliders died in the bloody battle.

return home. He reached Mankato the following day and held services in the church there. It was a sad day, and the bishop was exhausted.

When the year finally ended, Henry Whipple was no longer an obscure Western ecclesiastic. From then on, his name would be prominently connected in the public mind with the subject of justice for Indians.

The Indian camp at Fort Snelling in 1862. Sixteen hundred Dakotas—mostly children, women, and old men—spent the winter in tents in a fenced enclosure outside the fort. More than one hundred Dakotas died that season.

During the winter of 1862–1863, Bishop Whipple visited the Dakota internees often at Fort Snelling. Samuel Hinman, who had accompanied them to St. Paul, baptized more than 100 Dakota and had a regular congregation of 400. Whipple confirmed 47 of them on March 18 and 108 more on April 30. For this, he was roundly criticized in the press; one headline read "Awful Sacrilege: Holiest Rites of Religion Given to Murderers." In addition, Father Augustin Ravoux reported 184 new Catholics, and John Williamson was baptizing Presbyterians just as rapidly. Demoralized by the collapse of their rebellion and the condemnation of most of their adult males, the Dakota seemed convinced that the *wakan tanka* (Great Spirit) had failed them and were embracing Christianity as an alternative to despair.[191]

Outrage against the Dakota was still running high. Hinman was attacked by ruffians outside the camp one evening and badly beaten for his efforts on their behalf. Diatribes against Whipple appeared in the newspapers, accusing him of finding excuses for a race of bloodthirsty savages. In the camp, illness and hunger claimed many lives, especially among the children. Of the 1,601 Dakota who went into the camp in early November, 130 died before March 10. In May, 1,318 Dakota were loaded onto steamboats "like so many cattle" and shipped off to a new reservation on Crow Creek in Dakota Territory. Hinman (whom Whipple had ordained priest on March 9) and Williamson accompanied them. As the two boats left the docks, crowds gathered to jeer and throw stones.[192]

Commissioner of Indian Affairs William Dole estimated that nearly three-quarters of Minnesota's Dakota had fled into Dakota Territory after the Battle of Wood Lake, including the Sisseton and Wahpeton tribes, who had not taken part in the war but feared retaliation from the whites.[193] At General Pope's command, Sibley mounted an expedition to pursue the fugitives in the summer of 1863.

The "friendly Sioux," cleared of charges of wrongdoing, were allowed to remain in Minnesota, although their reservation no longer existed, thanks to that clever clause in the treaty placing their title at President Lincoln's discretion. The men who enlisted as scouts with Sibley's expedition, and others who had saved settlers during the Dakota War, were promised a monetary reward for their "loyalty," which Congress finally approved in February 1865. The "friendlies" needed the money badly by then, as the tribe's annuities were being paid only at Crow Creek.[194]

The Winnebago, who had remained peaceful throughout 1862, were also sent to Crow Creek. This was done, ostensibly, to protect them from attacks by outraged whites who, as Whipple wrote in his diary, "can't tell a Sioux from a Chippewa"—or a Winnebago. But the Winnebago refused to stay on their new reservation. Many traveled downstream to the Omaha Reservation in eastern Nebraska, where the Winnebago were granted a reservation in 1865.[195]

Whipple holding a confirmation service for forty-seven Dakotas at Fort Snelling in early 1863. Local papers railed, "Holiest Rites of Religion Given to Murderers!!"

Samuel Hinman's chapel at the Crow Creek Reservation site on the Missouri River in South Dakota, where thirteen hundred Dakotas were sent in the spring of 1863. In 1867 the survivors were moved from the barren site to the Niobrara River in Nebraska, where they were joined by the men released from prison in Iowa. Those men who had not taken part in the 1862 war, or who had volunteered to serve as scouts for the army expedition sent against Little Crow and others who escaped into Dakota Territory, were allowed to remain in Minnesota with their families for the time being, on land owned by Alexander Faribault and Henry Sibley.

The Dakota, regarded to some extent as prisoners of war, did not have this option.

Hinman wrote Whipple in June 1863 describing the appalling conditions prevailing at Crow Creek, where they were "separated from all arable land by at least 1,000 miles of desert." He could barely contain his anger with the government that had selected this godforsaken place. "If I were an Indian," he wrote, "I would never lay down the war-club while I lived."[196] G. W. Knox, the Indian bureau's school superintendent for the Winnebago, described Crow Creek as "totally unfit for the habitation of any human beings . . . destitute of any timber save in small strips along the Missouri . . . a vast plain of sand without water, without grass, without timber. Over 600 children alone died while I was with them owing to lack of vegetables and wild fruits."[197] Food supplies sent to the reservation the first year spent twenty days in transit, often arriving unfit to eat. Only the discovery of a buffalo herd near Redfield, South Dakota, enabled the people to survive their first winter. A group of women walked hundreds of miles to Faribault in the dead of winter, eating nothing but roots along the way, to tell Whipple how bad things were. Many of the children who had survived the first winter at Fort Snelling perished by the end of their first year at Crow Creek.[198]

The Dakota convicts who had not been sentenced to death were transferred in April 1863 to an army prison at Davenport, Iowa. In December, Whipple called on Iowa's Bishop Henry Lee and visited with the Dakota prisoners. After some early difficulties with a commanding officer who felt that his pris-

oners had "committed such heinous crimes that it is wrong to preach the Gospel to them," the 278 prisoners had settled into a relatively comfortable routine, reading, attending church services, and occasionally working in the surrounding community. The few women who accompanied them were hired as laundresses and cooks.[199]

Williamson and Hinman, having reestablished their respective missions at Crow Creek, visited the Davenport camp periodically, offering religious services and messages from the men's families. The two missions did not get along. The American Board felt the Episcopalians had preempted its plans for a Presbyterian mission at the Lower Sioux Agency in 1860. Hinman complained to Whipple that the American Board was "trying to alienate" the Indians, restricting the use of reading and writing materials to their own converts.[200]

John Williamson, a Presbyterian missionary with the American Board, accompanied the Dakota to Crow Creek and Niobrara. The son of Dr. Thomas Williamson, he headed the American Board Mission to the Dakota-speaking Indians after 1862.

Whipple was finding his job much more demanding than he had expected. With the initial excitement of the Civil War wearing off and the Dakota War successfully ended, immigration into Minnesota was again on the rise. The bishop was hard pressed to recruit and license missionary clergy, find a way to fund their work when the war was absorbing the public's time and money, organize and staff the schools at Faribault, and, at the same time, carry on a campaign to protect the Indians.

At least once a year Whipple visited the Ojibwe bands, preaching, confirming, and talking with them informally through various interpreters, although after a while he may have acquired a rough acquaintance with the language. He put together a small medical bag and, during an 1862 stop in Chicago, learned how to pull teeth. He used simple medical skills like this to good account on his journeys.

In February 1863 he took a ninety-mile round trip from Crow Wing to Mille Lacs with Enmegahbowh, Peake, and two Ojibwe guides, assessing the political and economic situation among the Ojibwe. Things had calmed down since Lucius Walker's death the previous August. Although Hole-in-the-Day had continued his depredations for a few weeks, support for a full-fledged war with the whites failed to materialize. The chief's actions brought the split between the tribe's warrior faction and its more conservative elders into the open, making it almost impossible for a time for the Ojibwe to form a consensus in their dealings with the U.S. government.

Commissioner Dole met with Hole-in-the-Day at Crow Wing on September 10, 1862, while the Dakota uprising was still active. The nervous commissioner brought a detachment of troops from Fort Ripley with him to the meeting. Not impressed, the chief had his warriors surround them. Instructing Special Agent Ashley Morrill, who had been appointed to investigate the Ojibwe claims, to sort things out and report back to him, Dole stayed only long enough to save face before departing.

Minnesota's Governor Ramsey then formed another delegation consisting of himself, Senator Henry Rice, missionary Frederic Ayer, former territorial judge David Cooper, and Edwin A. Hatch, a onetime agent to the Blackfeet, to negotiate with the Ojibwe. Ramsey did not consult with Agent Morrill, for reasons having more to do with local Republican politics than the necessities of the situation. When he reached Crow Wing, Ramsey found the Ojibwe returning to their homes, as Walker's death had satisfied their main complaints. A council was held (which Hole-in-the-Day did not attend), and a number of chiefs signed a treaty agreeing to continued

peace and friendship between the Ojibwe and the United States. Ramsey's delegation promised that a board of arbitrators would be appointed to review Ojibwe complaints and that the annuities would be promptly paid, without penalty for the depredations of Hole-in-the-Day's warriors.

The treaty was dismissed by Morrill and Dole as worthless. Yet another council was called in 1863. Whipple suggested that Rice be included in the negotiating team, citing the senator's long experience among the Ojibwe. Dole agreed and the treaty signed on March 11, 1863, was endorsed by Dole, Thompson, and Rice for the government and by the leaders of seven bands of Ojibwe—but not by Hole-in-the-Day, who was not present. A key point in the new treaty was that all of the Mississippi Ojibwe would move from their present scattered locations to a single reservation at Leech Lake.[201]

Whipple did not like the 1863 treaty. Although he approved concentrating the Ojibwe on one large reservation, away from the negative influences of white settlements, Leech Lake was not a satisfactory location. The land was not fertile enough to support so many people, he told Dole. Enmegahbowh, who had been an interpreter at the talks, noted there was already a large settlement of Ojibwe at Leech Lake (the fierce Pillagers) and they were not likely to agree to share their territory with the other bands. But Whipple's main objection to the treaty arose from his contention that the Ojibwe must be brought under U.S. law to protect their property, persons, and lives.[202] That issue had not been addressed.

Nevertheless, the treaty was signed. Among its lesser provisions was one giving the Episcopal Church title to the Gull Lake Mission property, including the house that Enmegahbowh and his family had inhabited. It was ratified by Congress just two days later.[203]

The chiefs who signed the treaty were aware of the fate of the Dakota, and that the Winnebago had been shipped out of Minnesota, although they had done nothing wrong. The chiefs hoped that by agreeing to a consolidated reservation at Leech Lake, they would not be forced to leave the state for an even less desirable location. Unfortunately, their reasoning was not clear to many of their people and the treaty was not popular.

Hole-in-the-Day, not unexpectedly, raised objections, particularly with regard to the amount of money offered for the land being ceded. He wrote to President Lincoln and Commissioner Dole, spelling out his concerns. After some haggling, yet another treaty was signed in May 1864. Honoring the promise he had made the Mille Lacs band for their support in 1862, Dole inserted a clause exempting them from removal.[204]

In May 1863, the Office of Indian Affairs named Whipple, Catholic Bishop Thomas L. Grace, and American Board missionary Thomas Williamson to a Board of Visitors, charged with supervising the Ojibwe's annuity distribution and determining the amount of land under cultivation by them in order to facilitate the proposed consolidation.

The Ojibwe payments were to be made in late October and early November. On September 6, Whipple preached to Sibley's expedition, preparing to start its pursuit of the Dakota fugitives. The next day, as he left the expedition's camp near Richmond, Minnesota, his wagon was upset and he was badly bruised. Slow to recover, he finally joined the Board of Visitors in Crow Wing on October 15.

The three leaders from rival denominations spent three weeks together under what Whipple described as "hard conditions," treating one another with extreme courtesy and developing a mutual respect that transcended their sectarian differences. In the report they sent to the commissioner of Indian Affairs on November 9, they complained of Agent Ashley Morrill's reluctance to cooperate fully, not permitting them to see invoices for the goods being disbursed. They criticized the practice of paying annuities through chiefs, suggesting that in the future the money and supplies be given directly to heads of

families. On the whole, however, the payment went smoothly, and with apparent honesty.[205] Morrill seemed to have been accepted by the Ojibwe, and the threat of violence had faded away.

The board also reported that the chiefs were not pleased with the latest version of their treaty. Few of the Ojibwe were willing to move to Leech Lake. The other bands argued that if the Mille Lacs band didn't have to move, why should they? The chiefs resented Dole's efforts to appease Hole-in-the-Day. Dole, they said, had promised to punish Hole-in-the-Day, but had failed to do so. In fact, he had rewarded the wily chief, promising him money to rebuild a house that they claimed Hole-in-the-Day had burned down himself.[206]

An exasperated Dole told Whipple that when he appealed to Ramsey for troops in 1862, he had been advised to give Hole-in-the-Day whatever he wanted. He admitted that the disparity in the government's treatment of Hole-in-the-Day and the Winnebago (rewarding one who had broken the peace and punishing others who had not) was wrong, but it had seemed expedient at the time. As for Whipple's report of the unacceptable conditions faced by the Dakota and Winnebago at Crow Creek, Dole said he had been assured by his subordinates that the reports of Indian sufferings were exaggerated. He suggested that Whipple bring a delegation of Dakota to Washington, concluding irritably, "I also have felt that I was misunderstood."[207]

Whipple had been asked by Commissioner Dole to serve on a treaty commission to meet with the Red Lake Ojibwe in September 1863, but because of his wagon accident, the bishop was not able to do so. A few months later, Chief Madwaganonint walked 150 miles across frozen lakes and streams to see Whipple at Crow Wing. He told the bishop the commissioners had manipulated the negotiations, persuading the other chiefs to sign a treaty that he could not accept. Whipple had advised him to insist the treaty include provision for houses, cattle, agricultural implements, and schools, but none of these

Madwaganonint, leading chief of the Red Lake Ojibwe, was a convert to Christianity. Whipple admired the chief's immense dignity and oratorical ability, which he likened to that of a Roman senator.

things had been mentioned. Madwaganonint, whose band constituted half of the Ojibwe at Red Lake, had therefore refused to sign the treaty. But the commissioner claimed that since the other chiefs had signed, the land had been sold. Was there nothing Madwaganonint could do? The bishop promised to help.

A man who met Whipple on a stagecoach traveling up the Mississippi from Minneapolis to St. Cloud in September 1863 left a vivid description of the Minnesota bishop in these early years. The bishop was "a most delightful chatty fellow. . . . [His] sweet briar pipe and free and easy manner rather upsets one's conceptions of episcopal dignity. . . . I found the Bishop belonged to the muscular school of Christians and believes devoutly in the Trinity and Isaak Walton, the 'Church' and Prof. Wilson (the Noctes Ambrosium Wilson), who he confessed was his beau ideal. . . . We chatted unintermittedly all day ranging through all possible fields of Literature, Theology, Ichthyology, Ornithology, Zoology, History and everything which the sights of the frontier suggest."[208]

In early December, Whipple went to Illinois to inspect some coal-bearing property that Dr. George Shattuck of Boston had given him to help finance the Faribault schools. Whipple then set out on his annual round, visiting parishes and missions, talking with the clergy in charge and performing confirmations; he visited ninety-three churches between December and March. In January, he agreed to write an article on the evils of the nation's Indian policy for the *North American Review*. He also received letters asking for his support for a bill being introduced into Congress exempting clergy from the draft.

In March 1864, Whipple accompanied the Mississippi Ojibwe, including Hole-in-the-Day, and the Red Lake delegations to Washington to sign the new treaties. He spoke with President Lincoln, cabinet members, and Congressmen, explaining that the naive Red Lake chiefs had not understood the terms of their treaty—which, he wrote in his diary, was "from beginning to end a fraud." The officials stood their ground. At last Whipple told Dole that, although he did not want to embarrass a government that was "on the verge of destruction" because of the Civil War, he had no option but to take the issue to the press. Frustrated, Dole asked what the Red Lakers wanted. The treaty was essential if the government was to open the Red River Valley to settlement.[209] At last, in early May, the Red Lake treaty was amended to address some of the issues Madwaganonint had raised and it was signed. It was, Whipple said, "one of the severest personal conflicts that I have had in my life."

Less familiar with the ways of the white men than their brothers from the Mississippi bands, the Red Lake delegates had spent their free time sampling Washington's low life. Enmegahbowh wrote Whipple at the end of April that he was embarrassed by their drinking and fighting. They had naively assumed, he said, that once they signed the treaty they would be paid immediately. They were more than disappointed to learn this was not how the process worked. It took the two Ojibwe treaties almost a year to make their way through the Senate and be officially proclaimed.[210]

Whipple also spoke to government officials about the situation of the Winnebago and Dakota at

Crow Creek, demanding they be moved to a more satisfactory site. He was not successful. Superintendent Clark Thompson insisted, against all evidence to the contrary, that the land was arable and could be made to support the population.[211]

After celebrating Easter Day 1864 with the Army of the Potomac, Whipple returned to Faribault in early May, in time to preside at the wedding of his eldest daughter, Lizzie. Yet he remained thoroughly frustrated by the difficulties he faced in getting what he considered to be just treatment for the Indians. He wrote to Wisconsin's Senator James R. Doolittle, chair of the Committee on Indian Affairs, thanking him for his help but lamenting the "total lack of interest" Congress as a whole had taken in the situation. Doolittle replied that he was glad someone appreciated the effort he was making.[212]

The stress of the past two years was beginning to show, and Whipple's friends became concerned that his heavy workload was endangering his health. In the summer of 1863, New York merchant Robert Minturn had invited Whipple to accompany him on a trip to Egypt. The bishop's friends urged him to accept, but he refused, citing his duty to the Indians and to his diocese in a difficult time.

Whipple's goal was to have an Episcopal religious service held monthly in every village in the state. He expected every priest and deacon in his jurisdiction to travel to neighboring towns on Sundays or weekdays as well as tend their own parishes. Divinity students at Seabury were included in this order as part of their training. In towns that could not be easily reached, lay readers were licensed to lead services in the absence of clergy. What Whipple asked of his clergy he himself did not refuse to do. In the first five years of his epis-

copate, he estimated that he had traveled over 46,000 miles (both within and outside of the state) on diocesan business. And the pace was increasing.

At the June 1864 diocesan convention (which he pronounced "delightful"), Whipple requested a diocesan synod be established to keep him informed on matters of concern in every corner of the diocese. The request was politely tabled as too expensive for a wartime budget, but the convention did authorize formation of missionary societies in every parish to collect funds for diocesan missions.[213]

By the end of July 1864, Whipple was approaching a state of nervous prostration. At the diocesan convention, his clergy begged him to take six months' leave for the

Sarah Elizabeth (Lizzie) Whipple was the oldest of Whipple's six children. In May 1864, she married Charles Augustus Farnum, a widowed lawyer from Philadelphia, on the Seabury campus. The couple lived in Philadelphia, a few doors down from influential banker Jay Cooke. Her father frequently stayed with them during his yearly visits to New York, Philadelphia, and Washington. "Brilliant and handsome," Lizzie fit well in Philadelphia society. She raised her husband's three children and three of her own: Cornelia, Henry, and Arthur.

sake of his health. Soon after, Robert Minturn wrote from Switzerland, sending money "for your personal use" and an invitation to come to England to attend his daughter Anna's wedding in October and remain as his guest through the Christmas holidays.[214]

This time, Whipple accepted his friend's offer. He stayed home long enough to ordain his brother George to the priesthood on August 28, then set out for New York. As he waited to embark on the ship for Liverpool, he wrote to his wife that he "had suddenly come to a standstill." The only solution was to get completely away from anything connected with his work.

He very nearly did not return.

Jerusalem as it appeared in the mid-1860s. Under Ottoman rule, Palestine was something of a backwater in 1865 when Whipple visited it. The first English mission was established here in 1833; the first Anglican bishop arrived in 1841. Today's Anglican Province of Jerusalem and the Middle East includes four dioceses, stretching from Libya to Iran. As railroads and steam-driven ships became more common in Europe and America, tourism began to flourish and trips to the Holy Land gained popularity among those who could afford them.

*T*he weeks spent aboard the ship were quiet and, except for a touch of seasickness, very pleasant for Whipple. He sat on the deck and wrote letters to Cornelia, describing the sighting of a whale and an iceberg. Arriving in England, he went to Auckland Castle near Durham to attend Robert Minturn's daughter's wedding on October 4, 1864. Afterward, he accompanied the Minturn family to Scotland. He assured Cornelia that he had promised his friend to refuse all calls to preach during his stay in Great Britain.[215]

In Edinburgh, Whipple met Edward Caird, a founder of the Free Church of Scotland. Caird's son James had visited Minnesota in 1863, shortly after the Dakota War, and took a deep interest in what Whipple referred to as "my Indians." He also met the dean of the Edinburgh cathedral, E. B. Ramsay, who told him charming tales about the people of Scotland. Whipple and Minturn accompanied Ramsay's brother, Admiral William Ramsay, and the chief of police on a tour of Edinburgh's slums, "where we saw scenes too awful for words."[216]

Whipple had brought letters of introduction from American bishops, including Presiding Bishop Thomas C. Brownell and Bishop William DeLancey, to their fellow divines in the Church of England. Whipple met Bishop Samuel Wilberforce, a leader in the restoration of ecclesiastical authority to English Church conventions and son of the celebrated British abolitionist. He talked schools with Charles T. Longley, the archbishop of Canterbury, and Archibald Tait, bishop of London, who had once been headmasters of Harrow and Rugby respectively. They advised him to "remember that your school has as real a life as an individual; its character is the sum of all its traditions." They also assured him that if God had called him to do this work, it would succeed.[217]

On a visit to Oxford, Whipple talked at length with Edward B. Pusey, a leader of the Oxford Movement that had caused such an upheaval in the Anglican churches. "I always felt that I was in the presence of a great intellect and a great saint," Whipple recalled.[218] Pusey had also helped to establish the first Anglican

Archbishop of Canterbury Charles Longley, with whom Whipple discussed his plans for the schools at Faribault. Longley had been headmaster at Harrow before becoming a bishop.

Edward B. Pusey, leading spokesman of the Oxford Movement. His teachings influenced the High Church party, whose fondness for formal ritual offended the more evangelical members. Professor of Hebrew at Oxford, Pusey was deposed as a preacher in 1845 for his views on the real presence of Christ in the Eucharist, but he continued to urge a closer union between the Anglican and Roman churches. Although he himself objected to the re-creation of medieval ceremonies in worship, many of his followers (influenced by the pre-Raphaelite movement in art) embraced the practice eagerly, and "Puseyism" became synonymous with Anglo-Catholicism, the most extreme High Church behavior.

order of nuns some twenty years earlier. Upon learning of Whipple's interest in charitable organizations, he gave him a letter of introduction to Priscilla Lydia Sellon, who founded the order in Devonport in 1848. Whipple visited her and became acquainted with her program.[219]

London in 1864 resembled the descriptions in Charles Dickens' novels. One stormy night in November, Whipple accompanied Minturn to a mission house in one of its slums. "The doors were guarded by policemen to prevent noted criminals from enter-

ing," he recalled. Women were sent upstairs, while men remained on the main floor. "When the rooms were full, bread and coffee were distributed, after which a hymn was sung, a chapter from the gospels read, and a prayer offered." One of the paupers was an American. Whipple and Minturn spoke with him for some time, listening sympathetically to his tale of misfortune. Later, Minturn arranged for the man's passage back to St. Louis.

Whipple found it "difficult to understand the English craze over the Confederate States." Although by the end of 1864 the Civil War was drawing to its end—Sherman had taken Atlanta shortly before Whipple's departure in September, and Grant had Lee bottled up at Petersburg—a segment of the English public still regarded the Confederacy as a noble, romantic experiment. The southern aristocracy, with its wide plantations and many servants, struck a kindred spark in the hearts of many English aristocrats, who shared its dislike for industrialization and modern methods of trade. Textile manufacturers were also distressed by the embargo on cotton, which had forced them to find new suppliers for their mills.[220]

This trip to England was especially meaningful to Whipple, for whom Anglo-American culture was the epitome of civilization. England in 1864 was at the height of her power, with a vigorous empire stretching around the globe. In his published sermons, Whipple often commented on the "work that . . . has largely been committed to the English-speaking race" and his conviction that English, along with Christianity, had become a unifying force for all peoples. English culture, English language, English law, and English religion had been largely responsible for shaping nineteenth-century America. The Episcopal Church was a direct descendant of the Church of England. The Congregational, Methodist, and Quaker churches all had English origins; even the Presbyterian Church had come to America through Scottish immigrants. Proud as he was of his American heritage,

Whipple was delighted by this opportunity to visit the people and places that had played a seminal role in his country's history.

It distressed him, however, to find the English Church still suffering from the paralyzing influence of its traditional role as a pillar of society. "On one occasion, while staying with friends in the country, I heard the parish incumbent say in a sermon upon the Holy Scripture, 'I think I may say, without reasonable fear of contradiction, that the Holy Scriptures promote good morals.' Which was certainly a safe assertion." To one accustomed to competing for congregations with camp meetings and frontier revivals, such bland sermons were painful to hear.[221]

London in the 1860s was a city of contrasts. Whipple was entertained by high-ranking clerics during his winter in England in 1864–1865, but also visited missions in the slums.

In London, Whipple consulted a Harley Street doctor, who assured him that his illness was not caused by any "organic disease," but simply "nervous prostration." What he needed, the doctor said, was a few weeks rest in a milder climate. The suggestion suited Whipple. He had recently encountered another old friend in London, William Aspinwall, whose trading empire extended from the Mediterranean to the East and West Indies and once included fur posts in Minnesota. Aspinwall was traveling to Italy with his family, and he invited Whipple to join them. The opportunity to see Rome was irresistible for a clergyman. After spending Christmas with the Minturns' daughter and her new husband, Whipple crossed the English Channel with the Aspinwalls to Paris.[222]

Paris was at the height of the Second Empire under Napoleon III, an autocrat with liberal aspirations. Whipple admired the city's grand boulevards and the monumental government buildings the emperor had built with the help of his friend, architect Baron Haussmann. The bishop attended services at the American Church of the Holy Trinity and was entertained by its warden, Dr. Theodore Evans and his wife, both highly respected members of the city's large American expatriate community.

In mid-January, the party left for Rome. By now, Whipple was feeling much more his old self and the urge to preach was becoming hard to resist. When he learned that there was no Anglican clergyman in Rome at the time, he agreed to undertake a little parish work at All Saints, the English church located outside the Vatican walls. One Sunday, following one of his services, Whipple heard an Englishwoman ask another, "Who was the bishop who preached today?" Her friend replied, "The Bishop of Mimosa; he comes from South Africa, you know." The bishop of Minnesota smiled.

In early February, an acquaintance of Minturn's who was going to the Holy Land invited Whipple to join him. If Rome had been hard to resist, it was impossible to refuse a trip to the Holy Land. Whipple accompanied his new friend to Naples, where they boarded a ship for Alexandria. Passing Sicily, they were enthralled by the sight of Mount Etna in eruption.[223]

On the ship, Whipple met a group of American clergy and laymen making the same pilgrimage as he. Among them was William Armitage, who would eventually succeed Jackson Kemper as bishop of Wisconsin.[224] The pilgrims spent a week in Egypt, at Alexandria and Cairo, and Whipple was fascinated by the markets and crowded streets of the ancient cities. He took a camel ride to Giza to see the pyramids and inspected the tombs at Memphis and Thebes.

They had arrived during the Muslim fast of Ramadan, and he observed with interest how the faithful went about their business the whole day without eating or drinking. "When the hour of prayer comes, they all kneel . . . with their faces towards Mecca. They take off their shoes, spread down a garment, then kneel and prostrate themselves kissing it and say their prayers as devoutly as a Christian. I am told," he added, "that their religion does not exercise any other control of their life. They are dishonest, liars, and very sadly deficient in morals."

The harbor at Alexandria was filled with ships. "Since our difficulties," Whipple reported, "Egypt had been the great depot of cotton. The sale has increased 20 fold. It has made Egypt rich and led to the orders of machinery in inconceivable quantities. Egypt is rich beyond our estimate. It has been literally sown with surveyors." There was now a railway from Alexandria to Cairo, and the Suez Canal was under construction. He was impressed by what he heard of the Khedive Ismail Pasha's wealth and force of character, unaware that the ambitious Egyptian prince would soon drive his country so deeply into debt that it would be bankrupt in little more than a decade.

On February 24, Whipple visited the ancient

Cairo was still technically a part of the Ottoman Empire in the 1860s, when Whipple first saw it. The city was ruled by the Khedive Ismail Pasha as an independent fiefdom. When the Civil War cut off European access to American cotton, Egypt profited, and Ismail Pasha used his new riches to fund an overly-ambitious modernization scheme that eventually bankrupted his country.

Coptic church in Old Cairo, "a very curious old church. The nave is divided into two compartments, one for the females & the other for the males—I think originally they separated the catecumens and the communicants. . . . They celebrate the Lord's supper every Sunday & Friday in both kinds, dipping the wafer in the wine. Beneath this church is a very old crypt, the oldest church I ever saw. . . . They connect this church with the Holy Family's residence in Egypt & however we may doubt it, I do not doubt that it goes back almost to Apostolic times."

By this time, Whipple had been away from home for more than five months and was beginning to feel homesick. "I confess," he told his wife, "however much my heart burns at the thought of going to the Holy Land, I long to be homeward bound and shall feel a light and happy heart when I can turn my face towards those dear ones I love so well and whom I have always in my prayers."

Whipple and his friends at last reached Palestine, "that land consecrated as the place where the Son of God tabernacled in the flesh." It was now the beginning of March. "My dear wife," he wrote, "I can hardly tell you how full my heart was of gratitude to God—To think that I was permitted to look upon the land overtrodden by the Son of God." From Jaffa they traveled on donkeys (the Greek Patriarch having arrived the previous day and hired all the available horses) to Ramleh through "waysides blooming with [anemones] and other wild flowers." Orange and lemon groves filled the plain of Sharon. They spent the night at a Greek convent, "and when they learned I was a bishop, it seemed as if their hospitality knew no bounds. [The lay brothers] brought me their children to bless, kissed my hands in token of love & respect."

As they approached Jerusalem, they were met by a party of the Sisters of Charity, coming out to meet two German Protestant nuns in their party who were coming to join the order. A school of Arab children accompanied them and "sang for me a song in praise of Jesus." Whipple was thoroughly charmed "by these descendants of Ishmail whom Christian love had won to Christ."

Whipple visited the Holy Sepulchre several times and sat to meditate on the Mount of Olives overlooking Jerusalem. He saw the Armenian Church of St. James, where the martyr was said to have been beheaded, and the Dome of the Rock, built on the ruins of Solomon's Temple. He traveled to Bethlehem, passing Rachael's tomb on the way, and then continued on to the shores of the Dead Sea, spending the night at an inn in Mar Saba, where "the heat and the fleas were so disturbing that sleep had been impossible." On the way back to Jerusalem, Edward Dean Adams, a young Harvard man who was a member of his group, asked Whipple to baptize him in the Jordan River. The bishop did so, "in the presence of a company of Christian pilgrims and a crowd of Arabs."

As they returned through Jericho to Jerusalem, Whipple began to feel feverish, and when he reached his hotel, he collapsed. The wife of the Anglican Bishop Samuel Gobat of Jerusalem had him brought to their home and sent for a Russian doctor, who diagnosed "Syrian fever."[225] For three weeks, Whipple lay in bed, weak and delirious. His weight fell from 170 pounds to 125. Often, as he hovered between life and death, his elderly Jewish guide, Abraham, came to pray at his bedside, raising his hands toward heaven and invoking the God of Abraham, Isaac, and Jacob.

At last, on April 6, 1865, Whipple was proclaimed strong enough to go by sedan chair to Jaffa, where he boarded the steamship for Alexandria. Too weak to leave the ship when it reached Egypt, he remained on board until it sailed again a few days later for Venice, where he rejoined the Aspinwalls and their friend, Richard Kingsland of New York, who took him back to Paris.

As they traveled through northern Italy, Whipple's fever returned. He arrived in Paris almost too weak to stand. He went immediately to see Dr. Evans,

The Dome of the Rock in Jerusalem was built in 687–691. It is revered by Muslims as the place from which Muhammad rose to heaven to receive instructions from Allah. The smaller building is the construction model.

whose wife put him to bed in their home, where he stayed for several weeks. Whipple recovered at last toward the end of May. During his recuperation, he learned of President Lincoln's assassination on April 14, which he found distressed the French nearly as much as the Americans.

The Minturns had returned to New York, but they made arrangements for the bishop to sail home again when he was ready. After a final dinner party at the Aspinwalls' Paris home, Whipple crossed to London on May 26 and revisited several friends he had met the previous fall. He paid a visit to Eton to discuss methods of secondary education with its headmaster. On June 15, Whipple sailed for Ireland, where Sir Curtis Lampson, the American deputy governor of the Hudson's Bay Company, had invited him to fish for salmon.[226] American financier and philanthropist George Peabody, a member of the fishing party, gave the bishop an Irish green-heart fishing rod as a memento of the occasion.

At last, on June 18, Whipple embarked for New York. It had been quite a vacation. He had recovered from nervous exhaustion, but nearly lost his life to an exotic eastern fever. He had made a number of influential friends in the English Church, with whom he would correspond for many years. Like their counterparts whom he cultivated in America, they would provide financial support for his projects and hospitality during his travels. He had spoken earnestly about the tribulations of America's Indians to an audience with a sincere if patronizing interest in native populations around the world, and had brought America's "Indian question" onto the international stage. His experiences in Rome, Egypt, and Palestine would provide fodder for educational lectures for years to come.

Now he was coming home, where all the old issues awaited him.

Altar cloth made of cotton, deerskin, and glass beads by Dakota Christians, ca. 1860-1910. Bishop Whipple Collection.

In August 1865, Enmegahbowh, who had moved to Mille Lacs when the Gull Lake Mission was destroyed, wrote Whipple that the proposal to concentrate the tribe at Leech Lake was meeting with strong resistance among the Ojibwe. The special agent sent to negotiate with the Ojibwe visited the bishop at Faribault, asking him to use his influence to get them to sign an agreement to the proposal. After examining it, Whipple said, "The Indians will not sign this treaty; they are not fools. This is the poorest strip of land in Minnesota, and is unfit for cultivation. You propose to take their arable land, their best hunting ground, their rice fields, and their fisheries, and give them a country where they cannot live without the support of the Government."

At the subsequent council at Crow Wing, the agent urged the Ojibwe to sign the treaty. "The winds of fifty-five winters have blown over my head," he declared, "and have silvered it with gray. In all that time I have never done wrong to a single human being. . . . I advise you to sign this treaty at once."

Sha-bosh-sgun, chief of the Mille Lacs band, stood and replied, "The winds of fifty-five winters have blown over my head and have silvered it with gray. But they haven't blown my brains away!" The other chiefs shouted their agreement, and the council ended.[227]

In September, the Office of Indian Affairs again appointed Whipple, Bishop Thomas Grace, and missionary Thomas Williamson to a Board of Visitors to supervise the annuity distribution for the Red Lake and Pembina bands, who had been brought under treaty the previous year. Whipple accepted the appointment reluctantly, reminding the bureau of the difficulties the last board had faced from the obstructions of Agent Ashley Morrill. The distribution was set for late October, when the General Convention was to meet in Philadelphia, so Whipple delegated his duties to David Knickerbacker, rector of Gethsemane Church in Minneapolis. Knickerbacker reported

Sha-bosh-sgun, chief of the Mille Lacs band of Ojibwe.

that the new Ojibwe agent, Edwin Clark, was no happier to have the board's assistance than Morrill had been, but the distribution was made properly.

The 1865 General Convention was an especially important one, and Whipple did not want to miss it. With the Civil War ended, the southern dioceses were to be welcomed back into the fold. The church had kept them on its roster throughout the war, in accordance with its decision to not acknowledge the split. When the convention opened, the bishop of North Carolina took his seat in the congregation. Several bishops, seeing him there, marched down the aisle in their robes of office and invited him to join them in the chancel. Texas and Arkansas also sent delegates, and in November the Second Gen-

David B. Knickerbacker was rector of Gethsemane Church in Minneapolis from 1857, when he was ordained a priest, until 1883, when he became bishop of Indiana. He was a trustee of Seabury and the Minnesota Church Foundation. As dean of the Northern District, he carried out missionary work throughout much of the area north and west of Minneapolis and also supervised the Ojibwe and railroad missions.

eral Council of the Protestant Episcopal Church in the Confederate States voted itself out of existence. By 1866, all the southern dioceses had reaffiliated with the mother church.[228]

Whipple spent two weeks in bed in February 1866 with severe bronchitis, from which he emerged to preside over the melancholy marriage of his daughter Nellie to William Davis, who was dying of tuberculosis. Whipple then departed for Maryland, where he had promised to make visitations for Bishop William R. Whittingham, who was ill. While

there, Whipple visited Washington to lobby on behalf of the Santee Sioux, as they were now called, at Crow Creek. Despite the arrival of a new, reasonably competent agent and the establishment of schools, churches, and farms on the reservation, the death rate at Crow Creek remained unacceptably high. Drought and grasshoppers had destroyed crops for two years running. When the Santees tried to organize another buffalo hunting expedition east of the James River, they were turned back. Hunting there, they were told, was reserved for the equally needy Sisseton and Wahpeton, now living on the plains beyond the western shore of Lake Traverse. Whipple visited General G. K. Warren at his headquarters on the Potomac, and asked the general, who had made a formal reconnaissance of the Crow Creek area, to write a description of it "with a view to the removal of the Santee Sioux." Warren complied, and Whipple used the report to bolster his lobbying efforts.

Success was not long in coming. Washington politics had changed with Andrew Johnson's succession to the presidency. His secretary of the interior, James Harlan, had thrown out the entire Indian Affairs staff, replacing William Dole with Dennis Cooley as commissioner and Clark Thompson with Edward B. Taylor as superintendent of the northern region.

During the previous summer, a six-man commission that included Taylor, General Henry Sibley, and Dakota Territory governor Newton Edmunds had traveled through the Lakota country to negotiate with the tribes for permission to build roads through their land.[229] While the commission's efforts were less successful than they had hoped, their report included a proposal to move the Santees to the mouth of Nebraska's Niobrara River. The climate there was not quite so harsh, the report said, and its location some 120 miles farther down the Missouri River would make it easier to supply them from the warehouses in St. Louis. Whipple and his allies supported this move, and in February 1866 Congress sanctioned it. At the same time, the Winnebagos were given a reservation on part of the Omaha Reservation. In May the Santee Sioux moved to their new home, where they were joined by the 247 former prisoners from Davenport, who had been released in April.[230]

Whipple was also concerned about the fate of the Dakota who had not been sent to Crow Creek. Because annuities were distributed only on the reservation, their situation was becoming desperate. Alexander Faribault had personally supported many of them for the past two years, but it was straining his resources. In March 1865, Samuel Hinman had been told that ten thousand acres of land would be set aside for these people near the old Lower Sioux Agency. This offer was withdrawn when white settlers expressed opposition to a permanent Indian settlement in their vicinity. Although the "friendlies" had committed no crimes—some had even risked

their lives to rescue settlers—the whites felt that if these Dakota were allowed to settle in Minnesota, their less innocent relatives might join them. These fears were heightened when a group of renegade mixed bloods murdered a family near Mankato in May 1865. The captured murderers were shown to have no connection with the Dakota at Faribault, but the settlers remained adamant. After a resolution against the proposal was introduced in the Minnesota Legislature, the plan was abandoned. Instead, Congress voted the "friendly Sioux" $7,500, in appreciation of their having saved the lives of many white settlers.[231]

Secretary Harlan asked

Cornelia Ward Whipple Rose, known as Nellie, was Whipple's second daughter. Educated like her sisters at St. Mary's Hall in Burlington, New Jersey, she was married in 1866 to William Davis, who died of tuberculosis days after the ceremony. A friend described her as "one of the most beautiful girls ever seen in the northwest . . . an exquisite revelation of loveliness." Nellie helped her mother organize St. Mary's Hall in Faribault and accompanied her father to Europe in the winter of 1869–1870. In 1876, she married the family's doctor, Francis Rose, a Civil War veteran from Ohio who had established a medical practice in Faribault in 1867. Of their four children, only their son Francis survived to maturity.

Whipple to draw up a list of those entitled to receive a share of the award, $2,500 of which was earmarked for John Other Day, a leader of the Dakota Presbyterian community who had saved many members of their mission. The rest—no more than $500 each—was to be distributed among "those specially entitled thereto."[232] Whipple's list consisted of thirty-three names, including Other Day's. To be sure it was accurate, he had it reviewed by General Sibley, who had employed some of the Dakota men as scouts during his campaigns in 1863 and 1864, and by the American Board missionaries, who were more familiar with the Dakota from the Upper Agency. As some of the men on his list had died, Whipple recommended that their share of the money go to their wives and children. In July, Dr. Jared Daniels, now living in Faribault, was appointed to distribute the money.

"It has been one of the most painful duties," Whipple wrote Commissioner Cooley, "to discriminate between men when I have no doubt of their fidelity." Angrily, he pointed out that $5,000 divided among thirty-two men was hardly fair compensation for the loss of land, family connections, and their share in the tribal annuities that had resulted from their actions.[233]

The government agreed that the annuity issue needed review. Certainly the "friendly Sioux" ought not to forfeit their annuities while the "guilty" ones continued to receive theirs. But making two separate distributions at such distant sites would be inefficient. The Indian bureau suggested that the "friendly Sioux" move to Niobrara. The possibility that the "friendlies," whom the other Santees considered disloyal, might not be welcome was considered irrelevant. Typically, Congress also failed to make any provision to pay the costs of moving the "friendlies" to Nebraska. When the order came, they were already plowing on land that Faribault let them use; by the time they reached Niobrara, it would be too late to get a crop in. "If we sow the seed of fraud and robbery the harvest must be sorrow," Samuel Hinman fumed to his bishop.[234]

There was some debate about whether the move should be voluntary or enforced. Finally, the bureau agreed that those who wanted to stay in Minnesota could remain, but they would forfeit their annuities. In July 1867 about half of the "friendly Sioux"—some thirty-nine people—departed for Nebraska. Good Thunder was among them; Taopi, who had testified against Shakopee in 1864 and feared

the chief's relatives might kill him, remained behind. Whipple continued to ask the government to give land to these men and their families, who had been so poorly rewarded for their courage in defending the white captives against their own people.

Busy as he was with Indian matters, Whipple still found time to deal with the challenges facing the Seabury schools. By the time he returned from Europe, the juvenile department had acquired three additional sections: a seventy-five-student primary department, a sixty-student female grammar depart-

Solon Manney, chaplain at Fort Ripley in the 1850s, was one of the first professors at Seabury, giving up an annual government salary of $1,800 for a $500-a-year teaching post. Manney had been one of Seabury Mission's three partners when James Lloyd Breck set it up in 1857. However, Breck invited David Sanford to join the teaching staff at Faribault, leaving Manney at Fort Ripley. Father Ezekiel Gear told Whipple it was because Manney "knew too many things about the *high jinks* over the *grass widow* [a divorced, separated, or wanton woman] up in his wilderness." Sanford left the mission in December 1858; Manney took his place in May 1859. He was Whipple's confidante and right hand in the early years of the schools' organization.

ment, and a forty-four-student coeducational intermediate department. Most of these students came from the town and its environs, and would become teachers in rural schools after graduation. In 1866, nearly four hundred students assembled for commencement.[235]

The boys' grammar school was now so large that it seemed wise to separate it physically from the divinity school. A small wooden building was constructed, and James Dobbin, who had returned to Faribault the previous year, was put in charge of the program. The school was soon overcrowded, and the cornerstone for a more permanent hall was laid in 1866. Before the hall was completed, the old building burned down, subjecting the students to "great inconvenience at an inclement season."

The new building was named Shattuck Hall, for Dr. George Shattuck, the Boston philanthropist who provided the funds for its construction. Bishop Whipple and Dr. Shattuck were old friends whose

George Cheyne Shattuck Jr., the Boston physician and philanthropist for whom Shattuck School was named. Dean of the Harvard Medical School, he was also patron of St. Paul's boys' school in Concord, New Hampshire, which Whipple's son Charles attended. Shattuck helped to establish the Church of the Advent in Boston, the Sisters of St. Margaret, and the Society of St. John.

The original Shattuck Hall, built in 1866, soon after the preparatory school was separated from the divinity school.

James Dobbin enrolled at Seabury in 1860, but went back East to teach for three years before returning in 1864 to resume his studies. Ordained deacon upon his graduation in 1866, he was appointed warden of Seabury Hall, with responsibility for oversight of the divinity students and care of the younger boys. He also taught Latin and literature. When Shattuck Hall opened in 1867, he became its rector, a position he held for forty-seven years.

Felix Brunot, director of the Allegheny Valley Railway, second chair of the Board of Commissioners for Indian Affairs, and a prominent lay leader in the Episcopal Church. In 1865, he bought the land Shattuck gave Whipple to raise money for his schools. A member of the Evangelical Education Society, Brunot was cofounder of the American Church Missionary Society. He was a trustee of the Philadelphia Divinity School and a donor to the Faribault cathedral fund.

paths had frequently crossed at General Convention. Shortly after his consecration, Whipple had shared his hopes for the Faribault school with Shattuck, and the doctor offered him a share in the proceeds of a piece of land he had acquired in Illinois. Shattuck had promised $4,000 to St. James School in Maryland, he told Whipple, but anything the bishop could get for the property over that would be his to use for his school.[236]

There was coal on the property, and Whipple sold it for a much better price than Shattuck expected. Felix Brunot, a prominent Episcopal businessman from Philadelphia, owned land adjoining Shattuck's property and wanted to buy eighty additional acres. He promised Whipple ten dollars an acre over the best offer anyone else made. "The land belongs to the church," Brunot told him grandly.[237]

In the end, Whipple paid St. James School twice what Shattuck had promised and still had nearly $30,000 left for his own schools. By then the Seabury Mission had acquired some forty-five acres of land, including its original site, on which the Shat-tuck and Seabury schools were built. The state had built a school nearby for the hearing impaired in 1863. When it added one for the blind in 1866, a sizeable educational campus began to take shape on the bluff above the Straight River.[238]

The Seabury library was given to Whipple by a friend who acquired it when St. Paul's College in Palmyra, Missouri, sold it to pay off debts.[239] The library was added to by other donors, including Augusta Shumway, the English bishop of Chester, and the Reverend F. J. Warner of Rhode Island.[240] In 1865, Whipple received an exceptional gift from Hiram Sibley, founder of Western Union. Sibley had visited Russia to advise the tsar on telegraphy, and as a token of the tsar's gratitude, was presented with a copy of the *Codex Sinaiticus,* a rare translation of the New Testament discovered at a convent on Mount Sinai. The Russians asked that it be given to "an American college." Sibley gave it to Whipple.[241]

Eager as he was to improve his schools' resources, Whipple refused to accept the offer of the library belonging to Bishop William Whittingham, for whom Whipple had performed church services while the Maryland cleric was ill. Whipple described the private collection as "the most valuable theological library in the American Church." Whittingham had intended to give the books to his own diocese "on the condition that they would provide a suitable library building." The diocese had not come up with the building, so Whittingham proposed giving it to Seabury instead. Whipple felt this would not be appropriate, and he urged the Marylanders to "see that a library building was at once provided." It was, and the library remained in Maryland.

Seabury's divinity school was acquiring a larger faculty. At first Whipple supplemented the efforts of Breck and Manney by inviting active priests from the diocese, like Sterling Y. McMasters, rector of Christ Church in St. Paul, and Edward P. Gray of Shakopee, to give occasional lectures. In 1864 Elisha S. Thomas came from Connecticut to teach Hebrew and New

Testament exegesis. Samuel Buel arrived in 1866 from New York to teach ecclesiastical history.

Although the parish school had a program for young girls, it did not offer them a secondary-level education. Early in 1866, Cornelia Whipple observed to her husband that some of their fellow Episcopalians were sending their daughters to Catholic secondary schools. "You know what that means?" she added ominously. The possibility of the young women's susceptible minds being seduced by Roman Catholicism was more than she could bear.

"Yes, but what can I do?" the bishop replied. "I have a divinity school without one dollar of endowment. Our boys' school has no buildings, and I have not one dollar of means."

"We can open it in our home," she said firmly. "The church must educate her own daughters."[242]

Bishop Whipple agreed. He borrowed money to enlarge their house, and on November 1, 1866, the

The Mission School House in Faribault (later the Church of the Good Shepherd). It was built on the bluff across from the town, on what would become the Seabury-Shattuck campus. Seabury's first classes were held here.

Cornelia Whipple in her middle years. Her desire for a non-Catholic secondary school for young ladies led to the foundation of St. Mary's Hall in 1866.

Sarah Darlington, first headmistress of St. Mary's. The daughter of a Philadelphia botanist, she bequeathed the school funds for a scholarship and the library.

The second graduating class of St. Mary's Hall. Whipple's picture is in the center. He had a close relationship with the young ladies of St. Mary's and was always delighted to meet them again after their graduation, sometimes in far corners of the world.

school—christened St. Mary's Hall in honor of his daughters' alma mater in Burlington, New Jersey—was ready to welcome its first students. As the bishop was extremely busy that summer, Cornelia supervised the renovations that would provide rooms for thirty-two young ladies. She also recommended that Sarah P. Darlington, a teacher in their parish and mission schools, be hired as principal. It was an inspired choice. Under Darlington's cultivated leadership, the school quickly acquired a reputation for excellence.[243]

In the early stages of its organization, the school had the added assistance of the Reverend Leonard J. Mills, a former instructor at St. James College in Maryland who had come to Faribault for his health. Mills served as chaplain and advised the Whipples on organizational matters until his death in May 1867, six months after the school opened.

St. Mary's flourished from the start, although it was some years before Whipple was able to achieve his dream of providing scholarships for the daughters of clergymen. In 1872 the school was incorporated and a board of trustees appointed. Leading Philadelphia financier Anthony Drexel donated a valuable library. The influence of Cornelia Whipple and Sarah Darlington may perhaps be seen in the school's curriculum, which included Latin, mathematics, and natural sciences as well as English, literature, music, elocution, drawing, and painting. German and French were offered as elective classes.[244] But the school's overriding philosophy was Bishop Whipple's. "It is the glory of our age," he said at the laying of the cornerstone for a new St. Mary's in 1882, "that it has enfranchised woman without robbing her of the gentle prerogatives of her sex. . . . Wherever a well trained childhood has had the privilege of higher culture woman has taken her rightful place in intellect, as in heart, as a helpmeet for man." The school's goal was "to train and mould into perfectness Christian womanhood." Its graduates would be prepared for "a life of usefulness here and the joy and bliss of Heaven hereafter."[245]

The success of Faribault's schools owed a great deal to Whipple's exceptional ability to wheedle money out of people of every income level. He could even pry funds out of hard-headed bankers.[246] He always ascribed his success to the will of God, but

donor Augusta Shumway observed that the bishop's appeal was more personal. Although initially reluctant to receive "the old man" who had come to ask her for a donation, she said, "When he had talked about his work for half an hour, I was ready to give him every penny I had."[247]

Over the next few years, Shattuck School changed its focus. It no longer only trained boys for admission to Seabury. Now it welcomed young men who would enter a wide range of professions—law and business, as well as the military—with an emphasis on public service. One of the biggest changes in the school's character occurred when Thomas J. Crump returned from the army after the Civil War and enrolled at Seabury. During his free time, he coached the younger boys in military drill. The drills became so popular that Whipple had them incorporated into Shattuck's curriculum, and when Congress voted to allow each state one regular army officer to teach military science at an educational institution,

St. Mary's Hall began as an addition to the Whipple house and by the late 1870s had expanded to fill much of the block. In its first decade, it graduated more than two hundred young women, many of them daughters of some of the state's most illlustrious families. In 1870, Whipple instituted a dress code for the girls to keep them from becoming frivolous and fashion-conscious. There was to be "no expensive jewelry, dresses of silk, silk poplin or velvet, no ruffled underwear."

Thomas Crump, a son of English immigrants living in Faribault, enrolled at Seabury after service in the Civil War and taught the younger boys at Shattuck how to drill military-style. The boys' enthusiasm led to Whipple's decision to pattern the school on West Point. After graduating from Seabury, Crump served as missionary to counties in west-central Minnesota from his parish at Litchfield.

aging school property, and reading unauthorized books or papers were all strictly forbidden.[249]

Whipple believed military discipline was excellent training for young men. "Perfect freedom only comes through perfect obedience," he said. In the next forty years, Shattuck sent more than one hundred young men into the military as commissioned officers. Both Ulysses Grant and William Tecumseh Sherman took an interest in the program, assuring the bishop the best men for the teaching post— sometimes, according to Whipple, even overruling the decision of the incumbent secretary of war.

Whipple took pride in the success of his education program. Seabury produced a steady stream of clergymen to fill the pulpits of churches throughout Minnesota and nearby states. Shattuck graduates achieved honor in a variety of colleges and professions, while the daughters of St. Mary's were to be found all over the world. Although Andrews Hall, the Indian school, had failed, Whipple encouraged many Indian students to attend Shattuck and St. Mary's; a few attended Seabury and became ministers. The inevitable faculty squabbles broke out now and again, causing the bishop a great deal of distress at the time, but they were usually smoothed over without serious repercussions.

Henry Whipple wasn't an innovative educator. Most of the schools he founded were modeled after similar schools elsewhere: Shattuck on West Point, with overtones of Harrow and Rugby, and St. Mary's on its namesake in Burlington, New Jersey. Seabury was James Lloyd Breck's creation, but Whipple adapted it over the years to come in line with Episcopal seminaries elsewhere. In setting the schools' curricula, he consulted people he considered experts, selecting those elements he thought most fitting. Whipple's genius lay in his assumption that a frontier community like Faribault, Minnesota, could produce a high-quality educational program and in his skill at finding talented staff and the financial support needed to make his dreams reality.

he applied to have one assigned to his school. The first officer, Major A. E. Latimer, arrived in 1868.[248]

The military course gave Shattuck cachet. The students wore gray uniforms like those of West Point and were subject to military-style discipline. Using alcohol or tobacco, playing cards, visiting saloons or billiard parlors, swearing, contracting debts, leaving the school grounds without permission, dam-

The Seabury-Shattuck campus on the bluff, ca. late 1860s. Seabury Hall is on the left, with Shattuck Hall hidden behind it; to the right is Ballyhack, Breck's original dormitory for Seabury students. The path to the school led up the hill past Fleckenstein's Brewery (the building on the lower right), a fact that annoyed Breck and Whipple considerably.

Shattuck cadets in formation in front of the Manney Armory (built in 1880). An off-duty army officer ran the military program at the school for many years. In 1871 Shattuck School was granted 120 stands of arms and two field pieces from the army's surplus weaponry. The military drills and uniforms were not abandoned until the 1970s.

The original St. Columba mission at White Earth, built in 1868. Although the government (and Bishop Whipple) had hoped to combine all Minnesota Ojibwe at White Earth, the Mille Lacs, Red Lake and Leech Lake bands remained where they were. Enmegahbowh was in charge of the mission until the arrival of Joseph Gilfillan in 1873.

*A*s he dealt with the business of organizing, building, and financing his schools and cathedral—and administrating his ever-growing diocese—Henry Whipple was being drawn even deeper into Indian matters.

In August 1866, he officially transferred Samuel Hinman to the oversight of Robert Clarkson, the new missionary bishop of Nebraska, who had been Whipple's colleague in Chicago seven years earlier. Whipple continued to take an interest in Hinman's work, however, sending him money until the Board of Missions agreed to support him in 1872. The bishop remained concerned about the welfare of the Dakota, though few of them were still in his jurisdiction. Many Dakotas continued to regard Whipple as their protector, writing to him for help with their personal problems.[250]

Enmegahbowh complained that the new Ojibwe agent, Edwin Clark, was showing signs of corruption and "was not the fit man for his position."[251] Clark had antagonized the trader establishment by closing the whiskey shops and giving the trading company of Aspinwall, Ruffee, and Nash a virtual monopoly on business with the Ojibwe. Rumors arose that Clark was colluding with traders to skim money from the annuity fund. The Indian bureau sent a special investigator from Washington in September 1866 to look into the matter.

Assuming that Clark would soon be replaced, Charles Ruffee started lobbying his friends in Washington to let him take Clark's place. Although Whipple knew and liked Ruffee, he felt this was too much like setting a fox to mind the chickens. He told Commissioner Cooley that Ruffee had boasted "he could make $75,000 out of this post."[252] The bishop's chief concern, however, was Ruffee's weakness for alcohol. "I would rather have a moral thief than an honest drunkard," he wrote a friend.[253] He used his influence to have Joel Bassett, an Episcopal Civil War veteran in St. Paul, appointed agent. He told Bassett this was the first time he had ever asked a political favor, and he hoped Bassett would not disappoint him.[254]

It is hard to say how many of the accusations of corruption lodged against Bassett over the next two years were true and how much was the result of political infighting, compounded by his unfamiliarity with the complexity of Ojibwe tribal politics. Enmegahbowh, who had had little good to say of Edwin Clark, at one point declared Bassett "the very worst agent we ever have."[255] Whipple believed Bassett was basically honest and well-intentioned, though unable to steer a straight path through the pitfalls surrounding him.[256]

Much of Bassett's trouble arose from a new treaty offered to the Ojibwe leaders in Washington in February 1867. Realizing that they would not accept concentration at Leech Lake, the bureau now proposed another site, a thirteen hundred-square-mile area farther west called White Earth. White Earth stood on the edge of the prairie, within the fertile region drained by the Red River. Much better suited to farming than Leech Lake, it also contained wide stretches of deciduous forest teeming with wildlife and several thousand acres of coniferous forest, home to the red and white pine that was Minnesota's greatest economic treasure. There were many small lakes and rivers on the proposed reservation, with wild rice beds, cranberry bogs, and maple trees for sugaring. Because it lay in an area formerly contested between the Ojibwe and the Dakota, it had never been occupied by any specific band. It was also fairly well removed from the whiskey shops in Crow Wing. Whipple thought it an ideal spot and urged the Ojibwe to accept it. The treaty was duly signed on March 19, 1867.

The new treaty included provisions designed to further another goal that Whipple and other "friends of the Indian" favored: allotment. The idea was that if Indians could be induced to acquire individual farms instead of continuing their communal lifestyle, they could be assimilated more quickly into the majority culture. Instead of relying on government annuities for support, they would become self-supporting farmers, imbued with the Protestant work ethic.

Over the next two decades, numerous plans were drawn up in an attempt to find a way to provide Indians with individual allotments that could not be taken from them by unscrupulous white men. The 1867 Ojibwe treaty provided that an individual cultivating ten acres of land would be entitled to claim forty acres. As the amount of land cultivated increased, the amount of the individual's titled property would increase as well, up to 160 acres. This land would be exempt from taxes or attachment for debt and could not be sold without permission from the secretary of the interior. White men could not purchase it, and only those mixed bloods who lived on the reservation would be eligible to participate in the program.

The Ojibwe were not happy with the new treaty. Many of them felt that leaving their homes for White

Earth would be the first step "toward the setting sun." Too many tribes had given up their homelands for "permanent" reservations that had proved to be anything but. When Whipple (whom they called *Kichimekadewiconaye,* the Great Black-Robed Priest) visited them that spring, they gathered around him, protesting the move. At last Nebuneshkung spoke up. "Kichimekadewiconaye has not a forked tongue," he said. If Straight Tongue—Henry Whipple—said that they would be safe at White Earth, he would go.[257]

Hole-in-the-Day, whose political clout was waning, approved many of the treaty's provisions—particularly the one that authorized a special annuity just for him—but he objected to the inclusion of mixed bloods in the program. Although he had previously allied himself with the mixed-blood traders at Crow Wing, he had quarreled with them after his house was burned in 1862. Despite Hole-in-the-Day's objections, leaders of the other Mississippi bands signed the treaty readily enough. They had already decided that farming offered the best hope for their people's survival.

The Ojibwe chiefs stipulated in the treaty that those who moved could choose the site of their village themselves and that improvements (houses, blacksmith shops, and the like) must be made before they arrived. But Bassett wanted them settled at White Earth in time to begin planting in the spring, so he began in September to pressure them to move immediately. The result was chaos. Many Ojibwe immigrants spent that first winter in tents or hastily constructed wigwams because there had not been time to build enough houses. They arrived too late in the year to plant gardens and had to depend on government rations to supplement their diet of wild rice, fish, ducks, geese, and prairie chickens.[258]

By January 1868, most of the Sandy Lake, Lake Pokegama, and Gull Lake bands had moved to White Earth. Having been assured that removal would not be forced, Whipple was angry to find that Bassett had given people little choice. When the bishop challenged him, Bassett replied he had been pressured by Washington to complete the removal in a timely manner—a claim that Chief Clerk Charles Mix of the Indian bureau denied.[259] Accusations against Bassett for incompetence and venality arose from various sources. Charles Ruffee in particular insisted that "the Indians are being swindled," though this may have been because he received none of the lucrative contracts for transporting the immigrants and building homes for them. Wrote Governor William R. Marshall of Minnesota to Whipple, "I fear that this Indian system is so inherently vicious and evil that the old traders can peculate and plunder at will in spite of honest agents."[260]

Washington sent a special agent, A. S. Paddock, to investigate Bassett's actions. The investigation took place against the background of a Congress determined to reduce the power of the chief executive. In March 1867, the Tenure of Office Act had made it virtually impossible for the president to fire a cabinet member. It also made it hard to dismiss an Indian agent such as Joel Bassett without clear proof of malfeasance. Paddock found no evidence of wrongdoing, although he claimed he was offered money to find it. Bassett was not dismissed until early 1869, when the incoming administration of Ulysses S. Grant replaced almost all of the nation's Indian agents.[261]

The relocation effort, meanwhile, moved forward. The mixed-blood families from Crow Wing, many employed by the government as teachers or mechanics, took up residence at White Earth, where the traders also set up shops. Enmegahbowh shifted St. Columba's Mission to White Earth in December 1867. The government had finally approved Whipple's $4,000 claim for damages sustained by the Gull Lake Mission buildings in 1862, and this money was used to construct new ones.[262]

By 1867, Minnesota—like Wisconsin before it—was filling up with farms and small towns, and—

After he was ordained priest in 1867, Enmegahbowh was able to perform all the rites of the church (except confirmation and ordination) for his people. Driven from Gull Lake in 1862, he reestablished the St. Columba Mission at Mille Lacs until the White Earth Reservation was formed in 1867.

again like Wisconsin—the needs of the growing numbers of new parishes was depriving the Seabury mission program of full-time workers. Whipple encouraged this trend, which ran counter to the vision of James Lloyd Breck. While Whipple generally left the day-to-day running of the school to Breck, there was never any doubt that the bishop was the man in charge. Breck, now forty-nine years old, no longer had ties to Faribault. His wife had died in 1862 and his house burned down in 1866, destroying all of his records and private papers. He decided to move to

California, where he founded a new mission at Benicia. On June 16, Whipple hosted a farewell party for Breck, inviting all of the diocesan missionaries to pay their respects to the man who had started it all.[263]

Enmegahbowh was now a full-fledged priest. In recognition of the loyal deacon's long-time work among his people, Whipple had received permission to waive the usual requirement of demonstrating literacy in Hebrew and Greek during the examination for ordination. It seemed more important, the bishop said, to have a priest who could preach and perform the liturgy in Ojibwe than to insist on his being able to read ancient texts in their original languages. "Enmegahbowh had a good English education and was devout and well-read in the Scriptures and Church history," he told the examiners. The test lasted all day, "and my Indian deacon did not miss an answer," wrote a proud Whipple. Enmegahbowh's competence reinforced his contention that Indians were as capable of learning as any white man. On June 19, 1867, he ordained John Johnson Enmegahbowh to the priesthood at Faribault.[264]

Following a trip back to his childhood home in Canada, where he showed some of his Ojibwe friends how Christianity had benefited Canada's Ottawa, Enmegahbowh returned to his work energized. To his surprise and delight, the number of Ojibwe converts to the Episcopal Church's version of Christianity at White Earth promptly mushroomed. The reasons for this sudden wave of conversion were many and complex. Undoubtedly many of the converts were sincere in adopting the white man's religion as presented to them by their old friend and fellow Algonquian. Others may have hoped that, by accepting Christianity and the outward signs of the white man's culture, their relations with the government and the settlers would improve. With the fur trade all but dead, and the amount of land available for hunting and gathering shrinking, farming offered the best option to feed their families. The white man

had offered to teach them his skills, but only as part of a larger program of cultural change, which the Ojibwe had refused to accept. Now the need to adapt was becoming more acute, and they decided to make the change.

Most of those who joined the Episcopal Church did so because of two men: Enmegahbowh, who was able to explain his faith to them in terms they could understand, and Henry Whipple, who was willing to use his influence in Washington and with the eastern philanthropists on their behalf. Kichimekadewiconaye was one missionary who had it in his power to do things for them, even if his goals and theirs were not always the same.

The Indian war begun in Minnesota in 1862 had spread into the Great Plains, as the construction of roads and railways carrying a flood of white immigrants across Indian lands led to violent confrontations with the Lakota, Cheyenne, and other Plains tribes. The huge buffalo herds were shrinking, victims of organized hunting and reduced pasturage. The tribes living off the buffalo found, as the woodland tribes of the East had earlier, that their economic base was vanishing. When U.S. soldiers under Major John Chivington massacred a peaceful Cheyenne village in November 1864 at Sand Creek in Colorado, the Cheyenne, Arapaho, and Lakota formed an alliance, staging bloody raids on wagon trains, stage stations, isolated farms, and small military outposts.

The settlers and travelers demanded increased military protection, as did the crews building the railroads. Agitation grew in Washington to transfer the Office of Indian Affairs from the Department of Interior to the War Department. Bishop Whipple opposed this idea as early as 1862, when he told Lincoln that soldiers were not trained in the skills needed to help Indians adopt a sedentary lifestyle. Putting an army officer in charge of Indian Affairs would inevitably politicize the military, he said. Although soldiers, trained to despise lying and theft, might be an improvement over the political hacks usually appointed as Indian agents, only men of strong moral character, paid a decent living wage, would be able to withstand the temptations the post offered.[265]

When Whipple attended the fall 1866 meeting of the Board of Missions in New York, he asked the board to restore the appropriations for Indian mission work that had been dropped from its budget during the war as donations dropped off. For the past year or more, he told them, he had been subsidizing the Ojibwe and Dakota Missions out of his own funds. Recently returned from a series of councils with the Red Lake bands, he had a bad cold and was in no mood to mince words. When the board passed a resolution expressing its "cordial sympathy with the Bishop of Minnesota in his efforts to carry the Gospel to the Indian race," he rose irritably to his feet. "If the object of that resolution is to help the Indians," Whipple said, "it is not worth the paper on which it is written; if it is to praise the Bishop of Minnesota, he does not want it. It is an honest fight, and if any one wants to enlist, there is room."[266] The board responded by making him chair of a committee to report on the subject the following year.

Whipple's report, "On the Moral and Temporal Condition of the Indian Tribes on Our Western Border," presented at the Board of Missions' annual meeting in October 1867, had a much wider influence than its title might imply. Published in 1868, it was read by all those concerned with the reform of the Indian system and is second only to Whipple's 1862 letter to President Lincoln in its effect on

On November 29, 1864, American soldiers led by Colonel John M. Chivington attacked an undefended Cheyenne village in Colorado Territory, killing between 150 and 184. Most of the dead were women, children, or old men, and some of the bodies were mutilated. The event touched off a major war with the Cheyenne, Arapaho, and Lakota. Chivington was severely criticized for his actions by government investigators, but no one was ever punished. Painting by Robert Lindneux.

U.S. Indian policy. In the report, he reviewed the history of America's relations with the various Indian tribes, with special emphasis on recent events concerning the Cheyenne, Arapaho, Kiowa, Comanche, and Navajo. "A Christian nation," he said, "has taken possession of the homes of heathen tribes without giving them one single blessing of Christian civilization." He pointed out the cost of war. "Today, forty millions of people, forgetful of the histories of the past, are clamoring for the extermination of a few thousand heathen, and are engaged in the work of blood at a cost which would purchase one of our most beautiful American homes for every man, woman and child in Indian country. . . . Every Indian slain has cost us over half a million dollars."

What, Whipple asked, is to be done? First, the Office of Indian Affairs must be purged of its present personnel, and "men of character, appointed for life, subject to as severe discipline as court-martial, with ample salaries" appointed in their place. The commissioner should have cabinet-level rank and be "selected for his Christian character, his philanthropy, his wisdom and his knowledge of the intricate interests to be cared for." There must be local boards of commissioners at each agency "to examine into all the details of every agency, arrange plans for civilization, government, schools, and mechanical pursuits." He cited British policy in Canada as an example of the way things ought to be done: in Canada "we see the Indians and whites living in friendship . . . and a century passed without one drop of blood shed in Indian war." The Canadian government's approach, he said, was to "localize them, guarantee them rights, place them under law, and give them individual rights of property." The ultimate goal of American policy should be "to give to this poor people the blessings of the Gospel and a Christian civilization."[267]

When the bishop read his report, "men and women wept." The noted philanthropist Peter Cooper invited him to read it again before a gathering of clergymen at Cooper Union in New York. Whipple was invited to address the Quakers' 1867 annual meeting in Baltimore, where he repeated the same themes. The Quaker report on the Indian situation contained many of his ideas and quoted extensively from a letter the committee had received from Enmegahbowh, saying "our only hope of salvation in the future is to embrace the Christian religion in hand and heart and pray to the God of the white man."[268]

Whipple was no longer alone in pressing for change in the government's Indian policy. Until the end of the Civil War, the Episcopal Church's missions to Native Americans had been limited largely to Wisconsin and Minnesota. That was changing, as the tide of settlement moved across the Mississippi. Awareness of conditions among the Indian population and of the hardships they were suffering as a result of official government policies began to grow. Other religious groups also became vocal advocates of change. The Society of Friends was among the first to take an active interest in improving the Indians' conditions. The Congregationalists, who had sent missions to Native Americans for years, also spoke up.

One of the most energetic advocates of Indian policy reform was a fellow Episcopalian named William Welsh, a wealthy Philadelphia merchant and philanthropist. Welsh was a close friend of Katherine Biddle, who had visited the Lower Sioux Mission with the Whipples in the spring of 1862. Miss Biddle's report on Whipple's work among the Dakota and Ojibwe piqued Welsh's interest, and when Whipple asked him to sign his 1862 letter from the General Convention to President Lincoln, Welsh agreed. Passionate and outspoken, Welsh became one of Whipple's closest allies during the following decade.

The bishop's battle to save the Indians was gaining momentum.

Back view of Mandan-Hidatsa man's shirt, made of deerskin, porcupine quills, glass beads, wool trade cloth, human hair, pigment, and weasel skin. Bishop Whipple Collection.

St. Paul in 1869. The population of Minnesota's capital was now slightly more than 20,000 and growing rapidly. By 1880 it would be 41,473. In the same decade, Minneapolis grew from 13,066 to 46,887.

From 1865 to 1868, Indian affairs frequently took a back seat to questions surrounding the reintegration of the southern states into the Union and the problems arising from the freeing of hundreds of thousands of slaves. Andrew Johnson's first secretary of the interior, James Harlan, and his Commissioner of Indian Affairs, Dennis Cooley, spent much of their tenure renegotiating the boundaries of the Indian Territory, that region which is now the state of Oklahoma. Because the Cherokee, Creeks, and others had supported the Confederacy, Harlan contended that their treaties were forfeit. Their reservations were therefore curtailed, and Harlan supported efforts to open the area to white settlement as Oklahoma Territory. He also began to move other Great Plains tribes from reservations in Kansas and Nebraska into Oklahoma. In the process, he stepped on too many toes, and in July 1866 he was replaced by Orville Browning. Browning's choice for Commissioner of Indian Affairs was Lewis Bogy, a St. Louis businessman whose chief interest in the post was the opportunity it provided for patronage. Bogy cancelled Commissioner Cooley's contracts for Indian supplies and made new ones with St. Louis firms in which his family had an interest. His financial shenanigans were too much for the Senate. In 1867 they replaced him with Nathaniel G. Taylor, who was considered an honest man without an ax to grind.[269]

In the summer of 1867, the government sent a second commission, consisting of Generals William Tecumseh Sherman, John Sanborn, and Alfred Terry, as well as Indian Commissioner Nathaniel Taylor, Senator John Henderson of Missouri, and Indian rights activist Samuel Tappan, to treat with the Lakota of the Great Plains. The Lakota, under Chief Red Cloud, had been at war with the United States for the past two years over the Bozeman Trail, which cut through their hunting grounds, connecting the Oregon Trail in eastern Wyoming to the gold fields around Virginia City in Montana. In 1865, the government had constructed three forts along the trail to protect travelers.

William Tecumseh Sherman advocated total removal of the Indians from the Great Plains. Nevertheless, as commander of the Department of the Missouri in 1868, he approved the sale of surplus army supplies to Whipple to feed the hungry Sisseton and Wahpeton Dakota.

This antagonized the Lakota, and in December 1866 they destroyed an army command led by Captain William J. Fetterman. Anxious to cut back on the size of the military following the end of the Civil War, Congress rejected the army's demand for a strong campaign against the Lakota in favor of negotiation.

The Peace Commission, as it became known, issued a report sympathetic to the Indian position. Confessing that the warfare resulted from U.S. policies that repeatedly deprived the Indians of their land, it suggested gathering the remnants of the tribes on two huge reservations, one in what is now Oklahoma and the other in the present states of North and South Dakota. Compulsory schools would be provided to teach agriculture and break down tribal differences, to "fuse them into one homogenous mass." Furthermore, "their barbarous dialects should be blotted out and the English language substituted." Annuities should be given in kind, not cash, as it was the availability of cash that had corrupted the Indian service.[270]

The Peace Commission's report reflected the views of Henderson, Taylor, and Tappan. The military members were less sanguine. The commission held a second meeting in Chicago's Fremont House in October 1868, which Whipple attended. It was the first time he had met General Sherman. Senator Henderson was unable to be present, but presidential candidate Ulysses Grant was. This time, the commission's report reflected the views of its military members, proposing the abolition of selected treaties, wider use of military force, and transfer of the Indian bureau to the War Department. As the commission never met again, these conflicting views were never resolved, but they brought the two positions most widely held in government circles at the time—the military and the civilizer—into sharp focus.

In the spring of 1867, the Sisseton and Wahpeton Dakota signed a new treaty in Washington. Although these bands had not taken part in the 1862 war, they had lost their reservation rights in Minnesota, as well as their annuities. Moving westward onto the Dakota plains, they were barely subsisting. After the 1864 establishment of Fort Wadsworth near the western shore of Lake Traverse, in what is now South Dakota, the two tribes began gathering there for protection from the violence spreading around them. They were almost completely dependent on the generosity of the commandant at Fort Wadsworth, who was hard pressed to find food for some sixteen hundred Indians in addition to his own troops.[271] The 1867 treaty assigned them two reservations: one to the north between Devils Lake and the Sheyenne River, and the other farther south between Lake Traverse and the headwaters of the Big Sioux River.

The Sisseton and Wahpeton were caught in a not uncommon dilemma: when they signed the 1867 treaty, they agreed to remain on their reservations at all times. If they did not, they ran the risk of being treated as hostiles by the armies then engaged in war with other Plains tribes. But there was not enough game on the reservation to feed them all, and they not only had little experience in farming, they also had few agricultural implements with which to attempt it. Although Superintendent Thompson had encouraged them to select farm sites and begin plowing, by 1868 only about 150 acres had been broken, mostly with hoes.

At the end of its summer session in 1868, Congress appropriated $45,000 for the relief of the Sisseton and Wahpeton and specifically stated that Bishop Henry Whipple was to take charge of its distribution. Whipple was dumbfounded. He was not a government official, he protested. But he was informed that, under the terms of the Appropriation Act (which could not be changed, because Congress was no longer in session), if he did not take charge of the distribution, the money would be returned to the U.S. Treasury unspent. Reluctantly, Whipple agreed.

Having done so, he determined to do the job

properly. He did not subcontract the purchasing, as others might have. Instead, he spent the next months gathering supplies of flour, salt pork, blankets, sugar, coffee, tobacco, axes, plows, and seed corn from merchants in New York, Philadelphia, and St. Paul. He recruited his friend Jared Daniels to help him deliver the goods. General Sherman, commander of all military forces on the Plains, wired permission for quartermasters at the forts to sell Whipple their excess pork, flour, and stores at cost.[272]

In July, just as Whipple was preparing to go to New York on his first government shopping trip, word came that his two elder daughters were seri-

Jared Daniels, former physician at the Lower Sioux Agency, whom Whipple baptized in 1860. He assisted Whipple at the Sisseton-Wahpeton distributions in 1868 and 1869. He became agent to the Sisseton and Wahpeton Dakota and later to the Lakota at Fort Laramie. After many years of medical practice in Faribault, he retired to California in 1900.

ously ill in Rome, New York, where they were spending the summer. Dropping Cornelia off in Rome to look after the girls, Whipple began to buy supplies and arrange for their shipment to the Dakota Territory.

When in November Whipple finally arrived at Fort Wadsworth, the condition of the Dakota was so appalling that he ordered immediate issuance of food and clothing to those in greatest need, regardless of their willingness to work. This was in direct conflict with government policy, as spelled out in the 1867 treaty on which the distribution was based. Agent Benjamin Thompson objected, but to no avail. Simon Anawangmani, a leading Sisseton chief, told Whipple, "The sky was iron above our heads, and the ground iron beneath our feet . . . but you have saved us." Then he burst into tears.[273]

The work requirement had resulted from complaints that the government annuity system discouraged Indians from making any effort to become self-sufficient. Whipple himself believed that "almshouses make paupers, and Indian almshouses make savage paupers." He made it clear to the Dakota that in the future, they must farm, chop

Simon Anawangmani, a chief of the Sisseton band, thanked Whipple for saving his people by bringing the food and supplies voted them by the government.

wood, or perform some similar form of task in exchange for the food, blankets, and other supplies the government gave them. He did not, however, share the common belief that Indians were lazy. "It would be as sensible to expect the wild man to take kindly to manual labor as it would be to expect the man of the city, suddenly thrust into a wilderness, to supply himself with food and clothing by skillful use of bow and arrow and knife."[274]

There were no railways west of St. Cloud, so to reach Fort Wadsworth, Whipple had driven nearly 150 miles across the open prairie in his buggy. On the way, he was caught in a "fearful storm," one of those fierce blizzards that often roar across the Dakota plains. Twenty miles from the nearest house, with the temperature well below zero, he had spent the night huddled in a haystack. By morning, he had a chest cold that became so severe that he could not remain at the fort to oversee the entire distribution. He asked Daniels and General Sibley to complete the task for him.

Before he left, however, Whipple stirred up a hornet's nest when he ruled that certain Dakota women, who were being kept by officers at the fort, were ineligible for payment. When the story appeared in the *St. Paul Pioneer,* army officers throughout the country took offense at the suggestion that any of them might be keeping Indian mistresses.[275] Whipple was also criticized by some of his fellow churchmen for accepting a secular assignment from the government. Annoyed, he asked the secretary of the interior for a letter explaining that he had not solicited the job, had in fact tried to evade it, and was persuaded to take it on only when the secretary assured him that no one else could legally do it.[276]

By January 22, Whipple had recovered from his illness sufficiently to go to White Earth for a council with the Ojibwe chiefs, but his cough lingered into the summer. Grief played a part in his debility, for he suffered two serious personal losses in the early

months of 1869. Solon Manney, who had done so much to make the schools at Faribault a success, died January 18 of blood poisoning from an infected corn on his foot. "If it were not that he had gone to a higher service, I should count it the greatest loss that had ever come to my diocese," Whipple said. A month later, Taopi, the Mdewakanton chief who had been one of Whipple's first adult Dakota converts, also died. Whipple was present at both deaths, providing comfort to the dying men.

In March, Whipple went to Washington to lobby the new Grant administration on behalf of the Indians. His reception was encouraging, and he wrote in his diary, "Thank God hope of reform." But to his dismay, Congress again specified him by name to dispense the $60,000 appropriated to get the Sisseton and Wahpeton settled into farming. The previous effort had cost him not only his health but "several hundred dollars of my own means & much valuable time which I could ill afford to spare from official duties," he complained to Secretary of the Interior Jacob D. Cox.[277] This time, however, Congress allowed him to delegate the job to Jared Daniels, although Whipple had to review all of Daniels' expenditures. He asked the Indian bureau to appoint Daniels agent to the Sisseton and Wahpeton, and it obliged. Exhausted, Whipple spent three days in bed at his daughter's house in Philadelphia before he was able to return home.

In April, he took his son Charles to New York to see him off for a summer with the Caird family in Scotland. He then performed confirmations at a number of churches around his diocese, taught his class at Seabury, attended graduation ceremonies at the schools, and presided over the annual diocesan convention.

The Cathedral of Our Merciful Saviour was officially consecrated on June 24, 1869. Bishop Jackson Kemper, in one of his last official acts, came from Wisconsin with his associate bishop, William Armitage, to preside over the ceremony. Bishop Henry

The Cathedral of Our Merciful Saviour, Whipple's see headquarters, was consecrated in 1869. Designed by Renwick and Company of New York, it was built of local limestone. The interior boasted a carved pine altar and communion rail, a pine pulpit, two rows of choir stalls in the chancel, and two ranks of pews able to seat six hundred "comfortably" in the nave. There are twenty-one stained-glass windows: seven in the chancel, six on the north aisle, and eight on the south.

Whitehouse of Illinois preached the sermon. Nearly all of the diocesan clergy took part, processing down the aisle behind the bishops while reciting Psalm 24 antiphonally with Kemper. More than a thousand persons crammed into the church, filling the pews, the side aisles, the empty organ chamber, and the unfinished base of the bell tower. A choir of students from the schools sang, and flowers by the hundreds scented the sanctuary. The following day, Whipple ordained four men to the priesthood in a formal demonstration of the new cathedral's proper purpose.[278]

Whipple then set off for Fort Wadsworth to meet with the Sisseton and Wahpeton and help Daniels with the annuity distribution. At this point, however, the pressure of events caught up with him. He was suffering from severe bronchitis; his breathing was labored and his persistent cough interfered with his sleep. Alarmed, Daniels sent him home. Whipple's family doctor, Francis Rose, ordered him to go abroad again, where the trials of the Indians would not tempt him to exceed his strength.[279]

Once again, friends came to his aid. Robert Minturn sent $500 in English pounds. Ellen Watkinson, who was financing a new church at White Earth, sent $500 more for the bishop's personal use. William Pierrepont, who had sponsored him at his baptism in 1842, also sent $500, which Whipple gave Cornelia to cover her expenses while he was away. Wisconsin's new bishop, William Armitage, agreed to take over Whipple's visitations until he returned.

Accompanied by his daughter Nellie, Whipple traveled to Philadelphia on September 27, where he prepared a written report on the Sisseton-Wahpeton situation for Secretary Cox. In New York on October 4, Whipple met Sir Henry Holland, a prominent English physician and world traveler, who would accompany the bishop and Nellie to London. They boarded the SS *Cuba* for England on October 6.

The ten days onboard worked their usual magic, and upon their arrival in Liverpool on October 17, Nellie was able to report that her father felt much

better. Once in London, however, he caught a fresh cold and was forbidden to leave the hotel for a week. "He is so imprudent," Nellie wrote her sister Lizzie in Philadelphia. "On Sunday he persisted in going to the Temple before eight. I sent for Sir Henry Holland."[280] Being unable to visit friends or attend church services was a severe strain on the sociable bishop, but his doctor and his daughter were firm.

Sir Henry prescribed a warm climate for his patient. After a few weeks in London, father and daughter sailed for Paris, where Whipple contacted Dr. Theodore Evans, who had treated him for Syrian fever five years previously. Evans consulted with several specialists, all of whom agreed with Dr. Rose's diagnosis: severe bronchitis with a strong tendency to asthma. The doctors said he had neg-

The "Indian Lambs" window in the cathedral, paid for by contributions from Indian children living at Faribault after the Dakota War of 1862. The children gathered berries to raise the $125 for this window, given in memory of children killed in the conflict.

The altar of the Cathedral of Our Merciful Saviour in 1976. The original pine altar (now in the Guild House) was replaced by this stone one in 1934. The central window depicts the Good Shepherd, in honor of the Reverend Ezekiel Gear, Minnesota's first resident Episcopal priest. Flanking it are windows depicting the four Gospels.

lected his cough "6 months too long" and insisted that what he needed most was a long rest.[281]

Whipple and Nellie spent the next six months at the Hotel des Anglais, a rest home run by English physician D. H. Bennett in Mentone, on the French coast near Monaco. An admirer of Whipple's, Dr. Bennett refused to charge for his services.[282] "I was much worse off than I feared," Whipple wrote Cornelia, "& nothing but my nervous energy kept me up. . . . The Doctor says I can never preach as I have, & must never make another winter visitation."

For the most part, he was confined to the hotel. "It is to me a strange life to be idle," he confessed to his wife on December 5, "to absolutely do nothing—all sight seeing forbidden, all calling or receiving calls forbidden—not permitted even to go to church—too weak for any rambles. Our only resource is to ride. . . . My daily life is this—I usually wake about 5½ a.m. and for an hour & a half lie and think of home. . . . At 7 a waiter comes in, bathes me in salt water from head to foot—I get up at 7½ & it usually takes me ½ to an hour to dress—at 8½ I go to our little parlour & read my bible till 9—Nell comes out about ¼ past & we have prayers—at 9½ we have our breakfast, usually some eggs & toast—or a mutton chop—always chocolate. If the day is fine we always go out as soon as the doctor has gone, he always comes at 10¼—we ride an hour or go & sit in the garden. We come home & dine at 3 (we have changed our dinner hour) read until tea—7 p.m. & go to bed at 9." Both Dr. Bennett and Sir Henry Holland were strong believers in mustard plasters, and "I am nearly a mustard pickle."

His greatest concern was for Cornelia and the responsibilities he had left her to face back in Faribault, especially the upkeep of St. Mary's, now in its fourth year. "I hope that you will receive from Judge [E. T.] Wilder the money on my salary, and that before long you may have some money I had used for missions & the money from Washington which Charlie credited Gen'l McPhail." (Twenty-year-old Charlie, having

Archibald Tait, archbishop of Canterbury from 1868 to 1882. Headmaster at Rugby from 1842 to 1849, he was bishop of London when Whipple first met him. He shared Whipple's interest in schools and in reconciliation between High and Low Churchmen.

returned from Scotland in August, was working in a bank in Faribault and had taken on some of his father's financial duties in Whipple's absence.) "It is my one great source of anxiety lest you should be so loaded with care as to give you anxiety & make you ill . . . ," he told her earnestly. "You have been one of the best and truest of wives and one of the most faithful of mothers." He praised Nellie's patience with a likely understatement: "You know I am sometimes nervous when ill."

As he grew stronger, the ban on visitors was lifted. Mentone was a fashionable resort, frequented by wealthy and educated people from many nations. "Every day we see troops of Americans," Whipple wrote Cornelia in January 1870. The Shattucks came from Torquay, where they were wintering for their daughter's health. The Evanses passed through on their way to the Holy Land. He saw the Shumways and Fabeaus, old acquaintances from Chicago, every day. The English author H. L. Sidney Lear was a fellow convalescent. Sir Henry Ackland, the Prince of Wales's physician, visited Whipple, bringing his two sons, whom the bishop regaled with tales of wild Indians. He even met Sir Hugh Cairns, lord chancellor of England under Disraeli the previous year, who invited the bishop to dine.

Whipple kept current on events at home with the *Faribault Democrat,* which arrived regularly by mail, supplemented by Cornelia's letters. Daniels sent regular reports concerning his purchases as Whipple's proxy for the Sisseton and Wahpeton. Henry Rice, Felix Brunot, and William Welsh wrote

Mentone, France, where Whipple spent the winter of 1869–1870 recuperating from severe bronchitis. He returned here again with his wife and sister in 1888, after the Third Lambeth Conference, to recover from an operation for nasal polyps. He stayed in the Hotel des Anglais.

about the condition of Indian affairs in Washington and the progress of Indian wars on the western plains. Bishop Armitage reported on his three weeks' visit to Minnesota, adding, "By the way, you must reform when you come home and give up some of your *long* visitations—they would kill a Hercules and wear out anybody's lungs and bronchial apparatus." On a more somber note, Whipple received notice of the death of his mother, Elizabeth Whipple, in March, at the home of his sister, Sarah Salisbury, in Blairstown, Iowa.[283]

During those long days spent lounging under the warm Mediterranean sun, Whipple talked at length with Augusta Shumway about the schools he had founded in Faribault. Before she left Mentone, she promised Whipple $10,000 to build a chapel on the Shattuck campus in memory of her infant daughter, Eunice. It was the beginning of a long and profitable relationship between the bishop and the wealthy widow.

At last, in April 1870, Whipple and his daughter left the Riviera. Nellie went to Italy with friends while her father took a leisurely tour of Spain. At Barcelona, he had to wait in the harbor while a street battle raged between government forces and Carlists.[284] He was received by several prominent Spaniards, including the Duke of Montpensier. In Madrid, he attended a meeting of the Cortez, the Spanish representative assembly, and, at the request of the British Minister, held services in the chapel of the U.S. Embassy. Easter week was spent in Seville. He admired the English cemetery at Malaga and was led around the Alhambra palace by an old guide who claimed to remember Washington Irving's visit many years before. A Catholic priest in the library of the Escorial monastery told him, "It is sad that they who love Jesus should differ."

Rejoining Nellie in Paris at the end of May, Whipple returned home via London and reached Faribault on June 18, just in time for the diocesan convention.

There had been a minor squabble among the Seabury faculty during his absence—the old argument between evangelicals and ritualists—but it had been settled amicably by the time he returned. Energized by Mrs. Shumway's offer of the chapel for Shattuck, Whipple resumed his diocesan work with enthusiasm.

Augusta Shumway, a wealthy Chicago matron, talked often with Whipple during his stay at Mentone in 1869–1870. His enthusiastic tales of his work at the schools impressed her so much that she promised to build a chapel at Shattuck. Most of her wealth was tied up in real estate, and the Chicago fire of October 1871 reduced her income considerably, but she insisted on sending Whipple the money she had promised him. Consecrated on September 24, 1872, the Chapel of the Good Shepherd, with its English stained-glass windows and Italian marble font, cost nearly $30,000. Mrs. Shumway continued to take an interest in the schools following her remarriage to M. C. Huntington in 1873. When she died in 1884, she left $300,000 to construct buildings at the schools in memory of her first husband, Horatio G. Shumway and her father, William S. Johnston.

Sign of the Episcopal Church of Santa María la Virgen in Itabo, Cuba, which was built in the 1930s and currently has about seventy active members. The sign bears the logo of the Episcopal Church of Cuba, which was founded in 1871 after Whipple visited the country. The Cuban Church became an independent entity in 1967.

*F*ollowing the June 1870 diocesan convention, Whipple set off on a round of visitations to parishes that were now much more accessible than when he and Bashaw rode their way from town to town almost by instinct. In August, he was in Tennessee, visiting his former brother-in-law George Fairbanks at Sewanee. He returned home in time to join a delegation sent by the new Board of Indian Commissioners to talk with the Ojibwe at White Earth. In November, he went east for the annual Board of Missions meeting, followed by the usual tour of parochial mission societies, including the one at Zion Church in Rome.

In the eleven years since Whipple's consecration, America had changed considerably. The rapidly expanding rail network provided even small towns easy access to major centers of trade and industry. Emigrants from Europe and the eastern states in ever-increasing numbers were claiming homesteads west of the Mississippi. Telegraph lines made instant communication possible over thousands of miles—even, since 1866, across the ocean to Europe. By 1874, the Episcopal Church nationwide would boast 282,359 communicants. Minnesota alone had 10,000 baptized Episcopalians, 3,500 of them full-fledged communicants. The Domestic and Foreign Mission Society coordinated mission work through its Board of Missions to Indian, black, and white populations in America, and to foreign lands such as China, Japan, Africa, and the Middle East. Its women's auxiliary, formed in 1868, had branches in every parish in the country, raising funds to support the board's missions.[285]

While many mission churches in Minnesota received support from the Board of Missions, diocesan growth had quickly exceeded the board's generosity. In 1865, Minnesota had formed its own diocesan missionary society, with branches in each parish, to supplement the board's efforts. The money the society raised went to the bishop to pay additional missionary stipends. In 1866, Whipple reported that nine of his missionaries were supported by the national board, two by the Philadelphia Association for Missions in the West, and another seven by the diocese. A year later, the diocese was supporting eleven missionaries, and the number continued to grow.[286]

Responsibility for the entire program rested on Whipple. At the 1869 diocesan convention, Whipple told the delegates, "There has been a steady increase in the liberality of our own people, but you will forgive me if I tell you that it is far behind what it ought to be. Your Bishop has had to take means provided for his own salary to prevent the withdrawal of missionaries from their field of labor. . . . Our missionary staff consists of nine missionaries of the domestic committee who receive $300 per annum, and twelve missionaries, who receive the same stipend and have been sent out by myself. I regret to say that in some instances this stipend is in many cases their only sure support." In response to his plea, the diocese appointed a Diocesan Board

Ulysses S. Grant was elected president on the strength of his military record in the Civil War, but his administration was marked by corruption and cronyism. The first president to make a serious effort to reform the nation's Indian policy, he established the Peace Policy, which gave U.S. churches a major role in the conduct of Indian agencies. However, increasing settlement on the Great Plains, the discovery of gold in the Black Hills, and the construction of intercontinental railroads through Indian hunting grounds led to another major Indian war in 1876, negating the Peace Policy's intent.

of Missions to relieve their bishop of this financial burden.[287]

Money was only part of the problem. The decade following the Civil War was one of great growth for the diocese of Minnesota. The state population by 1870 was 439,706, almost double what it had been in 1860, and church membership was growing in proportion.[288] For the past three years, Whipple had been pointing out the difficulties he faced in attempting to oversee the church's work in a state that was larger than many European countries. He proposed dividing the diocese into three rural convocations, each under a dean who would visit each parish several times a year and report back to him. This, he said, would make it easier for him to be aware of "all matters which require immediate attention." After extensive debate extending over several years, the delegates voted in 1871 to create three missionary districts—north, south, and central—each under a rural dean "whose powers and duties shall be defined by the several bodies of which they are heads, subject to the approval of the bishop."[289]

Whipple's optimism concerning the likelihood of reform in Indian affairs under the new administration seemed at first to be well founded. The election of Ulysses S. Grant in 1868 brought about a sea change in federal Indian policy. A Republican war hero, Grant did not face the political challenges that almost cost his predecessor his job. Moreover, the growing warfare on the Great Plains made it clear that previous Indian policies were not working to the government's benefit. Grant had discovered the complexities of Indian/white relationships during his pre-war service in the Oregon Territory. After his election, his friends in the Quaker community urged him to adopt the program that the Indian rights groups advocated, incorporating many of the ideas Whipple had promoted since 1860: gathering the tribes on reservations, converting them to Christianity, and educating them in EuroAmerican cultural concepts so they could be absorbed into the mainstream of American life. Once assimilated, the argument ran, they would cease to be a political and social embarrassment to a nation that prided itself on its advocacy of individual freedom for all people.[290]

Soon after his inauguration, Grant, like his predecessors, began replacing Indian agents. His first instinct was to rely on his fellow military men; thus, most of the new appointees were army officers rather than politicians. However, he permitted his Quaker friends to select the new agents in Kansas and Nebraska. He chose his wartime aide, Ely S. Parker, as commissioner of Indian Affairs. Parker was a Seneca Indian from New York State who had degrees in law and engineering and who supported assimilation and the end of the treaty system.[291]

Nonpolitical agents and an Indian commissioner were the first two legs of Grant's Peace Policy, as it came to be known. The third leg was the appointment of an independent Board of Commissioners for Indian Affairs, made up of wealthy volunteer philanthropists who would advise the Office of Indian Affairs on policy matters. The board was an extension of Whipple's proposal that local boards, made up of "men who would deem it a high privilege to work in the elevation of an heathen race," be appointed to oversee the activities of individual agencies.[292] Grant's board consisted of nine unpaid commissioners who were to act as auditors in financial matters at the Office of Indian Affairs, supervise and advise bureau personnel, and make "recommendations . . . as to the plans of civilizing or dealing with the Indians."[293]

William Welsh was elected president of the board; Felix Brunot was elected secretary. The other members were also prominent philanthropists: Nathan Bishop and William Dodge of New York City, Edward S. Tobey of Boston, George H. Stuart of Philadelphia, Robert Campbell of St. Louis, Henry S. Lane of Indiana, and John V. Farwell of Chicago. Whipple knew them all well.

Almost immediately conflict arose between Welsh and Commissioner Parker over the amount of authority the Board of Commissioners was to wield over Indian Affairs. Parker regarded the board as an advisory unit, while Welsh insisted that it had power to correct any instances of improper behavior it discovered. When Parker refused to act on advice from the board, Welsh resigned.

Whipple was out of the country in January 1870, when 173 Piegan Blackfeet (most of them women and children) were killed by an army unit in Montana. Using the public outcry that arose as evidence that the military could not be trusted with Indian relations, Congress in July passed a law banning military offi-

cers from holding civilian posts. Instead of returning to the previous system of political patronage, Grant asked his Quaker friends to recommend replacements for the military agents. The Board of Commissioners heartily approved of this idea but expanded

Ely Parker, a Seneca Indian, was Grant's aide-de-camp in the Civil War and the nation's first Native American commissioner of Indian Affairs. Parker considered Indian treaties inefficient and subject to abuse and persuaded Congress to end the treaty system in 1871. He supported allotment and assimilation of the Indians into the majority culture and accepted the use of force and economic pressure to induce change. His clashes with William Welsh, first chair of the Board of Commissioners for Indian Affairs, led to Parker's resignation in 1871. He died in New York in relative obscurity as a minor employee of the police department.

the policy to include eleven of the nation's major religious bodies.

Over the next two years, the seventy-three Indian agencies were divided among the churches. Each denomination formed a Committee for Indian Affairs to approve nominations for all Indian service employees. The churches were expected to keep a close eye on the reservations under their jurisdiction and to meet regularly with the Board of Commissioners to discuss problems that cropped up.

The Episcopal Church was assigned eight agencies, including the Shoshone agency in Wyoming; the Ponca, Yankton, and Red Cloud agencies in Nebraska; and the Spotted Tail, Yanktonais, Lower Brule, and Cheyenne River agencies in Dakota Territory. The Quakers were

Ojibwe knife case made of deerskin, glass beads, brass beads, yarn, and military braid, ca. 1860-1890. Bishop Whipple Collection.

given the Santee agency, even though most of the mission work there was being done by Samuel Hinman and the Presbyterian Alfred Riggs.[294]

The Ojibwe agency in Minnesota was initially placed under the Congregational Church. The rationale for this is not clear. Although the Congregationalists, through the American Board, were the first Protestants to send missionaries to Minnesota's Ojibwe, they had left the field more than a decade earlier. Whipple appears to have accepted this arrangement with equanimity, however, perhaps because he felt he had an ally in the Congregationalist camp through his Uncle George Whipple, who was a Congregationalist minister. In 1871, at George Whipple's recommendation, the Congre-

gationalists appointed Edward Parmalee Smith as agent to the Ojibwe.[295]

When Whipple preached at White Earth in July 1871, he was pleased by what he saw. Although "I have often visited these Indians & found them savages," he wrote in his diary, "I found them dressed as white men, living by toil, dwelling in houses." The change was "remarkable," reinforcing his belief that Indians could adopt the white man's ways if properly motivated and taught.

Earlier that spring, Whipple had become involved in yet another project. In December 1870, Bishop Whittingham of Maryland had asked the bishop to do him a favor. Whittingham was in charge of a mission in Haiti. The mission expected him to perform confirmation services, but he wasn't able to do it. Would Whipple mind taking his place? It sounded like a decent excuse to spend a few weeks in the Caribbean, away from the Minnesota winter, so Whipple agreed. But when he and Cornelia arrived in New York at the end of February 1871, they discovered that the ship for Haiti had sailed ahead of schedule and that there would not be another for several weeks. However, a ship *was* preparing to leave for Cuba. From there, they were assured, passage to Haiti could be easily arranged.

The Whipples arrived in Havana in early March, only to learn that there was, in fact, no ship available to take them to Haiti. But the expatriate community in Havana gave Whipple an enthusiastic welcome. The Cuban government, they told him, refused to allow Protestant clergy into the country. They begged him to hold services for them while he was there.

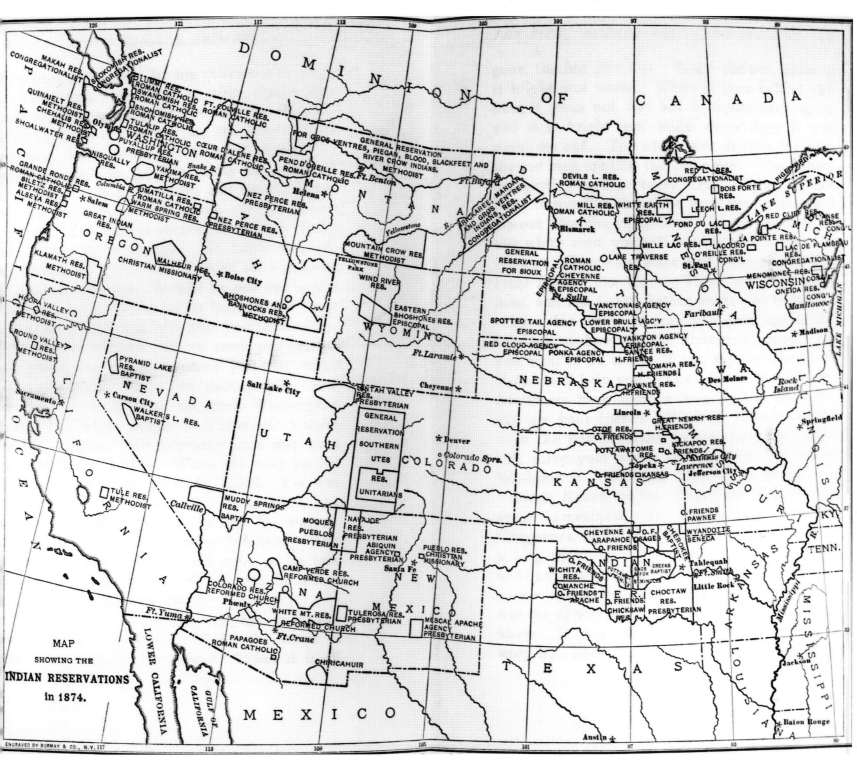

MAP

SHOWING THE

INDIAN RESERVATIONS

in 1874.

ENGRAVED BY BORMAY & CO., N.Y. 117

Cuba was still a Spanish colony in 1871, but an independence movement had begun more than a year earlier, and America's sympathy with the rebels had strained relations between the two governments. Not wanting to offend Cuban authorities, the U.S. consul-general refused to allow Whipple to hold services at his consulate in the city without the official permission of the Cuban governor. Whipple refused to apply for such permission. He had been in Spain only the year before, he said, and knew that the Spanish constitution of 1869 allowed freedom of worship to all foreigners living in Spain or her colonies. He did not want to force a direct confrontation with the authorities, however, so he held his service in the harbor, on the American man-of-war *Swatara*.

A large congregation of American, English, and German expatriates attended. The following Sunday, British consul-general Alexander Graham-Dunlop offered his hotel rooms for a service.[296] Afterward, Louis Wills, the German consul-general, asked if the bishop would perform a marriage at his consulate. Whipple did so, "as an act of international courtesy," for which he accepted no fee. Afterward, Wills allowed him to hold a public service at the German consulate. In his sermon, Whipple offered thanks for the recent restoration of peace between France and Germany.[297]

The coincidence of his original travel plans having been altered through no fault of his own convinced Whipple that God had sent him to Cuba for a purpose. At the General Convention in Boston that October, he asked the House of Bishops to approve the establishment of an Episcopal mission in Cuba. They declined, but had no objection to Whipple sending a man out on his own responsibility. Bishop Whittingham even had a candidate available: an energetic young minister named Edward Kenny. Whipple's appeal for funds to support Kenny's mission produced between $9,500 and $10,000 in pledges, and William Welsh, whose firm had an office in Ha-

vana, offered to serve as the mission's treasurer. Kenny departed for Havana in November 1871.

Whipple sent him a letter full of instructions concerning the work he was to do. "The object we seek is to give to our own people the privileges and the blessing of the Gospel. I believe that we shall also by example do much for those who are not of our communion—but it would fitter be our work if the idea went abroad that it was a mission. You must bear in mind that your flock are men of different religious training, Lutherans, Presbyterians, English and American Churchmen & the members of other religious bodies. You are to use the power of the love of God to draw these hearts as one into closest fellowship. . . . Use the service on all occasions but if you deem it best you may divide Morning Prayer Litany & Communion Office. . . . As yours will be a flock of all shades of opinion & where unity is absolutely necessary do not introduce any custom to awaken prejudice or raise the cry of ritualism—have your service however poor simple & as beautiful as you may—a plain altar, a white cloth, a few flowers, a hearty response & congregational singing will move all hearts. In preaching I would dwell much on the stories of the Gospel . . . dogmatic theology perplexes some & is never the seed to be sown on such fallow ground. . . . I believe that it is proper for you to allow all who feel that the address in the Communion office is addressed to them to come. I hope you may be able to get rooms in the U.S. consulate so your services may be under our flag. . . . I have said nothing of the Roman Catholic Church. You will hear & see much to grieve you, don't tell it, don't write it . . . avoid all associations which may turn you aside from your work. You may feel that by association with the Romish clergy you can do much as Langdon has to awaken a reformation—It is not your work now—you can do most by caring for our own & leave this to God."[298]

Kenny began cautiously, holding his services onboard ship in the harbor for the first few months, then moving to the U.S. consulate in April. Whipple came over at Easter in 1872 to hold confirmations. By the middle of 1873, Kenny had established a church on shore in "a suitable chapel," as well as a hospital and a mission outpost at Matanzas, sixty-two miles from Havana. The mission was then sufficiently well established for the Board of Missions to relieve Whipple of its oversight.[299]

Soon after he arrived in Havana in March 1871, Whipple received a letter from a representative of the archbishop of Canterbury that startled him con-siderably. At the request of the King of the Sandwich Islands (Hawaii), the archbishop proposed to appoint a new bishop "to preside over the English mission there, and to found, if so it please God, a Native Church there from the Mother Church." The archbishop wanted Whipple to take the position.[300] It was in some ways a tempting offer. The cold Minnesota winters were hard on his diseased lungs, and his doctor had told him a change of climate would bene-fit his health. His brother George had been doing mission work in Hawaii off and on for some time, so

The Episcopal Church of San Lucas in Ciego de Avila, Cuba, was established in 1933. It is one of the nine self-supporting parishes, twenty-eight organized missions, and forty-three smaller missions of the Iglesia Episcopal de Cuba.

he was familiar with conditions on the islands.

Whipple wrote to his friends and fellow bishops, asking their advice, but they were equally divided—some urging him to accept the offer for reasons of health or policy, others insisting he was needed more where he was. One asked whether he would be under the oversight of Canterbury or the American church. Although Hawaii was technically an independent state, American economic interests were pressing for political intervention. "Annexation is the manifest destiny of the Sandwich Islands," wrote Bishop Whitehouse of Illinois, adding that "the opening seems to be of obvious Divine guidance." Horatio Dyer of the Board of Missions pointed out that the American Board considered Hawaii its field. He reminded Whipple of "how much bad blood was stirred up by the course of the late [English] Bishop there," though he knew Whipple wouldn't "make such blunders."[301]

In the end, Whipple turned down the offer. He could not abandon Minnesota, he wrote to the archbishop's representative. "A change might imperil our schools, our missions, our Indian work, and fetter the Church at a time when the state is developing more rapidly than at any period of its history. . . . For me to voluntarily relinquish this field would dishearten some of the bravest of our clergy whose affection for me has helped them amid great trials."[302]

The General Convention of October 1871, which Whipple attended, made several landmark decisions: it established the Cuban mission; it set up an Indian Commission under the Board of Missions to work with President Grant's Board of Indian Commissioners on matters pertaining to the reservations assigned the Episcopal Church under the Peace Policy; and it authorized the first official hymnal for use in the church. But the most controversial item on the agenda was the report of a committee appointed three years earlier to review and make recommendations concerning ritual practices in use in the various dioceses. Their report brought the long-simmering battle between High and Low Church factions to a head.

The committee recommended the church forbid eleven practices and limit four others, mostly pertaining to the dress and behavior of ministers. The practice of infant baptism also came under fire. There followed the "stormiest session since 1844," the year the Oxford Movement reached America. The committee's report was approved by a majority of deputies but vetoed by the House of Bishops, who voted to limit church canons to matters of doctrine, not liturgy.[303]

As a result of this action, George D. Cummins resigned his position as assistant bishop of Kentucky in the fall of 1873 and founded the Reformed Episcopal Church, whose practices were based on a strict evangelical interpretation of the *Book of Common Prayer.* Eight priests and twenty laymen joined Cummins's new sect. Prominent among them was the Reverend Charles Cheney of Illinois.[304]

Whipple believed that the schism arose because "we were too ready to believe that if we compelled men to use words which we knew they did not believe we had preserved the faith."[305] In the spring of 1871, he had attempted to intervene in a dispute between Bishop Whitehouse and Cheney, whom Whitehouse proposed to dismiss from the ministry following a clerical trial at which Cheney claimed that "the words of the baptismal office were the cause of much erroneous belief." Cheney had appealed to a civil court, and the resulting publicity had embarrassed many churchmen. Whipple and Bishop Henry Lee of Iowa had gone to Chicago to try to talk Cheney into accepting the teachings of the church, with no success.

Whipple had no doubt that the church's position on infant baptism was correct. Early in his episcopacy, he had explained it to a frontier congregation that had just listened to a lengthy discourse from another minister on the impropriety of baptizing children. "If an angel from heaven came here tonight," Whipple said, "and said he had come to call the one best fitted to go . . . we would fix our eyes on this dear babe and say: 'There is the only one here who has never committed sin.' If an unbaptized child should ask its mother, 'Am I a Christian?' how could she reply, 'No, you are not a Christian; you are the child of the devil. I have taught you to kneel and say, "Our Father," but God is not your father. I hope that you will be a Christian some time.'"[306]

Whipple tried to convince Cheney that infant baptism was based on the Gospel stories of Jesus, who had taken children in his arms and informed his critics that "of such is the Kingdom of God." He was unmoved by Cheney's reply that baptism was said to involve regeneration, which he felt implied "a spiritual change which his experience did not show had been wrought" in so young a child.[307]

Whitehouse deposed Cheney as priest in June 1871. "A schismatic movement has been for two years a recognized purpose," he told Whipple. "There is no alternative left in Mr. Cheney's unyielding contumacy."[308]

Bishop Cummins, who had started out as a Methodist before joining the Episcopal Church, was well liked despite his extreme evangelical views, and his withdrawal from the episcopacy caused widespread dismay. This turned to outrage when, a few days later, he and four other like-minded priests "held a service, by which they declared that the Rev. Charles E. Cheney was consecrated a bishop." In his sermon, Cummins declared that there was "no inherent difference between the office of a presbyter and bishop," except that a bishop was given responsibility for "general oversight and superintendence."[309] This was completely contrary to the Episcopal Church's philosophy and practice. To elevate

Cheney, who had been formally dismissed from the ministry, to the episcopacy was unacceptable to the mother church's leadership. Cummins was officially deposed as bishop in December 1873.

A few months later, Edward Neal, a Presbyterian minister who had joined Cummins's church, opened a Reformed Episcopal Church in Minneapolis, which welcomed people from all Protestant denominations "except the Old Episcopal Church." Whipple recognized Neal's high standing in the community as a historian and gentleman, and could not publicly object to his presence in the diocese, but he was relieved when the church closed following Neal's death some

George Cummins, assistant bishop of Kentucky, founded the Reformed Episcopal Church in 1873 as a protest against the growing acceptance of High Church liturgical practices. Still in operation, the Reformed Episcopal Church has five dioceses in the United States and Canada and boasts 13,422 members in 137 local parishes and missions. Its *Book of Common Prayer* was recently revised to conform with the 1662 prayer book, although the 1928 version is also authorized.

years later.

Whipple was badly shaken by these events, which had occurred "when all the members of the Church were being drawn to a close union and when all thought that the spirit of God was moving us to concede each to the other all that a Christian may concede and yet preserve the precious deposit of faith. . . . The schism was not made until it had been prepared for by alienation and strife. There was on the one side too little charity for men who were really troubled by words in the Prayer Book which they thought taught erroneous devotion, and on the other side by too much impatience and too little confidence in brethren, or in the guiding care of God, for his Church."[310]

For once, the peacemaker had failed in his mission.

Whipple Hall, the second home of Seabury Seminary School, was built after the first was destroyed by fire in November 1872. Despite the national depression that arose in the fall of 1873, Whipple raised the $30,000 he needed to rebuild through a loan from Faribault's bankers.

*I*n January 1872, Whipple's beloved cousin Henry Halleck died in Lexington, Kentucky. Whipple presided over his funeral, describing Lincoln's former commander-in-chief as "a pure patriot, a loyal citizen, a noble soldier, a fine scholar and devout believer." Despite Halleck's mediocre showing in the Civil War, Whipple had always felt that his cousin was unequaled as a military leader. "Few men have had a more perfect knowledge of the science of war," he claimed.[311]

That August, the bishop consecrated the new St. Columba's Church at White Earth. On his way home, he visited the railway camps along the Northern Pacific route at Detroit Lakes and Brainerd. Railroads had burgeoned in Minnesota since the end of the Civil War. The state's first rail bridge to cross the Mississippi was built at Hastings in 1871. By the end of 1872, Minnesota had 1,906 miles of rail. In 1870, a rail line had been laid from St. Paul to Duluth, which quickly became a major shipping center for Minnesota's wheat and lumber, sending ships through the Great Lakes to Chicago, Cleveland, and Buffalo. The St. Paul and Pacific's main line opened in 1871; soon after, the Northern Pacific was extended from Duluth to Moorhead, the chief market town of the Red River wheat-growing region. The mines opening on the Iron Range in the early 1880s enlarged Duluth's economy even more as the railroad brought iron ore to the harbor.[312]

The construction of these lines brought thousands of rowdy railroad men to join the lumber-jacks in a throng of lawless laborers eager to spend their free time and money at the saloons, bawdy houses, gambling dens, and cockfights that sprang up along the right-of-way. The camp at Oak Point, where Whipple stopped that August afternoon in 1872, was typical of its kind, and a merchant who knew the bishop told him it was a waste of time to try to hold a service there. Undaunted, Whipple rented a tent and went from door to door, announcing his intention of hold-ing a service and inviting everyone to come. At four o'clock, his little tent was crowded with sinners of all stripes. Basing his sermon on the parable of the prodigal son, the bishop soon had many of his listeners in tears. Afterward, one man told him that he believed Whipple had been sent to him by God. The bishop later wrote, "There is no joy like that of being permitted to tell of the love of Jesus for sinners."[313]

Whipple confirmed one person in Detroit Lakes, and then went on to preach in a railroad camp three or four miles farther east. "This is a city of tents," he wrote in his journal, "nearly every place a whiskey shop,—dance houses, saloons, gambling hells,—an abode of wicked-ness. I visited from tent to tent and gathered a good congregation;—they listened with appar-ent interest." In December of the following year, Whipple visited Moorhead, where he confirmed three adults, "preached one of his wonderful sermons," and spent the night on a sofa at the home of a local doctor.

Recalling his work among the railroad men in Chicago, Whipple asked Joseph A. Gilfillan to

Joseph Gilfillan, missionary to the Minnesota Ojibwe from 1873 to 1898. Born in Ireland of Scottish parents, Gilfillan came to America at age twenty to work for his uncle's banking firm. Whipple encouraged Gilfillan to enter the ministry, and in 1865 he graduated from General Theological Seminary in New York. He began his ministry in the railroad camps of the Northern Pacific. In 1873, Whipple sent him to White Earth to oversee the work of Enmegahbowh and the Indian deacons. Energetic, opinionated, and self-confident, Gilfillan became Whipple's chief informant on Ojibwe affairs and exerted considerable influence over the bishop's policies in the area. In 1891 Whipple promoted him to archdeacon. He left Minnesota for Washington, D.C., in 1898.

leave St. Paul's Church in Duluth, where he had served since his ordination in 1870, to begin an itinerant mission to these men "who had graduated in wickedness on the Central and Union Pacific Railroads." Gilfillan made his headquarters at Brainerd, "one of the worst towns in the land." Men were crowded a hundred at a time into boardinghouses, "every house with a bar. . . . Even the best dry

goods store had its barrel of whiskey with a dipper for anyone to help himself." Gambling and drinking went on all night long, seven days a week, and it wasn't uncommon for a pistol shot to ring out in the darkness. There wasn't a single church in town. Gilfillan rented a building and soon had large numbers of men attending his services. "As we had the only church building in Brainerd, nearly all the people who went to church anywhere came to us," he modestly informed the bishop.[314]

Back in Faribault, Whipple consecrated Shattuck's Chapel of the Good Shepherd, which Augusta Shumway had donated, on September 24, 1872. He then visited Hinman's missions at the Santee, Yankton, and Ponca agencies in Nebraska, noting the unusual occurrence of an earthquake in the area on October 9. After a few days at home, he was off again for the East to attend meetings of the Board of Missions and the House of Bishops.

On November 11, 1872, he attended the funeral of another war hero, General George G. Meade, in Philadelphia, delivering an address at the widow's request. The congregation included President Grant and his cabinet, General William Tecumseh Sherman, and other distinguished officers. Whipple recalled the Easter service he had held at Meade's camp on the Rapidan back in 1864, where he had learned "that loyalty to God and loyalty to country are blended in brave, true hearts."[315]

By this time, Whipple was quite ill. He returned home, dragging himself out of his sickbed on November 24 to give an address at St. Mary's. Four days later, on Thanksgiving Day, Seabury Hall went up in flames. The loss was significant. The building had housed the rector, the divinity students, and some of the boys from Shattuck, many of whom lost books, clothing, and other personal effects. The school's library was destroyed. But despite the financial depression that descended upon the country in the following year, Whipple was able to begin building a new hall a mile farther south within six months.

Moving Seabury gave the Shattuck campus badly needed room to expand. The new seminary building was called Whipple Hall.[316]

In 1873, Commissioner of Indian Affairs Edwin P. Smith found himself in hot water as the result of a deal he had made, while he was agent on the Ojibwe Reservation, to sell a large tract of Ojibwe pine to a local lumber merchant named H. P. Wilder. The price paid turned out to be well below the pine's market value. Smith viewed the Ojibwe pine lands

Shumway Chapel at Shattuck School, built by Augusta Shumway in memory of her infant daughter, Eunice.

Northern Pacific Railroad construction at Brainerd, Minnesota, in 1872. The construction of the Northern Pacific (and later the Great Northern Railroad, which paralleled it slightly to the north) did much to open northern Minnesota to settlement and made Duluth a major city. It also contributed to the decline of buffalo herds on the Great Plains, forcing the Lakota and their neighbors to settle on reservations.

Flat Mouth, the fiery chief of the Leech Lake band of Ojibwe, with whom Whipple discussed the touchy issue of the tribe's rights to its pine resources. Flat Mouth presented a stole to Whipple soon after their first meeting in 1861. Flat Mouth told him he had noticed that the bishop wore something over his robes, which he assumed was a badge of office, and he had his wife make one like it as a gift for the white man who had shown himself to be the friend of the Ojibwe people.

When Whipple heard about the deal late in 1873, he wrote to the Board of Commissioners to object. The Indians had "indisputable title to their land," he said, and the timber was "a part of the realty." If the government wished to sell the timber for the Indians' benefit, it should be done properly. Even if all parties had acted in good faith in this matter, he added, a bad precedent had been set.[317]

Although the Ojibwe were highly offended by Smith's actions, they did not resort to violence, perhaps because they were aware that this time there were white men speaking up for them. They did not oppose the sale itself, explained the mixed-blood trader Clement Beaulieu—only the failure of Smith and his successor, Ebenezer Douglass, to consult them beforehand, and the price, which they knew was much too low.[318]

Agent Douglass, who handled the sale for Smith, told the Ojibwe chiefs that the sale had been authorized under a clause in the 1864 treaty permitting the government to substitute goods for annuity money. He added that "the Indians were infants, incapable of knowing what was for their own good," and offered them oxen in exchange for dropping their objections. Disgusted, the Ojibwe refused the oxen. Joseph Gilfillan, who was present when this happened, reported, "I never saw Indians act with such good sense and dignity."[319]

The Leech Lake Pillagers were not so polite. Their leader, Flat Mouth, was a hot-tempered man who had caused considerable consternation three years earlier when he led a raid against the Dakota at Lake Traverse, killing two men, despite having promised "everlasting friendship" with them the previous summer.[320] Whipple was in the midst of visitations in southern Minnesota when he received an urgent message from George Bonga, the African American–Ojibwe trader, that the Pillagers had killed cattle and stolen goods belonging to the government. "I fear an outbreak," he told the bishop.

Whipple telegraphed his warning on to Wash-

as a resource to be used to benefit the tribe. Unfortunately, he didn't consult the Ojibwe before signing the contract with Wilder and he neglected to advertise the sale beforehand, so that there had been no opportunity for competitive bidding.

ington. Within hours, Secretary of the Interior Columbus Delano replied, asking the bishop to go to Leech Lake and "resolve the difficulty. [The president] will ratify whatever you do." Whipple went. He took along an officer from Fort Ripley as a witness, explaining, "If I take a Republican and settle this trouble, I shall be accused of covering up rascality; if I take a Democrat and fail to settle it, I shall be accused of stirring up an outbreak."

After a three-day journey in below-zero weather, the two men arrived at the Pillager village on Leech Lake to find the Ojibwe "angry and turbulent." Flat Mouth harangued them at length, claiming the government had robbed them and making no secret of his responsibility for killing the cattle and stealing the goods. When he finished, Whipple stood and asked, "Flat Mouth, how long have you known me?"

"Twelve years."

"Have I ever told you a lie?"

"No, you have not a forked tongue," the chief admitted.

"I shall not tell you a lie today." Whipple told the chief that those who committed crimes against the government would be punished. Flat Mouth leaped to his feet and began to shout. Whipple folded his arms and waited until the chief paused, then asked, "Flat Mouth, are you talking or am I?"

The chief had committed a serious breach of etiquette. Among the Ojibwe, one did not interrupt another person in council before he finished speaking. Embarrassed, Flat Mouth sat quietly. Whipple went on to describe how he had been working to have the pine sale annulled. Flat Mouth's actions, he said, had "put a gag into my mouth." He could not ask good men to help him get justice for people who stole and killed cattle. He suggested that the Pillagers talk things over and let him know what they wanted to do.

After several hours, the Pillagers sent for him, saying, "We have been foolish. You are wiser than we are. Tell us what to do and we will do it."

Whipple advised them to wait and trust him and their other white friends who were working diligently on their behalf.[321]

William Welsh demanded proof that the bureau had the legal right to dispose of Indian property without their approval. In October 1873, a high court ruled the sale comparable to an 1831 case, where the Oneidas had attempted to sell timber on land they were leasing from the Menominees; the court in that case had ruled that the timber could not be sold for profit, but cut only to improve the land for farming. But the Oneidas were only "occupying" the Menominee land, whereas the Ojibwe owned theirs, so the situation was not identical. Welsh insisted that "timber growing on land is as much real estate as houses erected thereon" and demanded to know "under what Act of Congress the Indian Department gets authority for selling" Indian property.[322]

Henry Rice, the former Minnesota senator who had been Whipple's ally in previous battles on behalf of the Ojibwe, supported Welsh's attack on Smith. Smith took Rice's opposition personally, claiming that Rice had, during his time in Congress, frequently taken bribes to have legislation passed and received kickbacks from appropriations he supported, specifically the "half-breed scrip" system that allowed mixed-blood Ojibwe to receive shares of annuity funds that then could be sold to non-Indians. Rice "was largely instrumental in procuring the charges against me and my administration at White Earth," Smith alleged, acting through the mixed-blood traders Beaulieu, Morrison, Fairbanks, and Bonga. Pointing to the treaties negotiated by agents Bassett and Morrill (which Rice had helped to arrange), Smith noted they had caused the Ojibwe to cede hundreds of acres of pine land for less than 10 cents per thousand board foot. Smith had not taken their land. Selling the pine had brought them between $6 and $7 per acre, while the government sold land for only $2.50 per acre. While he regretted having made the sale because of all the trouble it had caused, he still thought it had been the right thing to do.[323]

Whipple's refusal to condemn Smith led Welsh to accuse the bishop of being soft on the pine issue because of lumber baron Wilder's gifts to the Faribault schools. Whipple replied he had never considered such a thing. "As soon as I heard of the sale . . . I wrote to the Secretary and demanded an investigation," he protested. He did not think Smith dishonest. While Smith was the Ojibwe agent, "as I had been cruelly deceived in the past, I watched him very closely. . . . I do not think he knew the value of this pine." Nor, he added, was Wilder an evil man. He was a sharp dealer, but not without integrity, and it was highly doubtful that he had bribed Smith; he had simply taken advantage of Smith's ignorance. Wilder had indeed donated money to the Faribault schools in the past, as had Welsh and many others, "but I hope I am man enough to do my duty" regardless of such considerations, he concluded angrily.[324]

The pine sale issue came to an end in mid-1874, when the shortage of funds in the tribe's agricultural fund became acute. Smith was investigated and exonerated of fraud charges. Problems continued, however, with Agent Ebenezer Douglass, whose high-handed methods irritated the Ojibwe. They suspected him of making illegal profits off their annuity supplies and accused him of taking liberties with girls at the agency school. The chiefs complained that Douglass had fired all the agency employees they liked and hired others they mistrusted. In May 1874, Douglass was replaced by James Whitehead, whom the Ojibwe leaders also disliked. George Bonga claimed Whitehead was a tool of the pine interests. The chiefs asked Whipple to choose an agent for them.[325]

At this point, the Board of Indian Commissioners decided to shift Minnesota's Ojibwe from the Congregationalists' oversight to the Episcopalians'. Whipple recommended Lewis Stowe, a farmer from Le Sueur County whom he had licensed as a lay reader in July 1873, as agent at White Earth. Whitehead was sent to Leech Lake as subagent and a second subagent, R. M. Pratt, was sent to Red Lake.[326]

Lewis Stowe had been active in the church for many years and had just completed a term in the state legislature.[327] He was honest and diligent, if somewhat cavalier, and his tenure would probably have been relatively uneventful except for the arrival on the reservation of a Roman Catholic priest named Ignatius Tomazin. Tomazin was one of sixteen young theology students from Laibach, Germany, who had come to America in 1865 in response to an appeal by Father Francis Pierz, priest for many years at Crow Wing. "My zealous helper," as Pierz called him, went to White Earth sometime in late 1872 and soon began an energetic campaign to win converts away from the Episcopal mission.[328]

Until this time, the Catholic Church had not had much of a presence among the Minnesota Ojibwe, confining its efforts to the mixed-blood descendants of French Canadian fur traders who were assumed to follow their fathers' religion. Tomazin was the first to begin widening its scope. His sermons emphasized the superiority of the Catholic faith, telling the Ojibwe that attending Protestant services or the government school would condemn them to hell. He claimed an agent selected by the Catholic Church would take their interests more to heart.[329] He accused Whipple of conniving with the government to steal from the Ojibwe, and when Whipple went to Florida for his health that winter, Tomazin told his parishioners that the bishop "had been degraded from [his] office and gone south to hide [his] shame and would never come back."[330] He even told Enmegahbowh that his wife, who was ill, would die of consumption unless she joined the Catholic Church.[331]

While Tomazin may have been inspired in part by genuine zeal for the faith, he was also following a policy recently established by the Bureau of Catholic Indian Missions, a lobbying unit established in Washington in 1873 to press for greater Catholic involvement in the Peace Policy program. The initial movement for Indian policy reform came from Protestant groups and the first Board of Indian Commissioners was made up solely of Protestants. When the agencies were parceled out, the Catholics received only seven. They contended that, as the country's largest Christian denomination (the Protestants being divided into numerous sects), they should have received as many as forty agencies. They began setting up new missions on the reservations, rousing disrespect for the agents and missionaries allied with them, and organizing petitions from the Indians requesting new, Catholic agents. Their agitation caused so much trouble that the Office of Indian Affairs finally denied them access to Protestant reservations.[332]

Tomazin's behavior was totally in line with this policy. Stowe took over the agency in July 1874 and immediately came under fire from Tomazin, who accused him of bias against Catholic Indians, whom he claimed made up two-thirds of the population on the reservation. In 1875, Tomazin convinced a group of Ojibwe to sign a petition to the Board of Indian Commissioners asking that Stowe be replaced by a Catholic and that the reservation be placed under the oversight of the Catholic Church.[333]

Whipple's response to the board stated that, until Tomazin's arrival, the Episcopal mission was the only active one in the region. He had often paid the mission's expenses out of his own pocket. After he had established a successful mission, the Catholics came, found a few mixed bloods who claimed to be Catholic, and began a character assassination campaign against the Episcopal priest Enmegahbowh.

Whipple told the board that Clement Beaulieu, whose name appeared on the petitions, had denounced the priest's allegations and claimed that his signature was a forgery. Whipple asked that an investigator be sent to White Earth to get to the bottom of the matter.[334]

Commissioner Edward Smith went himself. He attended services at Enmegahbowh's church, which were well attended, and spoke to many Ojibwe. The Catholic mission appeared to be closed, and he was told that the priest had been gone for the past two to three weeks. In his report to the interior secretary, Smith said that Tomazin had exaggerated the number of Ojibwe attending his church, and that the Episcopal Ojibwe seemed to outnumber the Catholics. Several signatures on the petition appeared forged or acquired under false pretenses. The Indians' chief complaint, he said, was their poverty. They seemed to think that a new agent—any new agent—might improve their economic situation. They assured him that they did not think Stowe was dishonest. Stowe then provided his own petition, with 125 signatures, asking the bureau to keep him on.[335]

The dispute raged for two more years, into the administration of Rutherford B. Hayes, whose secretary of the interior, Carl Schurz, was forced to make another investigation into Stowe's behavior as agent. Whipple felt that Tomazin was being encouraged by economic forces who "cannot use the agent" for their own pecuniary interests, and he went all the way to President Hayes to try to keep Stowe from being dismissed. In the end, however, the controversy became so embarrassing that Stowe was removed in the spring of 1878. The Catholic Bureau also recalled Tomazin, although Minnesota's Catholic bishop Thomas Grace complained that it would be difficult to find another priest who spoke such fluent Ojibwe. It was three years before the Catholic Church resumed missionary activity at White Earth.

The Seabury-Shattuck campus ca. 1875. The buildings are, clockwise from lower left, Phelps Cottage (housing the schools' library), Shattuck Hall, schoolhouse, Whipple Hall and Shumway Memorial Chapel of the Good Shepherd. Notice the young cadets training in the field behind the campus.

THE SHATTUCK SC

RT REV. H. B. WHIPPLE, D.D. PRES' REV. JAMES DOBBIN, A. M. RECTOR

...OL, FARIBAULT, MINN.
J.M. LANCASTER, COMMANDER OF THE MILITARY DEPARTMENT.

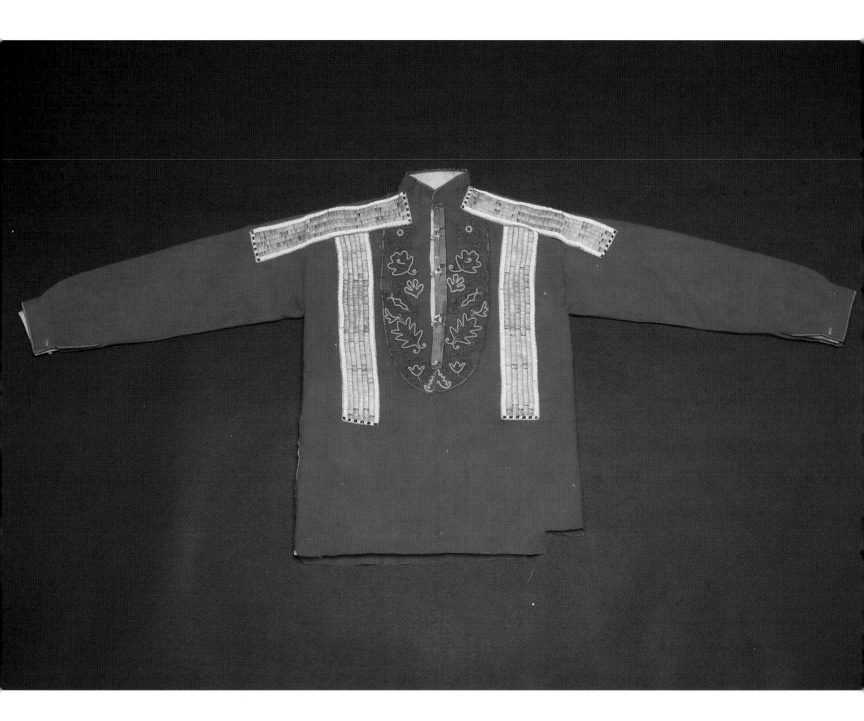

Ojibwe man's shirt made of wool trade cloth, bird quills, silk ribbons, glass beads, glass buttons, and buffalo hide. Bishop Whipple Collection.

The year of 1873 was stressful for the country as a whole. The Credit Mobilier scandal, a money manipulation scheme that involved several members of Congress and government officials, broke in January. That in turn led to the failure of the Jay Cooke and Company Bank in September. Headquartered in Philadelphia, with branches in New York, London, and Washington, the Cooke bank was one of the nation's most influential financial institutions. Its collapse brought about a severe financial panic that affected businesses throughout the world. It was especially painful in Minnesota, where Cooke had invested heavily in the Northern Pacific Railroad and the port of Duluth.

Many of the wealthy philanthropists on whom Whipple relied to support his programs were obliged to cut back on their donations in the ensuing three-year slump. Even after the economy began to recover, it took time for charitable giving to resume its previous levels. The Board of Missions was still showing a sharp decline in income two years later, when its general secretary, A. T. Twing, asked Whipple for a letter that the board could use in its solicitations.

The financial situation wasn't Whipple's only source of stress during 1873. In June, he officiated at the funeral of a Shattuck student who drowned while swimming in the river. In September, he was obliged to go to the Santee Reservation to investigate charges of financial impropriety against his protégé Samuel Hinman. He presided over the funeral of Ezekiel Gear, beloved patriarch of Minnesota's clergy, on October 15.

But there were happy times too. In January, Whipple attended a meeting of the Peace Commission for Indians in New York. In February, he went to a gathering of the Indians of the Six Nations at Brownsford, New York. He confirmed thirty-six Ojibwe at White Earth on June 1. On June 18, his youngest daughter, Fannie, married Frank Craw, a merchant from Cleveland. And in November, he rejoiced at the consecration of William Hare as missionary bishop of Niobrara, which he hoped would bring new strength to the church's mission efforts

Whipple in 1875. After fifteen years in office, he had seen fifty-three churches built, confirmed 4,116 new members, and added thirty-five clergy to his diocesan rolls.

among the tribes of the Great Plains.

That same year, Whipple was asked to become a trustee of the Peabody Education Fund. The fund had been founded in 1867 by George Peabody, the international banker and philanthropist with whom Whipple had fished for salmon on his way home from Europe in 1865. Its purpose was to "encourage the intellectual, moral and industrial education of destitute children of the Southern States." When he died in 1869, Peabody left the fund $2 million to help create a public school system in the South. The board met annually at a dinner held in Peabody's memory in New York, usually in October.[336] At the board's 1875 meeting, Whipple proposed that the fund "take into consideration the propriety

George Peabody, the American banker whose charitable foundations encouraged the arts and education. Often considered the "most liberal philanthropist of his time," Peabody went fishing with Whipple in Ireland in 1865 and gave him a fishing rod as a memento.

of establishing scholarships for the education of teachers in a limited number of schools or colleges in the more destitute portions of the South." Unanimously adopted, the resolution led to the founding of Peabody College in Nashville, Tennessee, in 1875, and Winthrop College in Rock Hill, South Carolina, in 1886.[337]

Whipple brought to the board not only his experience in school administration, but also the memory of his years in pre–Civil War Florida, when he preached to both slaves and poor "crackers." These qualifications were not familiar to some of the other trustees, who knew Whipple primarily as an advocate for the Indians. They questioned the chair's wisdom in selecting him until they heard him speak knowledgeably of the South's culture and its people.

Whipple's attitude toward African Americans had changed over the years, as he witnessed their aptitude for learning once freed from the confines of a society based on slavery. He no longer believed that they were lazy and inherently unable to accomplish as much as white people. He told those who opposed efforts to educate them, "for good or ill, these people are, and will be, our fellow-citizens. . . . We must take care of them or they will take care of us."[338] He praised the work of General Samuel Armstrong, founder of the Hampton Institute in Hampton, Virginia, to provide instruction for freedmen. He also supported the African Methodist Episcopal Church's efforts to raise funds to establish a college. "The education of eight millions of the colored race to be Christian citizens of our country is one of the gravest of problems. . . . I believe they will succeed," he wrote.[339]

Seabury Divinity School was open to all races. When the father of a St. Mary's student criticized Whipple for allowing a black Seabury student to attend social events with students of the other schools, the bishop replied, "For me to forbid the Principal to invite the Divinity students to our entertainments would justly destroy my Divinity school. . . . If they are invited to be present & I refuse this colored man who is my fellow citizen in the nation & the Kingdom of God, I believe I should put a stigma and a dishonor on a disciple of Christ who will give his life to his Master." He assured the man he would see that "no familiarity" took place between the girls and *any* divinity student, but he would not single out this one young man simply because of his color.[340]

Still, Whipple felt that the Indians were "far

superior to the negro, intellectually and in moral characteristics." African Americans were "by nature, trustful, affectionate, and as a race religious. They have made marvelous strides in a few years . . . [but] their energies lie dormant." On the other hand, "the capabilities of the North American Indians are equal to those of our own race." While he admired individual African Americans—Booker T. Washington "wrote one of the best essays upon Industrial Education that I have ever read," he said, and the young Seabury student was "one of the most modest, devoted scholarly men I have ever known"—Whipple felt that Indians, having made the transition from a primitive lifestyle to a modern one in a single generation, showed greater intellectual capacity.[341]

By the summer of 1873, railroad construction in Minnesota had virtually ceased, due to overbuilding and financial troubles. Signs of civil order were appearing in Brainerd and other towns along the line. Families arrived. Stores closed on Sundays. Churches were being built and additional missionaries appeared, eager to take on the work. Whipple decided to transfer Joseph Gilfillan to the Ojibwe Mission at White Earth.

Whipple made it clear to Enmegahbowh that he did not mean for Gilfillan to usurp his position. Enmegahbowh would continue as rector of St. Columba, while Gilfillan, with the title of dean, would

Peabody College at Vanderbilt University. Founded as a teacher training school for former slaves, it was governed by a board on which Whipple served from 1873 to 1901. Teachers trained at Peabody became educational leaders throughout the South.

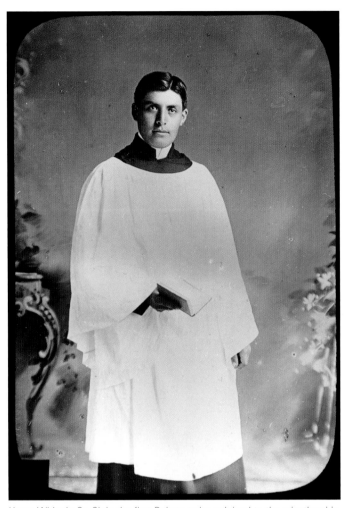

Henry Whipple St. Clair, the first Dakota to be ordained to the priesthood in the Diocese of Minnesota. The son of George Whipple St. Clair, who served as a deacon to the Minnesota Dakota for several years, Henry was educated at Shattuck and Seabury. Whipple ordained him as a deacon in 1899. Ordained priest in 1904, he served for many years at St. Cornelia's Church.

One of the new dean's first tasks was to train a cadre of native clergy to establish churches around the region. Whipple understood the value of priests who could not only preach the Gospel in the language of the people, but translate it in terms of their culture. "The church has never Christianized any people until she has given them a native ministry," he wrote the editor of the *St. Louis Evening Dispatch*. "The age demands scholars, but for this work they need most faith in God."[342] This became apparent to Whipple early in his service as bishop, as he watched Enmegahbowh among the Ojibwe at Gull Lake. Yet in his forty-two years as bishop, Whipple ordained only one full-blooded Native American—Enmegahbowh—to the priesthood. The reason for this anomaly may lie in the character of the man he chose to guide the mission at White Earth.

Joseph Gilfillan was outspoken, self-confident, and assertive, with little time for anyone who disagreed with his point of view. Though he accomplished much in his new post, he was not universally liked, and there were periodic squabbles with his staff, both Ojibwe and white. When he and Enmegahbowh disagreed on something, it was usually Gilfillan whose opinion was accepted by the bishop. Enmegahbowh understood the Ojibwe, but Gilfillan understood Henry Whipple. The two white clergymen spoke the same kind of "missionspeak," sharing a mindset that the native priest lacked. For the next twenty-five years Gilfillan was Whipple's chief source of information on what was happening in the Ojibwe country.

Gilfillan selected several young men, most of them sons of prominent Ojibwe, sent them to Seabury for religious training, and presented them to Whipple for ordination to the diaconate. The first four candidates—Samuel Madison, Fred Smith, and Charles and James Jackson—were ordained in 1876. Charles Wright and Enmegahbowh's son George Johnson followed in 1877; George B. Morgan, Mark

concentrate on forming new missions. The truth was, the venerable Ojibwe priest, earnest as he was, did not have the kind of organizational talent that Whipple felt was needed to expand the faith beyond the immediate vicinity of St. Columba's Church. The number of villages established at White Earth was increasing, though not all the bands had yet moved to the new reservation. Red Lake still had no mission. Bogged down by the needs of his parish, Enmegahbowh did not seem to have time to travel to more distant sites or to establish new parishes.

Hart, George Smith, and John Coleman in 1878.

The Jacksons don't appear to have followed up on their initial training, and Samuel Madison died in September 1877; but the other seven set to work energetically. By 1880 there were five new Episcopal missions on the Ojibwe reservations. There were occasional episodes of conflict between the deacons and their dean, who was constantly annoyed by their tendency to do things in Ojibwe rather than white fashion. Gilfillan assigned his native deacons in pairs to prevent them from resuming their old Ojibwe habits. In 1882, several of them went on strike, complaining of low pay and unfair treatment from their dean. But for the most part, the young men labored conscientiously, and Whipple was able to confirm significant numbers of Ojibwe on his annual visitations to the region.

Gilfillan's dissatisfaction with his Ojibwe deacons may explain why he recruited no more additional young men from the reservation, with the exception of Clement Beaulieu Jr. Beaulieu was the son of the prominent mixed-blood trader Clement H. Beaulieu, whom Gilfillan regarded as white. Beaulieau Jr. was ordained to the priesthood in 1881.

After 1862, only a few Dakota remained in Minnesota, primarily men who had served as scouts for General Sibley's expeditions and their families. In 1874, Whipple admitted one of them, George St. Clair, as a candidate for holy orders. Ordained deacon in 1879, St. Clair served the Dakota communities

St. Antipas Church at Red Lake, ca. early 1900s, where Whipple baptized Madwaganonint and most of his band. St. Antipas was built in 1878 with a gift from the will of Angie Robinson of Sing Sing, New York. Fred Smith and Samuel Madison were the church's first missionaries at Red Lake.

in Mendota, Red Wing, and Prairie Island until his death in 1881. His son, Henry Whipple St. Clair, was educated at Shattuck and Seabury, ordained deacon by Whipple in 1899, and became a priest in 1904.

The Ojibwe at White Earth by 1875 were no longer the wild denizens of the forest that Whipple remembered from his early visits to them. The bands from Gull Lake, Sandy Lake, Rabbit Lake, and Lake Pokegama especially had decided to co-operate to a large extent with the government pro-grams. They established farms and sent their children to the government schools. A large contin-gent of mixed bloods also moved onto the reserva-tion from Crow Wing and other parts of the region. In the area around the agency, the community ap-peared little different from white settlements in other parts of the state. Only in the woods and lakes on the eastern half of the reservation, where it was still possible to make a living from the tradi-tional seasonal round of hunting and gathering, were there groups who retained their old habits.

Red Lake, being farther from the influence of white "civilization," was more traditional. The Red Lake Mission had been acquired from the Congre-gationalists, who returned to the area in 1868 but made little headway. Whipple became interested in the band when he met its chief, Madwaganonint, during the 1864 treaty negotiations. The chief later visited him in Faribault; after several lengthy dis-cussions on religious matters, Madwaganonint ac-cepted baptism and asked Whipple to send a missionary to his people. Not wanting to offend the Congregationalists, with whom he maintained a cordial relationship because of his uncle's con-nection with them, Whipple wrote to M. E. Streiby, secretary of the American Missionary Association, in 1876 to ask if they would mind his sending one of the Ojibwe deacons to Red Lake. Acknowledg-ing that his own man, Reverend F. Spees, was hav-ing little effect, Streiby withdrew the mission. Gilfillan sent Fred Smith and Samuel Madison to

take over, naming the new mission St. Antipas, from a verse in the second chapter of Revelation referring to "Antipas, my faithful martyr, who was slain among you, where Satan dwells."[343]

Whipple confirmed Madwaganonint, who be-came a faithful attendant at the new church. The next time the bishop came to Red Lake for a confir-mation service, Madwaganonint accompanied the candidates to the chancel rail and carefully counted them off on his fingers, making sure they were all there. "As their chief," Whipple realized, "he consid-ered it his duty to see that the young men fulfilled their promises."

Whipple wrote to one of his East Coast corre-spondents in January 1874, describing for her the pressure of trying to satisfy the needs of his mis-sionaries, his schools, and the two Episcopal hos-pitals at Minneapolis and White Earth, not to mention "my Indian fights," which often brought criticism from the press. He had been preaching daily for at least a month, visiting not only estab-lished parishes but also lumber camps and places without churches. "I do not believe you can know the music there is in kind words to a weary heart," he told her.[344]

At the diocesan convention in June 1874, Whipple revisited the question of how he was to manage the care of such a large diocese adequately. Over the past fifteen years, fifty-three churches and sixteen rectories had been built; eleven churches had been enlarged. The diocese had thirty-five new clergymen. There had been 5,802 infant baptisms, 3,830 adult baptisms, and 4,116 confirmations. In the past year, he had delivered 310 sermons and addresses, baptized 113 infants and a dozen adults, confirmed 569 persons, celebrated Holy Communion 40 times, licensed 5 lay readers, or-dained 8 deacons, received a priest from the Catholic Church, laid a cornerstone, buried 2 people, and cate-chized 10 groups of children. He had consecrated 4 churches, a cemetery, and a hospital.[345] All of this, in addition to his advocacy for the Indians and his fundraising work in the East during his annual visit to the Board of Missions.

It was a mammoth undertaking for one man, even with the help of his rural deans.

Whipple then put forth three proposals: split the diocese in half, elect an assistant bishop, or set up a system of provincial synods like those in the Canadian diocese of Rupert's Land. The first proposal would require him to give up either the Indian missions in the north or the Faribault schools in the south, neither of which wanted to lose him. The second was rejected as too expensive; the diocese was barely able to support one bishop. A committee was appointed to look into the synod concept, but it was never adopted. Instead, the rural convocations were realigned to reflect changes in population in the rural deans' areas of responsibility.

Minneapolis's Cottage Hospital, mentioned in Whipple's report, had been founded in 1871 by the Brotherhood of Gethsemane Church, a lay service organization formed the previous year. It served patients of every race and creed, and ministers of all denominations were allowed to visit at the bedside of those who asked for them. It had recently moved into a "commodious building" at the corner of Sixth Street and Ninth Avenue in Minneapolis, which Whipple dedicated on April 14, 1874. Like most hospitals of the time, it served primarily the poor, who were often so ill when they arrived that more of them died than were cured. As a result, the Brotherhood also established an orphanage to care for their children.[346]

On June 12, 1874, following the diocesan convention, Whipple formally opened St. Luke's Hospital in St. Paul, founded by Christ Church.[347]

Some of the hospitals' nurses were deaconesses trained at schools in Philadelphia or New York. In January 1875, an order was formed in Minneapolis, with Sister Annette Relf as its first member. The women, who lived together in the Bishop Potter Memorial House, worked as nurses in the hospitals and assisted with parish work in local

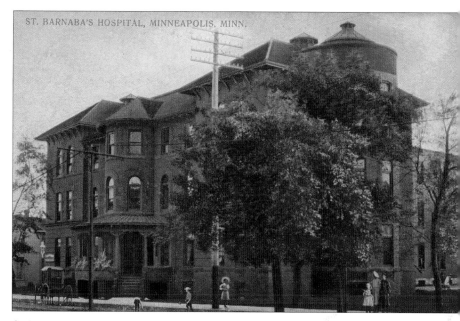

St. Barnabas Hospital in Minneapolis. Founded by Gethsemane parish in 1871, it was first known as Cottage Hospital and staffed in part by deaconesses trained at the Bishop Potter House in Philadelphia. Gethsemane subsequently founded its own house for training deaconesses, also called the Bishop Potter House. When this building was constructed in 1881, the hospital was renamed St. Barnabas.

Hospital established in 1873 by Joseph Gilfillan at the White Earth Mission. Founded with a gift from Ellen Watkinson, it was seldom used by the Ojibwe, who preferred being treated at home. It closed in 1895.

churches. Whipple approved of the concept and enjoyed formally commissioning the women. "Any plan which enables holy women to consecrate their lives unto Christ in His work will bring its own reward." Pointing to the order's historical origin in apostolic times, he added, "No plan for the work of such Christian women commends itself as does that Divine plan which the apostles established."[348]

A third hospital was established in 1873 on the White Earth Reservation by a generous gift from Ellen Watkinson of Hartford, Connecticut. Sister Maria Selby, one of the eastern-trained deaconesses, ran it. It was not a great success. The Indians were leery of the white man's medicine and generally preferred to remain at home when they were ill. If they did come to the hospital, they wanted their families around them, and often either did not take the unfamiliar medications they were given or supplemented them with tribal remedies. Friction between Gilfillan and the hospital staff also hampered its mission.[349]

On Sunday, August 2, 1874, as Whipple was attending services in the Faribault cathedral, a young man rose from his seat in the rear and walked purposefully up the aisle, brandishing a pistol. He pointed it at the bishop. Noticing that the pistol was not cocked, Whipple leaped over the altar rail and grabbed the youth by the elbow. The other clergy present came forward and seized the weapon. As the young man was led away, the bishop announced calmly that the danger was now over and instructed the organist to resume playing. The would-be assassin, George L. Nims, was described as "an intense student" at Seabury, so unbalanced that he had been told he could not be admitted to the ministry. Apparently blaming Whipple for preventing his ordination, he had been acting strangely for several days, wandering in the streets and mumbling to himself. Nims was committed to the insane asylum at St. Peter the following morning.[350]

The next week, Whipple headed for Minnesota's north shore to go fishing. Fishing was one of his life-long joys, and he acquired quite a reputation as an angler. Enmegahbowh claimed that the bishop had caught the largest fish ever seen in Minnesota: "I know this, for I saw it with my own eyes." On his first trip to Duluth in 1870, Whipple had brought back seven hundred trout from what he later described as an angler's paradise: "I have caught salmon in Scotland, bluefish off Nantucket, kingfish in the Gulf, tarpon in Florida, trout in the Yellowstone Park, but for the perfection of the angler's craft, give me the clear sparkling waters of the streams which flow into Lake Superior."[351]

Whipple lost three good friends and fellow bishops during 1874. Bishop Henry Whitehouse of Illinois, whom he had served under as a parish priest in Chicago, died August 20, followed the next month by Bishop Henry Lee of Iowa. Earlier in the year, Bishop William Armitage of Wisconsin had died. Over the past few years, Whipple had met with them annually, along with the bishops of Michigan and Indiana, to discuss issues common to their dioceses, which were no longer frontier establishments but not as deeply rooted as those in the East.

In the spring of 1874, a group of concerned churchmen, disturbed by the uproar that had occurred at the 1871 General Convention, established the American Church Congress as a national forum for discussion of thorny issues in a setting where no action need be taken. It held its first official meeting in September 1874, just before the opening of the General Convention. Five bishops were in attendance, representing all points of view held within the church. Whipple was asked to preside, as the organizers thought his reputation would lend the meeting prestige. In his opening statement, he was greeted with an ovation "when he asserted that most attendants believed that 'to the loyal, all things are loyal.'"[352]

Robert Machray, Canadian bishop of Rupert's Land, invited Whipple to the region's first annual provincial synod in Winnipeg in August 1875. The bishops of Rupert's Land had been frequent visitors to Minnesota, but this would be Whipple's first visit to their country. He and Machray shared an interest in Ojibwe and Dakota affairs; both tribes had bands in Manitoba and the United States. The diocese of Montreal, not to be outdone, asked Whipple to speak to their synod in October, on his way home from his annual meetings in New York. It was an excellent opportunity to compare the way the two nationalities managed their church administration and to discuss their different ways of dealing with the native communities in their midst.[353]

While Whipple was in St. Augustine during the winter of 1875–1876, he was asked to preach to a group of Indian prisoners at nearby Fort Marion. Considered among their peoples' most violent and intractable warriors, these men were under the supervision of Captain Richard H. Pratt, an army officer with a streak of humanitarian activism in his character. Determined to prove that these so-called savages could be assimilated into mainstream culture, Pratt dressed them in military-style uniforms, helped them build a comfortable wooden barracks, invited female volunteers from St. Augustine to teach them to read and write, and encouraged them to earn money by teaching archery, performing dances for tourists, decorating polished palm seeds, and drawing pictures to sell. The wealthy East Coast tourists who flocked to St. Augustine every winter were delighted at the opportunity to meet real Indians, and Pratt's experiment seemed to be a great success.

Wrote Whipple to President Grant: "I was never more touched than when I entered this school. Here were men who had committed murder upon helpless women and children sitting like docile children at the feet of the women, learning to read." He

TOP RIGHT: Bishop Whipple (on the left), preaching to Indian prisoners with an interpreter's help. Captain R. H. Pratt sits nearby. BOTTOM RIGHT: Trinity Church, St. Augustine, as seen by an Indian prisoner in 1875.

preached to the men frequently during their three years in Florida and gave several books of their drawings to influential people, along with a description of Pratt's work.[354]

By 1876, the men's campus at Faribault covered some fifty acres, with seven good-sized buildings. Shattuck had more than one hundred students, with another twenty-five on a waiting list. Seabury, with around twenty-five students, had just acquired a new oratory. St. Mary's occupied a square block of land in town across from the cathedral and accommodated seventy boarders and forty day scholars.[355]

The work at these schools, hospitals, and missions was supported largely by donations from benefactors large and small. In addition to the Board of Missions and the missionary societies of parishes throughout the diocese, Whipple relied on gifts from individuals, many of them amounting to no more than a dollar. He kept a regular mailing list of people he could approach when a special project arose, and he insisted that each gift be acknowledged by a personal note from him or one of his staff. Groups of churchwomen in the East sold handicrafts and sent their small profits to him. Wealthier people, like George Shattuck, Augusta Shumway, Robert Minturn, banker Junius S. Morgan and his son, J. P. Morgan, endowed larger projects. From time to time, Whipple would receive a sizable bequest from a benefactor's will.

Whipple enjoyed the company of these wealthy, powerful people—the intellectual, moral, political, and religious leaders of his time—not only for what they could do for him but also for their stimulating conversation. There were others whose company he did not seek—Charles Darwin, for example, whose theories seemed to challenge the basis of the bishop's ultra-traditional beliefs. Nor was he interested in the arts (beyond his encouragement of native craftsmen), except as they related to the church. He read Charles Dickens, but never sought him out in London, and he took little interest in America's artistic or literary scene. His primary focus remained man's religious duty to serve others—the poor, the undereducated, those in need of a closer relationship with God.

His missionaries were encouraged to write reports for publication in *The Spirit of Missions* or the diocesan *Minnesota Missionary,* to inform the faithful and keep the donations rolling in, but most of the money raised came from Whipple's own efforts. His warm, earnest personality, his willingness to speak anywhere, anytime, brought a steady stream of income to his diocese. In January 1872, Bishop Clarkson of Nebraska had written him, "You ask me if I am feeling the Hard Times—ah—my dear Brother—*you* can't have any conception how we ordinary Bishops, with few rich friends, and no persuasive tongues, are obliged to [skimp] and struggle."[356] It *was* hard work, as Whipple acknowledged to his friend William Cox Pope in 1900: "I know, better than you can, the heartache in trying to raise money for the Church's work."[357]

In June 1876, the diocese of Iowa asked Whipple to make a round of visitations in their state. They had been without a bishop for two years, and their new bishop, William Perry, would not be consecrated until October. Although he had just barely finished his own visitations in Minnesota, Whipple agreed. He had spent time in Iowa off and on since his sister, Sarah Salisbury, and her husband moved there ten years earlier, and he had occasionally performed confirmation services for the late Bishop Lee when the latter was unavailable.

"It has always been a cause of thankfulness," Whipple wrote in his autobiography in 1899, "that God has given me the ability to put aside the petty annoyances which fret out life. It is worry, not work, that kills men; and the man is happy who can shut out troubles when the day is done, for burdens are not lightened by hugging them to the heart."

INDIAN DEACONS

BETWEEN 1876 AND 1878, Whipple ordained ten young men from the Ojibwe tribe as deacons and assigned them to work under Joseph Gilfillan on the Ojibwe reservations. They founded missions at Red Lake (St. Antipas and St. John's), Wild Rice River (Epiphany), Leech Lake (Good Shepherd), and Cass Lake. The bishop sent all ten to Seabury, ordaining them upon their graduation.

The first four candidates—Samuel Madison, Fred Smith, and Charles and James Jackson—were ordained in 1876. Whipple had personally selected two of them, Smith and Madison, when their white employers told him they were more observant of Christian behavior than most of their white employees. Charles Wright and Enmegahbowh's son, George Johnson, followed in 1877. George B. Morgan, Mark Hart, George Smith, and John Coleman became deacons in 1878. Coleman and the two Smiths were sons of Crow Feather, who had been Hole-in-the-Day's chief warrior until his death in the 1850s. Wright was the son of Chief White Cloud. Madison's father, Shadayens, was a former Mediwiwin leader who had converted to Christianity. Morgan was the son of The Buck, the Mille Lacs chief. Only Mark Hart, an orphan, had no impressive family connections.

Gilfillan assigned his native deacons in pairs to prevent them from resuming their traditional habits.[358] His strategy did not always work, and in 1882, Wright organized a "strike" among his fellow native deacons, complaining of inadequate pay and unequal treatment of two deacons (one an Ojibwe, the other a Canadian mixed blood regarded as "white") who had fathered children out of wedlock.

Although no more clergy were recruited from the reservation until after Gilfillan's departure in 1898, several joined the mission from outside the state. Joseph Wakazoo, an Ottawa, came from Michigan, was made a lay reader in 1882, and ordained deacon in 1886. Louis Manypenny, who had been a Presbyterian minister in Wisconsin, arrived in 1887 and was ordained deacon in 1895. In 1894, Edward Kah-o-sed arrived from Walpole Island in Ontario and was licensed as a lay reader. He graduated from Seabury in 1900, became a deacon, and was ordained priest in 1907.

Samuel Madison

Fred Smith

Charles Wright

George Johnson

George B. Morgan

Mark Hart

George Smith

John Coleman

South Dakota's Black Hills. The government's 1868 treaty with the Lakota stated that any further cessation of land must be agreed to by three-quarters of the male population of the tribe. When the government redrew the reservation's boundaries in 1876 to allow gold mining in the Black Hills, that stipulation was ignored. The Supreme Court ruled in 1980 that the price paid to the Lakota for the land they ceded in 1876 was insufficient and awarded them $106 million for the Black Hills, with an additional $40 million awarded in 1989 for other land taken by the same treaty. The Lakota have not used the money, as many of them feel they should be given back the land instead.

*I*n the spring of 1876, America was once more engaged in a war against the Indians. It began escalating a year earlier, when the government attempted to talk the Teton Lakota of the Dakota Territory into ceding the Black Hills, whose gold was expected to offset some of the financial difficulties of the nation, which was still suffering from the depression caused by the Panic of 1873.

Rumors of gold in the area had been circulating for some time. In 1874, former Civil War general George Armstrong Custer—now a lieutenant colonel of the army's Seventh Cavalry—had led his force into the Black Hills on what was described as a reconnaissance mission. With him went a detachment of thirty Santee Sioux serving as scouts, as well as two veteran prospectors. When the prospectors found gold, Custer announced it to the press, sparking a massive influx of miners into the Black Hills, technically off-limits to white men under the treaty the Lakota had signed in 1868.

But the roots of the conflict went further back, to the wagons that began crossing the plains in 1842, disrupting the migration patterns of buffalo on which the Lakota depended for survival. The Oregon Trail was succeeded by trails made by Mormons en route to Utah. The discovery of gold in California in 1849, Colorado in 1859, and Montana in 1861 resulted in more roads through Lakota territory and further shrinkage of the buffalo herds.

A series of treaties had gradually decreased the amount of land "guaranteed" to the Lakota in return for annuity payments that were supposed to compensate for the loss of access to the buffalo. At Fort Laramie in 1851, the government recognized Lakota sovereignty over an area consisting of half of today's South Dakota, the northeast quarter of Wyoming, and a good third of Nebraska, with small portions of Montana and North Dakota as well. In 1868, it was reduced to that

Lieutenant Colonel George Armstrong Custer, whose announcement of the presence of gold in the Black Hills led to the 1870s Indian War. He was killed on June 25, 1876, with his entire detachment, on the banks of the Little Big Horn River in Montana.

portion of South Dakota west of the Missouri River, though hunting rights were still guaranteed in Nebraska north of the Platte River and Wyoming east of the Powder River. Included within this Great Sioux Reservation were the Black Hills, which the Lakota regarded as holy.

This was not achieved without considerable bloodshed, nor did the 1868 treaty bring peace to the area. Although the Lakota made a serious effort to keep the terms of the treaty, the government did not. Skirmishes continued between small parties of Lakota and white soldiers and settlers. Construction of the Northern Pacific Railroad added to the problem; the Lakota had seen white hunters shoot at buffalo herds from moving trains on the Union Pacific and watched the noise of the "iron horse" drive the herds from their traditional pastures.[359] Things grew worse when Custer announced his discovery of gold in the Black Hills in July 1874.

A commission had tried to treat with the Lakota in the spring of 1875, but the tribes refused to consider selling either the land or its mineral rights. The non-agency Indians (who had not signed the 1868 treaty) gathered around the dissident Lakota leaders Sitting Bull and Crazy Horse, harassing miners and settlers who attempted to cross Lakota hunting grounds in the Powder River region. William Tecumseh Sherman, the army's commander-in-chief, and his subordinate, Philip Sheridan, commander of the Department of the Missouri, which included the Great Sioux Reservation and its surrounding areas, decided that the time had come to end the Sioux "problem" once and for all. The Black Hills issue offered the perfect excuse for confining the Lakota to a small reservation where their actions could be controlled and for opening the rest of the region to white settlement.

In November 1875, special Office of Indian Affairs inspector E. T. Watkins informed Commissioner Edwin Smith that the Lakota living outside the Great Sioux Reservation were well armed and well fed, and presented a threat to the reservation system. Watkins recommended that they be forced to join their relatives on the reservation. Smith concurred and set a January 31 deadline for the roving bands of Crazy Horse and Sitting Bull to relocate.

It was winter, a poor time to move large num-

General Philip Sheridan was in charge of the Department of the Missouri during the Indian wars of the 1870s.

bers of women and children over long distances. The chiefs played for time, but the army was impatient. On March 17, soldiers destroyed a Cheyenne village on the Powder River (mistaking it for the camp of Crazy Horse). The Lakota and their Cheyenne allies responded by launching a full-scale war on the United States.

Whipple had forecast this situation in a letter to the *New York Times* on March 3, 1876, in which he stated that the government had promised the Lakota that their country, including the Black Hills, would not be invaded by whites. Custer's expedition in 1874, which had reported the presence of gold in the Black Hills, "was made in clear violation of a nation's faith. . . . At first we were ashamed to violate our own treaty. The noble men who made that treaty for us honestly tried to keep white men out of the Indians' country. It was impossible. Our only honorable course was to make such amends as we could by purchase. The government did send out a commission, but the plea for economy was made a pretext to tie the hands of the commissioners so that they were powerless. . . . The treaty failed. The evil has been done. . . . We shall have another Indian war."[360]

Red Cloud and Spotted Tail, the two most influential Lakota chiefs, were not actively involved in the fighting. Fearing they would join the hostile faction of Crazy Horse and Sitting Bull, the government sent a commission to confer with Red Cloud and Spotted Tail. The commission was instructed to get the reservation Indians to promise to remain peaceful and to transfer ownership of the Black Hills to the United States. It included such notable figures as former Dakota governor Newton Edmunds, former commissioner of Indian Affairs George Manypenny, Colonel Albert G. Boone (grandson of Daniel Boone), former lieutenant governor of Iowa Henry C. Bulis, Assistant Attorney General Augustine S. Gaylord— and Bishop Henry Whipple.[361]

Following the death of Custer and his men on June 25 in the Battle at Little Big Horn, the administration suspended the law against army officers acting as agents, removing the agents from the Spotted Tail and Red Cloud agencies and turning their duties over to the military commander in the area, Colonel Ranald S. Mackenzie of the Fourth Cavalry. Mackenzie was instructed to suspend issuance of rations at the agencies to any Indians who left the reservation at any time, either to hunt or to fight with Sitting Bull and Crazy Horse.

Bearing in mind the disaster that had occurred three years earlier, when a treaty commission had been fired upon during a council by members of the Modoc tribe in California, Mackenzie suggested that the commission take along a military guard. Whipple, Daniels, and Boone objected, saying that the presence of soldiers would antagonize the Lakota. It appears, however, that they were overruled.[362]

The commission met first with Red Cloud and Spotted Tail, at a point midway between their two agencies. It was not a treaty council. The government had abolished the signing of treaties with Indians in 1871, arguing that the various tribes were not independent nations, but wards of the United States, living within its boundaries.[363]

Manypenny began, reading out the conditions of the agreement as Congress had defined them. Whipple then tried to explain them (through interpreters) in simple language the Lakota would understand. There would be no negotiation, he said. The conditions had been laid down in Washington, and "we cannot alter them even by the scratch of a pen." If the Lakota wanted to continue receiving the supplies previously promised to them, they must do three things: give up title to the Black Hills, permit the building of three roads through the reservation, and agree to receive their rations at a site on the Missouri River.[364]

If they accepted these terms, the Lakota would be provided with ample food in return for labor. Those who showed a willingness to "live by labor" (that is, farm) would be given 160 acres of land per man or household. They must send their children under the age of fourteen to school. Whites would not be allowed to settle on the reservations. Agency employees would be married men living on the reservations with their families, to avoid any temptation they might have toward immoral relations with Indian women. Also, the Indians would be instructed in self-government (white-man style) and provided with an Indian police force.[365]

The commission gave the chiefs a week to discuss the situation. At the end of that time, realizing he had no choice, Red Cloud signed the agreement. Spotted Tail followed suit. The presence of armed soldiers (with artillery in support) and the bribes of whiskey and cash that the signers were offered were secondary to the threat of having all supplies cut off if the paper were not signed. Without the food they received from the agencies, the Lakota

BLACK-HILLS PEACE TREATY 1876.

Members of Red Cloud's Lakota band who signed the 1876 peace treaty ceding the Black Hills to the United States. Red Cloud is on the horse in the rear; the others are (from left) No Water, Hunts Horses, Fast Whirlwind, Iron White Man, Spotted Eagle, and Iron Horse. Given the choice of signing the treaty or not receiving the supplies their people had come to rely on to prevent starvation, Red Cloud, Spotted Tail, and the other reservation Lakota signed the treaty. Whipple was a member of the government's negotiating commission.

knew they would starve.

No attempt was made to abide by the clause in the 1868 treaty providing that any future land sale must be approved by three-fourths of all adult males of the tribe. Ten percent was considered sufficient by an American government still smarting from the loss of Custer and his men at Little Big Horn.

The commission went on to the agencies at Standing Rock, Cheyenne River, Fort Thompson on Crow Creek, Lower Brule, Niobrara, and Yankton, where the chiefs of those bands also signed away their rights to the sacred Black Hills. Numerous warriors at the Cheyenne River Agency had recently been with Sitting Bull, fighting in the region between the Missouri and Powder Rivers. As the council began near the agency buildings, two companies of the Eleventh U.S. Infantry under Lieutenant Colonel E. P. Buell, assigned to protect the agency, stood under arms behind the commissioners. When the commissioners presented their case, angry shouting broke out. Eyewitness Captain E. C. Bowen later recalled that Buell instructed his men to prepare to fire. As the soldiers raised their weapons, Buell called, "Ready—aim," when he was interrupted by Whipple, who rose to his feet and in his best pulpit voice exclaimed, "Don't fire, Colonel! For God's sake, don't fire!"

For several seconds, no one moved. The bishop

stood before the crowd, perfectly calm and composed. Finally, the colonel ordered, "Recover arms!" and the tension eased.[366] Whipple denied that he had been heroic. He insisted that two Lakota chiefs, Four Bears and Rattling Ribs, were the real heroes of the day. Four Bears was the first to agree to the commission's proposal; Rattling Ribs supported him, offering to kill any man who attempted to harm any of the commissioners.

Whipple has been condemned for his work with the commission, but he was to some extent trapped by his own arguments. He had always believed that the Indians had no hope of stemming the tide of EuroAmerican immigration, and that their only option was to get as good a deal for their land as was possible under the circumstances. He had dedicated himself to finding a way to end the blatant exploitation and threats of physical extermination that had previously characterized U.S. Indian policy. In this instance, Congress had decided what must be done, and—as he told the chiefs—he could not alter the paper's conditions. He could only try to minimize the damage by convincing the chiefs that their sole hope of living in peace lay in submitting to the inevitable. It was too late to stop white settlement in the Black Hills, where hundreds of mines were already in operation and towns were springing up to serve the miners. Sherman had made it clear that he intended to end the Lakota threat if he had to kill every last one of them. If the Lakota saw that even the most outspoken of their advocates among the white men believed signing this agreement was in their best interest, perhaps they would accept it.

Not long after the agreement was signed, an army detachment confiscated Red Cloud's pony herd. The commission members were outraged. The following year, when Whipple met with President Grant and members of his Indian Peace Commission in Washington, General Sherman was present. Whipple challenged him on the subject of Red Cloud's ponies, showing him a copy of the dispatch

In March 1876, a letter from Whipple to the *New York Times* foretold the likelihood of war if whites invaded the Lakota's sacred Black Hills.

Sherman had sent to the agent at Standing Rock that "pledged the Indians protection of their property as long as they were peaceful."

The general looked at the paper. "But this does not speak of ponies," he said.

Whipple smiled. "General, you are too old and too good a soldier to have said that."

Sherman acknowledged it. "Bishop, you're right. Lying is lying; we had better call it what it is. It did pledge protection."[367]

Sherman and Whipple often differed on questions relating to Indian policy, but they maintained a high respect for one another. The officer admired the bishop's determination to protect the interests of a people who Sherman believed were like a man "who sits by the ocean's beach, and knowing there is a flood-tide coming, is too lazy to change his seat."[368] The man who once equated war with hell was a realist. He could see that the goals of Whipple and his fellow reformers were, in the end, not so different from his own in their effect on the Indians and their way of life.

The Indian wars led to a sharp division between the people of the West, who were most at risk from Indian attacks, and the East, who were more sympathetic to the arguments of people like Whipple, who blamed the violence on the government's inability to keep the promises it made to the Indians. The rivalry between the Departments of War and Interior for control of the Office of Indian Affairs intensified. As

the army became more insistent on a military solution to the "Indian problem," the Department of the Interior became more determined to find a peaceful one.

By February 1877, the Dakota territorial legislature had organized counties in the Black Hills and was making plans to build the three roads through the Lakota reservations. Gold prospectors were hard at work, now that they could legally establish claim to the land. There had been delays in delivering the foodstuffs promised to the Lakota in the treaties, but the commis-

Spotted Tail, who signed the 1868 and 1876 treaties. As the government debated the location of a reservation for his band, he remarked, "The white man should put wheels on his red brothers so he can move them whenever he wants."

Red Cloud, chief of the Oglala Tetons, led the successful campaign against the U.S. Army that resulted in the Fort Laramie treaty of 1868. In 1876, under threat of starvation for his tribe, he signed the Black Hills treaty.

sioner of Indian Affairs assured Whipple that since the army had allowed his civilian agents to resume control of the delivery process, things would improve.[369]

The Sioux war continued until the fall of 1877, when Crazy Horse was captured and killed. Sitting Bull had fled to Canada the previous spring; Red Cloud and Spotted Tail remained, dispirited, on their reservations, abiding by the terms of the treaties they had signed in 1876.

In September 1877, Whipple again wrote to the newspapers on "The Present Montana Indian War: A Few Official Facts Concerning It." In presenting a defense of the Nez Perce rebellion, he spelled out in detail the treaties that had been made and broken with tribes across the western half of the country. It was a strong indictment of money not paid, unsuitable and inferior quality goods provided, murderers not prosecuted, "permanent" reservations opened to settlement. The capital of the Territory of Idaho had actually been built on the Nez Perce reservation. Was it any wonder the Indians had lost patience with the Americans?[370]

Grant's Peace Policy was publicly branded a failure. The quality of the men serving as Indian agents may have been improved, but graft remained hard to root out. Some church-appointed agents were little more familiar with the ways of their charges than their political-patronage predecessors. The infighting between various religious communities over who was to have what agency and whether the agents were interfering in the missionary efforts of people from rival churches was not especially edifying. Balancing the demands of the military against those of the humanitarians, President Grant laid the groundwork for an end to the war on the plains and for confining the majority of the remaining tribes to reservations, where their behavior could be manipulated through the issuance of supplies. But a great many people died before peace was established, and the pressure upon the Indians to give up their traditional way of life increased.

Whipple was less negative about the Peace Policy's achievements than most. On July 31, 1876, he wrote a letter to Grant, thanking him "for honestly trying to give us a better [Indian] policy. . . . The so-called peace policy . . . has done more for the civilization of the Indians than all which the government had done before. Its only weakness was that the system was not reformed. . . . The peace policy did not fail. It was a success until our faith was broken" through treaties that the United States did not keep. "My own conviction is that the Indian Bureau ought to be an independent Department . . . with one of the best men in the nation at its head." He again compared U.S. policy with that of Canada, where "the Indian treaty calls these men 'the Indian subjects of her Majesty.' . . . They are placed on ample reservations, they receive aid in civilization, they have personal rights of property, they are amenable to its law & protected by laws, they have schools."

Whipple made three further suggestions: "Concentrate the Indian tribes. . . . Whenever an Indian in good faith gives up his wild life & begins to live by labor, give him an honest title by patent of 160 acres of land and make it inalienable. . . . Provide government for every Indian tribe placed upon a reservation. . . . I do believe that a just and humane policy worthy of a great Christian nation will save our poor Indian wards and bring upon us the blessing of God."[371]

When Grant left office in March 1877, the Peace Policy was abandoned, a victim of the protracted warfare in the West and the prolonged bickering among the religious communities involved in its implementation. But, as Whipple had pointed out, a corner had been turned. The relationship between the American government and the native peoples living within its borders had not yet reached an acceptable resolution, but the days of blatant exploitation were over. No one any longer thought that the Indians could simply be removed from the country, although the desire to remove them from its more attractive portions remained.

What would happen next was anybody's guess.

The interdenominational Church of the Good Shepherd in Maitland, Florida, was built in memory of the Whipples' son John in 1883.

*I*n the late 1870s, Minnesota was invaded by locusts that devoured crops across much of the western part of the state. The Indians who were just learning to farm were especially devastated by the repeated destruction of the fruits of their hard labor. On April 26, 1877, Governor John Pillsbury declared a statewide day of prayer and fasting. Businesses closed and churches held solemn services. To the amazement of skeptics, a sudden spring snowstorm descended on the state and by the next morning the locusts were dead. Whipple regarded it as an act of God. Locusts, tornadoes, forest fires—Minnesota had them all, but the bishop remained confident that behind the horror was a God who loved his children. "When we see how these sorrows break through the crust of selfishness, drawing hearts together and knitting again the ties of brotherhood . . . we can see light in the darkness."[372]

Whipple's bronchial condition always seemed worse in winter, and his doctor recommended he spend the season in a milder climate. From 1875 on, he and Cornelia spent nearly every winter in Florida. He was especially fond of the Orange County area around Maitland, where his son John had spent a year on a citrus farm. In the spring of 1878, Whipple bought nine acres of land at the lower end of Maitland, building a house and planting a five-acre orange grove. He passed the time writing letters, fishing, and preaching now and then in nearby churches. A town "with high moral and religious standards, there being no barrooms nor drunken loafers in the place," Maitland was much more agreeable to Whipple than it had been to his fun-loving son.[373]

Whipple's youngest son, John Hall Whipple, was a born charmer, the darling of the family. After graduating from Shattuck, he spent half a year studying law, but the serious, conventional lifestyle followed by the rest of his family was too constraining for him. A schoolmate later recalled John's carefree manner, his fondness for boating and driving, and his eternal "party-party" outlook.[374] Whipple took him fishing, and sent him one year to grow citrus fruit in Florida, another to work on a ranch in Colorado, but John refused to settle down. He developed a taste for drinking and gambling that scandalized his father. In early 1878, not long after his twenty-first birthday, John walked out of the house, leaving behind a note saying, "I want to see the world. I'll get in touch with you later."[375]

John Hall Whipple, the Whipples' youngest son, was murdered in Cincinnati in 1878 at the age of twenty-one. The last year of his rebellious youth was spent drinking and gambling.

His departure left his father deeply depressed.[376] A month later John sent a brief note from Cincinnati; in May, he wired a telegram from Chicago. The bishop caught the next train to Chicago, hoping to persuade John to come home, but returned three days later without success. He was on a fishing trip on the north shore of Lake Superior when the next message arrived, this time from the Louisville police, who had recovered a man's body from the Ohio River on August 5. Letters in the dead man's pocket indicated that he might be one John H. Whipple of Faribault, Minnesota. Charles Whipple hurried to Louisville to identify his brother's body, which had been buried in a pauper's grave.

The newspapers reported that John had been a well-liked fellow with a gentleman's manners and a passion for gambling. He had worked briefly as a bartender in Chicago, moving to Cincinnati sometime in July. He brought a woman to his boarding house whom he introduced as his wife, although someone recognized her as a prostitute named Lillian Porter. When they quarreled, John left her, vanishing some two weeks before his body was found in the river, partially disrobed, with a pistol wound through the right cheek. Charles identified the badly decomposed body and had it packed in ice and shipped to Faribault for burial.[377]

It was unbearable irony, the bishop told Cornelia, that their children should survive infancy and childhood in perfect health, only to have this tragedy descend upon them in maturity. "I would give the world for one word from my boy. . . . My poor boy who when a child was one of the most beautiful beings on earth fell & got into bad company & was murdered. I am left with a great agony. . . . I can leave him to God whose love & mercy is infinite— who knew him as I could not & who knew every temptation & also knows why." Whipple cautioned Charles never to allow his children to touch a single drop of alcohol, lamenting that "the accursed stuff has taken all the light out of my home." The bishop said he drank nothing but communion wine and had never served alcohol on his table.[378]

The loss of his youngest child was the greatest grief Henry Whipple had faced. "I came to this Diocese 19 years ago," he wrote in his diary, "have borne great burdens, calmed everybody's sorrows, gave up my home and . . . out of anguish and gloom can only cry 'my son, my son.'" John's death inspired Whipple to build a chapel in Maitland in his son's memory. It would be open to people of all Christian persuasions, "a fold where the shibboleths which separate the kinsmen of Christ may be forgotten." Construction began in the fall of 1881 on property across the street from his home. The tiny neo-Gothic chapel, with its lovely stained-glass windows, was consecrated by Whipple (with the permission of Florida's Bishop John F. Young) on

John Whipple's grave in Maple Lawn Cemetery in Faribault.

William Hare, missionary bishop of Niobrara from 1873 to 1883 and bishop of South Dakota from 1883 to 1904. Hare supervised the development of a successful mission program among the Lakota. Son of George Hare, dean of the Philadelphia Divinity School, and grandson of the Reverend John Henry Hobart, bishop of New York, Hare was the Board of Missions' long-time secretary of foreign missions. In 1871, his nomination as missionary bishop to Cape Palmas in West Africa was withdrawn when the House of Deputies made a strong plea for his continuation on the Board of Missions. Whipple preached the sermon at Hare's consecration as bishop of Niobrara. Hare's belief that Samuel Hinman was unfit to serve as a minister resulted in a lawsuit that threatened Whipple's philanthropic base from 1881 to 1887.

Samuel Hinman in 1870, while he was still missionary at the Santee Reservation. Hinman had begun to establish an extensive mission program among the Dakota and Lakota with the assistance of native clergy when the church appointed William Hare as missionary bishop to oversee the work. After several years of successful work, he was dismissed in 1878 by Bishop Hare, who accused him of immorality and fiscal irresponsibility but did not deprive him of his status as a priest. After several years of disputes, including a lawsuit brought by Hinman against his bishop in 1881, Hinman was released from Hare's diocese in 1887 and returned to Minnesota to work among the Dakota living at Birch Coulee, near the old Lower Agency site. He died of pneumonia in 1890 and is buried beside St. Cornelia's Church at Birch Coulee.

March 17, 1883.[379] "It has been a great joy to me," Whipple wrote many years later, "that when I have been obliged to leave work dearer than my life, I have had this blessed Church of the Good Shepherd, with the close ties which bind pastor to people." He officiated in the church every winter from 1883 until 1901.

Earlier in 1878, Whipple had another shock when his colleague, Niobrara bishop William Hare, suspended Samuel Hinman from the Santee Mission on charges of immorality and fiscal irresponsibility. Both men were his friends; Whipple had personally nominated Hare in 1874 for the position of missionary

bishop and had supported Hinman as missionary to the Dakota since 1860. Cornelia Whipple regarded Hinman as "her oldest son."[380]

Hinman and Hare had been doomed to clash almost from the start. Under Whipple, and later Bishop Clarkson of Nebraska, Hinman had run his mission pretty much as he wished. Hare's ideas on mission operations, however, did not coincide with Hinman's. Hinman was a High Churchman, Hare an evangelical. Perhaps more significantly, Hinman had built up the mission program in the Dakotas, personally training many of its missionaries, especially the Dakota ones. Many people had expected

Mary Bury Hinman, the missionary's wife, who assisted him in his work. Her death in 1876 set in motion the factors that would lead to her husband's dismissal by Bishop Hare.

Hinman to be chosen as bishop of Niobrara, and Hare assumed Hinman resented being passed over, which undoubtedly colored his relations toward his unruly subordinate.[381]

The charges were based largely on rumors and half-truths. Stories of Hinman's improper relationship with Dakota women had been circulating since 1865, when Whipple convened a committee to investigate them and, finding them untrue, read the results of the investigation publicly to the citizens of Faribault. As Clarkson later remarked, "such rumors" were so common among those who dealt with Indians in the West that one tended to ignore them.[382] After Mary Bury Hinman's death in 1876, the rumors gained strength. As for the charge of fiscal irregularities, this referred to the period in 1870 when the mission funding changed from private donations to the Board of Missions. That had also been investigated, in 1873, when Hinman was again cleared of wrongdoing.[383]

A clerical trial convicted Hinman but declined to suspend him from the ministry. He appealed to the Board of Missions, and when details of his appeal were published, Hare likewise printed a pamphlet giving his side of the story, with graphic details. Hinman countered by suing Hare for libel in New York, where the national Episcopal headquarters was located.[384] The verdict went first to Hare, and then, on appeal, to Hinman. It was 1887 before Hare finally agreed to settle the matter.

The affair not only pained Whipple, as he tried to maintain friendly relations with both men, but also jeopardized his carefully crafted web of financial support, especially in Philadelphia, which had been Hare's home. Elizabeth Biddle, who had supported Minnesota's mission work since 1861, accepted Hare's account as accurate, leading Cornelia to refuse an invitation to dine at her home. "I feel so keenly that you have been wronged," Cornelia wrote Hinman in November 1879.[385]

During this time, Whipple acquired another protégé. Although Andrews Hall had closed in 1862, he liked to bring promising native youngsters to Faribault, enrolling them in Shattuck or St. Mary's. Sherman Coolidge was an Arapaho whose father died in an intertribal war in Wyoming in 1870. Captured by Shoshones, ten-year-old Sherman and his younger brother were given to the American soldiers at Fort Brown and renamed William Sherman and Philip Sheridan. Believing they would be safer with the soldiers, the boys' mother decided to leave them there. Sherman was taken in by Lieutenant and Mrs. Charles Coolidge, who had him baptized with their surname. Thinking to train him as a servant, Mrs. Coolidge sent him to the post school, but when she discovered he had a strong taste for learning, she asked Whipple in early 1877 if the boy could be enrolled at Shattuck.

Young Sherman was quick to adopt the manners and dress of the white community around him, and at Shattuck ranked consistently in the top quarter of his class. When he graduated, Whipple asked him what he planned to do next. Coolidge replied that he wanted to become a missionary. Whipple sent him to Seabury, where again he excelled; his senior thesis was one of the best in his class. During the summer vacation of Coolidge's senior year, one of Whipple's white missions requested a divinity student to serve as lay reader. The only student available was Coolidge. Whipple sent him for one Sunday and was delighted when the congregation asked him to stay for the summer. They also wanted him to return after his graduation as their pastor, but Coolidge had other plans. Ordained to the diaconate in 1884, he went to the Wind River Reservation in Wyoming, where he was reunited with his mother. In 1885, he was ordained to the priesthood by Colorado's Bishop John F. Spalding. Whipple considered Coolidge a fine example of successful assimilation.[386]

Whipple's health continued to worry him. He developed nasal polyps and underwent numerous operations to have them removed, but they always returned, causing him severe pain. At his first operation in April 1874, he spent two hours under ether and the next six days sick in bed. In November 1875, the procedure was repeated. In January 1877, he was given a hypodermic injection to relieve the pain. He consulted doctors in New York, Paris, Philadelphia, New Orleans, and St. Paul, all of whom followed much the same procedure, with much the same results. He always carried an assortment of pills with him; once when his purse was stolen he complained not about the lost money but the twenty or more prescription medicines that had been taken.[387]

Sherman Coolidge, an Arapaho priest whom Whipple educated at Shattuck and Seabury. Given by his mother to soldiers at Fort Brown when he was ten, he was raised by Lieutenant and Mrs. Charles Coolidge. He entered Seabury with the intention of becoming a missionary to his people and was ordained deacon in 1884 and priest in 1885. From 1887 to 1889 he attended Hobart College. In 1902, he married Grace Wetherbee, daughter of a wealthy New York family, who wrote articles about her experiences on the reservation for *Collier's Weekly* and *The Outlook*. Coolidge was one of the founders of the Society of American Indians in 1911.

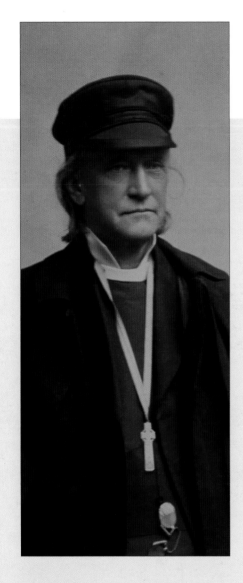

WHIPPLE'S ailments did not prevent him from maintaining a strenuous schedule. His diary for the year 1879 gives a good picture of his life in his fifty-seventh year:

January 1—left home with sister Susan [Hill] and wife; reached Nashville for breakfast; face very painful; Jennie, Nellie and I reached Sewanee at 4, found all well at George Fairbanks home.

January 3—bitter cold day, great suffering, read David Copperfield.

January 6—left for Florida via Nashville and Montgomery.

January 16—pleasant day, busy with article on Indians; Mrs. W. not well.

January 21 to February 24—in Maitland.

March 7—left Cedar Keys 9 a.m., on ocean [fishing], beautiful day.

March 11—left 7 p.m. for Havana.

March 19—left Havana for Key West.

March 29—in St. Augustine, received sad news of death of brother John [Whipple].

March 31—visited grave of [Cornelia's] sister Sarah [Fairbanks].

April 2—started for home via New Orleans.

April 5—unable to go out on account of operation [on] 4th.

April 14—left New Orleans.

April 16—Chicago.

April 17—home.

April 19—committed to the grave my dear son John—Lord remember him.[388] [The next six weeks are taken up with visitations to Minnesota parishes and the class he taught at Seabury every spring.]

June 11—20th anniversary council, full of love.

June 21—preach at White Earth.

June 26—at Red Lake.

July 2—back at White Earth.

July 21–22—family trip to Taylor's Falls [on the St. Croix River].

July 24—to New York. [The next few weeks are filled with fundraising trips to various places in New England, in connection with his visit to the Board of Missions meeting in Connecticut, and a short visit to Philadelphia.]

August 16—home.

August 22—Funeral of Mrs. McMasters [widow of Reverend S. Y. McMasters, rector of Christ Church St. Paul, first registrar of the diocese and one of Whipple's first rural deans].

[September is filled with more parish visitations.]

September 26—conference [in Davenport, Iowa] of bishops of Nebraska, Iowa, Kansas and Minnesota concerning missions and schools.

September 29—left for Chicago, met Mrs. W. there, left for New York.

October 1—Peabody Trustees, 5th Avenue, New York.

October 3—severe operation on nose, sick for a week.

October 10—New Mitford.

October 13—New York; Mrs. W. is in Philadelphia. [There follow several days of speeches in the New York area.]

October 17—to Philadelphia.

October 20—back to New York.

October 29—left for St. Louis [where his brother-in-law was on his deathbed].

November 1—John Wright died age 56.

November 5—buried John Wright beside my John [in Faribault]. [November contains more parish visitations.]

November 26—home.

November 29—my dear wife very ill, typhoid fever.

December 14—Mrs. Whipple came out to dining room—*Laus Deo* [Praise to God, a favorite phrase].

January 27—left for South via Davenport.

It was a schedule that would—and did—wear out many men, but the perennially infirm Whipple just kept on going.

Carlisle Indian School in Pennsylvania. Established by U.S. Army Captain Richard Henry Pratt in an abandoned military post, the school operated from 1879 to 1918. Some twelve thousand Indian children from more than 140 tribes attended the school, where they were instructed in EuroAmerican culture. Bishop Whipple corresponded regularly with Pratt and advised him concerning the school's curriculum.

hen Ulysses Grant's administration ended in 1877, Rutherford B. Hayes brought in an entirely new staff to deal with Indian Affairs. Newly appointed Secretary of the Interior Carl Schurz was much more involved with the day-to-day workings of the government's Indian policy than his predecessors. The German-born liberal opposed the interference of churches in government, but he was unable to make a strong enough case against the way the religious institutions were handling the Indian reservations to justify ending Grant's policy completely.

Schurz's Indian policy, proposed to Congress in December 1880, contained three major points: the Indians must be given rights to land in severalty; they must have protection under the law; and they must be educated so that they could achieve full citizenship. Whipple supported the plan, which included many of the ideas he had advocated for more than a decade. By this time, the bishop's reputation was so great that President Hayes told one of Whipple's friends in July 1877 that he knew him "like a book," even though the two had not yet met.[389]

In his first year in office, Schurz's commissioner of Indian Affairs, Ezra Hayt, replaced thirty-five agents, nearly half his force. Many new appointees were not church-approved, which led to complaints from the churches, if not from Secretary Schurz.[390] Among those who were replaced was Lewis Stowe, the Ojibwe agent at White Earth. Whipple had trouble finding an acceptable replacement. Jared Daniels refused to take the job, having just spent an unhappy year as agent to Red Cloud's band of Lakota at Fort Laramie. Whipple ended up asking Hayt to choose the next agent. Hayt chose Charles Ruffee, the wily old trader whose appointment Whipple had opposed ten years earlier. Hayt also closed the subagencies at Leech Lake and Red Lake, consolidating the agency's operations at White Earth.[391]

Although set in motion by the Grant administration, the bungled transfer in 1877 of the Ponca tribe from their ancestral land on the Missouri River in Nebraska to the Indian Territory (now Oklahoma) caused Schurz's Office of

Secretary of the Interior Carl Schurz overhauled the nation's Indian policies under President Hayes. Born in Germany, Schurz came to America after the government suppressed liberal reformists in 1848. He served in the Union Army in the Civil War, then entered politics. He is best known for his reforms of the U.S. Civil Service.

Indian Affairs considerable embarrassment and led to the formation of several organizations dedicated to securing justice for the American Indian.

The Poncas were a small tribe who had always lived in peace with the white people around them. However, the Poncas and Lakota were long-time enemies, and when the 1876 treaties were signed with the Lakota, the Ponca homeland was inadvertently included in the new Sioux Reservation. It was believed that the smaller tribe would not be safe if they remained where they were. Schurz appealed to Congress, which decided to move them to the Indian Territory. The Poncas were given no warning and no

This Thomas Nast cartoon, titled "Patience until the Indian Is Civilized," appeared in *Harper's Weekly* in 1878. It illustrates the attitude of many white Americans toward Carl Schurz's Indian policy in the years immediately following Custer's death at Little Big Horn.

appeal. The transfer—beset by heat, illness, and tornadoes—took six weeks, and the new reservation proved so unsuitable that within a year of their arrival one-quarter of the tribe had died.

Oddly enough, although the Ponca reservation was under the Episcopal Church's control, Whipple made no effort to intervene. Accepting the judgment of Bishop Hare, Whipple believed moving the Poncas was necessary to protect them from the Lakota. The result was a shock to him. "No one considered what the effect would be of changing these men from a high northern latitude to the Indian Territory," he later wrote.

In January 1879, Ponca chief Standing Bear led a group of his people back to Nebraska, without authorization from his agent, to bury his son. General George Crook, who had been sent to arrest the truant Poncas and take them back to Indian Territory, was so affected by their story that he enlisted the help of Omaha newspaper reporter Thomas Tibbles to publicize their plight. The city's churches petitioned for their release and a case was presented in the district court on their behalf. In *Standing Bear v. Crook,* Judge Elmer S. Dundy ruled that an Indian was a person, as defined by *habeas corpus,* and entitled to certain rights under the U.S. Constitution. The government, he said, had not had the right to remove the Poncas from their homes without their permission.[392]

The outcry over the Ponca case led Helen Hunt Jackson, a writer interested in the inequities of America's Indian policy, to search through government files for other similar episodes. In 1881 she published *A Century of Dishonor,* the first in-depth sympathetic study of America's Indian policies and their effect on Native American peoples. Whipple wrote the book's preface, repeating his assertion that all of the nation's Indian wars had been caused by the government's failure to live up to the promises made in its treaties with the tribes and by its tolerance of fraud among the employees of the Indian Service.[393]

In September 1877, Whipple had written an open letter to the press in which he reviewed the history of the government's relations with the Nez Perce, leading up to the war then in progress in Montana. Once again the government's determination to gather all members of a tribe onto a reservation (recently reduced in size due to the discovery of gold on it) had led to violence. It was easy, Whipple said, to criticize the Indian bureau officials, but they were "powerless unless Congress gives to them the means to do justice. . . . One wearies over the sickening story of the Minnesota massacre, the Modoc, the Sioux, the Cheyenne, the Apache, the Idaho war—and all in less than fifteen years. May God incline the whole nation to deal righteously. We have tried wrongdoing and reaped the harvest of sorrow."[394]

Among those wronged were the Turtle Mountain Ojibwe, a part of the Pembina band who had decided not to join their brothers at White Earth in 1876. About a thousand of them existed, some two-thirds of mixed-blood descent, with close connections to the Canadian Métis community in Manitoba. For years they had made their living off the buffalo trade. Then, as the herds vanished and white settlers began moving in and establishing farms, they began to feel significant economic pressure. They had never signed any treaties with the U.S. government ceding their rights to the Turtle Mountain area in north-central North Dakota.[395]

Despite this, the government had begun assigning homestead tracts on the land in 1870. As early as 1875, Enmegahbowh had informed Whipple about the tribe's situation. In 1882, Whipple wrote to the Indian bureau, citing several sources who affirmed that the tribe had lived on Turtle Mountain for more than twenty-five years—twice as long as the United States had shown any interest in the area. They ought, he said, to be reimbursed for whatever land the government had sold.[396]

A more serious issue arose in Minnesota in 1880, when the government decided to build a se-

Helen Hunt Jackson's *A Century of Dishonor*, published in 1881, brought the Indian question to the public eye. Daughter of a professor at Amherst College, she was educated at the Abbott Institute, where she became a close friend of Emily Dickinson. After the deaths of her first husband and two sons, she turned to writing in 1865. In 1884, she published *Ramona*, a best-selling romantic novel about the plight of California's Mission Indians.

ries of dams on the Upper Mississippi River to control the flow of water downstream. Although the U.S. Army Corps of Engineers had been investigating the issue for nearly three decades, it was the commercial interests in Minneapolis—wishing to maintain a constant flow of water over the Falls of St. Anthony for their mills—that succeeded in getting the proposal through Congress. Its backers suggested that river navigation above the falls would also be enhanced. Work began on a dam at Lake Winnibigoshish early in the year and plans were made for dams at Leech Lake and Lake Pokegama.

As the dam began to block the flow of water from Winnibigoshish, the Ojibwe discovered that the beds of wild rice that provided their chief staple were being drowned. The fish that formed a major part of their diet were no longer accessible in the deeper waters. Cranberry bogs were flooded. Villages on the lakeshore had to move away from the rising water, leaving behind burial grounds and garden plots cultivated for generations. The traditional Ojibwe economic cycle progressed from making maple sugar in the spring through fishing, gardening, and gathering berries during the summer, to harvesting wild rice and cranberries in the fall, supplemented by hunting for game to eat and pelts to trade. The dams threatened their entire way of life.

Missionary Joseph Gilfillan wrote Whipple in July 1886 that the water was so high at Leech Lake that no one could catch any fish, depriving the people of their main source of food for the summer. At Lake Winnibigoshish, things were even worse; though it had been a dry season, the hay meadows, roads, and graveyards were all under water. At Red Lake, fires were set in protest. Gilfillan wondered what would happen if the frustrated Ojibwe broke the dams: would Minneapolis be inundated?

Recognizing that the government's flooding of Ojibwe land might raise legal questions, the secretary of war requested an opinion from Attorney General Charles Devens. Devens ruled that while the right of eminent domain might have been applied, Congress had failed to exercise that power in its act of June 14, 1880, which offered to pay "all injuries occasioned to individuals by the overflow of their lands"—a sum not to exceed $5,000. This language, Devens said, referred only to individual landowners, not to tribally owned property. He suggested that further legislation be passed before the government proceeded with the project.[397]

As soon as he heard of the plan, Whipple began writing to his friends in Congress, opposing the dams. He recalled his awe, during his first visit to Red Lake in 1864, at passing a field of "not less than two hundred and fifty acres of wild rice" that produced as much as thirty bushels to the acre. "The crop seldom fails, and the Indians always leave enough ungathered for seed."[398] Now that resource was being threatened. Writing about his recent trip to Red Lake for the *St. Louis Evening Dispatch* in July 1880, he argued that the Ojibwe should be paid "just compensation" for the damage being done to their rice fields. He pointed out that their annuity, which came to about $5 per person, was hardly enough to survive on. Wild rice, he said, was their "manna."[399]

In March 1881, Congress voted an additional $225,000 for the project, of which not more than 10 percent, or $22,500, would go for damage payments to the Ojibwe. Wrote Whipple to Thomas Simpson of the Department of the Interior: "I fear the government does not appreciate the facts. . . . The Indians will never consent to any settlement which does not recognize their rights." Again he described the damage the dams had done to the Ojibwe economy, asserting that the 10 percent damage settlement voted them by Congress "would not be the damage for one year. . . . If the department wish you to secure the settlement of this damage without recognizing these facts you will fail. . . . The reservoir is a necessity I suppose for navigation and will be a great benefit to the water power at Minneapolis and other places but you can see that these benefits can best be secured by 'doing justly living wisely and fearing God.'"[400]

In August 1881, a three-man commission was appointed to assess the damages done by the dams. The commission recommended an award of $15,466.90, which the Department of the Interior approved. The Ojibwe—especially the Pillager band on Leech Lake—refused to accept it. The government asked Whipple, Henry Rice, and Henry Sibley to try to talk the Ojibwe out of interfering with the construction. A second assessment commission consisting of Sibley, former Minnesota governor William Marshall, and Joseph Gilfillan was formed in December 1882. Sibley was too ill to serve, and it took the commission nearly a year to prepare its report on what Marshall called "sentimental damages." Sibley observed glumly to Whipple that "government officials seem to learn no wisdom from experience."

While the reparations dispute continued, the Corps of Engineers stubbornly went about its business. The Office of Indian Affairs' request in 1883 to have work on the dams halted pending assessment of damages was rejected on the grounds that the public good would suffer. A Corps representative claimed the government had "stated fully, since 1879, the areas of Indian lands liable to damage," and there had been plenty of time since then to settle the question.[401]

Meanwhile, the Ojibwe—led by Pillager chief Flat Mouth—had settled on what they considered a reasonable amount: $250,000, to be paid every six months. This was unacceptable to the government. The Sibley commission recommended a one-time payment of $10,038.18 for property damage, plus an annual award of $26,800 for loss of wild rice, berries, maple trees, hay, and fish. "When we consider that over 46,000 acres were taken from the Indians without any compensation whatever," the report concluded, "it is believed that the estimate is not too high."[402]

Congress, however, declined to make the necessary appropriations and three more years passed. In 1885, Whipple approached President Grover Cleveland personally and got his promise to amend the situation. The following year, as part of yet another effort to concentrate all the Ojibwe at White Earth, the government agreed to pay $150,000 as compensation in full for the damage done by the dams. Congress approved the agreement, but again failed to appropriate the money. The issue was not finally resolved until 1985, more than a century after the first dam was built.[403]

During this time, Whipple's relationship with Enmegahbowh suffered a severe setback. At the request of some of the Ojibwe chiefs, Enmegahbowh

Dam built by the U.S. Corps of Engineers on Lake Pokegama as part of a project to control the flow of the Upper Mississippi River in Minnesota. Construction of the dams drowned thousands of acres of wild rice, disrupted fishing sites, and flooded several Ojibwe villages.

Stone church of St. Columba, built in 1881 at White Earth. It succeeded the 1872 wooden church, affirming the permanence of the church's presence on the reservation.

had gone to Washington in January 1881 to discuss the $84,000 his people believed Congress had neglected to include in its annuity appropriations over the past thirty years. Apparently whenever a new treaty was signed, Congress based the tribe's annuity payments on the amount agreed upon in that treaty, conveniently overlooking any other commitments it had made in earlier treaties involving land cessions. At some point, someone noticed the error and pointed it out to the Ojibwe, who now wanted their "back dues" paid.

Whipple, who was ill that winter, was in Florida recuperating, so Enmegahbowh was left to make the representations on his own. He was unsuccessful. Everyone shook his hand politely but told him he had come too late for Congress to do anything during the current session, which was nearing its end. The secretary of interior and the commissioner of Indian Af-

fairs both assured him that they would see that the arrears were voted "without fail," and he went home convinced that he had done all he could. While he was in Washington, he had been invited to speak at several churches, but had told them he could not raise money without permission from his bishop.[404]

On his return to White Earth, Enmegahbowh saw a letter from Whipple that seemed to speak disparagingly of him, implying that he was not as capable of dealing with the government as a white man would have been. He was highly offended.[405] For several years afterward, his once long and chatty letters describing Ojibwe political maneuverings and views of government policy became few and far between. Only after Joseph Gilfillan left Minnesota in 1898 did Enmegahbowh's letters to his bishop reflect again the warmth of a longstanding friendship.

In July 1881, after laying the cornerstone for a

stone church at St. Columba, Whipple ordained Clement Beaulieu Jr. to the priesthood. The Ojibwe deacons took part in the service, and Whipple noted that it was the "first time Indians joined in ordaining a white man."[406] The son of the influential trader Clement H. Beaulieu, the new priest was part-Ojibwe and the only man from the reservation whom Joseph Gilfillan had recommended for advancement.[407]

Enmegahbowh sympathized with the Ojibwe deacons' complaints about low salaries when they went on strike in November 1882. Gilfillan insisted they needed no more than their current dollar per day, plus their government annuities, to live on. He objected to Deacon John Coleman's working at a store in Cass Lake, which he thought demeaning; Coleman complained that his stipend was too low. (Enmegahbowh had tried several times to recruit young men from his native Quebec Province for mission work in Minnesota, but most of them refused to work for such low salaries.)

The Ojibwe deacons were also irritated by Gilfillan's severe treatment of Coleman for fathering a child out of wedlock—Coleman was suspended briefly and required to make a public confession and promise to pay for the child's support—as opposed to his leniency when Edwin Benedict, a mixed-blood

Reverend Clement Beaulieu Jr. (right) at White Earth in 1910. Son of the prominent mixed-blood trader of the same name, Beaulieu was ordained an Episcopal priest in 1881. After a short stint at a church in Austin, Minnesota, Beaulieu returned to the White Earth Reservation as a teacher. He was priest-in-charge at Le Sueur in 1920.

priest from Quebec whom Gilfillan considered a white man, was accused of the same crime. (Gilfillan accepted Benedict's denial of the charges without question. Later, however, when Benedict admitted the charges were true, an outraged Gilfillan insisted on having him tried in a clerical court and dismissed from the priesthood.)

On Gilfillan's advice, Whipple declined to intervene in the dispute. Gilfillan suspended the strikers' stipends, and after four months they returned to work.[408]

Despite these differences with church leadership, the Ojibwe clergy played a major role in keeping tempers in check throughout the dispute with the government over the dams. Whipple believed "the missions . . . have undoubtedly saved the country from an Indian war on account of the Government dam."[409] But they could not understand the bishop's support of the 1886 bill requiring all Ojibwe to move to White Earth and accept allotments of eighty acres each (forty for minors) to qualify, in time, for full citizenship. To Whipple, the bill would further Ojibwe assimilation, which he believed was necessary to their survival. To the Ojibwe, it was just another land grab. According to Gilfillan, Enmegahbowh called on his congregation "to throw overboard all white people connected with the mission (including yourself, though no names were given)."[410] The antagonism to this bill among his native clergy was so strong that Whipple cancelled his annual visitation to them that year.

He did, however, go to White Earth as a member of an official commission to treat with the Ojibwe on the proposal. After much discussion, three-quarters of the Mississippi bands—the Cass Lake, Winnibigoshish, and White Oak bands, with nearly two-thirds of the Leech Lake band—signed the agreement. The chiefs seem to have felt it was important not to jeopardize their alliance with Whipple with the dam issue still pending and lumber interests hovering on the sidelines, looking for any opportunity to get their hands on Ojibwe timber.[411]

Despite the uproar the 1886 bill caused, Congress did not pass it, and the issue was set aside until the passage of the Dawes Act the following year.

The 1886 Indian Commission appointed by Congress to discuss with the Ojibwe a new bill requiring them all to move to White Earth and accept allotments. Whipple is in the center. The bill was superceded the following year by the Dawes Act.

In 1883, Albert K. Smiley, a Quaker educator and philanthropist who had served on the Board of Indian Commissioners for the past four years, called a conference at his Mountain House resort on Lake Mohonk in upstate New York of all those interested in the welfare of the Indian. All the major Indian rights groups sent representatives, and various proposals for improving the welfare of Indians were discussed at length. Most of the religious groups with missions on the reservations sent delegates, but no Indians were invited. Assimilation, by means of the allotment of reservation land to individual Indians, was accepted as an article of faith; the reformers differed only as to how this goal might be best achieved. The delegates decided to make the conference an annual affair, and for the next three decades the Lake Mohonk Conferences wielded a powerful influence over America's Indian policy. Whipple attended frequently, addressing the meetings on several occasions.

One of the most popular themes among reformers in the 1880s was the use of education to transform Indians into mainstream Americans. From the earliest days, missionaries had taught EuroAmerican culture in their schools, and most treaties included promises of government schools to teach the Indians farming, housewifery, and allied trades. Now a new element was added: boarding schools, where young Native Americans were physically removed from their families' influence and forced to learn the ways of the white man.

The most famous of these schools was the one Richard Pratt opened at Carlisle, Pennsylvania, in October 1879. Whipple had corresponded with Pratt regularly since their meeting in Florida in 1875, and he was happy to advise the younger man on methods of running a school. Both men believed assimilation was the Indian's only hope. "The Indian must perish as a wild man," Whipple claimed.[412] The education reformers used his words as a guide. In 1881, one of them said, "Of all education, we think Bishop Whipple's words are as true as of Christian educa-

Mountain House resort at Lake Mohonk. Owned by the reformer Albert Smiley, this resort hotel was the site of the annual Lake Mohonk conferences on Indian policy. Whipple attended many of the conferences and addressed them frequently.

Richard Pratt with Indian children from New Mexico, who had just arrived at his Carlisle Industrial Training School. Pratt's goal was the total assimilation of the children committed to his care. They had to cut their hair, dress in EuroAmerican clothing, speak English, and sing only in American-style harmony, mostly hymns. They were educated in trade skills as well as academics, and after graduation went back to their reservations as advocates for their new lifestyle. Their new skills were often unsuitable for reservation life, however. No longer comfortable in Indian society, many of them became depressed and disoriented.

tion; 'With justice, personal rights, and the protection of law, the Gospel will do for our red brothers what it has done for other races: give to them homes, manhood, and freedom.'"[413]

Shattuck Hall.

Seabury Divinity School.

Bishop Whipple

Shumway Memorial Chapel

Cathedral Faribault

This collage of the schools at Faribault, published in *Harper's Weekly* on June 23, 1888, shows the two men's schools and the cathedral as they appeared at that time. Clockwise from upper right: Seabury Divinity School, the Cathedral of Our Merciful Saviour, Phelps Cottage (where the Seabury library was kept), Whipple Hall, the rector's residence, Shumway Memorial Chapel, and Shattuck Hall; only St. Mary's Hall is missing. Seabury combined with Western Theological School in 1933 and moved to Evanston, Illinois, where Seabury-Western Theological Seminary now occupies a prominent position on the Northwestern University campus. Shattuck abandoned its military program in 1974 and in 1985 combined with St. Mary's into a single coeducational institution for grades six through twelve, known as Shattuck-St. Mary's School.

ndian affairs were not Bishop Whipple's only concern during the 1880s. He stopped in Davenport, Iowa, in January 1880 for four days on his way to Florida to meet with the bishops of the states bordering Minnesota, where they formed an association to take charge of church land in the central states. Returning to Minnesota in April, he was pleased to find that among the nineteen confirmation candidates at Wabasha on April 19, twelve were Dakotas who had been prepared by the Dakota deacon, George St. Clair, whom Whipple had ordained the previous year.[414]

After the diocesan convention in June, Whipple consulted a doctor in St. Paul for nasal polyps, and, following another painful operation, he and Cornelia went to Kenosha, Wisconsin, to take a "water cure." He visited White Earth, Leech Lake, and Red Lake in July and spent a few days fishing on Lake Superior before returning home. In October, he attended the General Convention in New York, where a committee was appointed to recommend revisions to the *Book of Common Prayer*.[415] Whipple's triennial report to the convention for 1880 indicated Minnesota had 63 priests, 113 deacons, 33 licensed lay readers, and 4,836 communicants in 59 parishes, 21 organized missions, and 50 unorganized missions, worshiping in 95 houses of worship, 90 of which were free. The diocese now supported three hospitals and three schools.

In November, old Bashaw, the black thoroughbred who had served Whipple so well for so many years, died at the age of twenty-nine. The old horse had been sent to winter on a friend's farm. One day, some colts who shared his pasture began racing. Old Bashaw eagerly joined in, outran the youngsters, then dropped dead on the field. Whipple wept when he heard the news, and a brief notice appeared in the *Faribault Republican* the following week to mark the passing of the famous horse.

In February 1881 Whipple attended a special Peabody Fund meeting in Washington to discuss funding issues for the teacher training school the fund had established in Nashville. Tennessee had reluctantly approved the school's foundation in 1875, but provided no funding until 1880, when the Peabody Fund threatened to move it to Georgia. Now that the Tennessee legislature had promised to match the Peabody Fund's annual subsidy of $6,000 for the school, the fund could move ahead with its plans.[416] On his way back to Maitland, Whipple stopped in Atlanta, where he preached to black and white congregations. He returned to Minnesota in April, making his annual round of parish visitations before the diocesan convention convened in Stillwater in June.

On July 2, 1881, the nation was shocked when a disgruntled office-seeker shot President James A. Garfield in a railway station in Washington, D.C. The president lingered in agony for several months before dying on September 19 of infection and internal hemorrhaging. Whipple gave the memorial address at Garfield's burial service in Cleveland nine days later.

The new St. Mary's Hall (above), built in 1883 near the men's schools on the bluff across the river from Faribault, had space for one hundred students. Tuition, including French and German, was $300 a year, extra for painting and music lessons. The building had all the most up-to-date amenities, including steam heat and gas lighting.

The 1883 St. Mary's building burned down in 1924. It was later rebuilt in a much less flamboyant style that blended better with the other structures on campus. Today's St. Mary's Hall houses the middle school program of Shattuck-St. Mary's School.

Whipple was ill off and on through much of 1881. He went to Florida as usual in December and celebrated his sixtieth birthday at Maitland on February 15, 1882. Not even the moist, warm air

of Maitland could keep him from suffering repeated bouts of bronchitis, however, and he was too ill to attend a meeting in New York in March. Cornelia was ill several times that winter, too. When they returned north in April 1882, the bishop had to curtail his visitation schedule until his health improved.

After the diocesan convention in St. Paul in June, Whipple returned to Faribault to lay the cornerstone for a new St. Mary's Hall. Having outgrown the space adjacent to the Whipple home, the school was ready to expand into new quarters on the bluff overlooking the Straight River, near the men's schools. Completed in 1883, the $80,000 building was equipped with modern amenities, including steam heat and gas lighting. The school had its own museum and library, classrooms, offices, and thirty-six dormitory rooms.[417]

On June 23, Whipple left for Ojibwe country, where he met with the chiefs, listened to their accounts of how the government's new dams were destroying their livelihood, and assured them he was doing everything he could on their behalf. Feeling better, he managed to make a number of visitations in August. In October, during his annual trip east, he gave a speech at Cornell University. After attending the Peabody Fund dinner and the Board of Missions meeting, he went to Washington to lobby for the Ojibwe dam compensation claims.

The winter of 1882–1883 was exceptionally cold and stormy. Whipple held a meeting of the southern convocation at Faribault in January, then visited his sister and her family in Blairstown, Iowa. At the end of the month, he received notice of the dedication of the Bishop Whipple School at Moorhead at the meeting of the northwest convocation. The Ojibwe deacons were on strike, Flat Mouth was demanding increased damage payments for the dams, and smallpox had broken out near Leech Lake. It was March before Whipple could get away to Maitland, and he had to be back in Minnesota in April to teach his class at Seabury.

During his few weeks in Florida, Whipple wrote down some of the stories he had learned from his Ojibwe friends for the Northern Pacific Railroad's tourist guidebook. From his earliest days in Minnesota, Whipple had collected Indian tales and artifacts. He liked to share them with the public, to show native culture in a positive light. In 1862, shortly before the Dakota War, he had asked agent Thomas Galbraith for examples of Dakota handicrafts to send to the London International Exhibition, and he prepared an exhibit of "Indian curiosities and clothing" for the Paris Exhibition of 1867. In 1876, he sent materials to the Office of Indian Affairs for its exhibit at the Philadelphia Centennial Exhibition to help illustrate the history of efforts to "civilize" Native Americans.[418]

At the October 1883 General Convention in Cleveland, Whipple was asked to serve on a commission with Bishops William McLaren of Illinois

Whipple Hall at Concordia College in Moorhead, Minnesota. This building originally housed the Bishop Whipple School, founded in 1883 by Reverend Thomas Dickey. An outbreak of scarlet fever in 1889 caused the school to close, and it never recovered. The property was sold in 1890 to the Northwest Lutheran College Association, which reopened it in 1891 as Concordia College.

and Thomas Dudley of Kentucky to investigate the work of the church's mission in Mexico. Bishop Henry C. Riley, the man in charge of the Mexican mission, had come into conflict with the Board of Missions. The details of the dispute are rather vague. Riley had begun his work in Mexico while still a priest in 1868, when he purchased part of the great San Francisco church from the aggressively anticlerical government of Benito Juarez and started holding Anglican services there. The House of Bishops had appointed Riley missionary bishop of Mexico in 1875.

In 1880, Riley had gone to Spain and Portugal, at the behest of Archbishop of Canterbury Archibald Tait, to organize Anglican churches there. Once the churches were formed, they were placed under the supervision of Lord William Plunkett, Anglican bishop of Meath in Ireland, and Riley returned to Mexico. His efforts to establish a national Anglican church ran up against a resurgence of Roman Catholic activity under the dictator Porfirio Diaz, who ruled Mexico from 1876 to 1910.

Mexico's political situation led Whipple and his colleagues to conclude that "it was not advisable to visit Mexico" to investigate Riley's activities. As Whipple wrote Riley in 1884, "Circumstances have arisen which seem to make it necessary to hold in abeyance the present plan of establishing a National Church in Mexico, and to carry on the work as a mission of our own Church. The expectations of yourself and the Mexican Commission as to the adoption of a liturgy and order for the administration of sacraments have not been fulfilled. Grave dangers threaten the work—dangers which touch upon all which we hold dear." Contending the church's honor was at stake, Whipple asked Riley to resign. The Board of Missions then sent a priest, Henry Forrester, to take charge of the mission. The church leadership, embarrassed, considered the episode a "fiasco," but Whipple, the great peacemaker, was credited with having brought it to a satisfactory close.[419]

Whipple was not able to take much pleasure in his success, having suffered too many personal losses during the interim. Harry Scandrett, his daughter Jennie's husband, died of tuberculosis in September 1883; in February 1884, his infant granddaughter Mary Pell Rose died, followed in May by her mother, his beloved daughter Nellie. His longtime friend and fellow bishop Robert Clarkson died in March. A few months later, his close friend and benefactress Augusta Shumway Huntington was thrown from her carriage and killed while on a trip to Colorado.

Not even the gala celebration held in Faribault in June to mark his twenty-fifth anniversary as bishop could raise Whipple's spirits for long. Once again he asked the diocesan council for an assistant bishop, citing his poor health and the continuing growth of the state's population, which demanded ever-greater efforts to provide enough churches. This time the council agreed and a committee was appointed to work out the details.

The loss of a son-in-law, a granddaughter, a daughter, and two dear friends in little more than six months distressed the whole Whipple family. So much sorrow demanded a counterbalance, and one was offered by the invitation Whipple received to attend the centennial celebration of the consecration of Bishop Samuel Seabury, held in Edinburgh in October 1884.[420] Whipple took his wife and his sister, Susan Hill, with him to Europe, sailing from New York on September 20.

It was a delightful trip, a chance to share with Cornelia the sights and dear friends he had made on his two previous visits to Great Britain and the Continent. The party spent a few days with the Cairds in Scotland during the Seabury centennial celebration. The American church's presiding bishop, John Williams of Connecticut, was also present for the occasion. Whipple spoke to audiences in Carlisle, Glasgow, Aberdeen, and Dundee. Lord Hugh Cairns, the former lord chancellor of England, invited the Whipple party for a week at his country home near Leith, where they were entertained one evening at a baronial dinner given for the tenants on the estate.

In mid-October the party headed south into England, stopping in York, Oakham, and Lincoln, and then went on to London. A great meeting in honor of the centennial was held in Victoria Hall on November 14, attended by several thousand persons. Addresses were made by the bishops of Aberdeen, Winchester, Albany—and Minnesota. The following Sunday, at the request of the American House of Bishops, a special service marking the centennial was held at St. Paul's Cathedral, with the bishops of Iowa, Minnesota, and Connecticut in attendance. The archbishop of Canterbury preached the sermon.

The Whipples were entertained by Edward White Benson, the new archbishop of Canterbury, at Lambeth Palace. They visited Oxford and Stratford. Almost every post brought invitations to dinner or tea. The ladies spent several days shopping in London's shops, and Whipple ordered new clerical robes from his favorite tailor.[421]

They continued on to Paris in December 1884, where Dr. Theodore Evans and his wife made them feel at home.[422] Evans arranged for Whipple to see a specialist for his polyps, and the bishop underwent still more operations. He officiated at a service at the American Church of the Holy Trinity, on the south bank of the Seine. The Second Empire had ended after the Franco-Prussian War in 1871 and France was a republic again, with universal suffrage and trade unions; but it was a more conservative republic than before, now run by business and professional men. To the eyes of the American bishop, however there would have been few noticeable changes. Again there was shopping, sightseeing, and entertainment by wealthy American expatriates.

One of the sights Whipple visited in Paris was the McAll Mission, officially the Mission Populaire Evangelique de France. Founded in the early 1870s

Edward Benson was master at Rugby, first master of Wellington College, and bishop of Truro in Wales before being elevated to archbishop of Canterbury in 1882. He was archbishop during the Seabury Centennial as well as the Third Lambeth Conference, both of which Whipple attended.

by American Baptist clergyman Robert Whitaker McAll, it ministered to the Parisian poor. After nearly a century of wars, revolutions, and economic turmoil, the French had lost much of their former faith in the teachings of the Catholic Church. "I spoke to the people in many of the missions," Whipple said, "and they listened as if the Gospel were a new revelation from heaven." Laborers and soldiers packed the nightly services at the mission halls. The police claimed that the crime rate in the vicinity of the missions had dropped off noticeably.[423]

Charles Whipple, the bishop's oldest son, worked for First National Bank and Citizens National Bank in Faribault and as paymaster on the Northern Pacific Railroad. In 1881 he joined the army as paymaster with the rank of major; he retired in 1912 as paymaster general with the rank of brigadier general. His wife, Evelyn McLean, was the grandniece of Nathaniel McLean, government agent to the Dakota when the Traverse des Sioux treaties were signed.

Timothy Sheehan, Ojibwe agent from 1885 to 1889, had to deal with the sensitive issues of the Mississippi dams and illegal logging on reservation land. As a young army lieutenant, Sheehan supervised the defense of Minnesota's Fort Ridgely from attack in 1862 by Little Crow's forces. He was sheriff of Freeborn County from 1871 to 1883 and U.S. deputy marshal in St. Paul from 1890 to 1907. He was wounded during the Bear Island conflict in October 1898.

In January 1885, the Whipples went to Mentone, staying for a month at the Hotel des Anglais while the bishop recovered from his operations. Again he enjoyed warm baths, pleasant carriage drives through the countryside, and the stimulating company of Europe's elite. One day he took the ladies to Monte Carlo to see the casino. During February and March, they toured Italy—Genoa, Pisa, Rome, Venice, Milan—returning to Paris via Switzerland in mid-March. The bishop suffered yet another extended operation on his sinuses, and then continued on to London for some final visits and shopping. Their departure for home was delayed for several days when Cornelia became ill.

At last they reached Faribault on April 30, 1885. Whipple plunged back into work, teaching his Seabury class and spending two months on parish visits before the diocesan convention met in June. After it ended, he went to Iowa, where his sister Sarah had died in March. He visited his former missionary Edward Livermore in Kenosha, Wisconsin, in July, and the two men went fishing together. It was the last time they would spend together, as Livermore died in May 1886.[424]

Whipple made more visitations in August and September, then made his annual trek to New York for the Peabody and Lake Mohonk meetings, this time taking along his twelve-year-old granddaughter, Nellie Scandrett. On the way back, he stopped in Philadelphia and Washington to continue trying to persuade the government to offer the Ojibwe a better rate of compensation for the property destroyed by the dams.

In 1885, Timothy J. Sheehan was appointed agent at the White Earth Reservation. Whipple had

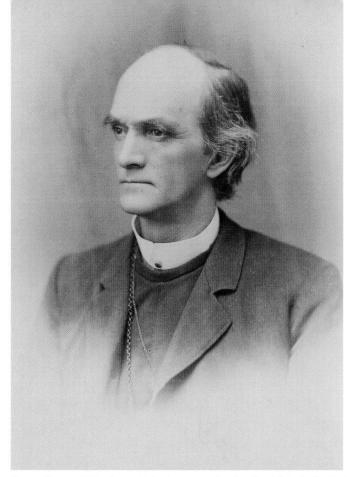

George Brayton Whipple, the bishop's youngest brother. Youthful rebellion led him to sign onto a whaling ship that left him stranded in Hawaii. On his return to America in 1860, he enrolled in Seabury's divinity school and was ordained in 1864. He returned to Hawaii as a missionary with his wife, Mary. Several moves later, he settled in Faribault in 1873 as chaplain and rector as well as the bishop's secretary and business manager for the Seabury Mission.

George Whipple married Mary Joanna Mills, sister of Jane Maria Mills, the wife of James Lloyd Breck. Mary came to Faribault in 1857 to teach at the Seabury Mission's primary school. When she and George were missionaries in Hawaii, they adopted two girls, both of whom died before reaching maturity. After their return to Faribault in 1873, Mary taught from time to time at St. Mary's, filling in once for Sarah Darlington as its associate principal.

first met him in 1862, when Sheehan was a lieutenant in the army and stationed at Fort Ripley. As a Catholic, Sheehan was acceptable to the Catholic Board, but he was also a friend of Whipple, who had recommended him for the post to President Cleveland.[425]

In Faribault, a new generation of young Whipples was playing on the grounds of the bishop's home on Fifth Street across from the cathedral. The four Scandrett children (Nellie, Harry, Ben, and Jeanie) now lived there with their mother and grandparents. His daughter Nellie's widower, Francis Rose, was the family's doctor, and Rose's young son Francis (born in 1881) often came to play with his cousins. Charles Whipple had left Faribault in 1881 to join the army, but he and his wife, Evelyn, brought their three boys (Charles, Henry, and Nathaniel) back often for visits. Whipple's brother George, now chaplain at St. Mary's, and his

wife had adopted two girls in Hawaii, who were also growing up in Faribault. The bishop's widowed sister, Susan Hill, had moved to Faribault in 1878, and often helped her brother with his office work. Her grown son Henry had married Jared Daniels' daughter and made his home in Faribault.[426]

The stress of caring for some 130 religious establishments, advocating for the Ojibwe and other tribes, and keeping his commitments to the Peabody Fund and other organizations was beginning to take its toll on the sixty-four-year-old bishop. His persistent health problems, the deaths of two of his children, and the long legal battle between his friends William Hare and Samuel Hinman added weight to his load. It was thus a great relief when, in June 1886, the diocesan council elected Mahlon Gilbert assistant bishop of Minnesota.

Andrew Good Thunder and his wife, Sarah, returned to Minnesota in 1884, buying land across from Morton, near the old Lower Sioux Agency site. In 1885, they gave the Episcopal Church land for a mission church for those Santees who had settled near them. Sarah Good Thunder (Mockpedaga) was the widow of White Dog, the former head farmer who was hanged after the Dakota War. She married Good Thunder after his previous wife, Snana (Margaret), left him in 1865.

The process for electing an assistant bishop began in 1884, when a committee was appointed to find a means of funding the new position. The question of funding had long been a stumbling block. Whipple reminded the delegates that he would not live forever and suggested that if he had an assistant, he might have more time for fundraising. He especially wanted to secure permanent endowments for the schools, which he described as "our children's inheritance."

When the diocesan council delegates gathered in Duluth in June 1886, the committee presented its report, asking that $15,000 for the support of an assistant bishop be pledged before the convention closed. "This having been made the order of the day," the diocesan historian reported, "the Council went into open session, and the entire amount of $15,000 was soon pledged."[427]

The next order of business was to choose the man for the job. There were two candidates: Mahlon Gilbert and Elisha Thomas.[428] As in Whipple's own election, the votes were close, and it was the laity's preference for Gilbert that carried the day. On the fourth ballot, the Reverend Mahlon Gilbert was finally chosen as assistant bishop of Minnesota. Although Gilbert was not Whipple's choice for the post, once he took office, Whipple was able to work with him exceptionally well. "There never was a Coadjutor Bishop who shared more thoroughly in his Diocesan's confidence, plans and hopes," Whipple wrote. The two men complemented one another perfectly.

This Dakota cap made of cotton, velvet, and glass beads from the Bishop Whipple Collection belonged to Andrew Good Thunder. During the Dakota War in 1862, Good Thunder risked his life to rescue white families. The Minnesota town of Good Thunder is named for him.

Gilbert's history paralleled Whipple's in an uncanny way. Born in upstate New York, he grew up in Rome and attended Zion Church, Whipple's former parish, where his father was a warden and his mother the organist. Like Whipple, Gilbert had been forced to end his education prematurely due to poor health and went to Florida to recover. Educated at Seabury, he was ordained to the diaconate by Whipple in June 1875. After serving five years in a mission church in Montana, he was called to Christ Church in St. Paul in November 1880. Like Whipple, Gilbert was a popular preacher and a competent fundraiser. He was consecrated assistant bishop of Minnesota at St. James Church in Chicago on October 17, 1886, during the General Convention.[429]

Mahlon Gilbert, Whipple's assistant bishop, took much of the load of administering the diocese off the bishop's back and worked himself to death in the process. Raised in Rome, New York, Gilbert attended Zion Church, where Whipple had once been rector. He was educated at Seabury and ordained by Whipple in 1875. After five years in a mission church in Montana, Gilbert was called as rector to Christ Church, St. Paul, in 1880, and elected assistant bishop in 1886.

On their way home from Gilbert's consecration, Whipple and his wife were in a train wreck near Rio, Wisconsin. The express in which they were riding was traveling 45 mph when it ran off the tracks. Coals from the stoves in the sleeper car scattered through the aisle, setting it aflame. Seventeen people were burned to death. The Whipples, whose car had been near the rear of the train, were not injured. Whipple helped those who were trying to free the passengers trapped by the inferno, rescuing two children from Winona. Cornelia, he observed, remained "calm, cool and brave" through the ordeal. The engineer, Thomas Little, was credited with preventing a worse disaster, and the bishop had a gold medal cast, which he presented to Little a month later.

Whipple's new assistant took on the responsibility for diocesan missionary work, leaving oversight of the schools to Whipple, and they divided the parochial visitations more or less equally. Whipple was relieved to be able to leave the day-to-day running of the diocese, to an increasing degree, in his assistant's capable hands. Gilbert was a highly organized man who took charge of his new responsibilities with enthusiasm, although he made sure to consult Whipple regularly. His fundraising skills were a bonus for the chronically cash-strapped diocese. He shared Whipple's knack of winning friends easily, and the younger clergy quickly became devoted to him.

The 1886 diocesan convention was also notable for the increased presence of Native American delegates and clergy. Enmegahbowh, in his mid-sixties, had attended nearly every convention since the 1856 formation of the diocese, but now he was accompanied by seven Ojibwe deacons and several lay delegates from the reservations. One afternoon, as Whipple was presiding over the meeting, he looked up to see his old friend Madwaganonint standing at the door. Aware that the elderly Red Lake chief had traveled more than two hundred miles to be there, Whipple invited him in. Turning to the assembly, he said, "I want to introduce to you the head chief of the Red Lake Indians, our brother in the Church of Christ, whose village is the only one I know in Minnesota where every man, woman and child is a Christian." The delegates rose to their feet in tribute. "Do they expect me to speak to them?" the chief inquired, and when Whipple said they would be pleased if he would, Madwaganonint dropped his blanket from one shoulder and "with all the grace and dignity of a Roman senator" made a brief but affecting speech, thanking them for sending Whipple to his people and asking for their prayers.[430]

Like Whipple, Mahlon Gilbert relied heavily on Joseph Gilfillan's advice in dealing with the Ojibwe. Gilbert had almost no previous experience with

Indian missions when he took office, but with Gilfillan's assistance he soon gained confidence. He visited the White Earth congregation often, especially in the winter months when Whipple was in Florida, performing confirmations and overseeing parish affairs. In 1887, Gilbert ordained Joseph Wakazoo, the Ottawa missionary, as deacon.

Although he detailed the administrative work to Gilbert, the Ojibwe Mission remained Whipple's special interest. He continued to lobby in Washington concerning the government's efforts to move all the outlying bands onto the White Earth reservation, as well as the pressure from lumber interests to gain access to the pine on the Red Lake Reservation and the ongoing struggle over the dams.

In the spring of 1887, Congress passed the Dawes Act, one of the most controversial pieces of Indian legislation ever produced in America. Its supporters, who included most of the white "friends of the Indian," regarded it as the best law ever made in terms of enlightened Indian policy. Named for its presenter, Massachusetts senator Henry Dawes (a long-time supporter of Indian policy reform), it required every Indian in the country to acquire a plot of land on which to live and raise food for his family. To protect the Indians from unscrupulous white land dealers, these allotments were to be nontransferable for a period of twenty-five years.

The act's downside was the provision stipulating that once all the allotments had been made, any reservation land left over would be placed on the open market. This meant that of the 138 million acres held by Indian tribes in 1887, only 48 million (much of it desert or semi-desert) were left by 1934, when the act was superceded.[431]

Minnesota's 1889 Nelson Act established a process for dismantling all Ojibwe reservations except White Earth and Red Lake. On the two remaining reservations, agricultural land was to be allotted and the remainder sold for $1.25 per acre. Pine land would be appraised and sold at auction in forty-acre

Senator Henry Dawes, author of the Dawes Act, which made allotment of reservation lands to individual Indians law. Despite its noble intention of making the Indian an independent land-owning citizen, the Dawes Act resulted in the greatest loss of Indian land in the history of America's Indian policies because of its provision that all "excess" land (reservation land not allotted to individual Indians) would be offered for sale on the open market.

plots. However, the act allowed those Ojibwe who wished to take their allotments where they were presently living to do so, and many of the Leech Lake and Mille Lacs band members in particular did just that. Only 1,898 additional Ojibwe took up land on the two official reservations, despite heavy pressure from their agents, who withheld annuities and offered to pay up to $40,000 in moving costs to encourage them to cooperate with the government's plan.[432]

The Dawes Act was popular with the general public because it promised to reduce the cost of running the Indian program, open large areas of land (particularly in the Indian Territory and the large Sioux Reservation) to settlement, and break up the tribal organization believed to be impeding the Indians' progress toward civilization. The major Indian wars had ended by 1880, agency-sponsored Indian police forces had brought law onto the reservations, and the Dawes

Act seemed to many the logical next step to bring the Indians into mainstream American society.

In May 1887, Whipple presided at Ethelbert Talbot's consecration as missionary bishop of Wyoming and Idaho. Three months later, Whipple went to Winnipeg to attend the synod of the Province of Rupert's Land and join in the consecration of W. C. Pinkham as bishop of Saskatchewan. Then, with his wife and Joseph Gilfillan, Whipple traveled to Alaska with the British bishop of Rochester, Anthony W. Thorold, whom he had entertained at White Earth a few years earlier. Although Thorold was a firm evangelical, he and Whipple were close friends, perhaps because they shared a love for the Indians. Thorold once told Whipple, "The North American Indians have all the dignity of the House of Lords, with the difference that the House of Lords never listen, and the Indians always do."[433]

The party traveled by way of Banff, Glacier, Victoria, Charlotte Sound, Sitka, and Wrangel. Whipple took note of the conditions among the native peoples along the way. America had purchased Alaska from Russia in 1867, but little had been done to develop the area. The land was not yet surveyed, and the only titles recognized were those transferred from the Russian government.[434] This situation was brought to Whipple's attention by the friends of the eccentric English missionary William Duncan.

Duncan ran a rigidly structured utopia of Tsimshian Indians called Metlakahtla. It had a sawmill, a salmon cannery, a newspaper, a police force, a brass band, and a church choir. Its people lived in houses, observed the Sabbath, refrained from drinking alcohol, and paid taxes. But Duncan's Christianity did not conform to Church of England norms, and soon he was in conflict with both church and state, primarily over property rights to the land on which his mission stood. With the encouragement of wealthy American philanthropist Henry S. Wellcome, Duncan moved his flock from Canada to Annette Island in Alaska in 1887.[435]

Whipple was disappointed by the U.S. government's refusal to allow Alaskan natives to claim land under the Dawes Act, which was preventing Duncan's community from acquiring title to the new mission site on Annette Island. He supported Duncan at the 1887 Board of Missions meeting in Philadelphia and was severely criticized by men who disapproved of Duncan's methods. Whipple admitted that he was not personally acquainted with Duncan; his concern was for the Indians at Metlakahtla, whom he felt deserved support as fellow Christians. "When Mr. Duncan goes to his rest," he said, "are these Indians to find a home in an historical Church, or are they to be left a prey to every form of error?"[436]

Returning from Alaska in September 1887, Whipple began urging the House of Bishops to send a missionary bishop to the territory and brought up the subject at every General Convention from 1889 to 1895, when he succeeded at last. In his autobiography, he noted that the election of T. P. Rowe as missionary bishop of Alaska was made possible by the offer of "a generous layman of New York" to pay the new bishop's salary for three years. Did Whipple have a hand in arranging this generous gift? It would certainly have been in character.

In October 1887, Whipple finally managed to secure the services of Samuel Hinman as missionary for the Dakota who were returning to Minnesota. Since his dismissal from the Santee Mission in 1878, Hinman had been in a kind of ecclesiastical limbo, still certified as a priest but unable to practice his calling. Whipple asked William Hare several times to release Hinman to him, in proper canonical fashion with a statement of good standing, but Hare always refused.[437]

Hinman had been assisting Whipple unofficially for some time. In 1883, Good Thunder had returned to Minnesota and purchased eighty acres of land across the river from Morton, near the site of the old Lower Agency. Other members of his band followed, and by 1885 a small settlement of some fifty-four Dakota had become established there. Good Thunder and Sam Johnson led prayer services every Sunday, using Hinman's Dakota prayer book.

In June 1885, Good Thunder wrote to Whipple, "I would like to have a church built on my place. My wife and I are old . . . and we would like to be buried there when we die." If he donated the land, he asked, could Whipple raise the money to build the church?[438] Of course Whipple could raise the money. With Hinman's assistance, he applied to the government for funds to purchase additional land for the settlement, now known as Birch Coulee. Congress approved the appropriation, and over the next five years enough land was purchased to provide for the community, as others arrived from the Flandreau, Santee, and Faribault settlements. Hinman supervised the construction of a mission church and school, brought his family to Birch Coulee, and set to work as a teacher (since Hare had not yet released him to serve as a priest).[439]

Over the next several years, other small communities of Dakota had grown up at Prior Lake, Prairie Island, Hastings, and Mendota. None of them was as well organized as Good Thunder's Birch Coulee band. Few in number and terribly poor, they were generally tolerated by a white community that no

The Birch Coulee Mission near Morton, Minnesota, ca. 1890, built on land donated by Good Thunder. Samuel Hinman served the Santees who returned to Minnesota in the 1880s at this site from 1887 until his death in 1890.

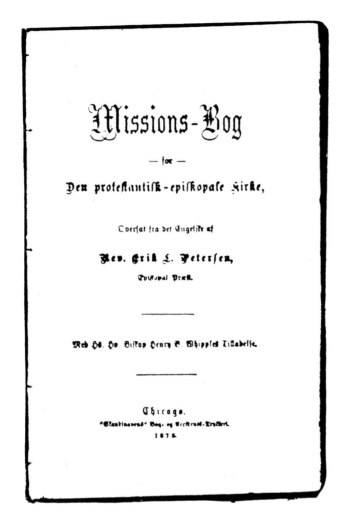

Norwegian-language *Book of Common Prayer,* translated by Eric Petersen, an Episcopal priest who served the Scandinavian community in Faribault. He suffered from depression and several physical ailments, and committed suicide in 1887.

longer regarded them as a threat.[440] Because Minnesota's Dakota lived on land they had purchased and not land reserved by treaty, they were not as affected by the Dawes Act as the Ojibwe were.

From 1884 to 1888, Whipple worked with Henry Sibley and others sympathetic to Minnesota's Dakota communities to persuade Congress to provide the communities with federal aid. Funds were appropriated in 1884, 1886, and 1888 to purchase land, farm equipment, and housing for them. Whipple wanted to concentrate the Dakota on a reservation at the Birch Coulee settlement, which was the

most prosperous, but only the Faribault community agreed to move there.[441]

As Whipple's assistant, Mahlon Gilbert's real expertise and primary responsibility lay with the state's steadily growing white communities. It was a big job. The development of iron mining in northern Minnesota spurred immigration to that region, as did the extension of the lumber industry into its vast white pine forests. By 1888 Gilbert was starting to feel the strain. At that year's diocesan convention, he proposed the council appoint a general missionary, with the rank of archdeacon, to coordinate mission work in the small towns and railheads in the northern part of the state. The delegates agreed, and T. H. M. V. Appleby, a missionary in the Red River Valley, was given the job.[442]

Gilbert's greatest achievement as assistant bishop, which pleased his superior the most, was the Swedish Mission. Minnesota's population had reached 780,773 by 1880; of the 267,676 Minnesotans who were foreign-born, nearly half were Scandinavian.[443] With his experiences in Chicago in the mid-1850s in mind, Whipple was eager to reach out to this large Scandinavian population. In the early days of the St. Paul Mission, James Breck had held services in Swedish, relying on a layman named Sorenson as interpreter. When Breck left to set up the Ojibwe Mission, those services lapsed. Later, Whipple hoped Joseph E. Lindholm, who graduated from Seabury in 1867, would take up work among the Swedes, but he did not.

Whipple kept the project in mind, however. Scandinavians were "a brave, virtuous, freedom-loving and law-abiding people," he told his diocesan council in 1874. "They have comparatively few attachments to the Episcopal government of their national churches, and are liable to be divided into sects, and this may lead to unbelief."[444] But the means eluded him. "Often and often I have tried to devise plans whereby these children of a sister church might become fellow-heirs with us. . . . At one time we had a

Norwegian clergyman of rare talents and a marvelous gift of oratory, who translated the Prayer Book into Norwegian; but his services left no permanent result."[445] This Norwegian clergyman, the Reverend Eric Peterson, was a former Roman Catholic received into the Episcopal Church in 1874. He held services in Norwegian for several years at the old mission chapel in Faribault. Whipple sometimes preached at the services, with Peterson translating. But after several years of attempting to organize missions in other towns in the area, Peterson observed that "the Scandinavians cling to the ancient Lutheran Service, and any alteration in that respect is useless."[446]

Under Mahlon Gilbert's direction, the Scandinavian outreach began at last to bear fruit. In 1891 another Seabury student, John Johnson, translated the *Book of Common Prayer* into Swedish. This translation was used by the Reverend Alfred Pinkham for services at his mission church in Litchfield. At the same time, an independent Swedish Lutheran congregation in Litchfield, Minnesota, led by the Reverend Olaf Tofteen, severed its connection with the Lutheran Augustana Synod and applied for affiliation with the Episcopal Church.[447] When Gilbert heard of this, he invited Tofteen to work among the Swedish people of Minneapolis. Under the leadership of Tofteen (who had been trained and ordained in the Episcopal diocese of Quincy, Illinois), the Swedish outreach finally took root. By the end of the century, Minneapolis and St. Paul boasted four Swedish Episcopal churches, and additional congregations had been organized in northern Minnesota and North Dakota.[448]

Although Gilbert's assistance lightened Whipple's workload considerably, the bishop was still extremely busy. By the mid-1880s, he was becoming an elder statesman. He still performed confirmations and other religious observances in his diocese. He continued to teach his class at Seabury every spring and attend graduations at all three schools as often

as he could. He took a strong interest in events on the Ojibwe reservation and at the new Dakota settlement at Birch Coulee. But his focus was shifting toward activities outside Minnesota, where he was in great demand both as a preacher and as a respected representative of his church.

Napoleon Wabasha, son of Wabasha, served as lay reader at the Birch Coulee Mission in its early years.

Lambeth Palace, official residence of the archbishops of Canterbury. Every ten years since 1867, a gathering of bishops from all Anglican churches around the world has been held here to discuss matters of mutual concern. Whipple attended in 1888 and 1897.

Whipple had been too busy distributing money and goods to the Sisseton and Wahpeton Dakota and developing the schools at Faribault to attend the first Lambeth Conference in 1867. The gathering of representatives from all the churches of the Anglican Communion was held at Lambeth Palace, home of the archbishop of Canterbury.[449] Archbishop Charles Longley invited bishops from Anglican churches around the world to England to discuss matters of common concern. He made it clear that attending the conference did not imply accepting superiority of Canterbury over other national churches, and that any decisions made would not be binding. It would simply be a family gathering of churches that followed the traditions of the English Church.

Over the years, several churches had been established around the world that used the 1662 *Book of Common Prayer* as their guide and followed the practices of the English Church. Many of them in their early years elected English clergymen as bishops, and for a time the majority of their clergy had come from English-speaking countries. While they all subscribed to Anglican doctrines, each daughter church had independently developed her own traditions.

Whipple's reply to Archbishop Longley's invitation expressed his approval of the movement toward unity: "We should no longer exhibit the painful spectacle of the same Church holding rival jurisdictions in heathen countries." He proposed that any changes in ritual be made "by authority, and that we do not symbolize doctrines which the Church does not teach." Recognizing that "the great deep of Society seems broken up by the efforts of the masses who seek enfranchisement and freedom," he argued that the church must win hearts by example and "brotherly love."[450]

When the second conference was held in 1878, Whipple was again too busy to attend, but when a third was called in 1888, he accepted the invitation. America's presiding bishop, John Williams of Connecticut, who was unable to attend the conference, suggested to incumbent archbishop Edward White Benson that Whipple, as the American church's senior bishop present, be asked to preach the opening sermon on July 3.

Whipple laid the cornerstone of Johnston Hall at Seabury on May 15, 1888, officiated at the wedding of its donor Augusta Shumway Huntington's daughter Clarina on the following day, then sailed for England with Cornelia and their granddaughter Nellie Farnum.

The Whipples spent a week in London, where the bishop attended the Lambeth Conference's preliminary meetings. When Whipple spoke about Indian missions at Cambridge University on June 9, the enthusiasm was so great that he was obliged to give the address a second time before a larger congregation in a larger hall. He then took his family to Scotland for two weeks with friends, returning to London in time to hear the great Jenny Lind sing at the Handel Festival on June 25. Two days later, Whipple addressed another meeting on the subject of protecting "native races."

Frederick Temple was bishop of London during the 1888 Lambeth Conference. He was headmaster at Rugby from 1858 to 1885, when he became bishop of London. Temple was archbishop of Canterbury from 1896 to 1902, when Whipple attended the Fourth Lambeth Conference. Like his predecessors, Temple was quite interested in Whipple's schools.

At last the conference began. The formal gathering in the Lambeth Palace chapel on July 3 filled Whipple with awe. Of 185 bishops whose dioceses were located outside of the British Isles, some eighty-nine were in attendance. Recalled Whipple: "There were present bishops from Africa, India, China, the isles of the sea, the icy regions of the North and from the scorching suns of tropic land—men who had given up home and country for Christ's sake, and had come together to witness as men of old witnessed to the faith." The Metropolitan of Guinea, Bishop Crowther, was a former slave, an octogenarian from Sierra Leone who had been consecrated in 1864. "Tears were on the aged bishop's cheeks as he stood in Westminster Abbey and read on Livingston's tomb the name of the man who gave his life for Africa."

Whipple's sermon at the conference opening was a strong plea for unity of purpose among Anglicans. "No one branch of the church is by itself alone the Catholic Church," he said, and he reminded his colleagues that a "divided Christianity cannot conquer the world." His own prejudices showed in his statement that God "has placed the Anglo-Saxon race in the forefront of the nations. They are carrying civilization to the ends of the earth." But, he said, they could only succeed if their hearts were pure. As was his habit, he presented his argument in the form of a list. To succeed, the church must 1) offer intercessory prayer for missionaries, 2) consecrate all to Christ, 3) have a full knowledge of Scriptures in order to preach, 4) love all whom Christ loves, and 5) partake of the "baptism of the Holy Ghost." It was important to understand that "wealth is a sacred trust for which they shall give account." And, as a High Churchman, he insisted that the "ritual of the church must be an expression of her life."[451]

One conference report in which Whipple was deeply interested concerned the relationship of the Anglican and Swedish churches. The committee, made up of fifteen of the church's most prominent theologians, urged close cooperation between the two institutions in the hope of "the ultimate establishment, if possible, of permanent inter-communion on sound principles of ecclesiastical polity."[452] This recommendation echoed Whipple's feelings on the subject, encouraging him to continue pursuing the Swedish Mission efforts in his own diocese.

America was well-represented at Lambeth. Twenty-nine bishops crossed the Atlantic for the event, including Whipple's dear friends David Knickerbacker (now bishop of Indiana) and Bishop Arthur Coxe of Western New York.[453] Whipple himself was perhaps the most popular with the English people, who bombarded him with invitations to dine or to speak, and sent many donations for his work among the Indians.

One American bishop, Samuel S. Harris of Michigan, became ill while preaching at Winchester Cathedral and died a week after the conference ended.

Whipple, who was at his bedside, preached at his funeral in Westminster Abbey the following Sunday. A large number of Americans attended the service, which Whipple recalled as having a "peculiar solemnity."

After Harris's funeral, Whipple went to Paris for a few days to consult his doctors. On his return to England, he was awarded an honorary law degree at Cambridge on July 18, 1888. When he appeared among the doctoral candidates in their scarlet robes, the crowd "cheered me like mad." His friend Bishop Anthony Thorold invited him to address a gathering at the Cathedral of Rochester on July 23, where the confirmation class numbered five hundred—an amazing number to a man whose entire diocesan membership was still less than ten thousand communicants.

On July 31, he received a doctor of divinity degree from Durham University, in company with Bishops Crowther, Coxe, and Henry C. Potter of New York. Sixty bishops gathered in the chancel of the university chapel for the service, where the choir of two thousand surpliced choristers suggested to Whipple the "voice of many waters" referred to in the Book of Revelation. But the most memorable service, to his mind, was the one at Canterbury Cathedral, where he felt himself in the company of St. Augustine, St. Anselm, Bishop Stephen Langton, and Thomas à Becket—all the great heroes of the English Church. Standing on the site of Augustine's first sermon before King Ethelbert fourteen hundred years earlier, Whipple reflected with pride on his church's long history and its recent spread to lands those early missionaries had not even known existed.

In the next weeks Whipple visited Harrow School, addressed the London YMCA, attended a missionary rally in Wales, and preached a sermon at the consecration of a church in Croyden. "The meetings for workingmen were thronged," he reported. He was impressed by the powerful orations of noted English bishops Wilberforce, Selwyn, Goodwin, and Magee. He ordered a single-breasted frock coat and a "poplin cassock like the last" from his London tailor.

Banker Junius S. Morgan of London promised him $50,000 for a new dining hall at Shattuck.

The only shadow on the entire experience was the news he received on July 20 that his ailing brother George had died two days previously while visiting Nantucket.

The conference's major accomplishment was the so-called Lambeth Quadrilateral, a statement of the historic fundamentals of Anglican faith. Based on a formula devised two years earlier by the American church at its General Convention in Chicago, its main elements were summed up in four articles: a) the Old and New Testaments contain "all things necessary to salvation," being the "rule and ultimate standard of faith"; b) the Apostle's Creed and the Nicene Creed are "the sufficient statement of the Christian faith"; c) the two sacraments of baptism and the Lord's Supper are to be ministered "with unfailing use of Christ's words of Institution, and of the elements ordained by Him"; and d) the historic episcopate is to be maintained, "locally adapted in the methods of its administration to the varying needs of the nations and peoples called of God into the Unity of His Church."[454]

In September 1888, Whipple returned home and resumed his accustomed routine, attending the Peabody Fund and Board of Missions meetings. He called on President Cleveland in Washington to discuss Indian affairs. In November, another friend and longtime colleague, Edward Welles, the bishop of Milwaukee, once rector of Christ Church Red Wing and dean of Minnesota's southern missionary district, died in Waterloo, New York. Welles was one of eight men from the Minnesota diocese Whipple had seen elevated to the rank of bishop during his term of office.[455]

The Whipples went south for the winter in December 1888, returning as usual in April so the bishop could teach his class at Seabury. On April 30 he laid the cornerstone of the Junius Morgan Dining Hall at Seabury, and in July he preached at the Birch Coulee Mission, where he baptized Samuel Hinman's infant daughter and confirmed six new members of the church.

The Birch Coulee Mission was flourishing. In his report to the diocesan convention in June, Hinman stated that he had ninety-two individuals from twenty-nine families in his congregation, fifty-eight of them full-fledged communicants. There were thirty pupils in the Sunday school, and communion was celebrated every Sunday, with morning and evening prayer read frequently on weekdays. Whipple returned in August to lay the cornerstone for a new church that would be built with stone from the mission's first church, abandoned half-built in the summer of 1862.

About this time, the idea was broached of building a school for farmers' children in the southwest part of the state, which had no large towns. The concept of a free school for poor pioneer children appealed to Whipple, who believed education was essential to the preservation of democracy and civilization, and he approved it wholeheartedly. In 1889, the Seabury Mission founded the James Breck Farm School in Wilder, a small town in Jackson County near the Iowa border.[456]

Whipple preached the opening sermon at the 1889 General Convention in New York. The sensitive question of revising the prayer book had again arisen. Although the 1883 proposals had been soundly defeated, the issue refused to die. Whipple himself hesitated to approve any changes to the church's sacred books. He had objected in 1871 when Samuel Wilberforce, bishop of Winchester, proposed a revision of the King James Bible. "I know of nothing in which all English-speaking people have a deeper interest than in the common inheritance of the English Bible. . . . That your Convocation will endeavor to do this work faithfully I do not doubt; but I do question whether its separate action can command that high degree of confidence which this work would have if it were the joint work of all Convocations of the Church of England, the Irish, the Scotch, the Colonial, and the American Churches." As for the prayer book, he said, "There never has been a liturgy broader in its spirit, more spiritual in its teachings, or clearer in its declaration of Christian doctrine."[457]

When the convention ended, he and Cornelia paid a visit to Rome, New York, then left for Florida via Chicago and Nashville. On November 23, near Albany, Georgia, the train they were riding in suffered an "awful crash." Whipple was only bruised, but Cornelia suffered a broken rib, concussion, and spinal

The Breck Farm School in Wilder, Minnesota, was founded in 1889 to offer higher education to poor farm children in the southwest corner of the state. It moved to Minneapolis in 1915. Its initial focus was abandoned after the public school system began to offer secondary education throughout the state. Now located in the Minneapolis suburb of Golden Valley, Breck is a private Episcopal college-preparatory day school.

injury, plus undiagnosed injuries to her kidneys. As soon as she could travel, they continued on to Maitland, but she was in constant pain the rest of the winter. Her memory, balance, and speech were affected, and she spent most of her time in bed.

Disaster piled upon disaster. In February 1890, Whipple rushed to Cleveland, where their daughter Fannie's husband, Frank Craw, was seriously ill. He died on February 15. After the funeral, Whipple returned to Maitland, where Cornelia was worrying over their daughter Jennie's pneumonia in Faribault. Though Jennie recovered, Samuel Hinman died of the same illness on March 24. Whipple received a letter written by Hinman the day before his death. "You will find my church papers all written out and vouchers for every expenditure, however small," Hinman assured him, adding, "You have been more than a father to me and Mrs. Whipple more than a mother. We can only thank you for it."[458]

In April, Whipple arranged for a special car to take his wife back to Faribault. She bore her discomfort stoically, saying only, "I do not think I can recover, but the Saviour knows what is best." The night before her departure from Maitland, a group of African Americans gathered outside her window, singing "The Sweet Bye-and-Bye" and "Shall We Meet Over There." Word of her illness reached the Dakota settlement at Birch Coulee, and several women traveled nearly one hundred miles to Faribault to say farewell to the woman who had taken such a deep interest in their welfare over the years.

Cornelia Whipple died on July 16, at the age of seventy-four. Her funeral was held in Faribault's cathedral, with Bishop Gilbert officiating. Nearly every business in town closed during the services. Three days later, Whipple "laid my blessed one in God's acre" in Faribault's Maple Lawn Cemetery beside her son and her brother, John Wright. On her tombstone her husband had the sculptor carve a portion of the verse from Mark 14:8: "She hath done what she could."

Cornelia Whipple in her later years.

Cornelia Whipple's grave in Faribault's Maple Lawn Cemetery. Located beside her son John and her brother John Wright, her gravestone bears the New Testament quotation, "She hath done what she could."

Victoria R. I.
Dec 7. 1890.

Presented to Bishop Whipple
by Queen Victoria
at Windsor Castle,
Nov. 10th 1890

Whipple was devastated by Cornelia's death. He took refuge in visits to Birch Coulee and White Earth, salving his spirit in conversation with his beloved Indians, and then went to Canada on a fishing trip. In September 1890 he went to Philadelphia for a week with his daughter Lizzie. He returned home by way of Montreal, and a week later was on the road again for the annual Peabody Fund meeting and Lake Mohonk Conference.

But his heart wasn't in any of it. In fact, he was having palpitations. He consulted Dr. Rose, who told him there was nothing physically wrong with his heart, only the stress of the past year with all its sorrows. Rose recommended against spending the winter in Maitland, saying it would only depress him further. When J. P. Morgan offered to pay his expenses for a winter in Egypt, Whipple accepted gratefully.

On October 8, he wrote to his former brother-in-law, George Fairbanks, telling him of his plans and asking for financial advice. His daughters were dependent on his support, he said, and he was thinking of selling his orange grove—about nine hundred trees on twenty acres, nearly all bearing well. He told Mahlon Gilbert that he had had to borrow $1,500 before he could leave the country.[459]

Whipple sailed for England on October 28, 1890, taking Fannie with him "to be my guide and helper." Father and daughter spent a week in Dundee and then went to London, which was "full of sweet memories of dear Cornelia." Death was still hounding him: on November 25, he received news that Dr. Theodore Evans had died in Paris. Mrs. Evans begged him to preside over her husband's funeral, and he agreed.

Whipple's English friends did their best to cheer him up. On his return to London after Evans's funeral, he was invited to Windsor Castle to meet Queen Victoria. He was honored by a twenty-minute private audience, during which he regaled her with tales of America's Indians and his work among them, including the story of how the Dakota women had traveled such a long distance to see his dying wife. The queen graciously asked him for a photograph of himself and sent him one of her own, accompanied by an inscribed copy of her book, *Journeys in the Highlands*. Afterward, acting

Frances (Fannie) Ransom Whipple attended St. Mary's Hall in New Jersey. In 1873, she married Frank G. Craw of Cleveland; he died in December 1889. In August 1891, she wed Freedom Ware Jackson, later the head of Standard Oil's Marine Department in Cleveland. Their daughter, Frances, was born in 1898.

Whipple attended meetings of the British Parliament during his 1890 visit to London.

American Minister Henry White wrote to tell him that the "Queen spoke of you in a very friendly and complimentary manner . . . you interested her." She wasn't at all bored, he added.[460]

Whipple preached in the Royal Chapel at Windsor and at the opening of a series of missionary sermons at Westminster Abbey. He and Fannie visited the House of Commons and observed William Gladstone in action. They were the guests of the archbishop of Canterbury and other notables, including the Duke of Argyll, who once wrote him, "I wish your spirit of liberality and common sense, as well as of Christian love, reigned in all hearts and heads as it reigns in yours!"[461]

London was full of talk about the latest Indian "war" in America and the death of Sitting Bull on December 15, 1890. Inspired by the Messianic prophecies of the Paiute prophet Wovoka, many Plains Indians had come to believe that the next spring the white men would vanish and all the Native American dead would return. They began to dance a special Ghost Dance to hasten the coming of that day. Some thought that painting a sacred Ghost Shirt on their chests would keep bullets from harming them.

The dancing was more of a disturbance than a threat—in fact, Wovoka advocated friendship and brotherly love among all races—but the authorities became worried as it spread from village to village and schools emptied, farms were abandoned, and trading houses lost trade. The government suspected that Sitting Bull, who had returned to the United States in 1881 and was living quietly on the Standing Rock Reservation (when he wasn't traveling with Buffalo Bill's Wild West Show), was behind

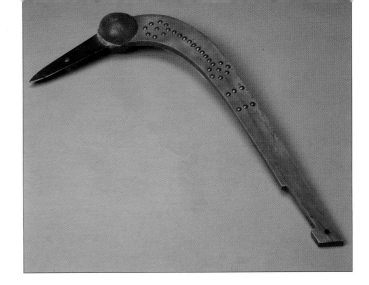

the unrest. They sent an Indian police unit to arrest the old chief, and in the ensuing riot, Sitting Bull was killed. Incensed by a London newspaper's report that Henry Sibley was involved in the episode, Whipple wrote an angry letter to the editor, assuring him that his old friend "was incapable of doing [the Indians] an injustice."[462]

On December 9 Whipple and Fannie left for Paris to spend the holidays with the Evans family. On New Year's Day, they sailed from Venice to Egypt for a month's cruising the Nile and examining antiquities. Egypt had changed considerably since Whipple was there in 1865. England had assumed an unofficial protectorship over the country when its ruler's debts plunged it into bankruptcy in 1875. Now it was one of the more popular tourist venues for wealthy travelers. Thomas Cook's travel agency arranged trips up the Nile for thousands of visitors every year on their steamer launches. Whipple took great pleasure in finding biblical references among the Roman ruins of Alexandria. In Luxor, his guide turned out to be one of the men who had carried his cot to Bishop Gobat's house in Jerusalem in 1865, when he was suffering from Syrian fever. Whipple held long theological conversations with a Coptic priest in Luxor, who asked if he could find a copy of the recent translation of the Coptic service into English. The bishop attended a Coptic wedding in Cairo, where the priest asked him to bless the newlyweds.[463]

Whipple celebrated his sixty-ninth birthday off the coast of Greece, reflecting in a melancholy fashion on the curious fate that had allowed a "frail, delicate boy" to survive so many hardships over the years. In

TOP RIGHT: From Bishop Whipple's personal collection, this Dakota club, ca. 1850-1880, is fashioned from maple, steel, and brass tacks.

LOWER RIGHT: Sitting Bull, the Teton Lakota leader who fought against the government's efforts to force his people onto a reservation following the loss of the Black Hills. He led his band to Canada in 1877. In 1881, he signed a peace agreement and returned to the United States. Government unease following the rise of the Ghost Dance in 1887 led to Sitting Bull's murder three years later by Indian police officers sent to arrest him.

Randall Davidson, archbishop of Canterbury from 1903 to 1928, was the son-in-law of Archbishop Archibald Tait. Whipple took part in Davidson's consecration as bishop of Rochester in 1891.

Athens, he visited a girls' school founded by the American Episcopal missionary Dr. J. H. Hill.[464] Whipple later called on the Greek Orthodox patriarch, who gave him a book of services of the Greek Church. In Constantinople, he talked at length with the British ambassador about American Indians and gave a speech at a Bulgarian girls' college in Scutari, where the teacher was a young woman from Minnesota. He also met the Armenian patriarch, who "showed a profound interest in the Church in the United States." After stopping in Cyprus to pay homage at the graves of the church fathers of Nicaea, he and Fannie returned (via Brindisi, Pompeii, and Rome) to Mentone in mid-March 1891.

The distraction of the extended trip had been good for him, but his grief for Cornelia remained. He had known her all his life; they had been married forty-eight years. He still found it hard to believe she was gone, "my precious wife [who] has not only been my right hand but to whom I owe all I am."

Whipple and Fannie returned to London at the end of April, and he assisted at the consecration of two English bishops, Randall T. Davidson as bishop of Rochester and Mandell Creighton as bishop of Peterborough. In June, they were back in Scotland, where Whipple attended the general assembly of the Scottish Presbyterian Church. Whipple had met its new moderator, James Macgregor, at the home of Edward Caird during an earlier visit to Scotland, and the two men had discovered a shared hope that the Anglican and Presbyterian Churches would one day be united.[465]

By mid-June, Whipple was back in Faribault. In July he consecrated Good Thunder's church at Birch Coulee, which the congregation decided to name St. Cornelia's, in honor of his wife. There were two memorial windows in the church: the chancel window in honor of Samuel Hinman and an oriel window dedicated to Cornelia Whipple. In an article written for the Episcopal newspaper *The Churchman,* Whipple said Cornelia probably wouldn't have wanted the church to bear her name, but it seemed appropriate nonetheless.

In August, Fannie married Freedom Ware Jackson of Cleveland. Her father officiated, then resumed his fall round of meetings and conferences. The Indian situation was relatively quiet. The "friendly Sioux" had finally been awarded the money they had been promised ten years earlier, although it had not yet been appropriated. There was a flare-up of dancing on the Ojibwe reservations, which Joseph Gilfillan complained "revives all the old barbarism." The Office of Indian Affairs' attitude toward the dancing was ambivalent; many agents felt it was a fad that would fade in time. Timothy Sheehan had been replaced as agent by B. P. Shuler in 1889, and Gilfillan claimed that Shuler was not just tolerating the dancing, but encouraging it. Gambling and drinking were also rampant.[466]

The popularity of the dancing was symptomatic of a general sense of disillusionment among the Ojibwe. They had tried for twenty years to follow the white man's path, cutting their hair, joining the Christian churches, and cultivating the soil. It seemed to make no difference. They were still poor, still at the mercy of avaricious traders, lumbermen, and officials, still largely ignored by Congress when their interests conflicted with those of the white men. The Dawes Act, so highly thought of by Whipple and his colleagues at Mohonk, seemed designed to undermine the Ojibwe's efforts to preserve their homeland and way of life. Many Ojibwes left the Episcopal Church, either returning to their old lifestyle or becoming Catholics. Some accepted allotments, but opposed the Dawes Act's underlying philosophy, reserving their right to object whenever possible.

During the 1890s, an Episcopal deaconess named Sibyl Carter brought the Ojibwe women a new outlet for their creativity and a new source of income. Carter had visited White Earth in 1886 and was impressed by the beautiful beadwork the women produced. There was not much of a market for it, although Whipple and others occasionally bought beaded items as gifts for their friends. A "general missionary" from a wealthy eastern family, Carter was then traveling around the world, observing missions in various places. She saw some lace schools during several months at a mission in Japan and was inspired to bring the craft to the women at White Earth.

Returning to Minnesota in 1889, she taught a small group of Ojibwe women how to make lace. The following spring she took the finished products east and sold them for enough money to hire two full-time lace teachers for the mission. Whipple encouraged the project. In 1892, his niece Susan Salisbury joined Carter's small cadre of lace teachers at White Earth, and the following year Carter set up a lace school at Birch Coulee. Other schools were founded in Wisconsin, Oklahoma, and Wyoming.

Annual lace sales were held in New York, Philadelphia, Boston, Cambridge, and Pittsburgh, with committees in each city to handle the transactions.

Mary Webster Whipple, Bishop Whipple's cousin, took charge of the lace school at the Birch Coulee Mission in 1895 from Whipple's niece Susan Salisbury, who had become Sybil Carter's chief assistant at the lace program's headquarters in St. Paul.

LEFT: Dakota women making lace at the Bishop Whipple Mission in Morton, Minnesota, in 1897.

Episcopal missionaries taught Ojibwe women at Leech Lake how to make lace. Sibyl Carter founded the lace program at the White Earth Reservation in 1889 to give Indian women a source of income. By 1898, the program had expanded to reservations in Minnesota, Wisconsin, Oklahoma, and Wyoming. The women in this photo are not identified, but Susan Salisbury and Carter are probably standing second and third from left.

The Indian women were delighted with this new industry, which was especially useful during the winter months, when their stores of foodstuffs began to dwindle. It pleased them to hear that their lace was being worn by fine ladies in the big cities. Carter entered samples of their work at the Paris Exhibition of 1889, where it won a gold medal. In 1892, Bishop Randall Davidson's wife presented a piece of "Red Indian lace" to Queen Victoria.[467]

In October 1891, Whipple served as presenter at the consecration of Phillips Brooks as bishop of Massachusetts. A hugely popular preacher, Brooks was a controversial divine whose election had not been unanimous. Iowa's Bishop William Perry complained that Brooks once failed to condemn a priest who doubted the Virgin birth and resurrection, saying that these things were "simply a difference of interpretation." Whipple, who considered Brooks "simple as a child," had no such misgivings. He recalled Brooks' surprise when several bishops spoke of a growing indifference to public worship; he had always found full congregations at the churches he addressed, Brooks said. "He looked surprised," Whipple said, "when we smiled."[468]

Whipple returned to Florida in December 1891, bringing with him his niece Susan Salisbury, his daughter Jennie, and her two sons, Harry (age sixteen) and Ben (nine). Francis Rose, Nellie's eleven-year-old son, joined them around the first of the year. Having the young people around made it easier for Whipple to bear Cornelia's absence. Maitland was now a substantial community, boasting two hotels and nine lakes within its corporate limits. It produced forty thousand boxes of oranges annually and was beginning to add grapes as well. Whipple had not, after all, sold his orange groves, which provided boxes of fruit for his many friends. The family threw him a party on his seventieth birthday in February 1892.[469]

A few weeks later, on a fishing trip with Judge E. T. Wilder of St. Paul, Whipple caught a 124-pound tarpon that was six feet, seven inches long. It was

Bishop Phillips Brooks, who wrote the words to "O Little Town of Bethlehem," was a popular, if somewhat controversial, preacher. Whipple was his presenter at his consecration as bishop of Massachusetts in 1891.

Whipple hooking a fish in Florida, possibly the six-foot-seven tarpon he hung on the wall in his den in Faribault. A devout fisherman, Whipple pursued his avocation in the waters of Minnesota, Florida, and Yellowstone Park, Canada, and Ireland. Enmegahbowh claimed he was present when the bishop caught the largest fish in Minnesota.

the largest tarpon caught to date off Fort Myers, and Whipple was ecstatic. "He leaped seven times at least out of the water & when I captured [him] I hurrahed like a boy," he wrote George Fairbanks. He had the fish stuffed and mounted and brought it back to Faribault to hang on the wall in his den.[470]

Whipple recalled that winter in Florida with fondness, "for it was full of blessed incidents, simple in themselves, but bearing out the wise man's saying, 'A word fitly spoken is like apples of gold in pictures of silver.'" He visited friends, ministered to the sick, preached in his Church of the Good Shepherd, and traveled around the countryside. He took up the cause of the Seminoles, who were trying to regain ownership of property in the Everglades that had been set aside in 1850 for their "sole and permanent use and benefit" before they were sent off to Indian Territory.[471] Although the majority of the tribe had left Florida between 1835 and 1858, a stubborn remnant remained, deep in the state's swamps, and Whipple argued that they should be allowed to stay.

Whipple returned to Minnesota in April 1892 and smoothed over a dispute that had arisen at Seabury between the professor of ecclesiastical history and the new warden. "The trouble in Seabury makes me sick," he confided in his diary. Its cause was the neverending squabble between evangelical and liturgical factions, between Low Church and High Church teaching. The crisis ended when the offending professor departed, much to Whipple's dismay, as he would have preferred to keep both men.[472]

Although Whipple had not involved himself in partisan politics since his ordination, he accepted an invitation in June 1892 to give the opening prayer at the Republican Convention that nominated Grover Cleveland for his second term. He had found Cleveland, during his first term, sympathetic to pleas for justice for the Indians. As the president had intervened on behalf of the Ojibwe in the dam reparations dispute, Whipple felt he owed him "a debt of personal gratitude."

After the convention, Whipple returned home to preside over his diocesan council. It seemed the time had come to divide the diocese in two. The question had come up off and on since 1864, but Whipple had opposed the division because of the conflicting needs of the schools in the south and the Ojibwe Mission in the north. He also felt that the General Convention would not approve it, as the low number of white Episcopalians residing north of the Twin Cities would make it hard to support a bishop there. But the growth of Duluth and the development of iron mining had brought increased population and many new Episcopal parishes, and the stress of dealing with it all was beginning to take its toll on his assistant bishop's health. The delegates authorized Whipple to take the proposal to the upcoming General Convention in Baltimore.

The 1892 General Convention dealt with several issues of interest to Whipple. After long years of debate, the *Book of Common Prayer* was at last revised, for the first time since the church's founding in 1789 (although the changes were minimal). The hymnal was also revised, with many new tunes added.[473] When Whipple made his request for a missionary bishop for northern Minnesota, the question was referred to a committee for consideration at the next meeting.

Then the question arose of where to hold the 1895 convention. San Francisco, Saratoga Springs, Denver, and Louisville all were mentioned, with no one site winning a majority vote. Judge Isaac Atwater, a delegate from Minnesota, then invited the convention to come to Minneapolis. He assured the delegates that Minnesota had something for everyone: "St. Paul for the old, conservative Churchmen, St. Anthony for those of more advanced views, and for all there would be the openhanded hospitality of the West, with the object-lesson of a household at unity with itself." To Whipple's delight, the invitation was accepted.[474]

The strain of the succeeding fall round of meetings wore out the elderly bishop. By December he was so ill that J. P. Morgan ordered a special railcar to take him to Maitland. By the end of February he had recovered enough to spend a week fishing on the ocean, but he became so ill after he returned to Faribault in the spring that he couldn't leave his bed for six weeks.

In July 1893 Whipple's doctor sent him to the seashore at Marblehead, Massachusetts. Susan Salisbury came along to care for him. The sea air seemed to do him good, but Cornelia's death continued to depress him, and on his return to Faribault in early September, he became ill again. He managed a short visit to the Ojibwe at White Earth and spent several days at the Chicago World's Fair at the end of September, speaking on Indian missions. He attended the Board of Missions meeting, the Peabody dinner, and the Mohonk Conference, then left for Florida on November 24, several weeks earlier than usual.

Again Florida's climate revived him. By January, Whipple was able to travel to Cuba with three of his grandchildren, bringing home two hundred cigars and a parrot. He was inducted into the Sons of the Revolution at Annapolis in April. In July he went west to Seattle, Tacoma, and Helena with his grandchildren, paying a short visit to Yellowstone Park. "The scenery is beautiful and varied, the hotels comfortable, and the transportation by four and six-horse coaches perfect," he later wrote. The geysers and sulphur springs were awe-inspiring. It reminded him of the Indian who had visited Yellowstone, and when he later heard a missionary describe hell, said, "What you say is true. I have been there." The trout fishing in the park was ideal—"the most prolific fishing ground that I have ever known."

Back in St. Paul, Whipple attended a conference on Indian affairs and suffered through three more nasal operations. In September 1894, he attended a ceremony dedicating a monument to the memory of the soldiers who had died at the battle of Birch Coulee in 1862.

The Birch Coulee battle monument, at whose dedication Whipple made an unwelcome speech recalling the woes of the Indians before 1862.

Charles Flandrau moved to Minnesota in 1853. A lawyer, he was active in state politics and served briefly as government agent to the Dakota in 1856. From 1862 to 1864 he served on the Minnesota Supreme Court.

There had been some controversy about where the monument should stand and whose names should go on the inscription, and at the dedication Governor William Marshall spoke at some length about the mistakes he thought it contained. Judge Charles Flandrau, thinking to compliment the bravery of the soldiers, described the "splendid fighting qualities of the Sioux." When he finished, Whipple said, "I would give ten dollars for five minutes' speech." Smiling, Flandrau turned the podium over to him, and Whipple spoke for several minutes on how the Dakota had been led to violence by the government's behavior. The audience was not pleased; one man complained that he had come to listen to tales of Indian wickedness and instead got "an attack on the monument and two glowing eulogies of the savage murderers."[475]

Whipple addressed the Mohonk Conference twice in October 1894. On November 25, his sister

Susan Hill died, and he took her body back to Rome, New York, for burial. While there he preached at Zion Church, noting that it was exactly forty-five years since he gave his first sermon there.

In February 1895, Whipple was appointed to the Board of Indian Commissioners. The board's duties were by now "altogether advisory," but Whipple considered the appointment an honor nonetheless. He used his position to lobby for the Seminoles, the Red Lake Ojibwe (who had been given allotments on unusable land), and the Dakota scouts (whose back annuities, though appropriated, still had not been paid).

The 1895 General Convention, held in Minneapolis' Gethsemane Church, was a triumph for Whipple. It was the first General Convention to be held west of the Mississippi, a symbol of how the Episcopal Church—and the country—had expanded since the church's founding in 1789. There had been four bishops at that first convention; now there were ninety, seventy of whom were present. Since John Williams, who as the eldest bishop held the title of presiding bishop, was not able to attend, the role of presiding over the meeting fell upon Whipple, the oldest bishop present.[476]

The citizens of Minnesota were so pleased at the prospect of hosting the convention that a full half of the committee in charge of arrangements were not even Episcopalians. The theme of Christian unity carried through the entire program. Archbishop Robert Machray of Canada served as lector at the opening service. Joseph T. Smith, moderator of the general assembly of the American Presbyterian Church, spoke to the House of Bishops on the subject of Christian unity. At a reception given by railroad magnate James J. Hill, Roman Catholic Archbishop John Ireland and several of his clergy mingled with the Episcopal delegates in sociable harmony.

On Saturday, October 12, the 750 convention delegates adjourned to Faribault for a gala celebration chaired by Whipple's son Charles and the

Reverend F. T. Webb, rector of St. Paul's and dean of the Minneapolis Convocation. The president of the Milwaukee and St. Paul Railroad arranged for special trains, and a fleet of carriages met the guests and took them on a tour of the schools, both church and state-owned. The streets were hung with floral arches and banners, and brass bands serenaded the crowds.

It was a perfect Minnesota fall day, with clear skies and moderate temperatures. The Women's Auxiliary of Faribault, under the wife of Shattuck's warden, James Dobbin, served a commendably efficient luncheon in the Shattuck armory. The menu included chicken salad, roast beef, tongue, veal loaf, dipped oysters, sandwiches, celery, olives, toasted crackers, cheese, bread, fruit, and coffee, served by "a whole army of bright-eyed, pretty Faribault maidens." The mayor, a graduate of Shattuck, welcomed the crowd. More speeches and a parade of the cadets under the direction of their commandant, Lieutenant Asa T. Abbott, followed. After a short service in the cathedral, the delegates were taken back to Minneapolis, where the Church Club hosted a dinner attended by fifty-seven bishops and many lay delegates. At the end of the convention, the House of Bishops presented Whipple with a silver loving cup.[477]

Henry Whipple had taken a rough frontier diocese and made it a place that compared favorably with any diocese on the East Coast. It was an accomplishment in which he could take an honest pride. But he was happiest with the convention's vote to create a separate missionary bishopric of Duluth. While this effectively removed the Ojibwe reservation from his jurisdiction, Whipple knew the time had come to give up part of his responsibilities, for his own health and that of his assistant.

By 1895, the state's population had surpassed 1.5 million, and Duluth—with its radiating railroads and harbor—was a secondary metropolis serving nearly half a million people in the Iron Range, the lumber camps, and the Red River Valley wheat farms. Even after the Duluth diocese was created, the Minnesota diocese still retained 150 parishes and missions and twelve thousand communicants.[478]

It had been a strenuous year. Whipple left for Florida on November 19, tired and weakened by another attack of bronchitis. It was snowing as he boarded the train in St. Paul. But this time, a lovely young woman was waiting for him in Maitland.

Remodeled in 1864, Gethsemane Church became a center of mission work in the diocese under long-time rector David B. Knickerbacker. In 1895 it hosted the first General Convention west of the Mississippi.

FUNDRAISING IN ACTION

Bishop Whipple

James J. Hill

BISHOP WHIPPLE was blessed with generous friends in this country and in Europe and had learned how to raise money for his churches and schools.

On May 23, 1889, writing from Faribault, he penned a letter to railroad tycoon James J. Hill in St. Paul:

Honorable & dear Friend,

For thirty years you & I have been laboring for this Northwest. You, to build up its material interests & I, Christian work to protect all our country holds dear. I have often wished I could show you the Oxford of the West. If I say it there is no place in the United States that can show better foundations. This year I must build a gymnasium, put in boilers & engine[s?] for steam heating & electric light for our St. Mary's Hall at a cost of $15,000. If you can aid your old friend in this work I shall be grateful & He who never forgets a deed of love will repay.

Your friend,
H. B. Whipple
Bishop of Minnesota

Hon. J. J. Hill

Within days, as noted on Whipple's letter, now in the James J. Hill papers held by the James J. Hill Reference Library in St. Paul, Hill sent Whipple $1,000.

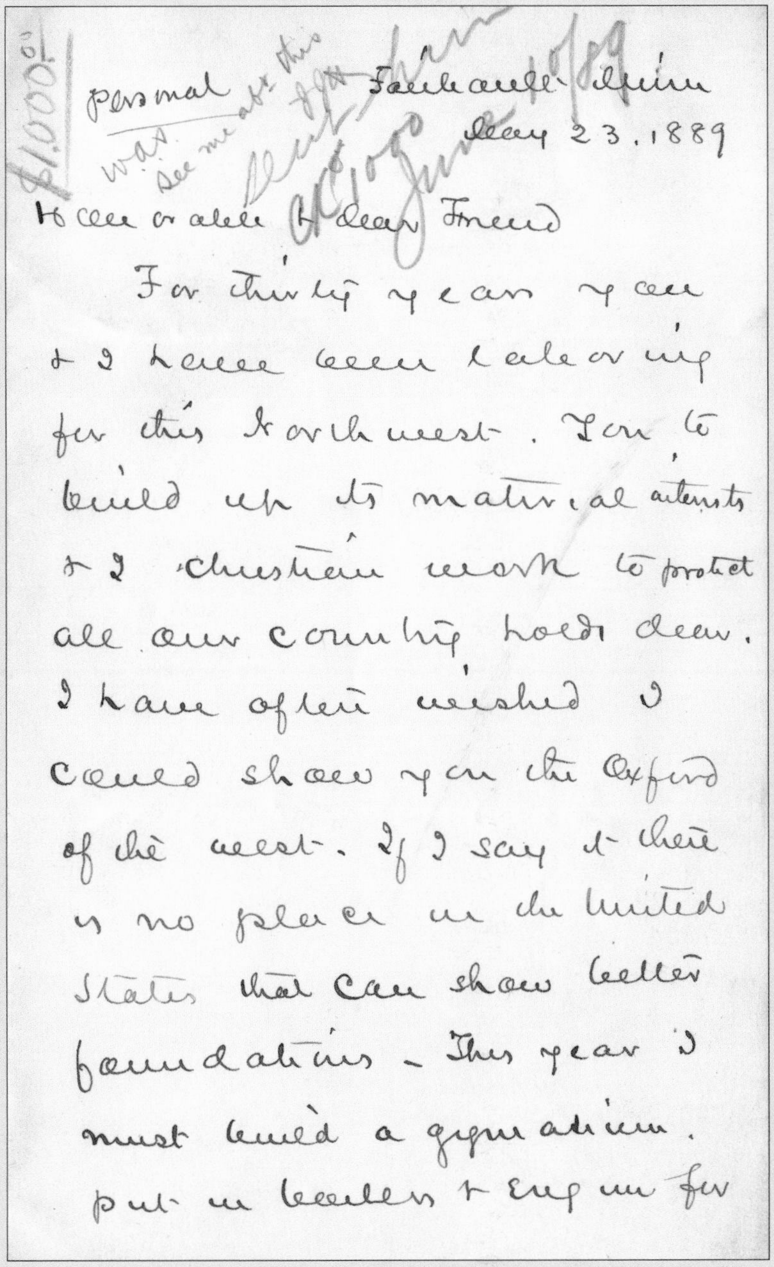

personal
see me at this [...]

Fairbault, Minn
May 23, 1889

To all or all? dear Friend

For thirty years you
& I have been laboring
for this Northwest. You to
build up its material interests
& I christian work to protect
all our country holds dear.
I have often wished I
could show you the Oxford
of the west. If I say it there
is no place in the United
States that can show better
foundations — This year I
must build a gymnasium.
put in boilers & eng. for

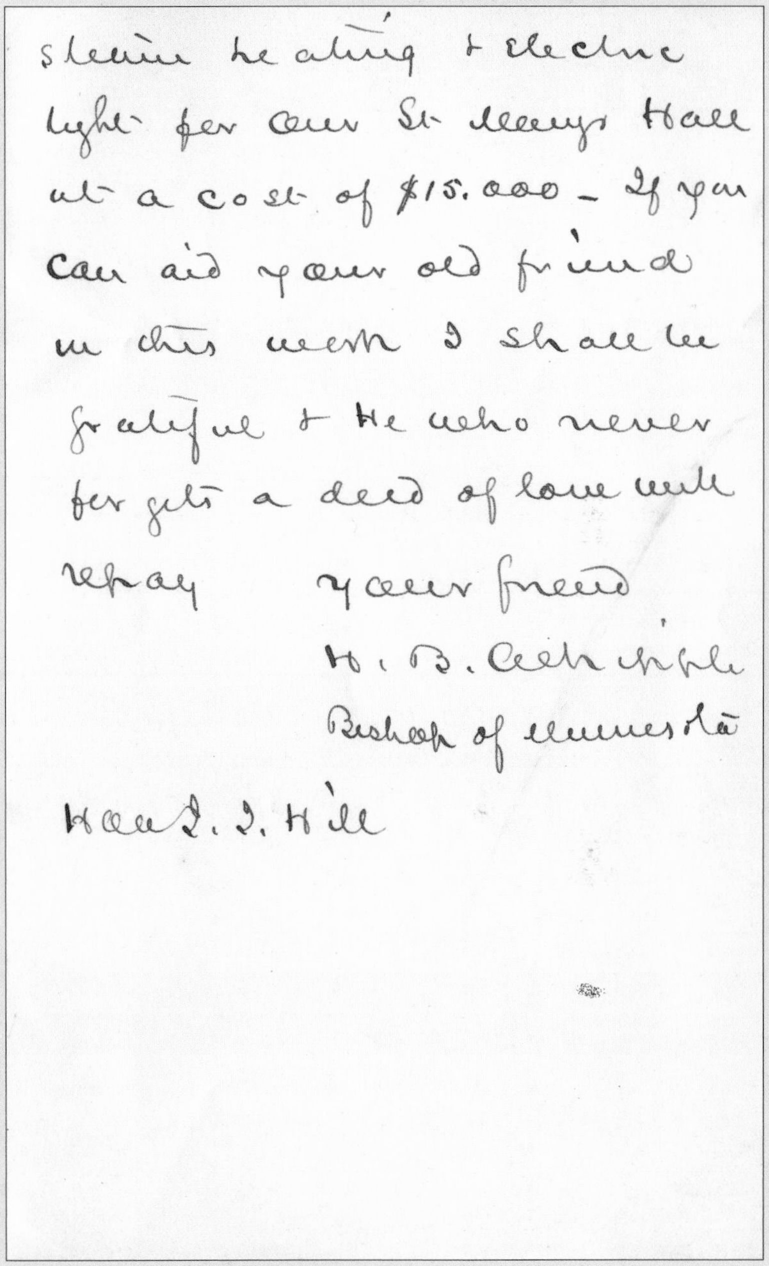

steam heating & electric
light for our St Marys Hall
at a cost of $15.000 — If you
can aid your old friend
in this work I shall be
grateful & He who never
forgets a deed of love will
repay   your friend
                  H. B. Whipple
                  Bishop of Minnesota
Hon. J. J. Hill

Evangeline Marrs Simpson married Henry Whipple in 1896. The bishop's new wife was the daughter of Dana Francis Marrs and Jane Van Poelan and the widow of Michael Simpson, a wealthy textile manufacturer in Saxonville, Massachusetts.

ELLIOTT & FRY   55, BAKER STREET. W.

W hile visiting the White House during Grover Cleveland's first term, Whipple had met Cleveland's sister Rose, who acted as the president's hostess until his marriage in 1886. In 1895, Rose Cleveland spent the winter at Maitland with her dear friend, Evangeline Simpson. The two women began attending services at the Church of the Good Shepherd. On March 29, 1895, Whipple baptized them.

The widow of Michael Simpson, a wealthy textile manufacturer, Evangeline Marrs Simpson came from a prominent Massachusetts family. Young, attractive, and cosmopolitan, she had traveled extensively in Europe, acquiring artwork and visiting cultural landmarks.[479]

Within weeks of their first meeting, Evangeline Simpson seems to have set her cap for the elderly bishop—or was it the other way around? By May, he was captivated, writing her passionate love letters such as he had never dreamed of addressing to Cornelia. In July 1895, he spent several weeks with Evangeline and her mother at their home in South Park, Massachusetts—"the pleasantest visit of an eventful life—are no words to describe it," he confided to his diary. Over the summer, he copied sermons for her, enclosing them with his letters. He could hardly wait to return to Florida, where he entertained her and Mrs. Marrs at Christmas dinner.

From then on, Evangeline Simpson was a frequent visitor at Whipple's home. She encouraged his writing and fussed over him when he was ill. He caught a chill on his way back to Faribault in April 1896, and Dr. Rose ordered him to the seashore again. The Hotel Victoria at Marblehead was near South Park, and Simpson soon found her way to Whipple's side, nursing him tenderly back to health.

On October 22, 1896 (following his usual fall round of meetings), Henry Benjamin Whipple and Evangeline Marrs Simpson were married at St. Bartholomew's Church in New York by Bishop Henry C. Potter.[480] The new Mrs. Whipple was thirty-eight years old; the bishop was seventy-four. "My dear wife [is] a perpetual joy, wise, thoughtful, cheerful, always loving," Whipple wrote in his diary. "My dear blessed wife . . . grows more lovely daily . . . anticipates my every wish. . . . God gave me a treasure in her."

Rose Cleveland, sister of President Grover Cleveland and Evangeline Whipple's dear friend. A teacher in private schools and editor for a time of *Literary Life,* Rose served as her brother's White House hostess until his marriage in 1886. She eventually moved to Bagni di Lucca, a center of expatriate American women writers and artists in Italy. In 1910, Evangeline joined Rose there. Those years are described in her book *A Famous Corner of Tuscany.*

Although he had raised hundreds of thousands of dollars over the years since his ordination, Whipple had never spent much of it on himself, believing the money had been entrusted to him for his work. His letters frequently reflected concern for the financial welfare of his family. Although he enjoyed the good life when he could as the guest of wealthy friends, and wasn't too proud to accept their help when he needed it, his personal lifestyle had remained simple. Now that had changed, as Evangeline had plenty of money to spare. He enjoyed being coddled by her, and Evangeline was good for him.

His health rebounded in the first year after their marriage, due no doubt to a combination of her tender care and the euphoria of an old man in love with an attractive young wife.[481]

With Evangeline's support, Whipple was able to resume his active lifestyle. In May 1897, the couple sailed to England to attend Queen Victoria's jubilee and the fourth Lambeth Conference. They spent several weeks in London, feted by British nobility. Evangeline's diary is filled with records of teas and dinners with earls and barons, as well as with bishops from Whipple's previous visits.[482]

Of the 195 bishops who attended the 1897 Lambeth Conference, 47 (including Henry Whipple and Mahlon Gilbert) were from the United States. England, Scotland, Ireland, Australia, Canada, South and Equatorial Africa, the West Indies, India, China, Japan, and the dioceses of Honolulu and Jerusalem all sent representatives.[483] Evangeline was thrilled by the sight of "700 surpliced clergy & about a thousand choristers" who attended the official opening service on June 6. Whipple's sermon was "splendid."

The Minnesota bishop preached four special sermons: one for the 1300th anniversary of the baptism

BELOW: One hundred ninety-four bishops attended the Lambeth Conference in 1897.

of Ethelbert, England's first Saxon king, at Salisbury Cathedral on June 3; Cambridge's annual Ramsden Sermon on Whitsunday; another at Holy Trinity in Stratford-on-Avon on Trinity Sunday; and a fourth at a missionary conference in Southwell Minster. The audiences loved him. A Cambridge newspaper called him "tall, graceful, with the figure of a sirdar and the face of a saint . . . this silver pine of Minnesota."[484]

There were secular pleasures too. The Whipples spent several days at Harrow School, where the bishop gave a talk to the boys on Indians. "On whatever soil a boy may be reared," he later observed, "interest in the North American Indian seems to be ingrained." At the Handel Festival at London's Crystal Palace, they heard four thousand voices perform the *Messiah.*

On June 22, the Whipples took part in Queen Victoria's jubilee procession. "There was no figure as striking as my Bishop in his Lambeth convention robes," Evangeline exulted. To her husband, she re-marked, "The most obdurate subject from the Celestial kingdom must have felt a dawning sentiment that there might be a corner for women hereafter." They met the Prince and Princess Christian, the Prince of Wales, and Queen Victoria herself. (Refusing to be impressed, Evangeline judged the prince pleasant but stupid, the princess plain and uninteresting, and pronounced smugly that "nobody is so *royal* as my blessed Bishop.")[485]

Whipple lunched at St. Augustine's College, preached at Westminster Abbey, and dined with the Lord Mayor of London. He gave a toast at the American Society's Independence Day Banquet at the Royal Palace Hotel in Kensington, attended missionary meetings in Southwark and at St. Paul's Cathedral, accompanied his fellow bishops on a formal tour of Glastonbury, and was the guest of the bishop of Lichfield, at whose request he gave a speech in the Lichfield cathedral.

The Lambeth Conference convened on June 30,

1897. The delegates approved the concept of deaconesses and agreed to establish a consultative committee representing all Anglican churches (the predecessor of today's Anglican Consultative Council).[486] Whipple opposed a proposal to establish an advisory council under the leadership of the archbishop of Canterbury: "In the past, centralization of authority beyond national bounds has been full of mischief and has brought sorrow to the Church." Recalling his sermon at the previous Lambeth Conference, he repeated that each national church had "its own peculiar responsibilities to God for the souls entrusted to its care," and although such a council might be beneficial for England's colonial churches, "an intervention of one national church in the affairs of another will certainly bring sorrow."

Since the last Lambeth Conference, several men with whom he had become closely acquainted had died. Archbishop Edward White Benson was gone, replaced by Frederick Temple. William Magee, the libertarian archbishop of York, who as bishop of Peterborough had sat beside Whipple during the 1888 conference and whose silver tongue Whipple envied, was dead, as was Joseph Lightfoot of Durham, whom Whipple considered perhaps the greatest biblical scholar in Britain. His good friend Anthony Thorold, bishop of Rochester, had passed away two years earlier, and longtime benefactors Junius S. Morgan and Alexander Duncan were also among the missing.

At the closing service at St. Paul's Cathedral, Whipple was privileged to serve as epistler and to assist Archbishop Temple in the celebration of Communion, along with the bishops of London and York. "It was a sweet and solemn service; and as we knelt to receive the Blessed Sacrament, our souls were full of gratitude to God for the spirit of love which pervaded all hearts, and which would make memorable the fourth Lambeth Conference."

When the conference ended, Whipple and Evangeline went to the Isle of Wight, where he gave a speech at the dedication of the Tennyson memorial beacon on August 6, 1897. The Whipples were guests of the poet's family at their home at Farringford. They then traveled north to Edinburgh, where Whipple renewed his acquaintance with James Macgregor, the Presbyterian divine. The bishop and Evangeline were the Duke of Argyll's guests at Inveraray Castle, and the duke's grandson, the bishop of Argyll and the Isles, took them to see Iona, site of St. Columba's sixth-century monastery. Inveraray was noted for its fine salmon, but the weather was too cold for fishing, much to Whipple's disappointment. Returning to England a week later, he attended a missionary celebration at Lincoln Cathedral and preached the sermon at an evensong service on August 22.

In September 1897, the Whipples returned to America, where they stayed with Mrs. Marrs at South Park for a month. Then it was time to go to Lake Mohonk, where Whipple delivered two speeches on the problems Minnesota's Ojibwe were still having with lumber interests over their pine forests. The sale of pine brought in a regular profit for the tribe, but also provided a regular source of plunder for those with weak consciences and ready access to funds. No matter how diligently the Indian bureau tried to root them out, "Indian rings" still flourished on nearly every reservation in the country.[487]

Aside from one day in March, when he reported severe facial pain, 1897 had passed without a day's notable illness for the bishop. Less euphoric was 1898, when he underwent two more operations in St. Paul in September at the hands of Dr. Paul Schadle, a specialist in throat conditions. But Whipple was able to carry out his usual activities without difficulty, and his infatuation with his young wife continued unabated.

Evangeline was determined to provide her new husband with the setting she felt he deserved. She remodeled the house in Maitland, adding a new

kitchen and fresh landscaping. She did the same for the Faribault house, adding a private chapel, a formal library, and a music room. In a secret closet off the bishop's library, its entrance hidden behind a large bookcase, he kept his personal papers and most valued mementos, including Indian beaded headdresses and ceremonial shirts, a peace pipe, and the cane William Gladstone had given him. Evangeline filled both houses with valuable paintings and furniture, some acquired at an estate sale held for Bavaria's late King Ludwig II.[488]

She built a deanery for the cathedral and a parsonage for the church at Birch Coulee. She also donated freely to the bishop's personal charities. Whipple was touched. "Her love and sympathy for the sorrowful and heavy laden, her deep interest in the brown and black races who have so long held a place in my heart drew us together," he wrote.

TOP: The Tennyson Memorial on the Isle of Wight, whose dedication Henry Whipple attended on August 6, 1897.
ABOVE: Inveraray Castle, home of the Duke of Argyll, where the Whipples were guests during their visits to England in the 1890s.

She even tried to rein in her husband's fondness for inappropriately colorful apparel. Charles Slattery, dean of the cathedral, was present once when the bishop came downstairs ready for a formal event wearing red socks. Evangeline made him go upstairs and change them. When he came back down, he whispered to Slattery, "I have on a pink undershirt anyway!"[489]

Whipple took Evangeline to White Earth in June 1898, where they were royally entertained with speeches and hymns by the Ojibwe Christians. At Leech Lake, they received a warm welcome at the mission church. There were changes on the reserva-

Bugonaygeshig (left), a Leech Lake Ojibwe, shortly before the 1898 Bear Island conflict, in which a group of his friends attacked an army unit and killed several soldiers. It was the last battle fought by the Ojibwe against the government.

tions. Joseph Gilfillan had left Minnesota earlier in the year, after twenty-five years' service among the Ojibwe. Enmegahbowh remained, now widowed, suffering from rheumatism and semi-retired. At Red Lake, Madwaganonint had died at the end of 1897, faithful to the last.

When Whipple first heard in October 1898 that the Bear Island band of Pillagers at Leech Lake had fired on a small army detachment, killing several men, he dismissed the incident as an "uprising by a small party of the Pillager Indians . . . who have always been in opposition to civilization and have refused our good Archdeacon Gilfillan to establish a mission among them."[490] The conflict began when an Ojibwe, Bugonaygeshig, refused to go to Duluth to appear as witness in a bootlegging trial. He was arrested, but friends forcibly freed him, and he fled back to his village on Bear Island. The government sent a military detachment to arrest the men who attacked the officers. The incident escalated; the troopers, mostly raw recruits, were pinned down by the Ojibwe and five men were killed.

The violence was short-lived. Commissioner of Indian Affairs William A. Jones arrived to talk with tribal leaders under Flat Mouth the Younger, and the matter was settled within a few days. Commissioner Jones claimed, "The Indians were prompted to their outbreak by the wrongs committed against them and chafed under unfair treatment. They now will go back to their homes and live peaceably if the whites will treat them fairly."[491]

On May 2, 1898, Whipple spoke to the Minnesota Historical Society on "The Civilization and Christianization of the Ojibways in Minnesota." Reviewing the history of the church's mission to the Ojibwe and other Native Americans, he concluded that, after many years of struggle, the "atmosphere is clearing." Of the 230,000 Native Americans in America, he said, 88,000 wore "civilized dress," 25,000 lived in houses, 25,000 had become Christians, 22,000 attended schools and 38,000 could

The Whipple house in Faribault, ca. 1897, after Evangeline had added a library, music room, and chapel.

read. In 1897 there had been 170 more births than deaths among Minnesota's Ojibwe. He was proud of his role in bringing this about. When he died, he said, he "would rather have [an Indian] say 'He helped us when he could' than the finest monument."[492]

At the 1898 General Convention in Washington, D.C., the delegates passed a canon approving Minnesota's action permitting her Swedish congregations to use the liturgy of the National Church of Sweden. Whipple was less happy with their refusal to pass a stringent canon on divorce, declaring that the "sundering of the marriage vow [is] contrary to the law of God." Four missionary bishops were elected, including one for the new Anglican church in Brazil. The high point of the convention was the dedication of the Peace Cross on the site of the future National Cathedral.

In the spring of 1899, Whipple and Evangeline returned to England to attend the centenary

Bishop Whipple's library at Faribault, ca. 1900. The portrait above the bookshelves is now at St. Mary's Hall. Whipple had a hidden closet behind the bookshelves, where he kept his private papers, his Indian artifact collection, and other prized items.

celebration of the Church Mission Society. As America's chief representative, Whipple spoke on Christian unity and the extension of missions. When he finished, the audience of six thousand rose to its feet, shouting "Minnesota! Minnesota!" A few weeks later, he received a doctor of divinity degree from Oxford.

On his return to Minnesota, his diocese held a grand celebration of the fortieth anniversary of his consecration as bishop. He was pleased by the presence of a large delegation of Ojibwe and a group of Dakota laymen from the Birch Coulee Mission, led by Good Thunder. The diocesan convention was one of "perfect harmony."

After another series of operations in St. Paul, he went east in mid-July for a few weeks at South Park. In September 1899, he launched his autobiography, *Lights and Shadows of a Long Episcopate* (published by Macmillan), in New York. He had begun writing his memoirs during the winter of 1894–1895, at the urging of his fellow bishops John Williams and William Doane. "It seems foolish," he said, but it passed the time. "It is pleasant to recall days long long ago—but it is hard work." Several early chapters appeared in the form of letters to *The Churchman* in 1896 and 1897.

The excitement of the book conference brought on an attack of bronchitis, and Dr. Daniels sent him home again to recover. A week later, he was back in New York to preside at the Peabody Fund meeting, giving an address on the "need of moral work and religious teaching for [the] colored race." He attended the Church Congress in Minnesota and the Missionary Council and House of Bishops meetings in St. Louis. On his way south to Florida in November, he paused in Nashville to meet with committees of Sewanee University and the Peabody Normal School trustees.

His eyes troubled him during January 1900, but by February he was able to sail to Puerto Rico to visit the church's missions there, performing confirmations on behalf of Illinois bishop William E. McLaren, who had official oversight of the mission. After touring the island, Whipple gave a speech on "Our Country" to a large crowd in the San Carlos amphitheater in San Juan on Washington's birthday. He later urged the House of Bishops to appoint a missionary bishop for Puerto Rico, but without success; Alabama's need for an assistant bishop was deemed more pressing.[493]

On March 2, 1900, Mahlon Gilbert died. Whipple

Whipple at St. Cornelia's Church at the Birch Coulee Mission, ca. 1898. Good Thunder suggested the church's name in honor of Whipple's wife, Cornelia, and her longstanding concern with the welfare of the Dakota. From left: Robert Hinman, son of Samuel, a teacher at the reservation school; Charles Good Thunder, son of Andrew Good Thunder; Reverend Henry W. St. Clair, a Dakota deacon; Mary Webster Whipple, Whipple's cousin; Evangeline Whipple; Bishop Whipple; Susan Salisbury, Whipple's niece; Andrew Good Thunder; Sam Wells; and George Crooks.

was still in San Juan at the time. "We had to break the news very gently to father," Charles Whipple reported to his sister Jennie. The bishop seemed more feeble than in the previous summer; "the exertion of preaching or any fatigue throws him into a violent perspiration."[494]

Throwing off his weakness, Whipple girded himself to resume the entire load of administering his diocese until a new assistant bishop could be elected. Even though three other bishops helped him with his parochial visitations, he was seriously stretched. There were also other commitments to keep, including the fiftieth anniversary celebration of Rome's Zion Church in September 1900, which he attended on his way to the Peabody Fund meeting in New York. At the end of October, he met with the church's Missionary Council in Louisville.

Andrew Good Thunder, who had done so much to keep the church alive among his people, died at Birch Coulee on February 15, 1901. When Whipple heard the news, he ordered a stone commemorative cross for the old chief's grave.[495]

In the six weeks between April 21 and May 5, 1901, Whipple preached and officiated at seventeen confirmation services, held one funeral, ordained one deaconess, and attended three diocesan meetings. ("Every hour up to June 5 is full," he informed the *Church Record*.) On July 1, he wrote Enmegahbowh, "I have never done more work in my life than I have done this year." Since Gilbert's death, he said, he had preached 239 sermons and confirmed 600 people. He had even visited the churches at White Earth (technically under Duluth's jurisdiction), whose people were still close to his heart.

At the June 1901 diocesan convention, Samuel Edsall, missionary bishop of South Dakota, was elected bishop coadjutor of Minnesota. Edsall, one of the men who had assisted Whipple with his duties during the previous year, had been his first choice for the position. Plans were made for Edsall to be installed at the General Convention in October.

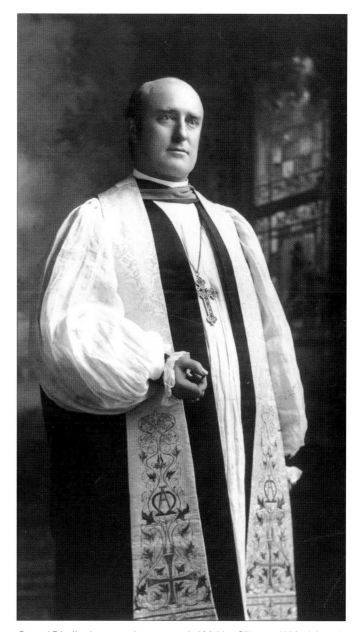

Samuel Edsall, who was to have succeeded Mahlon Gilbert as Whipple's assistant bishop in the fall of 1901, but instead succeeded Whipple himself.

Whipple was still fighting many of the old battles. On May 30, he asked the Board of Missions to restore Minnesota's appropriations to their previous level. He told them he was personally paying the stipend of Henry Whipple St. Clair, the Dakota deacon at Birch Coulee, and also funding schools for farmers and poor clergymen's daughters. The diocese also provided $650 annually to the

Swedish Mission. Minnesota gave more to the board's missionary fund than any other diocese west of Pittsburgh, he claimed, and deserved better treatment.[496] On August 29, he took on the Office of Indian Affairs on behalf of Madwaganonint's son, who was seeking the payment of arrears in annuities from 1864. Acknowledging that "the *books* at Washington" showed the money had already been paid, Whipple said he had no hesitation in taking the word of the old chief, whom he had known well, against that of Ashley Morrill, the agent at the time in question, who was "now a rich man in New York."[497]

By the end of August, Whipple was wearing out. Evangeline took him to the seashore, hoping the sea air would ease his lungs, but he caught a cold that settled in his chest. On September 5, he returned to Faribault to rest until it was time to leave for Octo-

ber's General Convention in San Francisco. He never made it. On September 16, 1901, the bishop's overworked heart finally gave out.

His body, garbed in the formal robes of his office, lay in state first in the private chapel in his home, then in the cathedral chancel. The cathedral was decked out in the purple and white of mourning, huge wreaths of oak leaves draping its arches and bishop's chair. The stained-glass window above the altar was framed in white from roof to floor, with clusters of oak leaves at its crown. Flowers covered the chancel floor. Crowds of mourners passed the coffin, wanting one last look at the man whom they had held in highest regard for forty-two years.

The burial service was held on Friday, September 20, in the cathedral, with Bishop Daniel Tuttle of Missouri officiating and seven other bishops in attendance. A line of Shattuck cadets stood at attention in front of the cathedral as the long procession of clergymen and laymen passed by. Forty Dakotas and twenty-five Ojibwes were present. Henry Whipple St. Clair, the Dakota deacon, and Fred Smith, an Ojibwe deacon, were among the pallbearers, as was the Swedish priest, Olaf Tofteen. As the bishop's body was interred beneath the altar, the Dakotas sang "Asleep in Jesus," one of Whipple's favorite hymns. The Ojibwes followed with "Jesus, Lover of My Soul," and then the entire congregation sang "For All the Saints Who from Their Labors Rest."

At a memorial service the following Sunday, the congregation sang more of his favorite hymns ("O God Our Help in Ages Past," "O Paradise, O Paradise," and "Ten Thousand Times Ten Thousand") and Psalms 1, 15, and 91. The choir performed John Stainer's anthem, "What Are These Which Are Arrayed in White Robes." Once more, the cathedral was packed.[498]

Many of those present must have felt like Enmegahbowh, who said wonderingly, "I did not think our bishop could die."[499]

In 1934, Whipple's remains were reinterred beneath the altar in the cathedral crypt, constructed in accordance with his widow Evangeline's will. At the same time, the family's private chapel was moved from the Whipple house to the cathedral.

Dedication of the Good Thunder memorial cross (which Whipple planned and Evangeline completed) at the Bishop Whipple Mission at Birch Coulee in September 1902. Charles Good Thunder, Andrew's son, kneels at left front; Bishop Edsall is to the right of the cross; beside him are Deacon Henry Whipple St. Clair; Sarah Good Thunder, Andrew's widow; and Evangeline. Henry St. Clair's son is the boy in the Shattuck uniform.

Dakotas and Ojibwes attended Whipple's funeral. The bishop's pallbearers included clergy from both tribes.

This portrait of Evangeline Whipple was painted in the garden of the palace of the late King John of Saxony, and includes her pet terrier. Evangeline left Faribault in 1910 and spent the remainder of her life in Bagni di Lucca, Italy. When she died in 1930, she left bequests to St. Mary's Hall and to the cathedral, where she hoped a museum would be built to commemorate her husband's work.

AFTER HER HUSBAND'S DEATH, Evangeline Whipple remained in Faribault for another nine years. She saw the stone cross the bishop had ordered for Good Thunder's grave put in place, blessed by Bishop Edsall. She purchased a peal of ten bells for the tower that was erected in 1902 by Dean Charles Slattery, funded by contributions from Whipple's friends from all over the country. She also continued her support for the Birch Coulee Mission, which was renamed the Bishop Whipple Mission, at her request.

Then, in 1910, Evangeline left abruptly for Italy, where her brother was seriously ill. Kingsmill Marrs recovered, but his sister did not return to America. She purchased a villa in the Tuscan town of Bagni di Lucca, where she and Rose Cleveland became members of a small community of expatriate women artists and literati. Her book, *A Famous Corner of Tuscany,* describes their life in those days. Evangeline and Rose were decorated by the Italian government for their work with the Red Cross during World War I. Evangeline remained in Bagni di Lucca after Rose died in the flu epidemic of 1917–1918. She took a strong interest in the welfare of the poor children and orphans in her adopted town, which repaid her kindness by naming a street for her. Evangeline Whipple died in London in 1930 and is buried beside Rose Cleveland in Bagni di Lucca.

Her will stipulated that her three Italian houses be sold and a fund established for Bagni di Lucca's poor. She left small bequests to family and friends, and larger ones to St. Mary's Hall and the Faribault cathedral. She asked that a crypt with a stone altar be constructed beneath the cathedral for her husband's remains, and a museum established to commemorate his work. The churches at Birch Coulee and Maitland also received gifts. The Faribault house, the deanery and a third house on the Whipple property were left to the diocese; they were eventually razed and the property sold.[500]

The Indian School at Morton, which Evangeline supported in her husband's memory. The former Birch Coulee Mission was renamed the Bishop Whipple Mission.

In 1933, the contents of the Whipple house were sold in a three-day-long estate sale. This included many of the art objects she had acquired before her marriage from the estate of Bavaria's mad king Ludwig II, as well as the 8,000-year-old stone frog from Egypt and a large sword said to have belonged to a crusading knight in the Middle Ages. Bishop Whipple's collection of Indian artifacts was divided between the Bishop Whipple Schools in Faribault and the Sibley House Association in Mendota. In 1980, both halves of this collection were brought together for a major exhibition at the Science Museum of Minnesota. The family chapel was moved to the cathedral in 1934, when the crypt and altar were installed.

Whipple's successor never lived in Faribault, preferring the more central location of Minneapolis. He used St. Mark's as his primary church, and in 1941 St. Mark's was officially designated the diocesan cathedral. The Faribault church was allowed to keep its cathedral status, however, in honor of Bishop Whipple.

The schools that were so close to the bishop's heart have survived into the twenty-first century, though not without change. Shattuck School and St. Mary's Hall were combined in 1972, and the boys' military program ended in 1974. Today's Shattuck-St. Mary's School maintains a high academic reputation and has developed nationally-recognized programs in the performing arts and ice hockey. The Breck School moved to Minneapolis in 1915; it is now a private college-preparatory day school for students from preschool through grade twelve. Seabury also moved, in 1933, to the Northwestern University campus in Evanston, Illinois, joining with Western Theological School to form Seabury-Western Theological Seminary.

The cathedral tower was erected by Dean Charles Slattery as a memorial to Bishop Whipple. Contributions came from donors as diverse as the archbishop of Canterbury and President Grover Cleveland to "Blind Charlie" of Eatonville, Florida. The tower was dedicated on November 1, 1902. Whipple's successors moved the diocesan headquarters to Minneapolis. When St. Mark's was designated the diocesan cathedral, the Cathedral of Our Merciful Saviour was permitted, because of its historic importance, to retain its cathedral status as "a perpetual memorial and shrine" to Whipple.

*I*n his forty-two years as bishop of Minnesota, Henry Benjamin Whipple saw Episcopal church membership in the state grow exponentially. By the time of his death, Minnesota had nearly 200 Episcopal churches, with more than 15,000 communicants, and was home to two dioceses. This was a significant increase from the 21 churches, 20 clergy, and 476 communicants that made up the original diocese of Minnesota in 1859.[501] In 2007, as it began its sesquicentennial year, the Episcopal Diocese of Minnesota had 25,260 active members in 107 parishes, ranging in size from St. Mark's Cathedral in Minneapolis (1,480) to St. Paul's in LeCenter (8). There were 296 resident clergy (priests and deacons together).[502]

As a preacher, organizer, fundraiser, and peacemaker, Henry Whipple had few peers. An unidentified Shattuck graduate in 1901 recalled the bishop's sermons as "an appeal, sometimes pathetic, sometimes stern, but always powerful. . . . His voice . . . seemed to reach and search the very souls of those that heard it. . . . His theme was the old gospel, but he gave it a very direct and practical bearing on the conduct of life. . . . As he talked, growing more and more earnest and impressive, it seemed as though he were one of God's prophets, divinely sent with a message from God to the youthful congregation hanging on his words."[503]

But he is best remembered in the country at large for his championship of Native Americans, and in that respect, his record is more controversial. Many modern scholars speak of Henry Whipple as a leading spokesman for "the cadre of Christian reformers who caused so much grief in the name of civilization."[504] They consider him and his fellow reformers misguided men whose attempts to help the Native Americans resulted instead in the near-extermination of that culture and the native popluation's collective sense of self-worth. This zeal to correct historical bias is misleading. Whipple may not have been the unqualified benefactor of the Indian his contemporaries thought he was, but neither was he the villain drawn by modern detractors.

Whipple believed that only completely adopting American culture would prevent the native peoples' extermination—a fate that many of his fellow Americans felt was deserved. His diligent efforts to speed up the assimilation process were made more out of concern for the Indians than from a desire to win members for his denomination. Unlike many missionaries, he had a sincere fondness for the Native Americans in his jurisdiction. He did not see them as mere counters in some game he played with God, nor did he regard their culture as inherently evil. He respected native intelligence and morality, though he objected to those practices that did not correspond to EuroAmerican ideas of propriety. His deep faith in Jesus as redeemer and embodiment of the principle of love made him want to share that conviction with those unfamiliar with it.

The society in which Whipple grew up assumed an inherent superiority of English culture, republican democracy, and Protestant Christianity. History was viewed as a steady ascent toward a perfect society, Christian in religion and democratic in government, where poverty, crime, and war would cease to exist. America's manifest destiny—the inevitable spread of her version of civilization across the face of the earth—was never questioned. Immigrants, wherever they were from, were expected to conform, to abandon their native language and "quaint" customs and merge, through the hypothetical "melting pot," into the larger community. Only those who managed to speak and look like "real" Americans were granted grudging acceptance. Roman Catholics and Jews, who stubbornly held to their nonconforming faiths, were regarded with deep suspicion. African Americans and Asians, set apart by their physical appearance, faced even greater challenges. In this context, it is hardly surprising that Whipple urged the native peoples to transform themselves into English-speaking, Christ-worshiping farmers who wore cotton shirts, wool trousers, and hair trimmed in the white man's fashion. Nor is it surprising that those who did so still faced discrimination from their "real" American neighbors.

"Oh, if they would only live as Christians, all the dark cloud would pass away," Whipple wrote Richard Pratt in 1876. But the challenge to the Indians was more complex than that. The German, Scandinavian, or Chinese immigrant who chose to separate himself from his historic past could, if he wished, return to his place of origin and resume his old ways. Even Africans, who had not chosen to come to America and whose native culture had been eradicated as completely as many white Americans wished the Indian culture to be, had the option (after 1865) of returning to Africa to regain contact with their ancestral traditions. But for the Indians, this was all they had. If they abandoned their culture, there was no way to recover it, no other place on earth where it remained intact.

The persistent breaking of promises made by the government to the Indians, and the seemingly in-eradicable corruption that pervaded the system of government support for the Indians on the reservations, were Whipple's chief concerns. These things not only offended his sense of morality, they also interfered with his goal of convincing the Indians that Christianity and EuroAmerican civilization were worthy of replacing their indigenous culture.

Although Whipple's proposals for improving the government's relationship with the Indians and improving the Indians' welfare were not original, he managed to express them more succinctly than most of his colleagues and to place them more advantageously in the public eye. His beautifully rendered reports and speeches were exceptionally persuasive. Whenever he visited Washington, Philadelphia, New York, Boston, or other centers of political power, he found opportunities to talk with those in a position to affect public policy for Indian affairs. Others may have conceived the ideas first, may have laid them before those able to carry them out, but in the end almost every proposal can be traced back at some point to Minnesota's bishop. From 1862 until 1888, he urged the government steadily in one direction, toward the total assimilation of the Native American population into mainstream society.

Whipple's influence extended well beyond the world of Indian affairs and the Minnesota diocese: It was felt in African American education through his work with the Peabody Fund, in the worldwide Anglican Communion through his work in Cuba and other nations, and in Minnesota through his schools and his connection with the state's historical society. When he died, the *Minneapolis Times* gave him equal space on its front page with the death of President McKinley.

Idealistic, gregarious, romantic, hard-headed—the bishop was all of these things and more. Perhaps a rephrasing of the epitaph he chose for his beloved Cornelia sums up the guiding principle of his life: Henry Benjamin Whipple always tried to do "what he could." And he did it on a grand scale.

They Catch the Eye | Want Ads in The Times are studied. They bring business.

THE MINNEAPOLIS TIMES.

THE WEATHER
Tuesday—Partly cloudy.
Wednesday—Fair; warmer.
Temperature: High, 59; low, 47

VOL. XXIV. NO. 4269. TUESDAY MORNING, SEPTEMBER 17, 1901.—TEN PAGES. PRICE TWO CENTS.

MARTYR PRESIDENT SLEEPS AT HOME

Bishop Henry Benjamin Whipple of Minnesota Passes Away at Faribault.

The End Came After an Illness of Some Weeks at an Early Hour Yesterday Morning.

For Forty Years He Had Been at the Head of the Episcopal Diocese of Minnesota.

His Work Among Indians Made Him Famous the World Over---Bishop Edsall Succeeds Him.

Faribault, Minn., Sept. 16.—(Times Special)—Right Rev. Henry Benjamin Whipple, bishop of the Episcopal diocese of Minnesota, died at his residence at 6 o'clock this morning after an illness of several days.

The bishop's death was a shock to the people of Faribault, where he has lived over forty years, although it was known that his illness was serious. He rested easily yesterday, but lapsed into unconsciousness during the early hours of the night, and shortly after midnight it was evident that he could not linger long.

His death was peaceful and painless.

At the time of his death there were present Mrs. Whipple, two daughters, Mrs. H. A. Scandrett of Faribault and Mrs. F. W. Jackson of Cleveland; his son-in-law, Dr. F. M. Rose, who has been in attendance upon him; his nephew, H. B. Hill; Mrs. George Whipple, his sister-in-law; several grandchildren, and Dr. A. J. Stone of St. Paul, who had been summoned early last week when it was learned that the bishop's illness was serious.

Major Charles B. Whipple, U. S. A., his son, who had been here during his father's illness, was called to Chicago Saturday on some important government business and was not here when his father died.

The hour of the funeral has been set for 2 o'clock Friday, and until that time the body will lie in state in the chapel of the bishop's residence. The services will be at the cathedral, and priests from all over the northwest will be in attendance.

The remains of the bishop will be interred in a tomb in the crypt of the cathedral.

The bishop was ill when he and Mrs. Whipple returned from the east on Sept. 5. He caught a cold on the cars, and this brought on an attack of angina pectoris, which proved fatal.

His family physician, Dr. F. M. Rose, and Dr. A. J. Stone of St. Paul did all in their power to prolong life, but their efforts were unavailing.

Hopes of recovery were entertained until the early hours of last night, when his heart began to weaken, and the family was notified that the end was near.

WHAT HE HAS DONE

Bishop Whipple's Efforts in Behalf of the Indians.

Henry Bishop Whipple, first Protestant Episcopal bishop of Minnesota and sixty-eighth in the order of the episcopate, was born at Adams, Jefferson county, New York, Feb. 15, 1822. He received an academical education; feeble health interfered with a college course and he entered his father's store, taking an active interest in politics. He married Cornelia, daughter of Benjamin Wright of Jefferson county in 1842 and her influence united him to the Episcopal church. He studied theology, became a lay reader and deacon in 1849 and was ordained priest by Bishop DeLancey at Sackett's Harbor in 1850. As rector he had charge of Zion church, Rome, N. Y.

In 1857 he removed to Chicago and in the Church of the Holy Communion inaugurated the free church system, inviting the men in the railroad workshops to attend these services. In 1859 he was elected first bishop of Minnesota and was consecrated at Richmond, Va., on Oct. 13, and late in the fall departed for his new field of labor, making the journey through Minnesota entirely by stage, for there was not a mile of railroad in the state.

Bishop Whipple at once entered on the work assigned him and even before the convention had finished its work he had written to St. Paul to secure a residence. Not succeeding in doing this, he left his family in Chicago and began at once the labor that was to endear his name to thousands and build up a lasting monument of glory.

Settles in Faribault.

That very fall and winter he visited every parish and mission in Minnesota. Having been offered a home by the citizens of Faribault, he selected that city, which was then a trading post, as his home and settled there in 1860. Already two clergymen had opened a school in a rude shanty of one room and this became a theological and academical training-school for both sexes.

But it was more especially as the brave

Continued on Fourth Page.

Right Rev. H. B. Whipple.

THE TRUST WOULD MAKE OUR VERY FIRES SOMBER.

THE OLD.
Old King Coal
Was a warm old soul
And a warm old soul was he;
He'd send for a match
And he'd send for some wood
And he'd blaze right merrily.

THE NEW.
New King Coal
Has a sad, sordid soul
And a sad, sordid soul has he;
He sends for his stocks
And he sends for his bonds
And, miserly, counts his "Divvee."

PRESIDENT'S WIFE COMES

Mrs. Roosevelt Arrives in Washington Very Quietly.

Guest of Her Sister-in-Law, Mrs. William Cowles.

Plans for the Immediate Future Not Complete.

SPECIAL—
TIMES' WASHINGTON OFFICE:

Washington, D. C., Sept. 16.—Mrs. Roosevelt arrived in Washington at 2 o'clock this afternoon. She was accompanied by ex-Governor Charles H. Allen of Porto Rico; her sister-in-law, Mrs. William Cowles, and her oldest son, Theodore Roosevelt, Jr.

Captain Cowles met the party at the Pennsylvania depot. They quietly left the station at the baggage entrance and entered a carriage which Captain Cowles had in readiness. The station and streets were filled with people who had been waiting all day long for the arrival of the funeral cortege. So quietly did the wife of the chief executive arrive that not one of the waiting crowd recognized her.

At the Cowles residence, whither the party was driven, no demonstration marked the arrival, and, so far as outward appearances go, the house might have been closed. A few rooms at the back of the house were opened and aired to-day and made ready for occupancy, but as this is the residence of the president and his family, the house will be closed and draped in mourning until after the body of the deceased executive is removed to Canton.

Immediately after the arrival of Mrs. Roosevelt and Mrs. Cowles they retired to their rooms to rest. A number of callers left messages, but none was received until after 6 o'clock. There are so few women in official and social circles now in the city that Mrs. Roosevelt is spared the burden of answering sympathetic calls.

Among those who have known Mrs. Roosevelt for some years is Mrs. William R. Merriam, wife of the director of the census. Mrs. Merriam spent some time with Mrs. Roosevelt and Mrs. Cowles. Mrs. Nathan B. Scott, wife of the West Virginia senator, also was among the callers.

Mrs. Roosevelt on her arrival was dressed in deep mourning, wearing a heavy crepe veil. This evening she re-

Continued on Second Page.

DUKE OF YORK DEPLORES THE TRAGEDY

SPECIAL—
NEW YORK HERALD SERVICE.

Quebec, Monday—In reply to the mayor's address of welcome the Duke of Cornwall and York said:

"I take this, my first opportunity to express, in common with the whole civilized world, my intense horror of the detestable crime which has plunged into mourning the great and friendly nation south of us, and deprived them of their great first magistrate. The duchess and I heartily join with you in sympathy toward the people, with whom we are connected by ties of kinship and esteem, and our hearts go out to the wife and family of the late distinguished and beloved president."

MRS. McKINLEY RESTING QUIETLY

Washington, Sept. 17.—At 2:15 o'clock this morning it was stated at the White House that Mrs. McKinley appeared to be resting quietly. Dr. P. M. Rixey, her physician, remained at the White House all night.

ROOSEVELT OUTLINES HIS POLICY

Buffalo, Sept. 16.—President Roosevelt has outlined in some detail the policy he will follow during his incumbency of office. It will be remembered that when he took the oath of office he stated with much definiteness:

> It shall be my aim to continue absolutely unbroken the policy of President McKinley for the peace (and he emphasized that word), prosperity and honor of the country.

Yesterday the president gathered together some personal friends in Buffalo and those cabinet members as were here and gave to them such ideas as he has already formulated for the conduct of public affairs and his own policy. In no sense are they divergent from what has been the policy of Mr. McKinley. His policy as outlined to his friends at yesterday's conference will be:

"For a more liberal and extensive reciprocity in the purchase and sale of commodities, so that the overproduction of this country can be satisfactorily disposed of by fair and equitable arrangements with foreign countries.

"The abolition entirely of commercial war with other countries and the adoption of reciprocity treaties.

"The abolition of such tariffs on foreign goods as are no longer needed, for revenue, if such abolition can be had without harm to our industries and labor.

"Direct commercial lines should be established between the eastern coast of the United States and the ports in South America and the Pacific coast ports of Mexico, Central America and South America.

"The encouragement of the merchant marine and the building of ships which shall carry the American flag and be owned and controlled by Americans and American capital.

"The building and completion as soon as possible of the isthmian canal so as to give direct water communication with the coasts of Central America, South America and Mexico.

"The construction of a cable, owned by the government, connecting our mainland with our foreign possessions, notably Hawaii and the Philippines.

"The use of conciliatory methods of arbitration in all disputes with foreign nations, so as to avoid armed strife.

"The protection of the savings of the people in banks and in other forms of investments by the preservation of the commercial prosperity of the country and the placing in positions of trust men of only the highest integrity."

ALASKAN NATIVES DIE FROM PLAGUE

Tacoma, Wash., Sept. 16.—(Times Special)—Father Rene, superintendent of Alaskan missions just returned from western Alaska, where his careful investigation proves that not less than [illegible] Alaskan natives died last fall and winter of disease seeming like cholera and grippe combined. Old Indians died in the largest numbers. The Indians believed a case was brought across from Siberia and its spread was aided by a shortage of fish and other foods, impoverishing their strength.

President McKinley's Body Now Lies in the East Room of the Executive Mansion.

Real Funeral Services of the People of Washington Held in the Grounds Last Night.

Ten Thousand Voices Sob "Nearer, My God, to Thee," as the Casket Is Taken In.

To-day the Imposing State Services Will Be Held in the Capitol's Rotunda at Washington.

MRS. McKINLEY BEARS UP BRAVELY

Washington, Sept. 16.—Mrs. McKinley has stood the strain of the trying ordeal following the death of the president without breaking down and her physician, Dr. Rixey, is encouraged to beleive that she will go through the state cermonial without collapse. The half hour she spent beside the coffin on the train this morning was followed by a period of depression, but Dr. Rixey induced her to sleep this afternoon. Now that she has gone through with the trials and fatigues of yesterday and to-day, those nearest to her feel there is little danger of immediate collapse. Their dread is for the future, when the nerve-tension of the present ordeal is over, and when she is back to Canton, with the flood of recollection that must come upon her.

SPECIAL—
TIMES' WASHINGTON OFFICE.

Washington, Sept. 16.—The voice of the people breathed over the city and the thunder of state power was not heard. To-morrow the guns of the soldiers of the sea and land will cry out the grim grief of the sons of war. To-night 10,000 people stood on the tender, green, White House lawns and sobbed "Nearer, My God, to Thee."

The real funeral ceremonies of the people of Washington were held to-night. To-morrow it is to be the funeral of state. The state grief shows to all the puissant powers of the earth in symbols, and all the states of the earth weep with Columbia of America. The colors of the German emperor will be dipped when the guns of the army and navy of America ring the death salute; the flags of British power will fly at half-mast; the state power of France will stand with bowed head, and all the powers of earth will murmur prayers.

> There was no formal ceremony in this plain and simple funeral of the people. No leader of song raised his baton; no plumed officer led a procession; the prayers were not read from books and will not be reported in the newspapers; there were no great personages who strutted for the pomp of personal greatness, and there was no one to say when to begin and when to cease; when to weep and when to go home.

When the flag-draped bier, in the plain, black hearse, drawn by the six black horses, held by the six ebony grooms, all without the heavy drapings of black, turned into the White House there was a deathly hush. Now one could hear the voice of a frightened child, then there was the low fluttering words of a vast multitude, then all was still and the staccato-like clackings of the horseshoofs gave sharp relief to the low, monotone of suppressed and smothered silence.

Familiar Scenes Brought to Mind.

Nearly everyone in that vast assemblage had seen President McKinley step from the portals of the white mansion. He always moved with lively step from the door to the carriage steps. With a half grave and half merry smile he bowed first to the right and then to the left.

> McKinley was always grave, but when greeting strangers the seriousness would give way to that smile which warm-hearted host always gives a visitor. And as he drove away he always bowed again, lifting his hat a little higher, giving an extra nod and wave of the hand to a child or timid woman, sometimes even stopping for a word from the carriage to a wistful, wide-eyed child.

Nearly all had seen that sight, many of them scores of times. It came vividly to the minds of the newspaper men, who had waited on those steps many days for men of state to come and go. McKinley always had the same genial greeting for them. It was never forgotten, it never extended beyond the half-grave pleasantry.

When Mrs. McKinley was along she was always placed in the carriage before she bowed, but she gave her salutes as she was led to the steps, and he always stooped down to see if the groom had carefully arranged the rugs about her feet, and he always took a look at the cushions. Then he saluted the ones who stood respectfully with uncovered heads a few feet away. He leaned back in his carriage as though he enjoyed the ride, the rest, and the wholesome freedom of it all. His horses clattered along rather lively, and he made good time to the outer section of the city.

All this was part of the funeral in the minds of all these people who stood with bared heads to-night. A dry sob choked

Mrs. Theodore Roosevelt.

timeline

1822 Born February 15, in Adams, Jefferson County, New York.

1838–
1839 Attends Oberlin.

1838–
1848 In business in Adams.

1842 Marries Cornelia Wright, October 5.

1843 Daughter Sarah Elizabeth (Lizzie) born, August 2.

1843–
1844 Southern tour (to restore health) November–May.

1845 Daughter Cornelia (Nellie) born, August 26.

1847 Daughter Jane (Jennie) born, March 10.

1848 Begins study of theology under W. D. Wilson in Albany.

1849 Ordained deacon, August 26. Son Charles born, June 12. Called to Zion Church, Rome, New York.

1850 Ordained priest, February. Builds church in Rome, New York. James Lloyd Breck founds Associate Mission in St. Paul.

1852 Brother-in-law Benjamin Wright dies in Florida.

1853 Daughter Frances (Fannie) born, June 5. Visits brother John in Minnesota. Winters in Florida with family; interim rector at Trinity, St. Augustine.

1857 Son John born, March 16. Accepts call to Chicago (Holy Communion Church). First Episcopal Convention in Minnesota (diocese organized).

1858 Minnesota becomes state. James Lloyd Breck establishes first school in Faribault.

1859 Elected bishop of Minnesota, June. Doctor of divinity degree, Hobart College. Consecrated, October. Travels to Minnesota, November. Father dies.

Enmegahbowh ordained deacon by Jackson Kemper, missionary bishop of the Northwest.

1860 Family moves to Minnesota. Seabury incorporated. Writes letter to President Buchanan. Holds first diocesan convention, June.

1861 Civil War begins. Dispute with Chamberlain.

1862 Seabury Hall and Cathedral begun. Dakota uprising, August. Visits D.C., Antietam, General Convention, New York. Writes letter to Lincoln.

1863 Seabury Hall opens. Serves on Board of Visitors to Ojibwe.

1864–
1865 Winters in Europe for health.

1866 Shattuck School and St. Mary's open. First bachelor of divinity degrees awarded from Seabury.

1867 Enmegahbowh ordained priest. Writes Report to Board of Missionaries.

1868 Hole-in-the-Day murdered. Distributes money to Sisseton/Wahpeton in Dakota. White Earth reservation founded.

1869 Grant's Peace Policy begins. Board of Commissioners for Indian Affairs formed. Cathedral consecrated. Winters in Mentone.

1870 Mother dies, March. Diocesan Mission Board formed. Piegan Massacre.

1871 Visits Cuba. Offered Bishopric of Sandwich Isles. Rural deans appointed. Episcopal Commission on Indian Affairs formed.

1872 St. Mary's incorporated. Begins missions to railroad camps.

1873 Named to Peabody Fund. Reformed Episcopal Church founded. Ojibwe pine controversy.

1874 Father Tomazin controversy. Assassination attempt. American Church Congress formed. Begins Swedish work in diocese.

1875 Attends Canadian synod.

1876 Ordains first Ojibwe deacons. Becomes member of Treaty Commission to Sioux (Black Hills).

1877 Ponca removal.

1878 Buys land in Florida. Son John murdered.

1879 Brother John dies. George St. Clair becomes first Dakota deacon.

1880 Writes preface for Helen Hunt Jackson book. Dam construction begins on Upper Mississippi.

1883 Daughter Jennie's husband dies, September. Lake Mohonk conferences begin.

1884 Daughter Nellie dies, May. Attends Seabury Centennial.

1886 Lace project begins. Bishop coadjutor elected (Mahlon Gilbert).

1887 Attends Conference of Canadian Bishops in Winnipeg. Visits Alaska. Dawes Act passes.

1888 Attends Third Lambeth Conference. Receives honorary law degree from Cambridge, doctor of divinity from Durham. Brother George dies.

1889 Breck School founded. Wife Cornelia injured in train wreck.

1890 Samuel Hinman dies, January. Son-in-law Frank Craw dies, February. Cornelia dies, July 16. Tours Egypt, etc. Meets Queen Victoria.

1891 Swedish Mission takes hold. Presides at Phillips Brooks' consecration, October.

1895 General Convention, Minneapolis. Appointed to Board of Indian Commissioners. Duluth diocese established.

1896 Marries Evangeline Simpson in New York. Duluth bishop elected.

1897 Attends Fourth Lambeth Conference and Queen Victoria's jubilee (audience).

1899 Attends centenary of Mission Society in England. Receives doctor of divinity, Oxford. Autobiography published. Fortieth anniversary celebration.

1900 Mahlon Gilbert dies, March.

1901 S. C. Edsall elected coadjutor, June. Dies September 16.

Bishop Whipple inscribed this photograph of himself made in London (by photographers Elliott and Fry in Baker Street) to his wife Evangeline: To my dear wife, ever yours, H. B. Whipple, Bishop of Minnesota.

notes

Much of the original source material for this book comes from three works: Henry Whipple's autobiography, Lights and Shadows of a Long Episcopate; *his diaries and letters, found in the library of the Minnesota Historical Society in the Henry Whipple Papers, the Whipple/Scandrett Family Papers, and the Diocesan Records of the Episcopal Diocese of Minnesota; and (for the history of the diocese and the schools)* Fifty Years of Church Work in the Diocese of Minnesota, 1857–1907 *by George C. Tanner. Information from these sources will not be noted, except as necessary.*

PROLOGUE

1. Henry Whipple, *Lights and Shadows of a Long Episcopate* (hereafter *Lights and Shadows*), 136; Whipple's diary, 9/16/1862, Minnesota Historical Society (MHS), Episcopal Church Diocesan Records, Box 42; HW to Ezekiel Gear, 11/5/1862, Whipple Papers, MHS, Box 41, letter book 4; HW to Henry Rice, 11/12/1862, Henry Rice Papers, MHS; Journal of the Episcopal Diocese of Minnesota, June 1863. The date and purpose of Whipple's meeting with President Lincoln has been debated for many years. In his autobiography, *Lights and Shadows*, Whipple says that it occurred in the fall, when he was on his way to the church's General Convention, held that year in New York on October 1-17. His letter to Gear says, "I went to Washington to lay before the President & Department [of Interior] a true statement of the causes of this fearful outbreak. He referred me to the Dept. I spoke very plainly in honest Saxon and charged this war upon a wicked and pernicious system which has & will thwart the kind wishes of the Government. I spent several days examining the books of the Indian bureau." The end of the letter refers to his visit to the battlefield at Antietam, where fighting had taken place on September 17. In his diary, Whipple tells of speaking with officials at the department of the interior on September 16, and of his visit to Antietam on September 18-19. He then returned to Washington, leaving for Philadelphia on the 27th en route to the convention in New York. There is no indication that he returned to Washington in 1862. Following the end of the convention, he embarked on a tour of New York, New Jersey, Rhode Island and Boston to raise funds on behalf of Minnesota settlers affected by the Dakota war. At the end of October, he took his father-in-law's body to Rome, New York, for burial. He then revisited Pennsylvania (still raising funds) and was in Carlisle, Pennsylvania, when he learned of the results of Sibley's trials, probably from the newspaper accounts. We know this from the letter he wrote from Carlisle to Minnesota Senator Henry Rice on November 12. He was back in Faribault on November 23. The fighting in Minnesota ended on September; the results of the trials were sent to Lincoln on November 5. In his address to his diocesan council in June 1863, Whipple clearly states, "I have never written or spoken a word to the president to shield any man who was condemned . . . for I have always feared to interfere with the administration of justice." All of this suggests that Whipple's meeting with Lincoln took place on September 16, before the battle of Antietam; that they discussed only the causes of the Dakota war, not its results; that he then (as he says in *Lights and Shadows*) visited the Bureau of Indian Affairs with Lincoln's permission to examine their records before going to Antietam on the 18th to visit the survivors of Minnesota's First Volunteer Regiment.

2. Pope to Edwin Stanton, 9/22/1862; Halleck to Pope, 9/23/1862, *Official Records,* series 1, vol. 13, 658, 663.

3. Some Ojibwe, under the leadership of Hole-in-the-Day, attacked the Episcopal mission at Gull Lake (then headed by the native deacon John Johnson Enmegabowh) and threatened war against the white, but they were a minority. The Mille Lacs band, in fact, sent warriors to protect the white communities at Fort Ripley and Crow Wing.

4. Whipple's diaries, in the Minnesota Historical Society (MHS) library, detail his meetings with leaders of the Ojibwe and Dakota tribes. Reactions to his letter to the press appeared in the *St. Paul Press* in December 1862.

5. Whipple's letter to Lincoln of 3/6/1862 is quoted in *Lights and Shadows,* 511.

6. Mark Diedrich, "Chief Hole-in-the-Day and the 1862 Chippewa Disturbance: A Reappraisal," 195.

7. In reminiscences written between 1893 and 1899, Whipple said that he had heard the story of Lincoln's reaction to his visit from Luther Dearborn, an Illinois lawyer whose wife's sister was married to Lincoln's law partner, William Herndon. Dearborn was in Minnesota in 1862, and a mutual friend in Washington told him that Lincoln asked, "Hasn't Luther Dearborn gone to Minnesota? When you see him, ask him if he knows Bishop Whipple. That man came here the other day and told me the story of the Indian's wrongs till he made me feel it to my boots." (These reminiscences are found in files owned by the Whipple family and in the MHS Whipple/Scandrett Family Papers. Whipple adds that Lincoln promised him, "If we live this system shall be reformed.")

8. Robert Kvasnicka and Herman Viola, eds., *The Commissioners of Indian Affairs, 1824–1977,* 91.

9. MHS Collections, vol. 10, 1900–1904, 714.

10. Many bodies were later dug up by local doctors who wanted skeletons for medical research.

CHAPTER 1

11. Henry Whipple's grandfather, Benjamin Whipple, had served in the American navy during the Revolution and was paralyzed as a result of his confinement in a British prison ship. His maternal grandfather, Henry Wager, was one of New York's electors in the presidential election of 1800. Other Whipple descendants include Stephen Hopkins (Rhode Island signer of the Declaration of Independence), Clara Barton, Susan B. Anthony, Calvin Coolidge, Franklin D. Roosevelt, James Russell Lowell, Tennessee Williams, and Brigham Young. Two Minnesota governors, Henry H. Sibley and John S. Pillsbury, had Whipple ancestors. From http://genweb.whipple.org, April 2005, and Charles Whipple, *Genealogy of Whipple-Wright-Wager, etc., Families* (hereafter referred to as *Genealogy*).

12. A third brother, David Wager Whipple, was born in 1839 but died the following year. Frances Ransom Whipple died in 1850, at the age of fifteen.

13. Frederick Ayer (1803–1867) first went to Minnesota in 1830, where he taught the children of the trader William Aitkin at Sandy Lake and developed an Ojibwe spelling book. In 1833, he and his wife, Elizabeth, opened a mission at Yellow Lake, near the St. Croix River, under the auspices of the American Board of Commissioners for Foreign Missions, which was founded by the Congregationalist Church in 1810. The Ayers went to Oberlin, Ohio, in 1840 to recruit missionaries from its divinity school. In 1855 the American Board withdrew its missionaries from the Ojibwe field, and the family settled in Belle Prairie. In 1865, they moved to Atlanta, where Ayer was superintendent of the American Missionary Association's schools for freedmen. (Source: Rebecca Kugel, *To Be the Main Leaders of Our People,* 25–50, 102; www.infoplease.com; online AMA Records, 1860–1888; William W. Folwell, *A History of Minnesota,* vol. I, 173.)

14. The Methodists built a church in Adams in 1828. The first Episcopal church in the town was not formed until 1849. (See *Our County and Its People: A Descriptive Work on Jefferson County*, 395-429.)

15. In contrast to the old Calvinist doctrines, the revivalists preached that man was not predestined to heaven or hell; he was a "moral free agent" who could obtain salvation by his own efforts, but he had only a limited time to do it in and would be well-advised to start now. (Andrew S. Brake, *Man in the Middle: The Reform and Influence of Henry Benjamin Whipple,* 19–20; see also Eric Foner and John Garraty, *The Reader's Companion to American History,* 975.)

16. In towns like Adams, teachers—often young men trying to earn money to pay their way to college or killing time while they looked for a job as a clerk or a minister—were hired by groups of parents or by the church.

17. *Genealogy*, 55–56. The school was probably chosen on the advice of his Wager grandparents, who still lived in Oneida County, where Clinton is located. Many of Whipple's relatives lived in Oneida County, including two of his father's sisters and most of his mother's family. It was probably at this time that he got to know his cousin Henry Halleck, who was eight years his senior.

18. Later known as the Jefferson Institute, the school was run by Professor James Robert Boyd, subsequently the author of a widely used textbook on rhetoric and literary criticism. Boyd's assistant, the Reverend John Covert, took the fourteen-year-old boy under his wing and they became close friends. (*Our County and Its People*, 319; *Appleton's Cyclopedia of American Biography*, vol. 1, 340.)

19. *General Catalogue of Oberlin College 1833–1908*, p. 1046 and Int. 181. The younger of John Whipple's two brothers, George Whipple (1805–1876) was educated at Oneida Institute and Lane Seminary and became a minister of the Congregational Church. He joined the faculty of Oberlin in 1836, first as principal of the preparatory department and then as professor of mathematics and natural philosophy. His wife, Alice Bridge Webster (a niece of Daniel Webster), served on the school's Women's Board of Managers from 1842 to 1847. George Whipple was elected secretary of a nondenominational abolitionist organization, the American Missionary Association, in 1847 and moved to Brooklyn, New York, where he remained until his death in 1876. An outspoken abolitionist before the Civil War, he was offered the presidency of Howard University in the early 1870s, but refused it. George and Mary Whipple had four children, including Mary Webster Whipple, who was involved in Minnesota's Indian lace project in the 1880s, and Ezekiel Webster Whipple, who taught for many years at Shattuck and was fondly known as "Old Zeke." (*Genealogy*, 19; *Faribault Republican*, 10/18/1876, 2.)

20. *Minnesota Historical Society Collections*, vol. 9, 1898–1899, 576, from a speech by Henry Whipple at the fiftieth anniversary of the state of Minnesota.

21. Author's conversation with Edward C. Rosenow, M.D., April 28, 2005, who analyzed Whipple's symptoms as described in his diaries and letters.

22. Carol Sheriff, *The Artificial River: The Erie Canal and the Paradox of Progress, 1817–1842*, 54–95.

23. Unrest in Canada in the late 1830s had made New Yorkers uneasy. They were afraid that the Canadian independence movement might lead to armed revolt, and if so, the United States could be drawn in. Many Americans thought that Canada should have been included in the original United States and were sympathetic to any signs of its desire for independence. But the anticipated violence never arose, and in 1867 Canada finally achieved a degree of autonomy when she was declared a separate dominion within the British Em-

pire. (Morison, *The Oxford History of the American People*, 461–67.) Although Whipple never saw active military duty, he was promoted in 1840 to the militia rank of major and in 1842 to lieutenant colonel.

24. He also joined the Adams fire department in 1845.

25. *Genealogy*, 42, 59.

26. 1892 memoir in Whipple family's private papers; message to 1891 diocesan council, published in *Minnesota Missionary and Church Record*, July 1891.

27. 1892 memoir.

28. The operation was probably to drain a peritonsillar abscess. (Dr. Edward C. Rosenow.)

29. Sarah Elizabeth (Lizzie) Whipple (1843–1918) married Charles Farnum (1825–1910) and moved to Philadelphia. In addition to Charles' three children by a previous marriage, she had three children of her own: Cornelia (Nell, born in 1865), Henry (born in 1868), and Arthur (born in 1879). Arthur became an Episcopal priest.

30. Much of the material on pages 21–24 comes from *Bishop Whipple's Southern Diary: 1843–1844*, published by the University of Minnesota in 1937. Mrs. Reid's husband had been governor of Florida under President Van Buren from December 1839 until his death from yellow fever in July 1841. Sarah Wright's marriage to George R. Fairbanks comes from the *Genealogical and Family History of the County of Jefferson, New York*, 51.

31. Whipple still felt much the same way at the end of his life, when he wrote to the bishop of Tasmania about the impropriety of marriage between races. It was undesirable, he wrote, because the differences of experience and culture would place an unbearable strain on the marital relationship. These differences were not insurmountable, but would require time and training to ameliorate. (HW to bishop of Tasmania, 7/1/1901, Whipple Papers, Box 11.)

32. As the boat passed Vicksburg, a fellow traveler told him it was the home of Judge Lynch, who had hanged a group of "desperadoes" without benefit of trial; he had the very tree used for the hanging pointed out to him. Whipple's leg was being pulled. The origin of the term "lynch" is still being debated; "Wordwatch" (a weekly Q & A newspaper column prepared in 2005 by the editors of *Merriam-Webster's Collegiate Dictionary*) identifies the most likely suspect as Captain William Lynch (1742–1820), who ran a vigilante-type operation in western Virginia around 1780. The first written use of the word lynch as a verb dates from 1836.

33. Twenty-two years later, when the first transatlantic cable joined England with Newfoundland, instant communication connected most communities in the United States, as well as the continents of Europe and North America.

34. The "foreign scum" were probably Irish immigrants who had come to America to escape starvation during the potato famine. At this stage of his life, Whipple was a supporter of the Native American Party, a nativist group sometimes called the "Know-Nothings." It was a phase he would grow out of as his experience of the world increased.

35. Cornelia Ward (Nellie) Whipple (1845–1884) was married twice. Her first husband, William Davis, died of tuberculosis eight days after their wedding. Her second husband was Dr. Francis Rose (1841–1916). Of her four children only one, Frances (1881–1965), survived. She died of tuberculosis and is buried in Faribault. Jane Whiting (Jennie) Whipple (1847–1932) married Henry A. Scandrett (1843–1883), who died of tuberculosis contracted during his service in the Civil War. Two daughters died in infancy, but their other four children—Cornelia (Nellie, 1873–1946), Henry (Buzz, 1876–1957), Jane (Jeanie, 1878–1970), and Benjamin (1883–1954) grew up in the home of their Whipple grandparents in Faribault after their father's death.

36. DeLancey's letter to Whipple describing requirements for study, dated January 12, 1848, is in the Whipple/Scandrett Papers, Box 1. William Dexter Wilson (1816–1900) was a founder of Cornell University. A graduate of Harvard Divinity School, he left the Unitarian Church for the Episcopal Church and was ordained priest in 1847. Rector of Christ Church, Sherburne, from 1842 to 1850, he then taught at Geneva (Hobart) College from 1850 to 1868 and at Cornell from 1868 to 1886. He was dean of St. Andrew's Divinity School in Syracuse from 1887 until his death. (www.episcopal-life.org/19625_13060_ENG_HTM.htm, September 2006.)

37. Charles Slattery, *Certain American Faces*, 104. See also Whipple, *Five Sermons*, "Address at the Burial of Mrs. J. Lloyd Breck," and "Niobrara," the sermon preached at the consecration of William H. Hare as missionary bishop of Niobrara. See also Andrew Brake, *Man in the Middle*, 22; first quote is from Whipple's Quarterly Message to the Diocese (July–September 1895).

38. Slattery, *Certain American Faces*, 111; Franklyn Curtiss-Wedge, *History of Rice and Steele Counties, Minnesota*, 265.

39. *History of Rice and Steele Counties*, 285–86.

40. Slattery, *Certain American Faces*, 107.

CHAPTER 2

41. Charles Henry Whipple (1849–1932) married Evelyn McLean (1851–1932). He spent most of his working life in the army as a paymaster, retiring in 1912. He served in the Philippines during the Spanish-American War. He had three sons: Charles (born in 1872), Henry (born in 1874), and Nathaniel (born in 1875).

42. HW's reminiscences to George Tanner 1892-93, Whipple Papers, MHS, Box 32. Episcopal mis-

sionary salaries during the 1840s ranged from $150 to $500 per year, depending on marital status, number of children and outside income. (Elinor Hearn, assistant archivist at Episcopal Church Archives, Austin, TX, to Mrs. Alton K. Fisher, 9/4/1981) According to George Tanner, *Fifty Years of Church Work in the Diocese of Minnesota* (hereafter *50 Years*), missionary salaries still averaged about $300 a year in 1867.

43. www.romenewyork.com, March 2006.

44. Frederick Reid, *Saints in Zion,* 8–9.

45. When one of his assistants approached the rector of a church in a large eastern city, appealing for funds for one of Whipple's projects, the rector replied, "Why, sir, a few weeks ago Bishop Whipple was in this city, and, sir, he stripped my parish clean, and I haven't been able to secure a dollar since then for anything." (Episcopal Diocese of Minnesota, *The Church Record,* vol. 25, no. 10, October 1901, "In Memoriam, Henry Benjamin Whipple, D.D., L.L.D.," 6–7.) In 1849, before sending him to Zion, Bishop DeLancey had used Whipple as a fundraiser for the newly founded Geneva (later called Hobart) College, and Whipple had purchased books for the college's library as DeLancey's agent.

46. The information on the financing and building of Zion Church, and Whipple's institution as its rector, comes from Reid 7–11.

47. Frances Ransom (Fannie) Whipple (1853–1940) was married twice, first to Frank Craw, who died in December 1889, and then to Freedom Ware Jackson (1857–1928). She lived in Cleveland, Ohio. Fannie had one daughter, Frances (born in 1898).

48. Reid, 12; see also Whipple's notes for the *National Encyclopedia of Biography* in the Whipple/Scandrett Papers, Box 3.

49. Whipple's brother-in-law Benjamin Wright was Trinity's rector from 1848 until his death in 1852. Wright had developed tuberculosis while serving at his first parish in Sackets Harbor, New York, and went to Florida partly in hopes of regaining his health. He was thirty years old when he died.

50. Whipple later observed that, during those pre–Civil War years, Charleston "was the most generous contributor to [Episcopal] Foreign Missions of any city in the United States."

51. Charlton Tebeau, *A History of Florida,* 138–43, 181, 196.

52. At 50 cents a dozen, the eggs represented a significant donation from these poor people.

53. Whipple wasn't the only one who admired the old man. When David died some years later, two bishops—William R. Whittingham of Maryland and Alonzo Potter of Pennsylvania—officiated at his burial.

54. The call from Grace Church was made at the recommendation of the Reverend Henry A. Neely

of Christ Church in Rochester, New York, brother of A. E. Neely.

55. For an example of pew rent rates, see George C. Tanner, *Fifty Years,* 124. Rome had a long history of financial problems before Whipple's arrival (see Reid, 5–6.)

56. Tuberculosis, or "consumption," was widespread in those days and almost inevitably fatal. Cornelia's brother Benjamin had died of it; her sister Sarah Fairbanks would die of it in 1858.

57. The letter to Neely is not in the Whipple papers; however, Whipple's letter of resignation to Zion parish, dated 3/19/1857, is in Whipple Papers, Box 2.

CHAPTER 3

58. A. E. Neely to HW, 3/5/1857, Whipple Papers, Box 2.

59. Donald L. Miller, *City of the Century,* 47–138. When an attempt was made in 1855 to close the German beer gardens on the Sabbath, it led to rioting in the streets.

60. All but thirteen-year-old Lizzie, who had entered St. Mary's School in Burlington, New Jersey. All of the Whipple daughters eventually attended St. Mary's.

61. Raymond W. Albright, *A History of the Protestant Episcopal Church,* 181–86, 226–46. Whipple's mentor, Bishop William DeLancey of Western New York, was a High Churchman, as was Bishop Jackson Kemper of Wisconsin, who would also play a role in Whipple's affairs. The Low Churchmen were led by Bishops Alexander Griswold of the Eastern Diocese (covering much of New England) and Richard C. Moore of Virginia.

62. For Whipple's views on ritual, see Tanner, *50 Years*, 436–441, and *Lights and Shadows*, 354.

63. The question of the unbroken line of succession of bishops from St. Peter to the present day remains important in Anglican tradition today.

64. Reverend John Elgar, *The Story of Nashotah,* and biographical sketch of Unonius, both on Project Canterbury, www.anglicanhistory.org, March 2005, and letters in the Whipple Papers, Box 2. Gustaf Unonius (1810–1902) was born in Helsinfors (then part of Russian Finland), graduated from the University of Uppsala, and immigrated to America in 1841. The first graduate of Nashotah House, he was ordained to the diaconate in May 1845. He did mission work among Scandinavian communities in eastern Wisconsin and Illinois before founding St. Ansgarius in the early 1850s. He left for Sweden in 1856 and never returned, spending the rest of his life promoting intercommunion between the Swedish and Anglican churches. His relationship with Bishop Whitehouse apparently deteriorated after his departure. An avid High Churchman, Unonius wrote to Whipple from Uppsala in March 1859, saying that

Whitehouse had replaced him at St. Ansgarius with a Mr. Gassman, who spoke Norwegian, and apparently didn't want him to return. Whipple (and probably Whitehouse) was under the impression that Unonius had "resigned his cure" when he left the United States. For Unonius's letters to HW on this subject, see Whipple Papers, Box 2.

65. One evening, as she entered a narrow alley to visit a dying woman whose husband was not at home, a rough Irishman, "who had seen the inside of a prison oftener than a church," tipped his hat to her and, knowing the nature of her errand, offered to wait for her outside the house, and then escorted her safely home. (*Genealogy*.)

66. Dedicated by Wisconsin's Bishop Kemper, Holy Communion Church remained active until it was destroyed in the Great Chicago Fire of 1871.

67. Clarkson later became bishop of Nebraska.

68. Albright, 181, 186, 226–48.

CHAPTER 4

69. William W. Folwell, *A History of Minnesota*, vol. I, 132, 213, 359, 360.

70. For information on the early history of the Episcopal Church, see Albright, 1–135, 161, 197, 216. The triennial General Convention is the governing body of the Episcopal Church. Today, it consists of a House of Bishops, to which all bishops belong, and a House of Clerical and Lay Delegates, consisting of up to four clerical and four lay (nonclerical) delegates from each diocese, plus one clerical and one lay delegate from each missionary jurisdiction. The presiding bishop was originally chosen for his seniority in office, but is now elected for a nine-year term.

71. Journal of the General Convention of the Protestant Episcopal Church in the United States of America, 1835, 82; also1838, as quoted on the Episcopal Diocese of Nebraska Web site, www.episcopal-ne.org, October 2004. See also *Spirit of Missions*, October 1, 1838, 331.

72. Albright, 161, 197.

73. Elgar, *The Story of Nashotah,* Project Canterbury.

74. The school was named for the first Episcopal bishop, Samuel Seabury. Information on early church history in Minnesota is from Tanner.

75. The quote is from *David B. Knickerbacker.* See also *Folwell*, vol. I, 359–61.

76. The procedure for selecting a bishop is somewhat complex. The candidate must be approved by a majority of lay and clerical delegations, voting separately, at the diocesan convention. The name is then submitted to the House of Bishops and the convention's Standing Committee, both of whom must approve the diocese's choice. Once the candidate passes these hurdles, a formal consecra-

tion service is held, in which at least three bishops must take part. Individual dioceses have their own rules for elections, which are set forth in their respective canons. Missionary bishops, who have no organized diocese to elect them, are appointed by the House of Bishops, but they too must be formally consecrated. Canons of the Episcopal Church of the USA, Canon 16.1.

77. Tanner, *50 Years*, 286-293, contains a detailed description of the circumstances of Whipple's election; the quote from Kemper is found on 286.

78. Arthur Coxe was later elected bishop of Western New York, succeeding William DeLancey after the latter's death in 1865.

79. In his 1893 notes prepared for the National Encyclopedia of Biography (in the possession of Whipple descendant Benjamin Oehler), Whipple identifies the man who recommended him to Paterson as the Reverend Mr. Clark.

80. John Whipple (1828–1879) worked as a dry goods merchant in Rome, New York. In 1856 he went to Minnesota as registrar for the township of Buchanan, near today's Duluth. Henry Whipple visited him at his office at Fort Ripley. In 1858 John opened a land office in Buchanan, but after the town collapsed in 1859 he moved to Portland, Minnesota, and served briefly in the state legislature in 1862. From 1862 to 1866 he served in the quartermaster corps of the Union Army. Soon after his discharge, he suffered a stroke, and a subsequent fall left him with a crippled leg. He never married and died in Fordham, New York. (Source: *Genealogy*. For information on John Whipple's experiences as land office receiver in the Duluth area, see Glenn Sandvik, "Land Office Buchanan," in *Minnesota History,* Fall 1991, 279–93.)

81. Mark Olds, as a deacon, was not allowed to vote.

82. Tanner, *50 Years*, 146.

CHAPTER 5

83. According to a letter from B. Dayton Ogden to HW, 3/13/1860, the cost of educating the Whipple daughters at St. Mary's School was $500 per year. Whipple Papers, Box 2.

84. *Minnesota in the Civil and Indian War,* vol. 1, 728. Charles Flandrau estimated that in 1849 there were approximately 8,000 Dakota, 7,834 Ojibwe, and 1,500 Winnebago in Minnesota; these numbers are not thought to have changed greatly in the ensuing decade. Douglas Linder *(The Dakota Conflict Trials)* estimates the Dakota population in 1862 at about 7,000.

85. Jackson Kemper was presenting bishop; other presenters were W. H. DeLancey of Western New York and Henry J. Whitehouse of Illinois. Also present were George Burgess of Maine, Nicholas H. Cobbs of Alabama, Thomas F. Scott of Oregon and Washington, Henry W. Lee of Iowa,

Thomas M. Clark of Rhode Island, and Samuel Bowman of Pennsylvania, all of whom joined in the consecration. At thirty-seven, Whipple was the youngest bishop in the church.

86. The child was not, as commonly believed, an Indian baby. Whipple's diary on 11/10/1859 (Episcopal Church Diocesan Records, MHS, Box 42, vol. 2) gives the child's name as Nathan Herrick Wright, born 10/24/1858, the son of William Warren Wright and Mary Wright of Wabasha. In the 1860 census for Minnesota, W.W. Wright and his family are described as white; William and Mary and their 7-year-old daughter were born in New York, while their son Nathan, 2, was born in Minnesota.

87. The report of J. W. Lynde, Ojibwe agent, to the commissioner for Indian Affairs, 9/15/1859 (1859 annual report of Commissioner for Indian Affairs, 19), mentions the prevalence of syphilis among the Ojibwe at this time.

88. Solon Manney was the boy's godfather.

89. St. Peter, located on the Minnesota River some seventy-five miles southwest of St. Paul, had been briefly considered as the site for the state capital.

90. Charles Bryant, *History of Rice County,* 322, 324.

91. Faribault's background: *Minnesota Historical Society Collections*, vol. 14, 1912; Edward Neill, *History of Minnesota*, 274; Charles Bryant, *History of Rice County*, 318, 320, 376-377. Son of a French-Canadian fur trader and his Dakota wife, Alexander Faribault (1806-1882) allowed several "friendly Sioux" families to live on his land after the 1862 Dakota war, providing them with work and supplies.

92. Reminiscences to Tanner; *History of the Schools at Faribault,* May 1876, published by *Faribault Republican.*

93. Bryant, *History of Rice County*, 350; see also Scott and Neslund, *The First Cathedral,* 14. The Indian school was named for William Andrews, an early Anglican missionary who translated the *Book of Common Prayer* into the Mohawk language. Its matron, Emily West, had been with Breck at Gull and Leech Lakes.

94. *History of the Schools at Faribault,* May 1876; *Faribault Democrat,* 7/3/1874, p. 1.

95. Whipple persuaded Breck to drop the school's claim to be a university. "I thought the public would honor a school which taught collegiate studies," he later told graduates of the University of Minnesota, "but they might despise a university which kept a parish school." (*Faribault Democrat,* 7/3/1874, p. 1.)

CHAPTER 6

96. Reverend William Cox Pope, in *Minnesota Historical Society Collections*, vol. 10, 1900–1904, 716.

97. Journal of the Episcopal Diocese of Minnesota, 1864, Appendix III, quoted in Tanner, *50 Years*, 164.

98. www.rupertsland.ca/history.htm, March 2005. For Whipple's opinions on Canadian Indian policy, see his 1868 report, "On the Moral and Temporal Condition of the Indian Tribes on Our Western Border," reprinted in *Lights and Shadows,* 522.

99. Stephen Riggs, "Protestant Missions in the Northwest," *Minnesota Historical Society Collections*, vol. 6, 1894, 164.

100. Details of the Chamberlain dispute are found in Whipple's diaries and in Tanner, *50 Years,* 174.

101. In 1867 the Chanhassen church moved to Eden Prairie. By the end of the century, only three of the churches Chamberlain founded were still flourishing: Holy Trinity and Gethsemane in Minneapolis and St. John's in St. Cloud.

102. Slattery, *Certain American Faces,* 102, 110. Whipple freely lent his clergy books from his personal library and showed them other kindnesses.

103. The weekly celebration of the Eucharist, not universal in the church, marked Minnesota as a High Church diocese. Low Church practice reserved the communion service for special occasions. (Albright, 187) Whipple once berated his protégé Samuel Hinman for dressing his choirboys in white surplices at Christmas. (Samuel Hinman to HW, 2/29/1868, Whipple Papers, Box 4.)

104. Address to English Society for the Propagation of the Gospel's 100th anniversary, 1899. The dispute with Chamberlain was more administrative than doctrinal.

105. Weekly reports of Seabury Juvenile and Primary Departments from 1860, Whipple Papers, Box 2. Expressing his respect for Solon Manney, who gave up a high government salary as an army chaplain to teach at Seabury, Whipple lists that salary as $1,800 in the 1876 "History of the Schools at Faribault" and $2,000 in *Lights and Shadows*. Regarding the nicknames: "canon" refers to church law, "rubrics" to the explanatory comments provided in the prayer book.

106. Tanner, *50 Years*, 194.

107. Whipple's speech to the teachers and professors of the church schools at Faribault, October 1881, Whipple Papers, Box 15.

108. *Faribault Democrat,* 7/3/1874, p. 1.

109. The continuing financial burdens of running a frontier diocese is a recurrent theme in Whipple's papers, which are full of notes from donors for his many undertakings; the amounts given run from less than a dollar to several hundreds of dollars. The cost of running the schools was aggravated by Whipple's practice of admitting needy students at little or no charge.

110. In his reminiscences to George Tanner in 1892 (Whipple Papers, Box 32), Whipple identifies the man only as an assistant secretary of state.

111. Whipple declined the army chaplaincy that was offered him in June, claiming that his diocese needed him more. Other Episcopal clergy were less hesitant. E. Steele Peake left Crow Wing in 1862 to join a Wisconsin regiment as its chaplain and served with them until the war ended.

112. Albright, 252. Whipple quote is from *Minnesota Historical Society Collections*, vol. 10, 1900–1904, 718.

CHAPTER 7

113. In 1848, lumber interests harvested some two million board feet of pine; by 1858 this had risen to more than forty-two million. (*Minnesota Historical Society Collections*, vol. 9, 1898, 361.)

114. Population figure is from *Minnesota Historical Society Collections*, vol. 10, 1900-1904, 693. The 1866 report of the commissioner of Indian Affairs cites a population figure of 4,000, which seems low (295); the 1870 figure is 6,367 (304).

115. Carol Berg, "Agents of Cultural Change: The Benedictines at White Earth," 159–61; Kevin Callahan, "An Introduction to Ojibway Culture and History, www.geocities.com/Athens/Acropolis/5579/ojibwa.

116. Stephen Riggs, "Protestant Missions in the Northwest," in *Minnesota Historical Society Collections*, vol. 6, 1894, 149; Rebecca Kugel, *To Be the Main Leaders of Our People,* discusses the missionaries' challenges in 25–44.

117. Unlike many converts, Enmegahbowh (ca. 1820–1902) did not abandon his Ojibwe name, but used both names interchangeably or in tandem, preferring to use the Ojibwe in his correspondence.

118. Kugel (26) also blames the influx of white loggers, miners, and farmers for disturbing the ecosystem, but game was already in seriously short supply before 1854, when the first large-scale land cession occurred.

119. www.dickshovel.com/win.html.

120. Kugel, 69–71.

121. One of these women, Jane Maria Mills, who arrived in 1853, would soon become Breck's wife. For a discussion of Breck's Ojibwe mission experiences, see Tanner, *50 Years*, 69-84, and Kugel, 76.

122. The Whipple Correspondence Papers contain many examples of Enmegahbowh's letters to Whipple and other clergy, giving them inside information on what is happening in the tribe. For example: 8/25/1862 letter from Enmegahbowh to Whipple describes his flight from the mission and the Ojibwe complaints that led to Hole-in-the-Day's attack; 9/6/1862 letter to James Lloyd Breck

expresses doubts of the long-term success of the government's settlement with the tribe; 5/3/1863 letter to Whipple claims that the Ojibwe are not happy with the recent treaty offered them.

123. The men were John Dix, G. S. Dickenson, Samuel Beardsley, C. Comstock of the Albany *Argus,* and Judge Hunt. Letter from HW to Buchanan, 4/9/1860, Whipple Papers, Box 2.

124. Whipple's letter to Buchanan, 4/9/1860, Whipple Papers, Box 2.

125. *Church Record,* In Memoriam, Henry Benjamin Whipple, DD, LLD, 1901, 14.

126. Possibly Father Francis Pierz, who founded the first Roman Catholic parish in Minnesota at Sauk Rapids in 1853. Pierz ministered primarily to the French Canadian mixed-blood community and the Irish soldiers at Fort Ripley. See Coleman *et al., Old Crow Wing,* 22–23.

127. Whipple's letter to Lincoln, 3/6/1862, Whipple Papers, Box 2.

128. Caleb Smith to HW, 3/31/1862, Whipple Papers, Box 3.

129. Morton S. Wilkinson to HW, 5/8/1862, Whipple Papers, Box 3.

130. Cyrus Aldrich to HW, 6/12/1862, Whipple Papers, Box 3.

131. George Whipple to HW, 4/26/1862, Whipple Papers, Box 3.

132. Henry Rice to HW, 4/26/1862, Whipple Papers, Box 3.

133. Diedrich, 195–97. For biographic data on Dole, see Kvasnicka and Viola, *The Commissioners of Indian Affairs*, 90.

134. Diedrich, 200; Kugel, 63, 90n14.

CHAPTER 8

135. www.flandreau.k12.sd.us/eldersspeak.

136. Background information on the Dakota comes from Gary Anderson, *Kinsmen of Another Kind,* xxix and 9–231; Roy Meyer, *History of the Santee Sioux,* 13–111; and Gary Anderson, *Little Crow,* 17–110. Most sources state that the Dakota were forced out of the lake country by the better-armed Ojibwe; Anderson says they moved south voluntarily to take advantage of new trade contacts with fur traders operating out of St. Louis along the Mississippi. See also Folwell, vol. I, 182–83, and Samuel Pond, "Dakotas or Sioux in Minnesota As They Were in 1834," *Minnesota Historical Society Collections,* vol. 12, 343, 383.

137. Folwell, vol. I, 92-94, 136. The payment was not made until 1819, when Fort Snelling was finally constructed.

138. Only Little Crow's village at Kaposia, near today's St. Paul, had to move; the others gave up hunting rights on the Mississippi's eastern shore.

139. Whiskey as an item of trade dated back to the fur-trading era, when competition led some traders to use whiskey to bribe native hunters away from their rivals. Whiskey cost relatively little, was easily transported, and could be counted on to muddle the minds of those who consumed it. It was so popular among the Indians that they used it themselves when trading with their neighbors on the plains; Little Crow spent a few years in the 1840s trading whiskey to the Yanktons and Tetons (Roy Meyer, *History of the Santee Sioux*).

140. The rationale for this was that after fifty years, the Dakota would be self-supporting and no longer need the money (Charles Flandrau to HW, 12/3/1897, Whipple Papers, Box 24).

141. Anderson, *Little Crow,* 66, quotes from a letter from Alexander Ramsey to Luke Lea, 8/28/1852.

142. There were cases of Indians who returned from their hunt to find a cornfield growing where their houses had been. (See Folwell, vol. I, 353.)

143. In *Minnesota Historical Society Collections,* vol. 9, 398, there is a description of the house by Mrs. N. D. White, who was a prisoner there during the Dakota War; *Minnesota Historical Society Collections,* vol. 12, 523, contains Dr. Asa Daniels's recollections of Little Crow.

144. www.crystalinks.com/sioux.html; Folwell, vol. I, p. 212. The American Board missionaries claimed their first adult male convert, Simon Anawangmani, in 1840 (see Riggs, *Mary and I,* 65). They had only thirty-one converts by 1852 (see John Willand, *Lac Qui Parle and the Dakota Mission,* 234), when they began to insist on the adoption by converts of EuroAmerican cultural forms, including farming, cutting of hair, and wearing of trousers.

145. Statistics from Whipple's diary for 12/12/1860, Episcopal Church Diocesan Papers, Box 42, vol. 2.

146. G. T. Bedell to HW, 10/4/1860, Whipple Papers, Box 1.

147. Much of the money came from Episcopal philanthropist William Welsh and from the Quaker establishment in Philadelphia.

148. Willand, 23; Gary Anderson and Alan Woolworth, ed., *Through Dakota Eyes: Narrative Accounts of the Minnesota Indian War of 1862,* 141.

149. Red Owl was a powerful orator who refused to attend the white man's church services. But Whipple was told that he was intrigued by the image of the crucified Christ, coming frequently to the mission school when the classes were over to sit before it in deep contemplation. Whipple was also told that, at his death, Red Owl asked that a cross be placed on his grave. (*Lights and Shadows,* 65.)

CHAPTER 9

150. The quote from Cornelia Whipple to her daughters, 7/27/1862, is quoted in Betty Oehler, *Bishop Whipple: Friend of the Indian*, 4.

151. See Big Eagle's statement, reprinted in Anderson and Woolworth, *Through Dakota Eyes*, 25. White Dog's wife would later become a Christian. She took the name Sarah and married Good Thunder after his first wife left him, ca. 1865.

152. William Welsh, *Journal of the Reverend Samuel D. Hinman, Missionary to the Santee Sioux Indians, or Taopi and His Friends*, 50.

153. Thomas Galbraith to HW, 5/31/1862, Whipple Papers, Box 3.

154. Samuel Hinman to HW, 6/19/1862, Whipple Papers, Box 3; Anderson, *Kinsmen of Another Kind*, 248. Charles Mix was the chief clerk in the Office of Indian Affairs for twenty years, often running the office in the absence of the reigning commissioner. He served one brief term as commissioner in 1858.

155. Mark Diedrich, "Chief Hole-in-the-Day and the 1862 Chippewa Disturbance," *Minnesota History*, Spring 1987, 195, quotes letters from Galbraith to Thompson, 1/31/1862 and 2/28/1862 (Clark Thompson Papers, MHS) which seem to support allegations of Galbraith's financial impropriety.

156. Folwell, vol. II, 236.

157. Centennial pamphlet, "Cathedral of Our Merciful Saviour," 1962. Over the next few years, the faithful around the diocese sent gifts of money and supplies, Whipple's wealthy friends in the East contributed their share, and Breck raised another $11,000 through his contacts. The ladies of the parish held ice cream socials to raise money for the organ, and at least two windows were given by the bishop's Indian friends. In the end, the cathedral cost perhaps $60,000.

158. Whipple, "Address on the Laying of the Cornerstone of the Bishop's Church," quoted in Scott and Neslund, *The First Cathedral*, 24–25. Whipple's cathedral was the first Protestant church to be built specifically for this purpose in the United States.

159. Completed in 1864, the stone structure was three stories high and seventy-five feet across the front. It cost $10,000, all donated by a few anonymous givers.

160. U.S. Department of Interior, Report of the Commissioner of Indian Affairs, 1863, 267.

161. Myrick, a twenty-eight-year-old New Yorker, had arrived in Minnesota a few years earlier with his brother Nathan, opened a trading post, and taken a Dakota wife. Myrick's wife, Nancy Stone, survived the fighting, along with their young daughter, Mary, and accompanied her Dakota family to Crow Creek and Niobrara. In 1884 Mary Myrick married Samuel Hinman, whose first wife had died in 1875. (US Census, Minnesota, 1860; also Samuel Hinman papers, MHS.)

162. Folwell, vol. II, 239.

163. "Taoyateduta Is Not a Coward," *Minnesota History,* September 1962, p. 115.

164. Folwell, vol. II, pp. 109–111. Hinman's wife was away at the time, visiting friends in Faribault.

165. Andrews Hall closed in 1862 and never reopened (Whipple, *Minnesota Historical Society Collections*, vol. 9, 134).

166. Folwell, vol. II, 115.

167. See Big Eagle's account of the battles in Anderson and Woolworth, *Through Dakota Eyes*, 147-153.

168. Three of the men later executed for their roles in the fighting were mixed bloods (*St. Paul Pioneer Press* account of execution, on www.law.umkc.edu/projects/ftrials/dakota). More than half of the women and children taken captive by the Dakota were mixed bloods.

169. John Other Day is credited with dissuading the Sisseton and Wahpeton from taking part in the fighting. (Anderson and Woolworth, 121.)

170. Report of the Commissioner of Indian Affairs, 1863, 32; Folwell, vol. II, 380.

171. Diedrich, "Chief Hole-in-the-Day and the 1862 Chippewa Disturbance," 197, quotes letters from Lucius Walker to Clark Thompson, September 13 and 24 and November 22 and 27, 1861, located in the Clark Thompson Papers, MHS. Diedrich covers this episode thoroughly.

172. Mooers, *St. Paul Daily Press* 5/3/1862 and *Pioneer and Democrat* 5/4/1862, 6/6/1862 (quoted in Diedrich, 199); Hole-in-the-Day to William Dole, 6/11/1862 (quoted in Diedrich, 200.)

173. Quoted in Whipple's letter to *The Churchman*, 2/11/1897. Two of Enmegahbowh's children died from exposure following their flight to safety.

174. This story appears on 110 of *Lights and Shadows;* Shaboshkung is identified on 249. See also www.millelacsojibwe.org/ojibhistory.asp.

175. Diedrich, 194.

176. *Lights and Shadows,* 317.

177. Folwell, vol. II, 178–82, 185, 192. As additional Dakotas straggled into the camp over the next few weeks, the number of prisoners reached more than seventeen hundred.

178. John Pope to Henry H. Sibley, Sept. 28, 1862, *Minnesota in the Civil and Indian Wars*, vol. II, 257.

179. Folwell, vol. II, 191, quoting Sibley's order book from *Minnesota in the Civil and Indian Wars*.

180. The three chiefs had sent a message to Sibley in mid-September, asking for the general's protection for themselves, their families, and as many captives as they could secure. (Folwell, vol. II, 172–73.)

181. Transcripts of trials of Sioux Indians, Case #200, Senate Records 37A-F2, cited in Anderson and Woolworth, 97.

182. Isaac Heard, "History of the Sioux War and Massacre," *St. Paul Press,* 1863, from www.law.umkc.edu; Riggs, *Mary and I,* 180.

183. Abraham Lincoln to John Pope, November 11, 1862, *Minnesota in the Civil and Indian Wars,* vol. II, 289.

184. Folwell, vol. II, p. 200.

185. Many of those who settled near Faribault were relatives of Alexander Faribault's wife. Whipple baptized some of them with the surname of Whipple, which their descendants bear proudly today. (Author's interview with Whipple descendant Ben Oehler, Jan. 3, 2005.)

186. Details of the Traverse des Sioux treaty (32 Congress, 1 session, *Senate Executive Documents* #1, pp. 279–82 [serial 613], *Statutes at Large,* 10:949–53) are found in Folwell, vol. I, 281; the 1858 treaty (*Statutes at Large,* 12:237) is in Folwell, vol. II, 218.

187. HW to Ezekiel Gear, 11/5/1862, Letter Book #4, Whipple Papers, Box 41.

188. Charles Slattery, *Felix Reville Brunot 1820–1989,* 84.

189. Albright, *History of the Protestant Episcopal Church,* 252.

190. The bishops who signed were John Williams of Connecticut, T. H. Clark of Rhode Island, Jackson Kemper of Wisconsin, C. S. Hawks of Missouri, George Burgess of Maine, Henry Whitehouse of Illinois, Alonzo Potter of Pennsylvania, Carleton Chase of New Hampshire, Alfred Lee of Delaware, Charles McIlvaine of Ohio, B. B. Smith of Kentucky, Manton Eastburn of Massachusetts, Horatio Potter of New York, Henry Lee of Iowa, George Upfold of Indiana, G. T. Bedell (assistant) of Ohio, William Stevens (assistant) of Pennsylvania, and Joseph C. Talbot, missionary bishop of the Northwest. The Minnesota laymen were J. Wilcoxon, Isaac Atwater, E. T. Wilder, and John Warren.

CHAPTER 10

191. Tanner, *50 Years*, 397-398, A. Ravoux, *Reminiscences, Memoirs, and Letters,* 82; Folwell, vol. II, 254. Ravoux also claimed to have baptized thirty of the condemned Dakotas at Mankato (Ravoux, 77). Although the missionaries tried to equate *wakan*

tanka (which they translated as the Great Spirit) with God, it was not quite the same thing.

192. Roy Meyer, *History of the Santee Sioux,* 137; Folwell, vol. II, 252, 259, 263. The quote is Folwell's.

193. U.S. Department of Interior, Report of Commissioner of Indian Affairs, 1863, 31.

194. Folwell, vol. II, 263; U.S. Department of Interior, Report of Commissioner of Indian Affairs, 1866, 244. Around two hundred "friendly Indians" were allowed to remain behind.

195. www.dickshovel.com/win. Some of the Winnebago went back to Wisconsin, where in 1875 the government purchased a second reservation for them. Today the tribal population is around twelve thousand.

196. S. Hinman to HW, 6/8/1863, Whipple Papers, Box 3.

197. G.W. Knox to HW, 3/25/1864, Whipple Papers, Box 3.

198. Folwell, vol. II, 260. In his *Report on the Moral and Temporal Conditions* (1868) Whipple tells the story of the women. For the mortality of children, see Welsh, *Taopi and His Friends,* p. vii. One child who survived was Mary Myrick, daughter of the hated trader Andrew Myrick.

199. Stephen Riggs, *Mary and I,* 194, tells about the women. The quote about the commandant is from T.S. Williamson to HW, 8/20/1863, Whipple Papers, Box 3.

200. S. Hinman to HW, 1/6/1864, Whipple Papers, Box 3.

201. For a discussion of these events, see Kugel, 77–86, and Folwell, vol. II, 377–79 and vol. III, 22–23.

202. Review of treaty by Whipple, 1863, in Whipple Papers, Box 3.

203. This may have been a record; Congress habitually sat on Indian treaties for months, if not years. A copy of the treaty is in HW Correspondence papers, Box 3, and includes the cession of the Gull Lake Mission lands.

204. Letter from Hole-in-the-Day to "Great Father in Washington," 6/7/1863, in 1863 report of Commissioner of Indian Affairs, 329–31. The clause regarding the Mille Lacs band contained the caveat that they must continue to cause no trouble. A copy of the treaty, signed on 5/7/1864, is in Whipple Papers, Box 3.

205. A copy of the Report of Board of Visitors, 11/9/1863, is in Whipple Papers, Box 3.

206. Hole-in-the-Day's house was burned on September 11. Hole-in-the-Day identifies two "white men," Peter Kelly and Ezra Briggs, as the arsonists; Melissa Meyer (*White Earth Tragedy*, 45) says

these "white men of Crow Wing" were mixed bloods connected with the traders. The mixed-blood population occupied an ambivalent position on the reservations: considered "white," they nonetheless often collected annuity payments for their blood connection to the tribe and were involved in tribal politics. Hole-in-the-Day had often worked through them in his dealings with Washington.

207. William Dole to HW, 3/3/1864, Whipple Papers, Box 3.

208. Joseph A. Wheelock to his wife, published in *Minnesota History,* vol. 16, no. 2, June 1935. The reference is to Professor W. D. Wilson, Whipple's tutor during his seminary years (see chapter 1). "Noctes Ambrosium" was probably something he wrote for publication.

209. William Dole to HW, 4/9/1864, Whipple Papers, Box 3.

210. Enmegahbowh to HW, 4/28/1864, Whipple Papers, Box 3.

211. Not until Thompson was replaced in 1865 did matters improve.

212. J. R. Doolittle to HW, 5/25/1864, Whipple Papers, Box 3. James Rood Doolittle served as Wisconsin's U.S. senator from 1857 to 1869 and was chair of the Committee on Indian Affairs in the 37th–39th Congresses.

213. Journal of the 7th Annual Convention of the Diocese of Minnesota, June 8-9, 1864, p. 11. In his autobiography, Whipple estimated his travel within the diocese at three thousand miles per year during those pre-railroad days.

214. Robert Minturn to HW, 7/14/1864, 10/2/1864, Whipple Papers, Box 4; letter from clergy, dated June 1864, suggesting he take six months' leave, Whipple Papers, Box 3.

CHAPTER 11

215. Most of the information concerning Whipple's trip to Europe comes from letters written to his wife, Cornelia; some of them are in Box 4 or in a letter book in Box 41 of the Whipple Papers; others appear in Box 1 of the Whipple/Scandrett Papers.

216. The Caird family became close friends of Whipple's, and he often visited them on his trips to England. In 1869, Whipple's son Charles spent the summer with them. The family also included Edward Caird (1835–1908), a leading neo-Hegelian philosopher who taught at Glasgow and Oxford, and John Caird (1820–1898), one of the Church of Scotland's most eloquent preachers. The Free Church had left the official Church of Scotland in 1843 in a dispute over the right to govern itself without interference from the government.

217. The quote is from *Lights and Shadows,* 190. Tait succeeded Longley as archbishop of Canterbury.

218. For information on Edward Pusey, see Albright, 226-228; www.newadvent.org/cathen/12582a.htm; www.ccel.org/s/schaff/encyc/encyc09/htm/iv.v.ciii.htm.

219. In addition to observing a daily cycle of prayer, these women frequently served as nurses during the epidemics that swept through Victorian England. Subsequent houses later opened in London, and by 1852 the movement had expanded to the United States, where houses were established in New York City and Philadelphia. (www.anglicanhistory.org/bios/plsellon.html, December 2005; www.womenshistory.about.com/cs/religion/p/ann_ayres.htm, December 2005.)

220. Ferguson and Bruun, *A Survey of European Civilization,* 785.

221. Whipple, *Five Sermons,* 85, 128.

222. Background on William Aspinwall from *Appleton's Cyclopedia of American Biography,* vol. 1.

223. The 1865 eruption of Mount Etna was the largest to occur in nearly two centuries. It removed 170 feet from the top of the volcano and was followed by a 4.7 magnitude earthquake that killed seventy people. (www.boris.volcanoetna.com and www.wikipedia.com, July 2, 2006)

224. Names of Whipple's companions are found in a letter of introduction written by Charles Hale, 2/21/1865. Robert Minturn's friend J.C. Hooker also wrote to HW on 1/7/1865. Both letters in Whipple Papers, Box 4.

225. This was possibly a form of malaria, although it may have been his old bronchiectasis, combined with pneumonia. (Drs. Edward C. Rosenow and John Joyce, conversations with author.)

226. Lampson, a native Vermonter who had lived in England for many years, received a knighthood in 1866 for his role in laying the first transatlantic telegraph cable. He was also deputy governor of the Hudson's Bay Company and a trustee of the Peabody Donation Fund, which benefited London's poor. He and Whipple had a common interest in Indians.

CHAPTER 12

227. *Lights and Shadows,* 248–49.

228. Albright, 252–54.

229. They were especially concerned with ending Lakota harassment of travelers on the Bozeman Trail from Fort Laramie to Montana's gold fields.

230. The Crow Creek agency was not completely abandoned, however. It was used for a time as a point of distribution of supplies for the tribes of the eastern plains under treaties signed in 1866 and 1868 (Lazarus, 56). Later it became a reservation for the Lower Brule Lakota, and a mission was established there by the Episcopal Church in 1871. See the 1st Annual Report of the missionary bishop of Niobrara (W. H. Hare) dated September 30, 1873.

231. S. Hinman to HW, 3/23/1865, Whipple Papers, Box 4.

232. "An Act for the Relief of Certain Friendly Indians of the Sioux Nation in Minnesota," 2/9/1865, Whipple Papers, Box 4.

233. HW to commissioner of Indian Affairs, 6/22/1866, Whipple Papers, Box 4.

234. Samuel Hinman to HW, 6/1/1866, Whipple Papers, Box 4.

235. Information on the founding and development of the schools at Faribault is from Tanner, chapters 24, 32, and 37.

236. *Lights and Shadows,* 191–92.

237. *Lights and Shadows,* 192–93. As Whipple told the story, a man (possibly Brunot, though Whipple didn't identify him) made him an offer for the land. Whipple asked him if he didn't own a coal mine on the adjoining property, which could be more efficiently mined by tunneling from Whipple's property? The man said yes. And wasn't there another man who owned a coal mine on the other side of the property? Yes, there was. "Then have I not the same right to take advantage of the peculiar position of my land that I would have if it were a corner lot in a city?" Whipple asked. "Of course you have," the man agreed, and raised his offer to $12.50 over the market price.

238. Bryant, *History of Rice County*, 339, 341. Another state school was added for the mentally impaired in 1881, and St. Mary's Hall was relocated nearby in 1883.

239. St. Paul's had acquired it from the defunct Kemper College in similar circumstances. The nineteenth century saw the birth and death of hundreds of small colleges as the nation's boundaries moved steadily westward.

240. Whipple does not identify the bishop of Chester, but it was probaby William Jackson, who held the position from 1865 to 1884.

241. Hiram Sibley to Whipple, 2/10/1865 and subsequent, Whipple Papers, Box 4. The original is housed in the British Museum in London.

242. Tanner, *50 Years*, 414.

243. Darlington (1829–1881) headed St. Mary's until 1881, when she succumbed to typhoid pneumonia.

244. Bryant, 352.

245. Quoted in Bryant, *History of Rice County*, 353, and in Tanner, *50 Years*, 419-420.

246. When the nationwide financial panic of 1873 threatened to halt construction on some of the school buildings, Whipple managed to get a $30,000 loan from one of the town banks to complete the work. (*Lights and Shadows,* 194.)

247. Slattery, *Certain American Faces,* 103.

248. Tanner, *50 Years*, 278-279, 425.

249. Catalog and Circular, 1873, 22, quoted in Scott and Neslund, *The First Cathedral,* 84; Bryant, *History of Rice County*, 347–49.

CHAPTER 13

250. See, for example, letter from Iron Shields at Faribault to HW, 8/9/1867, Whipple Papers, Box 5.

251. Enmegahbowh to HW, 8/12/1866, Whipple Papers, Box 4.

252. HW to D. M. Cooley, 9/28/1866, Whipple Papers, Box 4.

253. HW to H. M. Ruin, 4/19/1866, Whipple Papers, Box 4.

254. HW to Joel Bassett, 11/14/1866, Whipple Papers, Box 4.

255. Enmegahbowh to HW, 11/26/1867, Whipple Papers, Box 5.

256. The BIA's chief clerk Charles Mix informed Commissioner of Indian Affairs O. H. Browning on 12/2/1867 that because of Whipple's belief in Bassett's honesty and good intentions, the agent would not be censured. (Whipple Papers, Box 5.)

257. This anecdote, from *Lights and Shadows,* is apparently the origin of Whipple's purported nickname of Straight Tongue. Nebuneshkung, who was baptized Isaac Tuttle (after a prominent member of the Board of Missions), was an active leader of the White Earth Episcopal mission.

258. Enmegahbowh to HW, 9/13/1867, and C. A. Ruffee to HW, 10/14/1967, Whipple Papers, Box 5.

259. Joel Bassett to HW, 11/15/1867, Whipple Papers, Box 5.

260. C. A. Ruffee to HW, 12/29/1867, and W. R. Marshall to HW, 11/23/1867, Whipple Papers, Box 5.

261. A. S. Paddock to HW, 8/28/1868, Whipple Papers, Box 5.

262. The claim had been held up by former agent Edwin Clark on the grounds that while the mission had sustained damage in 1862, it had later burned down in 1864. Since the fire was not a result of hostile action, he opposed paying the church the full amount claimed, saying that it was impossible to determine how much damage had been done previously.

263. James Lloyd Breck married again in 1864 (to Sarah Styles of St. Louis). He died in California in 1876 and is buried in Wisconsin, at Nashotah.

264. In his autobiography, Whipple said that he had hoped to hold Enmegahbowh's ordination three days earlier (on Trinity Sunday), but the papers were delayed.

265. See the draft of Whipple's letter to President Lincoln, 3/6/1862, Whipple Papers, Box 3, and his 1868 "Report on the Moral and Temporal Condition of Indians."

266. *Lights and Shadows,* 255.

267. "Report on the Moral and Temporal Condition of Indians," 1868. The Canadian government's Indian policies would be tested during the next few decades as it struggled with the conflicting priorities of white and Indian populations on the plains of Manitoba and Saskatchewan. The issue was complicated by the presence of a large minority population of Métis, mixed bloods of Indian and French Canadian ancestry. Led by Louis Riel, the Métis took up arms against the Canadian government in 1869 and again in 1885; the first resulted in the establishment of Manitoba as a member of the Canadian confederation; the second was a failure and resulted in Riel's execution as a traitor. Yet the government did resurvey and provide the land grants requested by the métis in 1887, though much of the land quickly found its way into the hands of speculators.

268. Enmegahbowh's letter of 2/24/1867 is quoted in the Quaker Meeting report of 10/31/1867, 31, Whipple Papers, Box 5. Whipple addressed the Quakers' annual meeting on the same subject again in October 1871, following the Episcopal General Convention in Baltimore.

CHAPTER 14

269. Kvasnicka, *The Commissioners of Indian Affairs,* 99–115.

270. Report of Indian Commission to Congress, 1/7/1868, Whipple Papers, Box 4.

271. The situation was even worse among the roughly three hundred Sissetons who had settled near Devils Lake in northern Dakota Territory (see Charles Jewett to HW, 11/16/1868, Jared Daniels to HW, 11/17/1868, and HW to "General," 11/30/1868).

272. William Sherman to HW, 9/14/1868, Whipple Papers, Box 5.

273. *Lights and Shadows,* 286.

274. *Lights and Shadows,* 287–88.

275. Henry Jones to HW, 1/29/1869; C. H. Hall to Whipple, 2/9/1869; unidentified army officer at Fort Wadsworth to HW, 2/9/1869, all in Whipple Papers, Box 6.

276. HW to Orville Browning, 5/20/1869, Whipple Papers, Box 5.

277. HW to Secretary Jacob D. Cox, 3/22/1869, Whipple Papers, Box 6.

278. Centennial pamphlet, "Cathedral of Our Merciful Saviour," 1962, 11–12, 43–44.

279. When Daniels became involved in Indian matters, Rose—who became medical adviser to the Seabury Mission schools following his discharge from the Union army in 1865—took over the role of family physician to the Whipples.

280. Nellie Davis to Lizzie Farnum, 10/29/1869, Whipple/Scandrett Papers, Box 1.

281. Much of the following information comes from letters Whipple wrote to his wife Cornelia between November 1869 and May 1870, which are in the Whipple/Scandrett Papers, Box 1.

282. D. H. Bennett to HW, 12/18/1869, Whipple Papers, Box 7.

283. The Salisburys had moved to Iowa in 1866, where Hiram bought a farm in Clinton County and opened a store in Blairstown. Sarah Brayton Whipple (1824–1885) married Hiram Salisbury (1810-1887), a prosperous merchant in Adams, in 1844. The Depression following the Panic of 1857 damaged his business, and in 1859 he moved with his family to Indiana, where he was for a time connected with St. Mary's School in Terre Haute. Hiram and Sarah had one daughter, Susan (1854–1934), who later became involved in her uncle's work with the the Indians in Minnesota. (*Genealogy*, 20, 47–48.)

284. The Carlists took their name from their candidate for the throne, a male descendant of King Charles IV, as opposed to Queen Isabella II, who ruled from 1833 to 1868. Between 1868 and 1875, Spain's government was bandied about between Carlists, Liberal Monarchists, and Republicans; the offer of the throne in 1870 to Prince Leopold of Hohenzollern-Sigmaringen precipitated the Franco-Prussian War. (Ferguson and Bruun, *A Survey of European Civilization*, 732.)

CHAPTER 15

285. Albright, 197, 256, 269; Episcopal Church Archives, Austin TX; statistical report of the Episcopal Diocese of Minnesota, 3/30/1877, Whipple Papers, Box 12.

286. Tanner, *50 Years*, 311. The Philadelphia Association for Missions in the West, which eventually joined the Board of Missions, supported its own missionaries in Minnesota for many years.

287. Tanner, *50 Years*, 312.

288. Folwell, vol. III, 58.

289. Above information is from Tanner, *50 Years*, 418-421. Two of these men would eventually become bishops: Edward Welles in Milwaukee in 1874 and David B. Knickerbacker in Indiana in 1883.

290. For an extensive analysis of Grant's Peace Policy, see Pritchard, "Grant's Peace Policy," www.vts.edu/resources/classnotes/CH205, March 2005.

291. Robert Kvasnicka and Herman Viola, *The Commissioners of Indian Affairs*, 123-131. Ely Parker (1828-1895) was the nation's first Native American commissioner of Indian Affairs. Despite his law degree, he was unable to practice law because Indians were not considered U.S. citizens.

292. HW letter to the press, 1862, quoted in *Lights and Shadows,* 518.

293. 16 Statue, L.40, quoted in Robert Pritchard, "President Ulysses S. Grant's Peace Policy toward Native Americans and the Ministry of the Episcopal Church," as footnote 40.

294. Report of Commissioner of Indian Affairs, 1872, p. 386. The Quakers had 16 agencies; Methodists, 14; Presbyterians, 10; Roman Catholics, 7; Episcopalians, 8; Congregationalists, 3; Baptists, 5; Reformed Church, 5; Church of Christ, 2; Unitarians, 2; Lutherans, 1.

295. The only American Board missionary still active in the Ojibwe area, Sela Wright, operated a school at the Red Lake agency. After two years as Ojibwe agent, Edward P. Smith became commissioner of Indian Affairs (following the resignation of Ely Parker).

296. Alexander Graham-Dunlop to HW, 3/11/1871, Whipple Papers, Box 8.

297. *Lights and Shadows,* 359. The Franco-Prussian War had just ended.

298. HW to Edward Kenny, 1871, Whipple Papers, Box 8. William Chauncey Langdon, rector of St. Paul's within the Walls, the American Episcopal church in Rome, Italy, had been advocating a new approach to the Catholic Church that would combine the best qualities of the Catholic and Episcopal doctrines. (www.anglicanhistory.org/usa/whittingham/defects.html, January 2006.)

299. Whipple visited Cuba again in 1875 and 1879. Kenny continued to work diligently until his health gave out; by 1883 he was back in America. (Edward Kenny to HW, 1/17/1883, Whipple Papers, Box 16.) The mission continued, however, surviving years of the nation's political chaos. In his memoir in 1899, Whipple remarked that "Cuba ought to be a paradise, but lotteries, bull fights, and cock fights have debased the morals, and a corrupt government has oppressed the people." (*Lights and Shadows,* 360.)

300. S. Winton to HW, 3/8/1871, quoted in *Lights and Shadows,* 339.

301. H. Dyer to HW, 4/25/1871, Whipple Papers, Box 8. Whipple was quite aware of the previous bishop's troubles. Bishop Staley was a contentious man whose conflicts with the American Board missionaries were notorious. George Whipple had crossed swords with him on several occasions during his attempts to establish an American Episcopal mission on the islands. For Whipple's discussion of the unexpected offer, see *Lights and Shadows,* 339–48.

302. HW to S. Winton, 5/1/1871, Whipple Papers, Box 8.

303. Albright, 282–83.

304. George D. Cummins (1822–1876) was ordained priest in the Episcopal Church in 1847. A fervent evangelical, he quarreled frequently with Illinois's Bishop Henry Whitehouse before leaving the church to found the Reformed Episcopal Church (which is still active today). (www.chronicles.dickinson.edu/encyclo/c/ed_cumminsGD.html.) Charles Edward Cheney (1836-1916) was rector of Christ Church in Chicago until deposed by Bishop Whitehouse in 1871 in a dispute over the church's understanding of the sacrament of baptism.

305. *Faribault Democrat,* 6/19/1874, p. 4.

306. HW letter to *The Churchman,* July 1896, 37; *Lights and Shadows,* 94.

307. *Lights and Shadows,* 335.

308. Henry J. Whitehouse to HW, 5/16/1871, quoted in *Lights and Shadows,* 337.

309. *Lights and Shadows,* 328.

310. *Faribault Democrat,* 6/19/1874, 4.

CHAPTER 16

311. HW diary, 1/13/1872, Episcopal Church Diocesan Papers, Box 42; *Lights and Shadows,* 100.

312. Folwell, vol. III, 61. Construction on the Northern Pacific ceased in 1873, when the company went bankrupt, but resumed in 1879. It reached Seattle in 1883, becoming the nation's second intercontinental railroad line. The St. Paul and Pacific later became the Great Northern. The fifth intercontinental line to be completed, it followed a parallel path from Duluth to Seattle, reaching the coast in 1893.

313. HW letter to *The Churchman,* 12/26/1896, 867.

314. Tanner, *50 Years*, 460-465.

315. *Lights and Shadows,* 103–04.

316. The building's $30,000 mortgage would strain the school's budget for several years.

317. HW to "Gentlemen of the Indian Peace Commission," 12/27/1873, Whipple Papers, Box 10.

318. Clement Beaulieu to HW, 9/4/1873, Whipple Papers, Box 10.

319. Joseph Gilfillan to "Doctor," 11/10/1873, Whipple Papers, Box 10.

320. J. W. Daniels to HW, 5/8/1869, and Enmegahbowh to HW, 5/18/1869, Whipple Papers, Box 6. The fact that Flat Mouth's action did not result in intertribal war went far to prove how drastically Dakota culture had changed in the past decade.

321. *Lights and Shadows,* 45–48.

322. Supreme Court U.S. #161, October 1873; William Welsh to Secretary of Interior Columbus Delano, 11/8/1873, Whipple Papers, Box 10.

323. Undated, incomplete letter from E. P. Smith to HW, Whipple Papers, Box 10.

324. HW to William Welsh, 1/19/1874, Whipple Papers, Box 10.

325. Joseph Gilfillan to HW, 2/25/1874, 4/8/74; George Bonga to HW, 5/28/1874, Whipple Papers, Box 10.

326. U.S. Department of Interior, Report of Commissioner of Indian Affairs, 1875, 78.

327. Bio notes from Lewis Stowe papers, MHS; see also U.S. Census records, 1870, LeSueur County, T-132, Roll 7, 61.

328. Carol Berg, "Agents of Cultural Change," *Minnesota History,* vol. 48 (Winter 1982), 162.

329. U.S. Department of Interior, Report of Commissioner of Indian Affairs, 1875, 298.

330. Joseph Gilfillan to HW, 3/21/1877, Whipple Papers, Box 12.

331. Enmegahbowh to HW, 12/10/1880, Whipple Papers, Box 15. A worried Enmegahbowh, who had already lost several children to the dread disease, was sorely tempted, but he remained faithful to his church. His wife recovered and lived another fifteen years.

332. See H. E. Fritz, *The Movement for Indian Assimilation,* 87–95, for a discussion of the Catholic Church's activities at this period.

333. U.S. Department of Interior, Report of Board of Indian Commissioners, 1875, 44. One of the signers was Ignatius Hole-in-the-Day, presumably a son of the deceased chief.

334. U.S. Department of Interior, Report of Board of Indian Commissioners, 1875, 48–50.

335. Ibid., 61–62.

CHAPTER 17

336. www.peabodylibrary.org/history/george, May 2005. Among those who served on the board with Whipple over the next twenty-five years were past and future presidents Ulysses S. Grant, Rutherford B. Hayes, and Grover Cleveland, as well as Chief Justice M. R. Waite, Senator and Secretary of State Hamilton Fish, and philanthropists J. Pierpont Morgan and Anthony J. Drexel. Its president was Robert C. Winthrop, who had taken Daniel Webster's seat in the U.S. Senate.

337. Peabody College is now part of Vanderbilt University; Winthrop College is now Winthrop University. By 1898, nearly three million children were attending public schools in the southern states that had been initiated by the Peabody Education Fund.

338. HW letter to *The Churchman,* 3/28/1896, 405.

339. HW to R. Fulton Cutting, 3/14/1893, Whipple Papers, Box 22. The Hampton Institute was founded in 1868 under the auspices of the American Missionary Association, whose secretary was Whipple's uncle George.

340. HW to Stuart Fulton, 8/29/1889, Whipple Papers, Box 21.

341. HW to the bishop of Tasmania, 7/14/1901, Whipple Papers, Box 26; *Lights and Shadows,* 383–84.

342. HW to *Evening Dispatch,* 7/31/1880, Whipple Papers, Box 14.

343. M. E. Streiby to HW, 12/6/1876, Whipple Papers, Box 12; see also U.S. Department of Interior, Report of Commissioner of Indian Affairs, 1874, 198; 1875, 296; 1876, 78. This episode occurred two years after the Episcopal Church assumed oversight of the reservation under Grant's Peace Policy. The naming of the mission is described in *Lights and Shadows,* 145. (Quotation is from the King James Bible.)

344. HW to Mrs. A. L. Bigelow, 1/14/1874, Whipple Papers, Box 10.

345. *Faribault Democrat,* 6/19/1874, p. 1. Some of those confirmed were in the Diocese of Wisconsin.

346. Joel Bassett, the former Ojibwe agent and a communicant of Gethsemane, gave the hospital $200 toward an endowment fund. This was increased later that year by a legacy of $1,000 from Mrs. Horatio Seymour of Buffalo, New York, one of Whipple's network of philanthropic donors. Both patients and endowments continued to grow in number, until in 1881 a second building was added and the name of the hospital changed to St. Barnabas.

347. Diocese of Minnesota, Triennial Report, Whipple Papers, Box 14. St. Luke's Hospital in St. Paul was founded in 1874 under the direction of Sister Maria Matice, who had trained at the Bishop Potter House in Philadelphia. (Andrews, *History of St. Paul,* 503.) In 1882, a typhoid epidemic in Duluth would lead to the foundation of St. Luke's Hospital in that city, at the instigation of J.A. Cummings, rector of St. Paul's Duluth. (MacDonald, *This Is Duluth,* 90.)

348. *Lights and Shadows,* 218–19. The house was named for the Bishop Potter House in Philadelphia, from which Minnesota's earliest deaconesses had come. Whipple credited the Reverend C. Edgar Haupt as the instigator of Minnesota's deaconess program.

349. Joseph Gilfillan's authoritarian nature and short temper led to disputes with Sister Maria, who left at the end of 1876. He also quarreled with Dr. W. T. Parker, whom Whipple recruited for the hospital in 1879 from Lenox, Massachusetts. Parker left a year later, telling Whipple, "How deceived you have been in Mr. Gilfillan." (W. T. Parker to HW, 3/12/1880, Whipple Papers, Box 14.) When the hospital closed in 1895, Miss Watkinson's $10,000 endowment was still intact.

350. *Faribault Republican,* 8/5/1873, 3.

351. HW letter to *The Churchman,* January 1896; *Lights and Shadows,* 322.

352. Albright, 307. These meetings would continue to be held until well into the twentieth century and helped to defuse some of the most controversial issues before they could become serious causes of disunity in the church.

353. The original diocese of Rupert's Land had been divided by 1874 into four smaller dioceses, which were joined in 1875 into a regional province under Bishop Machray as Metropolitan.

354. Quote is found in Herman J. Viola, *Warrior Artists: Cheyenne and Kiowa Ledger Art by Making Medicine and Zotom,* p. 13. The seventy-one prisoners were from the Cheyenne, Kiowa, Comanche, Arapahoe, and Caddo tribes. When they were released in 1878, Pratt took several of them along with a group of young Nez Perce to Hampton Institute in Virginia, a training school for freed slaves. The next year, he set up a similar school strictly for Indians on an old cavalry post in Carlisle, Pennsylvania.

355. Statistics from "History of the Schools at Faribault," May 1876.

356. Robert Clarkson to HW, 1/ 26/1872, Whipple Papers, Box 9.

357. William Cox Pope, address to Minnesota Historical Society, 10/14/1901, *Minnesota Historical Society Collections*, vol. 10, 1904, 720.

358. See Gilfillan letters, Whipple Papers, Box 12, and Kugel, 149.

CHAPTER 18

359. The Northern Pacific ceased construction in 1873 when the Jay Cooke company went bankrupt. It resumed in 1878, when James J. Hill bought it back from a group of Dutch bondholders, and was completed in 1893. It was a major facilitator for the settlement of white farmers on the plains.

360. HW to *New York Times,* 3/3/1876, Whipple Papers, Box 11.

361. Also a member of the commission was Whipple's friend Jared Daniels, who had until recently been the agent for Red Cloud's band.

362. Curtiss-Wedge, 274. Two of the commissioners were killed in the Modoc affair.

363. Whipple had made this argument in his 1868 report to the Board of Missions (*Lights and Shadows,* 523).

364. U.S. Congress, 44th, 2nd session, Senate document 9, 5.

365. HW to R. H. Pratt, 11/13/1876, Whipple papers, Box 12.

366. Curtiss-Wedge, 274; also *Lights and Shadows,* 303–05. The incident was described in a letter from Captain Bowen to Whipple's son Charles.

367. Whipple made a habit of carrying documents relating to Indian questions with him whenever he went to meetings, "never knowing when the occasion might come to make use of them." (*Lights and Shadows,* 307–09).

368. William Sherman to HW, 12/10/1888, quoted in *Lights and Shadows,* 311.

369. J. Q. Smith to HW, 2/28/1877, Whipple Papers, Box 12.

370. HW, "The Present Montana Indian War," Whipple Papers, Box 11.

371. HW to the President of the United States, 7/31/1876, Whipple papers, Box 11.

CHAPTER 19

372. Folwell, vol. III, 105, 108–110; *Lights and Shadows,* 323–24. The effect was not quite as miraculous as Whipple claimed, but hatching was retarded, and that summer the hatchlings migrated out of the state. The year's harvest was exceptionally good that year.

373. Pamphlet, "Dedicated to all who served the Lord Jesus at the Church of the Good Shepherd" (Maitland, Florida: Church of the Good Shepherd, 2004), 3.

374. Unsigned letter, Whipple/Scandrett Papers, Box 1; *Genealogy,* 22.

375. *1975 Handbook for Tours,* Faribault Cathedral.

376. After a brief note, "poor John," on April 20, there are several days when the only entry in Whipple's diary is the word "sad."

377. *Faribault Republican,* 8/14/1878, p. 3; clippings from unidentified newspapers from Cincinnati or Louisville in Whipple Papers, Box 13.

378. HW to H. R. Pratt, 8/17/78, Whipple Papers, Box 13; HW to Charles Whipple, 8/15/1878, Whipple/ Scandrett Papers, Box 2. By 1878, Charles Whipple (1849–1932) had three children, aged three, four, and six.

379. Pamphlet from the Church of the Good Shepherd, Maitland, Florida, 10–12. By then, his daughter Nellie Whipple Rose had contracted tuberculosis, and was not expected to live. Windows in the narthex bear the names of Nellie and John. The altar was dedicated to the memory of Nellie's infant daughter, Mary Pell Rose, who died early in 1884, only a few months before her mother's death.

380. HW to Samuel Hinman, 6/28/1870, Hinman Papers, MHS, folder 2.

381. *Hinman v. Hare* trial transcript, 107.

382. *Hinman v. Hare,* 176, 166.

383. *Hinman v. Hare,* 89, 176. Mary Hinman's death was related to the aftereffects of injuries she received in a tornado that destroyed the mission buildings in 1870. Hare's allegation that her husband had infected her with syphilis was based on highly suspect evidence. In 1873, Hare was on the investigating committee that cleared Hinman of fiscal malfeasance.

384. *Hinman v. Hare,* introduction, Hinman's charge.

385. Cornelia Whipple to Samuel Hinman, 11/22/1879, Hinman Papers, MHS.

386. *Faribault Democrat,* 6/27/1884, p. 2. Coolidge became embroiled in a dispute with the Wind River agent in 1886–1887, allying himself with the agency school teacher (a Baptist minister) in an effort to keep Catholic missionaries from being allowed on the reservation. The priest in charge of Coolidge's mission supported the agent (who was also Episcopalian), reservation politics became involved, and there was a good deal of invective on both sides. Finally Coolidge and the Baptist teacher were expelled from the reservation. Coolidge went east to attend Hobart College in 1887. He returned home in 1889 to resume his mission work. In 1911 he was one of the founders of the Society of American Indians, the nation's first Indian-controlled rights organization. (Letters concerning Coolidge's troubles on the Wind River reservation are in Whipple Papers, Boxes 16 and 17. Additional biographic data is from www.coolidge.hmco.com/history/historyreader-scomp/naind/html, March 2005.)

387. Charles Slattery, *Certain American Faces,* 113. Neither the operations nor his periodic bouts with bronchitis affected his speaking voice, which remained strong and melodic.

388. Although John Whipple died in August 1878, he was not buried at Faribault until April 1879. This may have been due to the poor condition of the body, which had been buried without being embalmed in a pauper's grave in Cincinnati before Charles Whipple arrived to claim it in September 1878. Why it should have taken so long for the family to re-inter the body after it was brought back to Faribault is unclear. Whipple's brother John died in New York and is buried there.

CHAPTER 20

389. H. Dyer to HW, 7/3/1877, Whipple Papers, Box 12.

390. Hayt was one of the philanthropists who served on the Board of Indian Commissioners during Grant's administration.

391. J. W. Daniels to HW, 9/22/1877, and HW to Ezra Hayt, 9/29/77, Whipple Papers, Box 12; U.S. Department of Interior, Report of the Commissioner of Indian Affairs, 1879, 87–89.

392. Although Standing Bear won his case, he found that it did not guarantee that the government would abide by the ruling. Only Standing Bear and the 66 Poncas with him were permitted to remain in Nebraska; the remaining 530 Poncas had to stay on the Oklahoma reservation.

393. Helen Hunt Jackson, *A Century of Dishonor,* xix–xxiv.

394. HW letter "On the Present Montana Indian War: A Few Official Facts Concerning It," 9/1877, Whipple Papers, Box 12. For a discussion of the Nez Perce situation, see Merrill D. Beal, "I Will Fight No More Forever," 31–53.

395. U.S. Department of Interior, Report of Commissioner of Indian Affairs, 1881, L.

396. HW to commissioner of Indian Affairs, 12/4/1882, Whipple Papers, Box 16. Eventually the bureau agreed to make a treaty with the Turtle Mountain band, and their reservation was recognized and brought under the Indian bureau's purview. The nearest Indian agency was at Devils Lake. Around 1889 the government assigned E. W. Brenner, a government farmer from the Devils Lake agency, to live among them as their government contact. They settled into farming and sent their children to the Catholic schools at Devil's Lake. But when instructed to take allotments under the Dawes Act in 1889, they refused. They still had not been paid for their land, they said, so it remained theirs to use as they liked. (See Reports of Commissioner of Indian Affairs, 1884, 35; 1889, 144, 146.)

397. For a discussion of the dams issue, see Jane Lamm Carroll, "Dams and Damages," *Minnesota History,* Spring 1990.

398. *Lights and Shadows,* 80.

399. HW to *Evening Dispatch,* 7/28/1880, Whipple Papers, Box 14.

400. HW to Thomas Simpson, 8/19/1881, Whipple Papers, Box 15. Whipple paraphrases a Biblical verse from the Prophet Micah.

401. Major C. J. Allen to Secretary of War Robert Lincoln, 4/6/83, Whipple Papers, Box 16.

402. Carroll, 29, quoting from the government's report on Damage to Chippewa Indians.

403. The Ojibwe sued the government in 1972, and the issue was finally settled out of court in 1985, the tribe receiving compensation for 178,000 acres of land taken by the reservoirs plus

5 percent accumulated interest since 1884.

404. Whipple was strict about this point; it was one of his chief quarrels with Jacob Chamberlain in the early 1860s that Chamberlain insisted on making money-raising trips to the East without consulting his bishop in advance.

405. Enmegahbowh's letters to David B. Knicker-backer, dated 2/19/1881, 3/14/1881, and 3/15/1881 (Whipple Papers, Box 15) describe this episode. Presumably the letter in question was one written by Whipple to Gilfillan, who had little confidence in his fellow priest.

406. Whipple's diary for 7/6/1881, MHS, Episcopal Church Diocesan Records, Box 43.

407. In December 1892, Whipple asked Gilfillan if any of the Ojibwe deacons was ready for priest-hood. The only one whom Gilfillan thought was "reliable" enough was George Morgan, but he does not appear to have made any formal recommendation to the Standing Committee on Morgan's behalf. (Gilfillan to HW, 12/23/1892, Whipple Papers, Box 22.)

408. See Gilfillan's letters to Whipple in Box 16. After his dismissal from holy orders in 1884, Benedict returned to his native Canada. He tried to get Whipple to reinstate him in 1887, but Gilfillan wrote a strong letter to the Standing Committee in opposition, and Whipple had to refuse.

409. Tanner, 513.

410. J. Gilfillan to HW, 7/19/1886, Whipple Papers, Box 18.

411. Meshakigishick (Fine Day), who supported Whipple in this affair, reported that Charles Wright, the most outspoken of the Indian deacons, had refused to sign the agreement.

412. HW to *Evening Dispatch,* 7/31/1880, Whipple Papers, Box 14. With Pratt's example as a guide, the Indian bureau began to enforce tougher standards on reservation schools. Indian Commissioner Thomas J. Morgan in 1890 published "Rules for Indian Schools," which stressed the necessity of eradicating Indian culture. Additional government boarding schools were built on the Carlisle model near several reservations, including one at Flandreau, South Dakota, which opened in 1893. The teachers in the reservation schools began to complain that all their best students were being taken away from the reservations and sent to boarding schools, making it that much harder for them to achieve their own educational goals. (See U.S. Department of Interior, Report of Commissioner of Indian Affairs, 1893, p. 169.)

413. Francis P. Prucha, *Americanizing the American Indian,* 153, quotes William Justin Harsha, who was responding to an article by Carl Schurz in the *North American Review* in 1881.

CHAPTER 21

414. HW diary, 1/28/1880, 4/4/1880, 4/19/1880; Episcopal Church Diocesan Papers, Box 43, vol. 10. George and his mother were among the Dakotas who settled on Henry Sibley's farm near Mendota in 1863. Whipple had first noticed him at the Lower Agency in 1860, when the ten-year-old boy sat entranced by the music and ceremony of the church service. Whipple baptized, educated, and ordained him.

415. HW diary, 1880, Whipple Papers, Box 43. The proposed revisions were not approved until 1892. (Albright, 270, 296)

416. The Tennessee Historical Society, Nashville, 1998; online edition 2002 The University of Tennessee Press, Knoxville, TN. The school, Peabody Normal College, is now part of Vanderbilt University.

417. *Faribault Republican,* 9/19/1883, p. 3, and Bryant's *History of Rice County,* 346–53. Whipple proposed selling the old St. Mary's buildings to the government for a school for Indian girls, but while the Indian Bureau favored the idea in general, it had no money available just then to acquire and staff the school, and the proposal was dropped. An earlier proposal to use the abandoned Fort Ridgley as an Indian school met a similar fate. (Mary A. E. Twing to HW, 10/11/1884, E. S. Wilson to HW, 1/12/1885, Whipple Papers, Box 17; H. Price to HW, 4/5/1882 and 2/9/1883, Whipple Papers, Box 16.)

418. See Galbraith to HW, 7/8/1862, Whipple Papers, Box 3; Agency for Paris Exhibition of 1867 to HW, 9/24/1866, Whipple Papers, Box 4; John Eaton to HW, 4/20/1876 and 4/21/1876, Whipple Papers, Box 11. Whipple's extensive personal collection of Native American artifacts is now in the possession of the Science Museum of Minnesota and the Minnesota Historical Society.

419. For information on Riley's work in Mexico and Portugal, see www.historicaltextarchive.com/ sections.php, May 2005; www.diosemexico.org/ Dio2History, May 2005; 29.1911encyclopedia.org/ s/ sp/spanish_reformed-church.htm, May 2005; www. teceurope.org/partners/Lusitanian_partner.htm, May 2005. Whipple's letter to Riley is in *Lights and Shadows,* 485–87. In a letter to Whipple dated 2/8/1885, A. Littlejohn of Brooklyn on this matter uses the term "fiasco." In 1904, the General Convention created the Missionary District of Mexico under Bishop H. D. Aves; in 1995 the Anglican Church of Mexico became an autonomous Province within the Anglican Communion (www.diosemexico.org, 5/2005).

420. Seabury's consecration is generally conceded to mark the founding of the American church.

421. Most of the material in these paragraphs is from Whipple's diaries in Whipple Papers, Box 44. Service bulletins for the Seabury Centennial services in Aberdeen and at St. Paul's in London are in Whipple Papers, Box 17.

422. James Caird assured them that the reported cholera epidemic was only affecting the poor, so they should be quite safe. (James Caird to HW, 11/23/1884, Whipple Papers, Box 17.)

423. *Lights and Shadows,* 279. Background on the mission is from the March 1932 issue of the McCall Record, vol. L #2, Whipple Papers, Box 26.

424. After retiring as dean of Minnesota's western convocation, Livermore became chaplain of Kemper Hall, an Episcopal college in Kenosha. (Tanner, *50 years,* 346-47.)

425. In a letter dated 10/29/1885, Timothy Sheehan thanks Whipple for speaking to the president on his behalf. For Sheehan's actions in 1862, see Folwell, vol. II, 128–30, 229–30.

426. See Whipple's *Genealogy,* 21–22, 48–52, 110–111; *Faribault Republican,* 6/14/1911, p. 3, and 7/25/1888, p. 3. Susan Letitia Whipple (1826–1894) married Zaccheus Hill (1818–1877), a partner in the Hill Brothers store in Rome, New York, in 1850. When Hill Brothers went broke in 1857, Zaccheus turned to banking. By 1864, he had progressed from bookkeeper in the Bank of Rome to cashier of the Oneida Central Bank; in 1874 he became part owner of the Bank of Clinton. He was elected to the board of trustees of the village of Rome and served on its board of education. He and Susan had three sons, John Whipple Hill, William Squier Hill, and Henry Benjamin Hill. The three boys operated the Hill Brothers Bank in Janesville, Minnesota, for several years. The older two eventually left Minnesota, but Henry remained and in 1895 married the daughter of Whipple's friend, Dr. Jared W. Daniels. (*Genealogy,* pp. 20, 48-49; *Faribault Republican,* 12/5/1894, p. 3.)

CHAPTER 22

427. Tanner, *50 Years,* 476-77.

428. Elisha S. Thomas, who Whipple had hoped would be chosen as his assistant bishop, came to Minnesota in 1864 to teach at Seabury and served for many years as its warden. In 1876 he succeeded Andrew Paterson as rector of St. Paul's in St. Paul. He and Whipple were old and dear friends; "few men have shared more deeply in my love," Whipple recalled. Several weeks after Mahlon Gilbert's election as Whipple's assistant, Thomas became assistant bishop of Kansas under Thomas Vail, whom he later succeeded.

429. Francis L. Palmer, *Bishop Gilbert.* Gilbert developed a "severe hemorrhage of the lungs" in his sophomore year at Hobart College in Geneva, New York. He was ordained priest in October 1875 by Montana's Bishop Daniel Tuttle. He received the first doctorate of divinity degree ever granted by Seabury in 1887.

430. *Lights and Shadows,* 147–48.

431. Under the Roosevelt administration in 1934, government policy abandoned the allotment scheme and encouraged Indian self-government and the preservation of native cultures.

432. Melissa Meyer, *White Earth Tragedy,* 51–56.

433. *Lights and Shadows,* 268–69.

434. Only after gold was discovered in 1899 did Alaska became a magnet for EuroAmerican settlement.

435. Information on William Duncan from www.abcbookworld.com/?state=view_author&author_id=2714, April 2005.

436. *Lights and Shadows,* 158.

437. Hare's agreement in 1887 to sign the necessary affidavit proclaiming Hinman's "good standing" appears to have been connected with Hinman's marriage in 1884 to Mary Myrick, the mixed-blood daughter of the trader Andrew Myrick and his Dakota wife, Nancy Stone. In explanation of his action, Hare told his clergy that "a Bishop is bound to grant such a request unless he has evidence of the misconduct of the Presbyter concerned, within the three years preceding the request." By 1887, Hinman and Mary Myrick had been married for three years.

438. Good Thunder to HW, 6/21/1885, Whipple Papers, Box 18.

439. Betty and Edward Sheppard, *The Mission at the Lower Sioux,* 10-11.

440. Gethsemane Church in Minneapolis ran an outreach program to the settlements near the Twin Cities, but the impoverished Prairie Island band had little assistance from anyone. (See Tanner, *50 Years,* 260, and Roy Meyer, *History of the Santee Sioux,* 281.)

441. Hinman, as Whipple's associate in this endeavor, was accused of pressuring the government agent assigned to distribute the 1888 allocation to secure an overly large share for Birch Coulee. The agent denied the charges, which arose mostly from bureaucratic delays and rivalries among the Dakota communities. The reluctance of the other bands to move to Birch Coulee was likely due to their reluctance to submit to the leadership of Good Thunder and his band. The political divisions of the bands dated back to the pre-treaty period, when each village was an independent entity. Although much of the pre-1862 tribal government had been broken down, the family loyalties on which band membership was based remained strong.

442. During his nine years as archdeacon, Appleby traveled 142,846 miles, raised more than $123,000, and helped to build twenty-five churches in the region between Duluth and Moorhead.

443. Folwell, vol. III, 139–40.

444. Tanner, *50 Years,* 489.

445. *Lights and Shadows,* 435.

446. Peterson, who suffered from depression, committed suicide in 1887. The ambivalent relationship between the Anglican and Scandinavian Lutheran churches sometimes led to confusion even among the clergy. In 1880, Whipple read in the newspaper that a Norwegian clergyman named Egeland had been serving as priest in an Episcopal church. He wrote to the minister (and the paper), reminding him that although he might be a Lutheran minister, he was not authorized to serve communion in an Episcopal church; he had been licensed only as a lay reader.

447. The Augustana Synod was founded in 1860 by Swedish immigrants and is the forerunner of today's Lutheran Church in America. A rival Scandinavian Lutheran organization, the Norwegian Synod, was founded in 1853 and is the forerunner of today's Evangelical Lutheran Church in America (ELCA).

448. Of the ten Swedish Episcopal churches originally established in Minnesota in Litchfield, Cokato, Minneapolis [4], Duluth, Aitkin, Lake Park, and Strandvik, four remain active. Tofteen's congregation in Litchfield, which was admitted to the Episcopal Church in 1903, merged with Trinity Episcopal Church of Litchfield in the 1920s. Messiah moved from Minneapolis to St. Paul. St. Anskar in Minneapolis was destroyed in a tornado and its congregation combined with that of Holy Trinity; the parish is currently called Holy Trinity/St. Anskar. St. John's continues to exist in Aitkin.

CHAPTER 23

449. The term Anglican Communion was first used during the 1851 jubilee celebrations of the founding of the Society for the Propagation of the Gospel, a private missionary society that financed the sending of English missionaries to Britain's colonies and other "heathen" lands.

450. *Lights and Shadows,* 376.

451. A copy of Whipple's Lambeth sermon, given July 8, 1888, is in the Whipple Papers, Box 20. Anglican churches use the term "Catholic" in its generic sense, to mean the entire Christian community.

452. *Lights and Shadows,* 438.

453. A list of bishops attending the third Lambeth Conference is in the Whipple Papers, Box 20.

454. *Book of Common Prayer,* 877–78.

455. The others were David B. Knickerbacker (bishop of Indiana 1883–1894), Mahlon Gilbert (assistant bishop of Minnesota 1886–1900), Elisha S. Thomas (bishop of Kansas 1889–1896), Anson R. Graves (missionary bishop of the Platte 1890–1931), William M. Barker (bishop of Western Colorado 1893–1894 and bishop of Olympia 1894–1901), John H. White (bishop of Indiana 1895–1925), and Frank R. Millspaugh (bishop of Kansas 1894–1916).

456. Whipple was constantly looking for ways to provide funding for students from poor families. He tried to guarantee low rates to clergy offspring at Shattuck and St. Mary's, and often paid the costs of impoverished divinity students at Seabury himself.

457. *Lights and Shadows,* 357; address to 1874 Diocesan Convention, *Faribault Democrat,* 6/19/1874, p.1.

458. The letter is quoted in Sheppard, 16.

CHAPTER 24

459. HW to George Fairbanks, 10/8/1890, Whipple Papers, Box 21. Apparently Lizzie had begun teaching piano lessons in a small school in her home, but she had developed severe pain in her arms (possibly carpal tunnel syndrome) and could no longer play. Jennie Scandrett and her family had been living in the Whipple home for several years, and Fannie had been recently widowed.

460. Henry White to HW, 12/18/1890, Whipple Papers, Box 21.

461. *Lights and Shadows,* 475.

462. The paper even managed to confuse Minnesota's Henry Hastings Sibley with another Civil War general with a similar name, Henry Hopkins Sibley, inventor of the Sibley tent.

463. Whipple found the book with the help of his English publishing friend, Alexander Macmillan, and sent it to the priest.

464. The girls at the Hill School presented the bishop with an embroidered screen, which he raffled off to raise money for mission work. The purchaser gave it back to Whipple as a memento, and it remained in his home until 1934, when his wife's heirs sold the house and its contents. The Hill Memorial School is still in existence in Athens.

465. Whipple's diaries contain details of this trip.

466. Gilfillan to HW, 7/15/1891 and 7/29/1891, Whipple Papers, Box 21. The dance had been brought in by Dakota visitors and was probably a form of the Ghost Dance that had caused so much concern among the Plains tribes the previous year. Its use of Christian symbolism seemed to make it acceptable to the Christianized Ojibwe. For more information on the government's response to the Ghost Dance phenomenon, see Edward Lazarus, *Black Hills/White Justice,* 114.

467. Tanner, *50 Years,* 406-407. The missionaries were pleased to find that making lace encouraged Indian women to keep their hands and homes clean, fitting in well with their attempts to teach EuroAmerican concepts of housekeeping. The lace program continued to flourish until Sibyl Carter's death in 1909, by which time there were nine schools in Minnesota alone.

468. Brooks did not live long enough for his theological opinions to trouble the church; he died in early 1893.

469. Information on Maitland is taken from the back of a letter dated 3/22/1893 in Whipple Papers, Box 22.

470. HW to George Fairbanks, 3/9/1892; 1892 Tarpon Record citation from Fort Myers, Florida; both in Whipple Papers, Box 22. The *St. Paul Pioneer Press,* 9/14/1930, p. 11, lists the fish among the furnishings of the Whipple house following Evangeline Whipple's death.

471. Congressional Joint Resolution of 6/8/1891, in Whipple Papers, Box 21.

472. The professor in question appears to have been the Reverend Charles L. Wells, professor of ecclesiastical history from 1887 to 1892, and the Reverend John Hazen White's successor as (acting) warden of Seabury from 1888 to 1891.

473. Albright, 270, 293, 296.

474. *Lights and Shadows,* 431.

475. MHS Historical Collections, vol. 9, 208, and Folwell, vol. II, 386–89. Flandrau was highly amused by "the predicament we had got the ceremonies into." The dispute concerning the inscription centered on who should have been given credit for leading the expedition, Major Joseph Brown (the former Dakota agent) or Captain Hiram Grant. Grant and Brown's son Samuel fought the issue all the way to the State House. Why anyone would want to claim credit for leading such a disastrous expedition is another story. In 1899 a second monument was raised nearby to honor the "friendly Indians."

476. In 1926, the rules were changed to permit the House of Bishops to elect the presiding bishop, who serves a nine-year term. Bishop Williams, who found the practice of making the position a lifetime sinecure for the church's oldest bishop extremely distasteful, had begun to argue for this change before the 1895 convention. Williams held the post for twelve years. He died in February 1899 and was succeeded by Rhode Island's Bishop Thomas March Clark, who served until 1903.

477. *Faribault Democrat,* 10/18/1895, p. 1.

478. Journal of the Episcopal Diocese of Minnesota, 6/15/1895, Whipple Papers, Box 23. The new diocese consisted of the state's northern counties and more than half its land area, if only a third of its population. It would be another year before James Morrison was elected bishop of Duluth; until then, Mahlon Gilbert was in charge of creating the new diocese's administrative machinery and visiting its parishes.

CHAPTER 25

479. www.masshist.org/findingaids/ doc.cfm?fa=fap033, March 2005; Scott & Neslund, 69–70.

480. The wedding guests included Bishop Mahlon Gilbert, Susan Salisbury, Fannie Whipple Jackson, and Evangeline's brother Kingsmill Marrs.

481. When Evangeline Whipple left Faribault forever in the fall of 1910, she and Rose Cleveland settled in a villa in the Tuscan town of Bagni di Lucca in Italy, where the two presided over a colony of female expatriate writers and artists. Cleveland died in the influenza epidemic of 1919, and after Whipple's own death in London in 1930 she was buried beside Cleveland in the Bagni di Lucca cemetery. (MHS, Whipple/Scandrett papers, Box 3; also online articles at www.episcopalmn.org in 2003.)

482. Evangeline Whipple's diary for 1897 is in the Whipple Papers, Box 44a.

483. The list of bishops who attended the 1897 Lambeth Conference is in Whipple Papers, Box 24.

484. The newspaper quote is from Curtiss-Wedge, 282. The text of his Ramsden Sermon is in Whipple/Scandrett Papers, Box 3.

485. Evangeline Whipple describes these events in her 1897 diary. The invitation from the Lord Chamberlain is in Whipple Papers, Box 24. In a memorial tribute to Whipple at the 1901 Lake Mohonk meeting, President Smith recalled that the Queen's personal attendant had pushed aside two bishops at a garden party, saying, "Make way for the Lord Bishop of Minnesota, whose presence the Queen desires!"

486. www.episcopalspringfield.org/Heritage/ LambethConference.htm, March 2005.

487. U.S. Department of the Interior, Reports of Commissioner of Indian Affairs, 1897, 994. An Indian ring is a collaboration between government officials and private contractors to siphon funds from Indian annuity payments.

488. Many of Evangeline Whipple's treasures were left in her will to St. Mary's Hall and to the cathedral in Faribault. (Conversation of the author with the Reverend James Zotalis, dean of the cathedral, and Dr. Robert Neslund of Shattuck/St. Marys School.)

489. Slattery, *Certain American Faces,* 112.

490. HW to unknown, 10/6/1898, Whipple Papers, Box 25.

491. *New York Times,* 10/27/1898. Bugoneygejig does not appear to have been related to the more famous Hole-in-the-Day (Bugonaygeshig), the chief who had resisted government programs in the past and who died in 1868. For more information on this incident, see William Matsen, "The Battle of Sugar Point," *Minnesota History,* Fall 1987. W. A. Mercer, who took over the Leech Lake agency in 1899, attributed the outbreak to frustration over timber and "matters in general under . . . the Nelson law." (U.S. Department of Interior, Report of Commissioner of Indian Affairs, 1899, vol. 1, 213.)

492. MHS Collections, vol. 9, 142.

493. The appointment was not made until after Whipple's death.

494. Charles Whipple to Jennie Scandrett, 3/6/1900, Whipple/Scandrett Papers, Box 3.

495. Unfinished when Whipple died, the cross was installed by Bishop Edsall the following year.

496. HW to Dr. Lloyd, DFMS, 5/30/1901, Whipple Papers, Box 26.

497. HW to commissioner of Indian Affairs, 8/29/01, Whipple Papers, Box 26.

498. Details of the services are found in Curtiss-Wedge, 289–290, and in Charles Slattery's memorial sermon, filed in the Whipple Papers, Box 26. Attending bishops were Daniel Tuttle of Missouri, Samuel Edsall of North Dakota (soon to be Whipple's successor as bishop of Minnesota), William H. Hare of South Dakota, Elisha S. Thomas of Kansas, Theodore H. Morrison of Iowa, James Morrison of Duluth, and Charles C. Grafton of Fond du Lac, Wisconsin.

499. The Church Record, vol. 25, no. 10, October 1901, 14.

500. Copies of Evangeline Whipple's wills (dated 1906 and 1908) are in the Whipple/Scandrett Papers, MHS, Box 3. A later will, dealing only with her Italian property, is in the possession of Whipple descendant Benjamin Oehler.

EPILOGUE

501. Statistics from Tanner. The 1906 Census reported 14,769 communicants in the Diocese of Minnesota, with another 3,994 in the Diocese of Duluth. The two dioceses recombined in 1944.

502. For diocesan statistics, see 2007 Journal of the Episcopal Diocese of Minnesota, pp. 376-379; national statistics from Episcopal News Service, cited in Episcopal Life Online, October 29,2007.

503. The Church Record, vol. 25, no. 10, October 1901, 31.

504. Charles M. Robinson III, *A Good Year to Die: The Story of the Great Sioux War,* 261.

bibliography

ARTICLES, BOOKS, AND PAMPHLETS

Albright, Raymond W. *A History of the Protestant Episcopal Church*. New York: Macmillan, 1964.

Anderson, Gary C. *Kinsmen of Another Kind*. St. Paul: Minnesota Historical Society, 1997. Revised from University of Nebraska Press, 1984.

———. *Little Crow: Spokesman for the Sioux*. St. Paul: Minnesota Historical Society Press, 1986.

———, and Alan R. Woolworth, eds. *Through Dakota Eyes: Narrative Accounts of the Minnesota Indian War of 1862*. St. Paul: Minnesota Historical Society Press, 1988.

Anderson, Grant. "Samuel D. Hinman and the Opening of the Black Hills." *Nebraska History* (Winter 1979).

Anderson, Owanah. *Four Hundred Years: Anglican/Episcopal Mission among American Indians*. Cincinnati, Ohio: Forward Movement Publications, 1998.

Anderson, Stephanie. "On Sacred Ground: Commemorating Survival and Loss at the Carlisle Indian School." *Central Pennsylvania Magazine* (May 2000).

Andrews, C. C. *History of St. Paul*. Syracuse, New York: D. Mason and Company, 1890.

Babcock, W. M. "Minnesota's Indian War." *Minnesota History* 38, no. 3 (September 1962).

Bailey, Thomas A. *The American Pageant*. Boston: D. C. Heath and Company, 1956.

Beal, Merrill. *"I Will Fight No More Forever."* Seattle: University of Washington Press, 1963.

Berg, Carol J. "The Benedictines at White Earth." *Minnesota History* 48, no. 4 (Winter 1982).

Bliven, Bruce Jr. *New York: A History*. New York: W. W. Norton Company, 1981.

Book of Common Prayer. New York: Seabury Press, 1977.

Brake, Andrew S. *Man in the Middle: The Reform and Influence of Henry Benjamin Whipple, First Episcopal Bishop of Minnesota*. Lanham, Maryland: University Press of America, 2005.

Brown, Dee. *Bury My Heart at Wounded Knee.*

New York: Holt Rinehart & Winston, 1970.

Brown, J. H., ed. *Lamb's Biographic Dictionary of the United States*. Boston: Federal Book Company of Boston, 1903.

Bryant, Charles S. *History of Rice County*. Minneapolis: Minnesota History Company, 1882.

Burnquist, Joseph A. *Minnesota and Its People*. Chicago: S. J. Clarke Publishing Company, 1924.

Carley, Kenneth. "As Red Men Viewed It." *Minnesota History* 38, no. 3 (September 1962).

———. "The Sioux Campaign of 1862: Sibley's Letters to His Wife." *Minnesota History* 38, no. 3 (September 1962).

———. *The Sioux Uprising of 1862*. St. Paul: Minnesota Historical Society, 1961.

Carroll, Jane Lamm. "Dams and Damages: The Ojibway, the United States, and the Mississippi Headwaters Reservoirs." *Minnesota History* 52, no. 1 (Spring 1990).

Castle, Henry A. *History of Minnesota*. Chicago/New York: Lewis Publishing Company, 1915.

Cathedral of Our Merciful Saviour. Centennial booklet. Faribault, Minnesota: 1962.

Christianson, Theodore. *Minnesota: The Land of Sky-Tinted Waters*. Chicago/New York: American Historical Society, 1935.

Clark, Greenleaf. "Bishop Whipple as a Citizen of Minnesota." *Minnesota Historical Society Collections*. Vol. 10, part 2, 1900-1904.

Coleman, Sr. Bernard, Sr. Verona LaBud, and John Humphrey. *Old Crow Wing: History of a Village*. 1967. Reprint, Brainerd, Minnesota: Evergreen Press, 2000.

Curtiss-Wedge, Franklyn. *History of Redwood County*. Chicago: H. C. Cooper Jr. and Company, 1916.

———. *History of Rice and Steele Counties, Minnesota*. Chicago: H. C. Cooper Jr. and Company, 1910.

"Dedicated to all who served the Lord Jesus at the Church of the Good Shepherd." Maitland, Florida: Church of the Good Shepherd, 2004.

Dictionary of American Biography. Vol. 10. New York: Charles Scribner's Sons, 1964. Original version ca. 1936, vol. 20.

Diedrich, Mark. "Chief Hole-in-the-Day and the 1862 Chippewa Disturbance." *Minnesota History* 50, no. 5 (Spring 1987).

———. *Famous Chiefs of the Eastern Sioux*. Minneapolis: Coyote Press, 1987.

Durant, Samuel. *History of Oneida County, New York*. Philadelphia: Everts and Fariss, 1878.

Elgar, John. *The Story of Nashotah*. Milwaukee: Burdick and Armitage, 1874. www.anglicanhistory.com.

Episcopal Diocese of Minnesota. *1934 Church Yearbook*. St. Paul.

———. *2004 Journal and Directory.*

Fielder, Mildred. *Sioux Indian Leaders*. New York: Bonanza Books, 1981.

Flandrau, Charles E. "The Work of Bishop Whipple in Missions for the Indians." *Minnesota Historical Society Collections*. Vol. 10, part 2, 1900–1904.

Folwell, William W. *A History of Minnesota*. Vol. 1–3, 1924. Revised edition, St. Paul: Minnesota Historical Society, 1961.

Fritz, Henry E. *The Movement for Indian Assimilation*. Philadelphia: University of Pennsylvania Press, 1963.

Genealogical and Family History of the County of Jefferson, New York. New York: Lewis Publishing Company, 1905.

General Catalogue of Oberlin College 1833–1906. Oberlin, Ohio: 1909.

Gilman, Rhoda R. *Henry Hastings Sibley: A Divided Heart*. St. Paul: Minnesota Historical Society Press, 2004.

Handbook for Tours. Faribault Cathedral, Faribault, Minnesota, 1975.

Hawkinson, Ella. "The Old Crossing Chippewa Treaty." *Minnesota History* 15, no. 3 (September 1934).

Hein, David. "Straight Tongue: Bishop Henry Benjamin Whipple." *The Historiographer*. Vol. 41, no. 2

(Pentecost 2003).

History of St. Paul. St. Paul, Minnesota: D. Mason and Company, 1890.

Holbrook, Franklin F. *Minnesota in the Spanish American War and the Philippine Insurrection 1898–1902*. Minnesota War Records Commission. St. Paul, Minnesota: Riverside Press, 1923.

Homstad, Daniel W. "Lincoln's Agonizing Decision." *American History Illustrated* 36, no. 5 (December 2001).

Howe, M. A. DeWolfe. *The Life and Labors of Bishop Hare, Apostle to the Sioux*. New York: Sturgis and Walton, 1911.

"In Memoriam, Henry Benjamin Whipple, DD, LLD." *The Church Record*. Vol. 25, no. 10 (1901). Minneapolis.

Jackson, Helen Hunt. *A Century of Dishonor*. 1881. Reprint Norman: University of Oklahoma Press, 1995.

Josephy, Alvin M. Jr. *The Indian Heritage of America*. New York: Alfred A. Knopf, 1968.

Journal of the 7th Annual Convention of the Diocese of Minnesota, June 8-9, 1864.

Journal of the Proceedings of the bishops, clergy and laity of the Protestant Episcopal Church in the United States of America, Philadelphia: S. Potter & Co., 1835 and 1862.

Kelly, Lawrence. *Federal Indian Policy*. New York and Philadelphia: Chelsea House Publishers, 1990.

Kugel, Rebecca. *To Be the Main Leaders of Our People*. East Lansing: Michigan State University Press, 1998.

Kvasnicka, Robert M., and Herman J. Viola, eds. *The Commissioners of Indian Affairs, 1824–1977*. Lincoln: University of Nebraska Press, 1979.

Lazarus, Edward. *Black Hills, White Justice: The Sioux Nation Versus the United States, 1775 to the Present*. New York: HarperCollins, 1991.

Long, E. B. *The Civil War Day by Day: An Almanac*. Garden City, New York: Doubleday, 1971.

Macdonald, Dora M. *This Is Duluth*. Duluth, Minnesota: Central High School Printing Department, 1950.

Mardock, Robert W. *The Reformers and the American Indian*. Columbia: University of Missouri Press, 1971.

Marquis, A. N., ed. *The Book of Minnesotans*. Chicago: A. N. Marquis and Company, 1907.

Matsen, William E. "The Battle of Sugar Point: A Re-Examination." *Minnesota History* 50, no. 7 (Fall 1987).

Meyer, Melissa. *The White Earth Tragedy*. Lincoln: University of Nebraska Press, 1994.

Meyer, Roy W. *History of the Santee Sioux*. Lincoln: University of Nebraska Press, 1967.

Miller, Donald L. *City of the Century: The Epic of Chicago and the Making of America*. New York: Simon and Schuster, 1996.

Milner, Clive, and Floyd O'Neil, eds. *Churchmen and the American Indians, 1820–1920*. Norman: University of Oklahoma Press, 1985.

Minnesota in the Civil and Indian Wars, 1861–1865. Vol. 2. St. Paul, Minnesota: Pioneer Press Company, 1899.

Minnesota Historical Society Collections. Vol. 6, 1894; vol. 9, 1898–1899; vol. 10, 1900–1904; vol. 14, 1912. St. Paul: Minnesota Historical Society.

"Minnesota Historical Society Notes." *Minnesota History* 16, no. 2 (June 1935).

Morison, Samuel Eliot. *The Oxford History of the American People*. New York: Oxford University Press, 1965.

Moyer, L. R., and O. G. Dale. *History of Chippewa and Lac Qui Parle Counties*. Vol. 1. Indianapolis: B. F. Bowen and Company, 1916.

Neill, Edward D. *History of Minnesota*. New York: Lippincott, 1858.

Nevins, Allan. *The Ordeal of the Union*. Vol. 1. New York: Scribner's, 1947.

"News and Notes." *Minnesota History* 47, no. 3 (Fall 1980).

Nichols, David A. "The Other Civil War: Lincoln and the Indians." *Minnesota History* 44, no. 1 (Spring 1974).

Oehler, Betty. *Bishop Whipple: Friend of the Indian*. Privately published, 1976.

Oehler, C. M. *The Great Sioux Uprising*. New York: Oxford University Press, 1959.

Osgood, Phillips E. *Straight Tongue*. Minneapolis: T. S. Denison and Company, 1958.

Our County and Its People: A Descriptive Work on Jefferson County, New York. Boston: Boston History Company, 1898.

Palmer, Francis L. *Bishop Gilbert*. Milwaukee: Young Churchman Company, 1912.

Pond, Samuel. "The Dakotas or Sioux in Minnesota as They Were in 1834." *Minnesota Historical Society Collections* 12, 1905-1908.

———. *Two Volunteer Missionaries among the Dakotas*. Boston: Congregational Sunday School and Publishing Society, 1893.

Pope, William Cox. "The Work of Bishop Whipple for the Episcopal Church." *Minnesota Historical Society Collections*. Vol. 10, part 2, 1900–1904.

Prucha, Francis P. *Americanizing the American Indians*. Lincoln: University of Nebraska Press, 1978.

———. *The Churches and the Indian Schools*. Lincoln: University of Nebraska Press, 1979.

Ravoux, Augustin. *Reminiscences, Memoirs, and Lectures*. St. Paul, Minnesota: Brown Treacy and Company, 1890.

Reid, Frederick. *Saints in Zion*. Rome, New York: Zion Episcopal Church, 1975.

Riggs, Stephen. *Mary and I: Forty Years with the Sioux*. Williamstown, Massachusetts: Corner House Publishing, 1880. Reprint 1971.

Robinson, Charles M. III. *A Good Year to Die: The Story of the Great Sioux War*. New York: Random House, 1995.

Robinson, Doane. *History of the Dakota or Sioux Indians*. Minneapolis: Ross and Haines, 1904.

Rosenblatt, Judith. *Indians in Minnesota*. Minneapolis: Elizabeth Ebbott for the League of Women Voters of Minnesota, University of Minnesota Press, 1971–1985.

Sanborn, John B. "Bishop Whipple as a Mediator for the Rights of the Indians in Treaties." *Minnesota Historical Society Collections*. Vol. 10, part 2, 1900–1904.

Sandvik, Glenn N. "Land Office Buchanan." *Minnesota History* 52, no. 7 (Fall 1991).

Scott, Benjamin I. "Episcopalians in Minnesota." Leaflet, 1995.

———. "The Right Reverend Henry Benjamin Whipple, D.D., L.L.D., 1822–1901." Faribault,

Minnesota. Leaflet, September 16, 2001.

———, and Robert Neslund. *The First Cathedral.* Faribault, Minnesota: Cathedral of Our Merciful Saviour, 1987.

Sheppard, Betty P., and Edward L. *The Mission at the Lower Sioux, 1860–1980.* Minneapolis: Episcopal Diocese of Minnesota, 1981.

Sheriff, Carol. *The Artificial River: The Erie Canal and the Paradox of Progress.* New York: Hill and Wang, 1996.

Shortridge, Wilson P. "Sibley and the Frontier." *Minnesota History* 3, no. 7 (August 1919).

———. *Certain American Faces.* New York: E. P. Dutton, 1918.

Slattery, Charles L. *Felix Reville Brunot 1820–1898.* New York: Longmans Green and Company, 1901.

Smith, Charles A. *A Comprehensive History of Minnehaha County, South Dakota.* Mitchell, South Dakota: Educator Supply Company, 1949.

Smith, Jane F., and Robert M. Kvasnicka. *Indian-White Relations: A Persistent Paradox.* Washington, D.C.: Howard University Press, 1976.

Sneve, Virginia Driving Hawk. *That They May Have Life: The Episcopal Church in South Dakota, 1859–1976.* New York: Seabury Press, 1977.

Spirit of Missions, Domestic and Foreign Mission Society of the Protestant Episcopal Church in the United States of America, Burlington, New Jersey: J.L. Powell, 1836-1901.

"The State Historical Convention of 1937." *Minnesota History* 18, no. 3, (1937).

Strock, G. Michael. *By Faith, With Thanksgiving.* St. Augustine, Florida: Trinity Episcopal Church, 2004.

Swisher, Clarice, ed. *Victorian England.* San Diego, California: Greenhaven Press, 2000.

Tanner, George C. *Fifty Years of Church Work in the Diocese of Minnesota.* St. Paul, Minnesota: 1909. Published by private committee.

Tebeau, Charlton W. *A History of Florida.* Coral Gables, Florida: University of Miami Press, 1971.

Tinker, George. *Missionary Conquest: The Gospel and Native American Cultural Genocide.* Minneapolis: Augsburg Fortress Press, 1993.

Trenerry, Warren. "The Shooting of Little Crow."

Minnesota History 38, no. 3, (September 1962).

U.S. Biographical Dictionary and Portrait Gallery of Eminent and Self-Made Men, Minnesota. New York: American Biographical Publishing Company, 1879.

U.S. Census Bureau. *1906 Special Report of the Bureau of the Census, Religious Bodies.* Part II, Separate Denominations.

U.S. Census Records 1820, 1850, 1860, 1870, 1880, 1900.

U.S. Department of the Interior. *Reports of the Commissioner for Indian Affairs,* 1859–1901.

Viola, Herman J. *Warrior Artists: Historic Cheyenne and Kiowa Ledger Art Drawn by Making Medicine and Zotom.* Washington, D.C.: National Geographic Society, 1998.

Waldman, Carl. *Encyclopedia of Native American Tribes.* New York: Checkmark Books, 1999.

Warren, William W. *History of the Ojibway People.* St. Paul: Minnesota Historical Society Press, 1984. First edition 1885.

Welsh, William, compiler. *Journal of the Reverend S. D. Hinman, Missionary to the Santee Sioux Indians, or Taopi and His Friends.* Philadelphia: McCall and Stavely, 1869.

Westerhoff, John H. *A People Called Episcopalians.* Harrisburg, Pennsylvania: Morehouse Publishing, 1998.

Whipple, Charles H. *Genealogy of the Whipple-Wright-Wager etc. Families.* Salem, Massachusetts: Higginson Book Company, 2004. Original privately published 1917.

Whipple, Henry B. "Address at the Burial of Mrs. J. Lloyd Breck." Faribault, Minnesota: Central Republican Book and Job Office, 1862.

———. *Bishop Whipple's Southern Diary: 1843–1844.* Lester B. Shippee, ed. Minneapolis: University of Minnesota Press, 1937.

———. *Five Sermons.* New York: E. F. Dutton and Company, 1890.

———. *Lights and Shadows of a Long Episcopate.* New York: Macmillan, 1902.

———. "Niobrara: Sermon Preached at the Consecration of William Hobart Hare, S.T.D." Philadelphia: McCalla and Stavely, 1873.

Willand, John. *Lac Qui Parle and the Dakota Mis-*

sion. Madison, Minnesota: Lac Qui Parle Historical Society, 1964.

Williams, J. Fletcher. *History of Hennepin County.* Minneapolis: North Star Publishing Company, 1881.

Wilson, J. G., and John Fiske, ed. *Appleton's Cyclopedia of American Biography.* New York: Appleton and Company, 1887.

NEWSPAPER CITATIONS

The Churchman—August 15, 1891; January 1, 1895; February 22, 1896; March 7, 1896; March 28, 1896; June 27, 1896; July 11, 1896; October 17, 1896; November 14, 1896; February 13, 1897.

The Church Record, Episcopal Diocese of Minnesota—vol. 25, no. 10 (October 1901); vol. 28 (February 1904); vol. 38 (January 1914).

Faribault Central Republican—August 14, 1861, p. 3:1; April 16,1862, p. 2:8; April 30, 1862, p. 2:3; May 7, 1862, p. 2:2; June 3, 1863, p. 2:6; November 27, 1861, p. 3:1.

Faribault Daily News—October 12, 1932, p. 8:2; October 14, 1932, p. 10:1.

Faribault Democrat—June 20, 1873; June 27, 1884, p. 2; June 19, 1874, p. 1, 4; October 18, 1895; July 3, 1874, p. 1; June 20, 1873, p. 1; June 19, 1874, p. 1; July 3, 1874, p. 1; June 27,1884, p. 1; October 18, 1895, p. 1.

Faribault Journal—May 6, 1904, p. 1:1; May 24, 1916, p. 8:1; May 31, 1916, p. 7:1; June 13, 1906, p. 6:2; September 18, 1901, p. 8:3, p. 1:5; February 20, 1918, p. 8:5.

Faribault Republican—April 28, 1875, p. 3:1; August 14, 1878, p. 3:3; March 8, 1876, p. 3:1; April 5, 1876, p. 3:3; October 3, 1883, p. 3:4; September 19, 1883, p. 3; June 18, 1873; August 5, 1874, p. 3; April 6, 1870, p. 3:2; October 18, 1876, p. 2:3; November 3,1880, p. 3:2; December 5, 1894, p. 3:3; June 18,1873, p. 1; August 5, 1873, p. 3; June 14, 1911, p. 3:4; July 16, 1890, p. 3:2; July 23, 1890, p. 3:4; July 25, 1888, p. 3:4; May 23, 1918, p. 4:2.

New York Times—January 10, 1872, p. 1.

Soundings—June 2002.

ONLINE CITATIONS

Callahan, Kevin. "An Introduction to Ojibway Culture and History." www.geocities.com/ Athens/ Acropolis/5579/ojibwa. April 2005.

Hare, William H. "The First Annual Report of the

Missionary Bishop of Niobrara." www.anglicanhistory.org/indigenous/hare1873. March 14, 2006.

———. "Reminiscences on the Occasion of His 15th Anniversary as Bishop of South Dakota." www.anglicanhistory.org/usa/whhare/reminiscences 1888. July 2006.

Linder, Douglas. "The Dakota Conflict Trials." www.law.umkc.edu/faculty/projects/ftrials/dakota. April 2005.

Prichard, Robert W. "President Ulysses S. Grant's Peace Policy toward Native Americans and the Ministry of the Episcopal Church." www.vts.edu/resources/classnotes/CH205. March 2005.

www.abcbookworld.com/?state=view_author&author_id=2714. April 2005.

www.algebra.com/algebra/about/history/Anglicanism.wikipedia. November 2005.

www.anglicanhistory.org. March 2005.

www.anglicanjournal.com. December 2005.

www.americanpresident.org/history/grovercleveland/firstlady. March 2005.

www.ats.edu. December 2005.

www.boris.vulcanoetna.com/ETNA_erupt1. July 2006.

www.ccel.org/s/schaff/encyc/encyc09/htm/iv.v.ciii.htm. May 2005.

www.chronicles.dickinson.edu/encyclo/c/ed_cumminsGD.html. September 2006.

www.college.hmco.com/history/readerscomp/naind. March 2005.

www.cord.edu/dept/registrar/workingcatalog/ history. March 2005.

www.cr.nps.gov/nagpra. July 2006.

www.cr.nps.gov/nr/travel/pipestone/history.htm. August 2006.

www.crystalinks.com/sioux.html. February 2005.

www.cuba.anglican.org. December 2005.

www.culturagay.it/cg/bio. March 2005.

www.dickshovel.com/win.html. April 2005.

www.diosemexico.org/Dio2History.html. May 2005

www.ehistory.com. April 2005.

www.episcopalchurch.org/3577_48147_ENG-HTM.htm. December 2005.

www.episcopalmn.org/Feature_Milligan. March 2005.

www.episcopalmn.org/GC2003_Daily_0806_Exhibit-Closes.htm. March 2005.

www.episcopal-ne.org. October 2004.

www.episcopalspringfield.org/Heritage/Lambeth-Conference.htm. April 2005.

www.famousamericans.net. Edited Appleton's Encyclopedia, copyright 2001 Virtuality, March 2005.

www.flandreau.k12.sd.us/~eldersspeak. February 2003.

www.floridahistory.org. April 2005.

www.genweb.whipple.org. March 2005.

www.historicaltextarchive.com/sections.ph?op. May 2005.

www.infoplease.com. March 2005.

www.isd77.k12.mn.us/schools/dakota/conflict/good_thunder.htm. March 2005.

www.justus.anglican.org/resources/pc – Project Canterbury papers. January 2005.

www.kstrom.net. January 2005.

www.law.umkc.edu/faculty/projects/ftrials/ dakota. April 2005.

www.masshist.org. March 2005.

www.newadvent.org/cathen/12582a.htm. April 2005.

www.oberlin.edu/archive/holdings/finding/RG30/SG1912/biography.html. May 2005.

www.peabodylibrary.org/history/george. May 2005.

www.petersons.com/pschools/announcements. December 2005.

www.rechurch.org/history.htm. January 2006.

www.recus.org. March 2005.

www.romenewyork.com. April 2005.

www.rupertsland.ca., March 2005.

www.seabury.edu/mt/archives/2004. December 2005.

www.spartacus.schoolnet.co.uk/USAschurz. April 2005.

www.stpaulsrome.it/english/history/early.html. January 2006.

www.st-petersweb.org/lesson28.html. May 2005.

www.usd.edu/iais/siouxnation/1877act. April 2005.

www.womenshitory.about.com/cs/religion/p/anne_ayres.htm. December 2005.

http://97/1911encyclopedia.org/C/CO/COLENSO-JOHN-WILLIAM.htm. April 2005.

http://160.36.208.47/FMPro?-db=tnencyc&-format=tdetail.htm, Tennessee Historical Society, Nashville, 1998; online edition 2002 University of Tennessee Press, Knoxville.

ORIGINAL MANUSCRIPTS

Mary Myrick Hinman LaCroix, Oral History, Minnesota Historical Society, St. Paul.

Samuel D. Hinman Papers, Minnesota Historical Society, St. Paul.

Henry Benjamin Whipple Papers, Minnesota Historical Society, St. Paul.

Whipple/Scandrett Papers, Minnesota Historical Society, St. Paul.

OTHER SOURCES

Conversations with Benjamin Oehler, Whipple descendant.

Conversation with Reverend Benjamin I. Scott, retired archdeacon, Episcopal Diocese of Minnesota.

Conversations with Robert Neslund, historiographer, Episcopal Diocese of Minnesota.

Conversation/e-mail with John Joyce, M.D.

E-mail conversation with Edward C. Rosenow, M.D.

E-mail message from Episcopal Archives, Austin, Texas.

E-mail message from Oberlin College, Oberlin, Ohio.

illustration credits

The Whitney Arch, Shattuck-St. Mary's School, Faribault. Drawing by the Very Rev. James Cly Zotalis, Dean, Cathedral of Our Merciful Saviour, Faribault, Minnesota.

**AFTON HISTORICAL
SOCIETY PRESS**
Afton, Minnesota
p. 10, *Dacotah Village* by Seth Eastman; p. 26, Zion Episcopal Church, postcard; p. 34 (top), General George B. McClellan, 1863; p. 56, Faribault, drawn by Prof. A. Ruger, 1869; p. 73, Boundary map, artist: Seth Eastman, 1851; p. 88, *Beggar's Dance*, artist: Seth Eastman; p. 113, Cheapside, engraving 1851; p. 145, Archibald Campbell Tait, photographer: The London Stereoscopic & Photographic Company, Carte-de-visite, ca. 1870s; p. 171, Peabody College, postcard; p. 180, Custer State Park, postcard; p. 186 (right), Red Cloud, postcard, photographer: Charles M. Bell, Washington, D. C., 1880; p. 196, Carlisle Indian School, postcard; p. 222, Lambeth Palace, ca. 1890s; p. 247 (bottom), Inverary Castle, ca. 1870; p. 256, Cathedral, postcard.

ANNE BEISER ALLEN
Fitchburg, Wisconsin
p. 27, from *Saints in Zion* by Frederick Reid, published in 1975 by Zion Church; p. 82 (bottom), Trading Post; p. 144 (bottom), Cathedral of Our Merciful Saviour, postcard, ca. 1976; p. 190, grave of John H. Whipple; p. 227 (bottom), grave of Cornelia Whipple.

AMERICAN PHILOSOPHICAL SOCIETY
Philadelphia, Pennsylvania
p. 85, Wa-Pa-Sha, Zeno Shindler Photographs.

AARON BENNEIAN
Lancaster, Pennsylvania
p. 112, Edward Pusey, Carte-de-visite.

JOSEPH D. BJORDAL
Minneapolis, Minnesota
p. 188, Church of the Good Shepherd, Maitland, Florida.

**THE CATHEDRAL OF
OUR MERCIFUL SAVIOUR**
Faribault, Minnesota
p. 126 (top left), Cornelia Whipple, photographer: Chuck Johnston; p. 144 (top), Cathedral window, photographer: Chuck Johnston; p. 206, collage of the schools at Faribault, published in *Harper's Weekly*, June 23, 1888, photographer: Chuck Johnston; p. 208 (top), St. Mary's Hall, photographer: Chuck Johnston; p. 208 (bottom), fire

at St. Mary's Hall; p. 220, title page from the Norwegian translation of the *Book of Common Prayer*, 1872; p. 240 (top), Henry Benjamin Whipple, photographer: Chuck Johnston; p. 249 (top), Whipple house, 1897; p. 249 (bottom), Whipple library, photographer: Chuck Johnston; p. 252, crypt; p. 254, Evangeline Whipple, photographer: Chuck Johnston.

CHICAGO HISTORY MUSEUM
Chicago, Illinois
p. 32, Metropolitan Hall, 1858; p. 36, St. Ansgarius Church.

COLORADO HISTORICAL SOCIETY
Denver, Colorado
p. 135, *Sand Creek Massacre*, artist: Robert Lindneux, oil, 1936.

DENVER PUBLIC LIBRARY
Denver, Colorado
p. 193, Rev. Sherman Coolidge, 1893.

DICKINSON COLLEGE LIBRARY
Carlisle, Pennsylvania
p. 157, George D. Cummins.

**THE EPISCOPAL DIOCESE
OF MINNESOTA**
Minneapolis, Minnesota
p. 9, Bishop Whipple's pectoral cross, photographer: Marilyn Jelinek.

GEORGE EASTMAN HOUSE
Rochester, New York
p. 110, Jerusalem Rue et Mosque d'Omar, photographer: Chusseau Flaviens, ca. 1900.

NANCY RING KENDRICK
Adams, New York
p. 16, Adams, New York, postcard, 1909.

JAMES J. HILL REFERENCE LIBRARY
St. Paul, Minnesota
p. 240 (bottom), James J. Hill, 1916; p. 241, letter from Bishop Whipple to J. J. Hill, 1889.

JAMES KOLSTER
Atlantic Beach, Florida
p. 148, Sign of the Episcopal Church of Santa Maria la Virgen in Itabo, Cuba; p. 155, The Episcopal church of San Lucas in Ciego de Avila, Cuba.

LIBRARY OF CONGRESS
Washington, D.C.
p. 11, Abraham Lincoln, photographer: Alexander Gardner, 1863; p. 13, Maj. Gen. Henry W. Halleck, photographer: John A. Scholten, ca. 1860-65; p. 34 (bottom), Major General Ambrose E. Burnside, ca. 1860-65; p. 40, Bishop Jackson Kemper, ca. 1855-65; p. 64, Lieut. Gen. Leonidas Polk, ca. 1860-65; p. 100, Brig. Gen John Pope, ca. 1860-65; p. 101 (top), Antietam, 1862; p. 101 (bottom), Antietam, Lithographer: Kurz & Allison, c. 1888; p. 117, Mosque of Omar, photomechanical print, ca. 1890-1900; p. 122, Prof. S. Manney, Brady-Handy Photograph Collection, ca. 1855-65, p. 139, Gen. William T. Sherman, Engraver: John Chester Buttre; p. 146, Mentone, Riviera, photomechanical print : photocrom, color, ca. 1890-1900; p. 150, President Ulysses S. Grant, Brady-Handy Collection; p. 170, George Peabody, steel engraving by Johnson, Fry & Co., ca. 1867; p. 181, Gen. George A. Custer; p. 182, Lieut. Gen. Philip H. Sheridan, engraving; p. 197, Hon. Carl Schurz, ca. 1870-80; p. 198, Illustration, wood engraving, 1878; p. 199, Helen Hunt Jackson; p. 217, Hon. Henry L. Dawes, ca. 1870-80; p. 230, Westminster Abbey, c. 1909; p. 231 (bottom), Sitting Bull, photographer: D. F. Barry, c. 1885; p. 232, Randall Thomas Davidson, photographer: Bain News Service, 1922.

LOUISIANA STATE MUSEUM
New Orleans, Louisiana
p. 23 (top), *Mississippi River at New Orleans*, ca. 1845, woodcut.

RICHARD J. MAMMANA, JR.
Stamford, Connecticut
p. 35, Bishop Henry J. Whitehouse, carte-de-visite; p. 59, Archbishop Robert Machray; p. 191 (left), Bishop Wm. Hobart Hare from *The Life and Labors of Bishop Hare: Apostle to the Sioux*, by M.A. DeWolfe Howe, New York: Sturgis & Walton Co., 1911; p. 211, Archbishop E. W. Benson from *Reminiscences of Bishops and Archbishops*, by Henry Codman Potter, New York: G.P. Putnam's Sons, 1906; p. 224, Frederick Temple, from *Frederick Temple, Archbishop of Canterbury. Memoirs by Seven Friends*, ed. E. G. Sandford. London: Macmillan, 1906, volume two.

MINNEAPOLIS PUBLIC LIBRARY
Minneapolis, Minnesota
p. 45 (center), Henry Titus Welles.

MINNESOTA HISTORICAL SOCIETY
St. Paul, Minnesota
p. 15, *Execution of Dakota Indians* by J. Thullen, 1884, pastel on paper; p. 17 (top), John Hall Whipple; p. 17 (bottom), Elizabeth Wager Whipple; p. 38, View of St. Paul, 1859; p. 41 (top), Rev. James Lloyd Breck, photographer: Denison & Potter, 1866, Carte-de-visite on paper; p. 41 (bottom), Mission House, St. Paul, 1850; p. 42 (top), Christ Episcopal Church, ca. 1860; p. 42 (bottom), St. Paul's Episcopal Church, ca. 1870; p. 43, Rev. Andrew Bell Paterson; p. 44 (left), Ezekiel Gilbert Gear by Grace E. McKinstry, oil, ca. 1905; p. 44 (right), Napoleon Jackson Tecumseh Dana, photographer: E. Anthony, Carte-de-visite, ca. 1865; p. 45 (left), Hon. E. T. Wilder; p. 45 (right), Isaac Atwater, engraving by W. G. Phillips, ca. 1880; p. 47, Henry Whipple, by Whitney's Gallery, Carte-de-visite, 1859; p. 49, Crow Wing, 1863; p. 50 (left), Church at St. Columba Mission, photographer: Ralph D. Cleveland, ca. 1854; p. 50 (right), St. Mark's Episcopal Church, photographer: William Brown, ca. 1875; p. 51 (top), Holy Trinity Episcopal Church; p. 51 (bottom), Gethsemane Episcopal Church, ca. 1865; p. 52, Rev. E. Steele Peake; p. 53 (bottom), *Alexander Faribault House*, artist: Josephine Lutz Rollins, watercolor 1948; p. 54, Fowler's Store, ca. 1850; p. 60, Jacob Chamberlain, photographer: Leonard & Martin, ca. 1890; p. 63, Officers of the 1st Minnesota Volunteers, 1861; p. 65, Camp of the First Minnesota, January 1862; p. 68, Rev. John Johnson, photographer: Rockwood, Carte-de-visite, ca. 1870; p. 69, Rev. John Johnson, Isaac Manitowab, and Rev. J. L. Breck, ca. 1865; p. 70, Iron Sky Woman, photographer: Rockwood, Carte-de-visite, ca. 1870; p. 71 (left), White Fisher, photographer: Whitney's Gallery, Carte-de-visite, ca. 1860; p. 71 (right) Bad Boy, photographer: Whitney's Gallery, Carte-de-visite, ca. 1860; p. 72, Hole in the Day, photographer: A. H. Rose, Carte-de-visite, ca. 1865; p. 74, George Bonga, photographer: Charles A. Zimmerman, ca. 1870; p. 75, Henry M. Rice, artist: George Peter Alexander Healy, oil, 1857; p. 78, *Fort Snelling in 1848*, artist:

Seth Eastman; p. 79, Upper Sioux Agency, photographer: Eugene Debs Becker, 1960; p. 80 (top), Joseph R. Brown, ca. 1860; p. 80 (bottom), White Dog, artist: John Stevens, ca. 1862; p. 81, Gideon H. Pond and Samuel W. Pond, ca. 1860-70; p. 82 (top), Stephen R. Riggs, ca. 1870; p. 83, Samuel D. Hinman, Carte-de-visite, ca. 1865; p. 84, Andrew Good Thunder, ca. 1895; p. 86, *Attack on New Ulm*, artist: Anton Gag, oil, 1904; p. 87, Wounded Man, ca. 1860; p. 89, Cathedral of our Merciful Saviour, ca. 1863; p. 90, St. John's Church, 1862; p. 92, Little Crow, photographer: Joel E. Whitney, 1862; p. 94, John Other Day, photographer: Whitney's Gallery, 1862; p. 96, William P. Dole and John G. Nicolay, photographer: Whitney's Gallery, 1862; p. 97, Buffalo, photographer: Whitney's Gallery, ca. 1860; p. 98, *The Battle of Birch Coulee*, Lithographer: Paul G. Biersach, 1912; p. 99, Henry H. Sibley, photographer: Whitney's Gallery, ca. 1863; p. 102, Captured Sioux Indians, photographer: Benjamin Franklin Upton, 1862; p. 104 (top), Confirmation of Sioux, photographer: Benjamin Franklin Upton, 1863; p. 108, Metheganonent, photographer: A. H. Indrelee, ca. 1884; p. 109, Sarah Elizabeth Farnum; p. 119, Passed Through Everything (Sha-Bosh-Sgun), photographer: Martin's Gallery, Carte-de-visite, ca. 1860; p. 120, Rt. Rev. D. B. Knickerbacker; p. 124 (left), Rev. James H. Dobbin, photographer: James A. Brush, ca. 1905; p. 124 (right), Felix Reville Brunot; p. 128, Thomas G. Crump, photographer: Denison & Potter's Photograph Gallery, Carte-de-visite, 1866-69; p. 130, St. Columba Mission, Cabinet photograph, ca. 1890; p. 133, Reverend John Johnson (Enmegahbowh), photographer: N. E. Grantham, Cabinet photograph on paper, ca. 1890; p. 138, St. Paul, photographer: Benjamin Franklin Upton, 1869; p. 141 (top), Dr. Jared W. Daniels, ca. 1895; p. 141 (bottom), Simon Anawangmani, photographer: Joel W. Whitney, 1862; p. 143, Cathedral Church of Our Merciful Savior, photographer: A. F. Burnham, Carte-de-visite, ca. 1870; p. 151, Colonel Ely S. Parker, ca. 1870; p. 153, Map of Indian reservations in 1874; p. 158, Seabury Divinity Hall, ca. 1873; p. 160, Joseph A. Gilfillan, photographer: G. Dobkin, ca. 1875; p. 161 (top), Shumway Chapel, postcard on paper, ca. 1905; p. 161 (bottom),

Brainerd, photographer: Caswell & Davy, ca. 1872; p. 162, Flatmouth, 1896; p. 172, Henry Whipple St. Clair, ca. 1904; p. 173, St. Antipas Church, ca. 1900; p. 175 (top), St. Barnabas Hospital, postcard, 1905; p. 175 (bottom), Hospital at the White Earth Mission, ca. 1890; p. 179, Rev. Samuel Madison, tintype, ca. 1870; p. 179, Rev. Fred Smith, photographer: Fredricks, 1898; p. 179, Rev. Charles Wright, photographer: Frank E. Loomis, ca. 1885; p. 179, Rev. George W. Johnson, photographer: Frank E. Loomis, ca. 1885; p. 179, Rev. George Morgan, photographer: Frank E. Loomis, ca. 1885; p. 179, Rev. Mark Hart, photographer: Frank E. Loomis, ca. 1885; p. 179, Rev. George Smith, photographer: Frank E. Loomis, ca. 1885; p. 179, Rev. John Coleman, photographer: Frank E. Loomis, ca. 1885; p. 186 (left), Spotted Tail, Carte-de-visite, ca. 1875; p. 189, John Hall Whipple, II; p. 191 (right), Samuel D. Hinman, photographer: A. F. Burnham, ca. 1870; p. 192, Mary B. Hinman, photographer: A. F. Burnham, ca. 1870; p. 201, Pokegama Dam, photographer: Harry C. Varley, ca. 1900; p. 202, St. Columba Church, ca. 1882; p. 203, White Earth, ca. 1910; p. 204, Indian Commission, 1886; p. 209, Main building and dormitories at Concordia, postcard, ca. 1910; p. 212 (right), Timothy J. Sheehan, photographer: Charles A. Zimmerman, ca. 1895; p. 213 (left), Rev. George B. Whipple, photographer: Hoerger and Peterson, ca. 1885; p. 213 (right), Mary Joanna Mills Whipple; p. 214, Good Thunder and wife, photographer: George Eldon Keene, Cabinet photograph, ca. 1890; p. 216, Bishop Mahlon N. Gilbert, photographer: Louis Peavey, ca. 1898; p. 219, Birch Coulee Mission, ca. 1890; p. 221, Napoleon Wabasha, photographer: N. B. Andersen, 1899; p. 226, Breck School, photographer: Jesse O. Thompson, 1909; p. 233, Mary Webster Whipple, from *Certain American Faces, Sketches from Life* by Charles Lewis Slattery, New York, 1918; p. 234 (top left), Lace Makers at the Redwood Mission, photographer: Edward A. Bromley, 1897; p. 234 (bottom), Lace Makers at Leech Lake, 1894; p. 237, Birch Coulee Monument, postcard, ca. 1930; p. 238, Judge Charles E. Flandrau, photographer: Charles A. Zimmerman, ca. 1895; p. 239, Gethsemane Episcopal Church, ca. 1890; p. 248, Bugonaygeshig and two tribe members, 1897; p. 250, St. Cornelia's Church, photographer: N. B. Andersen, ca. 1895; p. 251, Samuel C. Edsall, photographer: George Kraft, ca. 1910; p. 253 (top), Dedication of monument, ca. 1901; p. 253 (bottom), Funeral of Bishop Henry Whipple, photographer: Minneapolis Times, 1901; p. 255, Indian school at Morton, photographer: N. B. Andersen, ca. 1905; p. 259, The Minneapolis Times, 1901.

NEBRASKA STATE HISTORICAL SOCIETY
Lincoln, Nebraska
p. 104 (bottom), Episcopal Chapel at Crow Creek; p. 184, signers of the 1876 Black Hills treaty.

THE NEW YORK PUBLIC LIBRARY
New York, New York
p. 19, *View on the Erie Canal*, artist John William Hill, watercolor, 1829, I. N. Phelps Stokes Collection, Miriam and Ira D. Wallach Division of Art, Prints and Photographs, The New York Public Library, Astor, Lenox and Tilden Foundations.

BENJAMIN OEHLER
Wayzata, Minnesota
p. 4, Henry Whipple; p. 12, Henry Whipple; p. 25, Henry Whipple with daughter Jane; p. 46, House of Bishops; p. 62, Stained glass Seal of the Diocese, photographer: Doug Ohman; p. 121, Cornelia Ward Rose; p. 127, St. Mary's Hall; p. 169, Henry Whipple, photographer: Elliot & Fry, Carte-de-visite, ca. 1875; p. 185, Henry Whipple, ca. 1876; p. 194, Henry Whipple; p. 212 (left), Charles Whipple; p. 227 (top) Cornelia Whipple; p. 228, Queen Victoria, photograph, 1890; p. 235 (bottom), Henry Whipple; p. 244-245, Lambeth Conference attendees, 1897; p. 261, Henry Whipple.

COLIN PALMER, WWW. BUYIMAGE. CO.UK
Hertfordshire, United Kingdom
p. 247 (top), Isle of Wight, photographer: Colin Palmer.

PRIVATE COLLECTION
p. 66, *Chippewa Burial Ground*, artist: Cameron Booth, photographer: Chuck Johnston; p. 242, Henry and Evangeline Whipple.

RICE COUNTY HISTORICAL SOCIETY
Faribault, Minnesota
p. 53 (top), Alexander Faribault, artist: Ivan Whillock.

ST. AUGUSTINE HISTORICAL SOCIETY
St. Augustine, Florida
p. 29, View of St. Augustine; p. 31, Trinity Church.

ST. PAUL'S SCHOOL, OHRSTROM LIBRARY
Concord, New Hampshire
p. 123 (top), George Shattuck.

THE SCHLESINGER LIBRARY, RADCLIFFE INSTITUTE, HARVARD UNIVERSITY
Cambridge, Massachusetts
p. 235 (top), Phillips Brooks, 1898.

SCIENCE MUSEUM OF MINNESOTA
St. Paul, Minnesota
p. 2, beaded cross; p. 6, stole; p. 118, altar cloth; p. 137, man's shirt; p. 152, knife case; p. 168, Ojibwe man's shirt; p. 215, Dakota cap; p. 231 (top), Dakota club; p. 234 (top right), lace; p. 288, Ojibwe Bandolier or shoulder bag, ca. 1850-1900, cotton, wool, deerskin, glass bead, silk, yarn.

SEWANEE: THE UNIVERSITY OF THE SOUTH SPECIAL COLLECTIONS, PERMANENT COLLECTION, AND UNIVERSITY ARCHIVES
Sewanee, Tennessee
p. 30, George R. Fairbanks, by George Peter Alexander Healy, 1858, oil on canvas.

SHATTUCK-ST. MARY'S SCHOOL
Faribault, Minnesota
p. 20, Cornelia Whipple, photographer: Chuck Johnston; p. 55, Ballyhack, photographer: Chuck Johnston; p. 123 (bottom), Shattuck Hall, photographer: Chuck Johnston; p. 125, The Mission School House, photographer: Chuck Johnston; p. 126 (top right), Sarah Darlington; p. 126 (bottom), graduating class, photographer: Chuck Johnston; p. 129 (top), Seabury/Shattuck Campus, 1867, photographer: Chuck Johnston; p. 129 (bottom), Manney Armory, photographer: Chuck Johnston; p. 147, Augusta Shumway, oil; p. 166-167, Shattuck campus, photographer: Chuck Johnston; p. 229, Frances Ransom Whipple,

photographer: Chuck Johnston.

SMITHSONIAN AMERICAN ART MUSEUM, Washington, D. C. / ART RESOURCE
New York, New York
p. 22, *Osceola*, artist: George Catlin, oil on canvas mounted on aluminum, 30 7/8" x 25 7/8", 1838; p. 76, *Sioux Village*, artist: George Catlin, 1835-36.

SMITHSONIAN INSTITUTION, NATIONAL ANTHROPOLOGICAL ARCHIVES
Suitland, Maryland
p. 205 (bottom), Capt. Richard H. Pratt, 1880.

SMITHSONIAN INSTITUTION, NATIONAL MUSEUM OF THE AMERICAN INDIAN,
Suitland, Maryland
p. 177, 2 crayon drawings by Kiowa artist James Bears Heart, Fort Marion, St. Augustine, Florida, ca. 1875, photographer: Katherine Fogden.

STATE HISTORICAL SOCIETY OF IOWA
Iowa City, Iowa
p. 23 (bottom), *City of Cincinnati*, artist: A. C. Warren, Engraver W. Wellstood, from *Picturesque America*, p. 161, D. Appleton & Publishers, Vol. II.

UNIVERSITY OF PENNSYLVANIA ARCHIVES
Philadelphia, Pennsylvania
p. 24, William Heathcote DeLancey.

VICTORIA & ALBERT MUSEUM
London / ART RESOURCE
New York, New York
p. 115, *The Gate of Metawalea*, artist: David Roberts, 1843.

WIKIPEDIA.ORG
p. 111, Charles Thomas Longley, photographer: Lewis Carroll; p. 205 (top), Mohonk House, 2000; p. 243, Rose Cleveland.

JEFF WILLIAMSON
Rosemount, Minnesota
p. 105, Rev. John P. Williamson.

JAMES ZOTALIS
Faribault, Minnesota
p. 280, The Whitney Arch, 1988.

index

This book was designed by

Mary Susan Oleson
NASHVILLE, TENNESSEE